GALES OF CHANGE

GALES OF CHANGE

RESPONDING TO A SHIFTING
MISSIONARY CONTEXT

THE STORY OF THE
LONDON MISSIONARY
SOCIETY
1945 - 1977

EDITED BY
BERNARD THOROGOOD

WCC Publications, Geneva

Cover design: Edwin Hassink

ISBN 2-8254-1126-4

© 1994 Council for World Mission, Livingstone House,
11 Carteret Street, London SW1H 9DL, England

Published for CWM by WCC Publications, World Council of Churches,
150 route de Ferney, 1211 Geneva 2, Switzerland

Printed in Switzerland

Table of Contents

In thanksgiving for
that Spirit which
sent witnesses
        healers
        teachers
        liberators
        and friends
to share the grace of
the Lord Jesus Christ
with the Father's world

Preface

The title of this volume, *Gales of Change*, refers to the broad context within which the London Missionary Society (LMS) and its successors, during the period 1945-77, sought to fulfil the purpose for which the LMS had been founded in 1975, namely, "to send the glorious gospel of the blessed God..." The sub-title, *Responding to a Shifting Missionary Context*, refers to the ways in which "the glorious gospel of the blessed God" was proclaimed and received in local situations on which global changes also had an impact. Though there is a continuity in the story of the London Missionary Society over the last two centuries, there have been several shifts of emphasis in mission work, particularly during the period covered by this volume.

External pressures and internal developments also brought about changes in the policy and structure of the LMS itself. In 1966 it ceased to be a society and became the Congregational Council for World Mission. This signalled the change from mission understood as the work of a few dedicated individuals, who formed a society for mission, to mission understood as the activity of the whole church, expressed in a council of the church. The year 1977 saw a further change with the formation of the new Council for World Mission. As a consequence of the work of the London Missionary Society, the Commonwealth Missionary Society and the Assembly Missionary Committee of the Presbyterian Church of England, churches came into being in all the countries where they were present. The new Council for World Mission was also the mission council of these so-called "younger churches".

The story of the London Missionary Society and its successor bodies from 1945 to 1977 continues a history that began in 1795. It is a story of Christian obedience in the context of major, rapid and even revolutionary changes — changes that are aptly described in the title, *Gales of Change*.

The introductory chapter sketches the contours of change in the world scene and in the ecumenical church scene, both of which influenced the work of the London Missionary Society. The subsequent chapters show how these changes, to a greater or lesser degree, had an impact on local situations and shaped the missionary response. Chapter 11 deals with developments in Britain and the factors and trends which led to the forming of a "council" for mission. Chapter 12 rounds off the story with a summary of the outstanding qualities of the London Missionary Society and its successor bodies, and how these need to be reflected in the work of the Council for World Mission (CWM), which continues the story albeit in a new form in a new age.

In its founding document, "Sharing in One World Mission" (1975), the Council for World Mission itself reflected on the task for mission in a new form in a new age in these words:

> We believe that we become participants in mission not because we hold all the answers and all the truth, but because we are part of the body of Christ. All of us are still searchers. We have glimpsed the glory of God in the face of Jesus Christ, and what we know we love. But there are varieties of Christian experience and of Christian community we have not entered. There are doubtless many ways in which Christ comes to men and women that we have never seen. Therefore, we seek a form of missionary organization in which we may learn from each other, for in that fellowship we believe that the Holy Spirit speaks to all through each. (section 2:7)

The first volume of the history of the London Missionary Society, by Richard Lovett, was published in 1895 for the centenary. This volume, the third in the series (the second, by Norman Goodall, covers the period 1895-1945), is being published in time for the bicentenary in 1995. Because it was felt that the period 1977-95 is still a history in the making for the Council for World Mission, and therefore too close for a proper historical evaluation to be made, it was decided to end the present story at 1977, and indicate in the last chapter the directions and challenges before the Council. Another generation will have to tell the story from 1977 onwards.

Though of multiple authorship, this volume is not an anthology of essays on mission. It has a clear purpose which has been described above. The authors worked as a team under the leadership of Bernard Thorogood, the chief editor. The first chapter was written first and formed the background for all the others. Besides the particular expertise each author brought to the project, all of them were also part of the missionary history of this period. In a real sense, therefore, this is also their story. However, lest the chapters reflect only one perspective, each was revised in the light of criticism and comments from local readers.

Much hard work has gone into the shaping and writing of this volume. In saying "thank you" to Bernard Thorogood and his team, the Council for World Mission, which commissioned this history, says "thank you" also to those of an age and a spirit who gave us this story of faithfulness in response to God's continuing faithfulness. Joe Wing of South Africa died shortly after his chapter was completed. Friends say that, even though he was terminally ill, he wanted to complete what he spoke of as "my last task on earth". He represented that "indomitable spirit" and "sanctified audacity" which characterizes the whole story. Barrie Scopes, the former general secretary of the CWM, worked long and hard as research officer and then administrator for the whole project. To him also the Council says "thank you". The CWM is grateful to the Office of Communication of the World Council of Churches for agreeing to publish this volume, thereby recognizing it as an important part of Christian ecumenical history.

"Now to him who by the power at work within us is able to do far more abundantly than all that we ask or think, to him be glory in the church and in Christ Jesus to all generations, for ever and ever" (Eph. 3:20). These are the words with which any history of Christian mission should appropriately both open and close. For the story of our obedience is set within the mystery of God's mission as well as God's forgiveness and grace.

Easter 1994

D. PREMAN NILES
General secretary
Council for World Mission

1. The Gales of Change

Bernard Thorogood

This volume relates the story of the London Missionary Society (LMS) and its successor bodies during the period 1945-77. The earlier parts of this narrative are told in the two-volume history by Richard Lovett published for the centenary in 1895 and the volume by Norman Goodall covering the period 1895-1945.

It was evident that the emphasis of this volume would be distinct. It was no longer possible to construct the story around the lives of outstanding missionaries. Such individuals were still at work but they were no longer the prime movers in the enterprise, nor was it possible to regard the institution known as the LMS, with its Board of directors in London, as the initiator and controller of events. The focus had begun to change well before 1945 and in this period moved decisively towards the development of local churches with local leadership.

The chapters which cover the regional work and witness have been prepared by various authors, each with a particular expertise, and each chapter has been discussed with national colleagues to ensure that no single viewpoint determines the selection and interpretation of such a large body of source material.

This introductory chapter looks at the background of these 32 years. I write as a minister in the Congregational and Reformed tradition, involved in the missionary enterprise during a large part of this period, and therefore with that particular slant. The years between 1945 and 1977 saw major, rapid and permanent changes in the political map of the world community, in the social context of many countries, and in the witness of Christian churches.

The political background

Occasionally a short period of history sees upheavals in thought, power, habit or invention which sweep aside the established pattern of many years and enable new ideologies to be born. One such period was from 1520 to 1550 when the insight and courage of Luther and Calvin were placed alongside the venal follies of the popes, the wisdom of Erasmus and the growth of nationalism to create a religious divide, a private conscience and a new order for Europe. Another climactic period was from 1780 to 1815 when there was a combination of new worlds challenging the old, new classes challenging the superiority of aristocrats, new industry challenging the old routines of agricultural life.

Ours is such a period. Living through it, we were only occasionally aware of the great changes around us. Looking back we know it for fact. All the muddled politics and the developing sciences, all the post-war guilt and economic weakness, all the disillusion with conventional Christianity were shaping a radical change in the life of the human family. If we are to place the Christian missionary movement in this context we have to note that the era of the great missionary expansion from the West also came to an end with the second world war.

Missionary expansion had been intimately related to the colonial era — not subservient to colonialism always but deriving from it assurance and security — and that era was swiftly closed by the war. This did not make the headlines at the time. The fall of Singapore to the Japanese was not then seen as a turning point in human history: we can now recognize that it marked the power failure of one of the great empires. British military power, always dependent on local forces throughout the empire, was unable to hold one of its principal bases against a well-organized Asian power. Throughout Singapore, Malaysia, Hong Kong, Sarawak, Java and Sumatra, colonial security was dislodged, with Europeans reduced to those haunting skeletal figures in prison camps. The weakness became visible. The lion was elderly and had lost many of its teeth.

In India this fact had been recognized by political activists for many years and when the security arrangements during wartime were lifted the pressure for change became intense, leading to a swift response from the Attlee government in Britain and so to the hastily drawn plans for partition and independence. Reading that story one has the feeling that any plans would have been accepted in London provided they were for rapid disengagement. The jewel in the crown of the empire was always too splendid, too vast, too diverse for Britain to assimilate; it could only be administered bureaucratically, mapped beautifully and romanticized in song and story. The story of national awareness and independence was lit by the personality of Gandhi who brought a rare vision of human worth to the world of politics and whose assassination in 1948 was one of the tragedies of our period. It is one of the ironic lessons that this exemplar of non-violence came not from the Christian tradition and not from the West but from the Hindu tradition of a more ancient culture which knew both suffering and hope to their limits.

The decolonization of Africa involved Britain, France, Belgium and Portugal. These countries had very different approaches to that process. France was deeply involved in the struggles of the colonists in North Africa and this embittered the closing years, but wherever there had been French government the cultural legacy was very significant, language was taught with care and the French style of life was established. It is, therefore, not surprising that Roman Catholicism remained in the former French territories as the major Christian presence. For Belgium and Portugal, the story was a grim one. Neither power had prepared the African people for independence, nor had they developed the infrastructure, the industry or the education, and in the Congo basin, Angola and Mozambique violent, dirty civil wars marred the independence years. The shift from an underdeveloped colony to a modern nation able to take its place in the international community was not an evolution but a tragic revolution. There was loss of life in British Africa as well but for different reasons. Here the colonial power had firm ideas about future development and the political framework which should be adopted. We knew what was good for them. Colonial boundaries, a unitary state, universal suffrage, elected parliaments, an independent judiciary — it all sounded splendid. Yet it took only limited account of what people wanted and what they could sustain. Parliamentary democracy proved to be a fragile system when tribalism became violent, as in Biafra and Zimbabwe. The great personalities of the independence struggle could not easily accept a secret ballot which could remove them from the scene, as Hastings Banda, Kenneth Kaunda and Julius Nyerere knew.

In Southern Africa, this period witnessed the legal entrenchment of apartheid in the Republic of South Africa. What was customary for generations and even for centuries was so built into the constitution and so supported by the theology of the Dutch Reformed Churches that it became the inflexible barrier to change. This dominated relationships with the emerging nations south of the Sahara, with particular pain for Namibia, Botswana, Mozambique, Lesotho and Swaziland to which refugees most naturally escaped. It is significant that it was in South Africa that Harold Macmillan, hardly a revolutionary, was moved to speak of the winds of change. It was to take many years and frequent gales before that defensive shield around white privilege was slowly battered down. For many Christians the great sorrow was that churches could defend apartheid as a biblical precept, hallowing a heresy and so strengthening the oppression of the majority for many years. The question has to be asked whether Protestant theology today is constitutionally weak when confronted by a determined establishment. Was it so in Germany?

Without so many headlines the decolonizing process reached the islands of the Caribbean and the South Pacific. Here there were no famous political struggles. For some places in the Pacific there was little overt pressure to be separated from the colonial power which provided generous subsidies; the Gilbert and Ellice Islands, for example, had to be chivvied along the road to independence by the foreign and commonwealth office in London. A much larger unit was Papua New Guinea, under the care of Australia, consisting of the most diverse of human communities. To bring its people together in anything resembling a modern nation state was almost miraculous, for its 700 tribes had, before 1945, very little appreciation of their neighbourhood as a great island. With a host of small islands it became surprisingly stable until massive mineral exploitation in Bougainville caused resentment and violence. By the end of our period only France retained its island colonies in the Pacific, but endeavoured to remove the stigma of the name by incorporating the territories into the French republic with representatives sitting in Paris. This tactic did not remove the problem and this is where political violence was most common.

Across the world the colonial powers left the field and one after another nation-states were born. The military and economic exhaustion of the European powers was a strong reason but there was also a growing sense of the rightness of independence. Politicians in Europe were beginning to appreciate the absurdity of arranging peoples' lives on the other side of the world. Some Westerners said: "But they are not ready." The best reply came from Julius Nyerere: "To ask if I'm ready for independence is like asking if I'm ready to be a man." What was usually meant was that "they are not ready" to run a political and economic society like ours, with our values and objectives. By such a test many have failed. But the test was so offensive, so paternalistic that few today would consider it valid. Twentieth-century European civilization has not been so wonderful that we can claim it to be a model for anyone. The ending of the empires has stimulated much self-criticism. It has changed the European perspective of the world. It has deeply affected the churches.

Two major factors stood on the other side of the balance sheet. The first was the expansion of the communist empires at exactly the same time as when withdrawal from the colonies was the western theme. In Europe the boundary of communist power followed the advance of Russian armies after the collapse of Germany. In China the growth of the communist popular base overwhelmed the authoritarian structures of the nationalists. In both these vast areas of human society there were early years of hope that the ideology, the upheaval, the centralized planning, the new education, the expropriation of old landowners and the corporate ownership of wealth would remove the old burdens of slavery and poverty. It is not surprising that this hope touched people around the world, from Burma to Cuba, from Nicaragua to Zimbabwe. It was not just a confidence trick used by a power-hungry party boss. There were genuine idealism and intention behind the revolution, and early commitment to "trust the people". In China, the mass appeal of the Maoist movement not only scattered the forces of Chiang Kai Shek but replaced them with the most effective central apparatus in China's history, reforming every branch of society and elevating the little red book into the gospel for a quarter of humanity.

It is now easy to describe the weaknesses and follies of the socialist economic system. But it is more important for our purpose to note the strength of the ideology, for that is what has affected Christian witness in many parts of the world. Can society be radically reshaped so that the ancient power of the wealthy becomes the shared power of all? Some Christian radicals, like early American settlers, have attempted this, but without a tough social discipline. It was the conviction of the socialists in the 1940s and 1950s that such a change was possible. This conviction was a missionary creed to be heard by the oppressed everywhere. Often it was a naive belief, forgetting that human sin can corrupt every system and that the larger the enterprise the less was the responsibility felt by each participant. It was also a regressive creed, for the discipline required to enforce the economic plan was a throwback to serfdom. Despite this the incentive to believe was strong. Who does not long to eradicate poverty? Christian liberal values often seemed a nervous weakling beside the tough socialist doctrine.

Christian workers were often caught in two minds as socialism was installed in the seats of power. They saw a social responsibility and the need to care for the poor which were directly in line with the efforts of missionaries over the past years. Here at least was a government which would share in the mission "to announce good news to the poor, to proclaim release for prisoners and recovery of sight for the blind, to let the broken victims go free". So the social programme was to be welcomed. But the Marxism which fuelled the politics was also an atheism which denied any place to the spiritual realities and was ready to destroy the church itself. That had to be resisted. This double focus was evident in the last years of missionary presence in China. The ambivalence did not appear as a strong, coherent policy but it was the honest reaction of those who loved the people in a way which Mao could not understand. The LMS annual report for 1947 commented:

> The hope expressed in last year's report that the genius of the Chinese for compromise would enable them to resolve their political conflict has not been fulfilled.

But those who had followed the Long March could not expect compromise; that was the British word, not the Chinese.

The knock-on effects of the Chinese revolution were of great severity. In Malaysia, Indonesia, Korea and Indo-China the expansion of communist influence met resistant regimes. In Malaysia and Indonesia a programme of physical containment with the killing or capture of communist agents was successful; in Korea a conflagration brought the Chinese army into the fight resulting in a great loss of life and a divided country. In Indo-China the French and the American armies fought a merciless but losing battle. In Burma the communist ideology won the day with persistent tribal resistance continuing. The island of Taiwan appeared as a rock in a stormy sea, resisting the tide but suffering from the domination of the exiled Chinese nationalist regime. All this testified to the powerful thrust of communism and led to the 1951 LMS annual report's statement that "restlessness, revolution and war are the main features of the background against which the story of the year's work must be told".

The second major influence on decolonization was the continued exercise of economic power when political power was withdrawn. This was a subject which embittered international relations. It seems to have been something of a surprise to the leaders of newly independent states. They discovered that the modernizing of communications, the growth of health care and education, the introduction of new industry and the creation of a defence force required far greater investment than could be generated locally from a mainly agricultural economy. So the organs for international investment were quickly developed. The International Monetary Fund and the World Bank were firmly located in America. The multinational industrial giants kept their headquarters in Europe or America. Donor agencies also sprang up in the North. All three forms of capital transfer meant that the controlling hand was not that of the new government in the new state but that of the same politicians and managers of the old colonial powers. This, too, had its effects on the life of the international church.

Effects of this economic dependence on the secular world have been far-reaching. The first has been instability. When the flow of investment is controlled from a distance many extraneous factors can affect what happens. A change in the government of the United Kingdom or in German interest rates or a drop in demand for a particular quality of oil could alter the economy of an emerging nation fundamentally. Local planning was subject to these fluctuations totally outside local control. For an economy like that of Zambia, very dependent on one export commodity, this brought a high risk of riots and urban poverty.

But a deeper psychological effect has been frustration and distrust in the family of nations. In Africa and Latin America particularly all social evils could be blamed on the economic grip of the capitalist powers. Here was a devil to bear all the failures of the local planners and economists, a scapegoat to be mentioned in every election. The blame was never wholly justified. But it was a splendid oratorical device with some truth in it. The strange reality was that the western powers took so little note of this economic imbalance and therefore appeared unconcerned about the frustration that resulted. It was almost as though the powers were content that their political control had become economic, an undercover colonialism that was beyond democratic accountability. The short-sightedness of governments in Europe and America was remarkable.

In the later part of our period this imbalance has led to the debt crisis. We have reached the point where debt repayments by many poorer nations exceed all that they receive as aid and cripple their economic plans. It is easy to criticize the banks and few could commend them for far-sightedness. The heavier charge has to be levelled at governments which have signally failed to grasp the gravity of the issue. The economic plight of many countries leads to thousands of unnecessary deaths every week and the wealthy nations generate no dynamics for radical change. It is not surprising that anger results.

It was against this political background of decolonization by the West, colonization by the communist East and the vast economic imbalance that the United Nations was born and developed. The East-West struggle in Europe greatly undermined its growth but also made its existence essential. The cold war was played out on the floor of the assembly and in all the specialized committees and agencies. On every controversial matter positions were decided in advance not by the merits of the case but by the camp to which the nation belonged. The surprise is that in such a context the UN survived and was able to do significant work, particularly in the fields of health care, literacy and refugee service, and in some places as a peace-keeping force. The work done through the specialized agencies of the UN touched voluntary agencies at many points; often they worked in harmony. Comparisons with the League of Nations were frequent. We commonly referred to the League's failure at a time when aggression had to be faced but there was no instrument available to do this with authority. Now the UN meets similar crises. In the cold-war period the division between the permanent members of the Security Council prevented effective action in many conflicts. Yet the fact that the UN was available as the widest international forum, committed to an extensive programme for human rights, was of profound importance for the peace of the world. It was an instrument, ready for use, as soon as the major powers recognized that justice is a common cause and not a party label.

And it was the struggle for justice which formed a background to all the political change of our period. Is it just for one nation to rule another from a distance? Is it just for one tribe to dominate its neighbours? Is it just that so many people should starve in God's good world and that expenditure on arms should come before health care? Is it just that a wall should divide a city and a nation, and is it just that a person's faith in God should lead to torture and death? The series of questions has no end. Politics fumbles towards an answer.

The social context

Great changes in the patterns of human society accompanied the shifting political map and were partly responsible for it. We would define these changes in different ways so this is no more than a personal assessment of the major elements which fundamentally altered our relationships with one another.

Power
Our period begins with the Hiroshima nuclear blast, the weapon which concluded the military adventure of Japan and began the guilt-ridden journey of the great nations as they developed ever-greater explosive power. The civilian uses of nuclear energy were problematic. It was neither an easy route to cheap electricity nor a wholly safe technology. The military uses were horrific. The USA, Britain and France quickly seized on their Pacific territories as the right place for experimentation without regard to the wishes of the indigenous people. When Britain exploded its H-bomb at Christmas Island, I was living on an island nearly 1,000 miles away, and our night sky turned mauve with flickering aurora-type light. Sir William Penny, the physicist, had to attempt to reassure us that the natural world was unharmed. It was a reminder of the new, impressive power in human hands. This leap in the availability of power

continued with the silicon chip, the micro circuit and the computer, so that a great many individuals commanded elaborate machines without physical labour. We have therefore seen the kind of revolution in our lives that accompanied the arrival of the steam engine and electricity.

The results are both psychological and social. In our minds there is far greater expectation of human power to solve problems, a new regard for humanity as the crown of all creation, able to dispose of all the ingredients of a troublesome life. Careful observation shows how naive is any such assumption, but it has considerable impact on religious awareness. The omnipotence of human beings is a powerful defence against the fear of God. If "man has come of age" in the skills applied to everyday life, all props can be removed and much of the biblical imagery will belong to the past. This is an unreal scenario but has had influence on the technological societies of the 1960s and 1970s.

This particular technical advance has produced a shift in how we work. The earlier industrial revolutions (coal, iron and steel) brought people together in great numbers to operate the new machinery. Now technology enables people to operate while being scattered. So a very powerful financial operator can live in an isolated cottage in the green hills of Vermont or the sands of Saudi Arabia without loss of effectiveness. Distant operators can be linked together across the globe. This means that an individual style of operation as distinct from the deep community life of the old industries developed. Here is one of the buttresses of western individualism which has increasingly affected every aspect of life including our approach to the community of God.

Communication

These technical advances have made possible the next major shift in our lives together, that of communication. Immediate, visual, dramatic, the images and words reach us. No part of the world can be secure in its isolation for the camera in the satellite may be looking down. To those at the console in the command bunker the life of the world is an open book. And to those in management offices of the bank the finances of the nations can be revealed. For teaching, entertainment or propaganda the power is enormous. One result of this is to make possible the awareness of a global community, not just as an intellectual concept but as flesh and blood. Famine comes into our homes. War stains our complacency. This factor has had a great effect on the international church in two ways. First, it has stimulated face-to-face meeting across the oceans and continents, and when we do not meet in person, then it is voice-to-voice. One of the paradigm shifts in missionary service occurred when it became possible to fly home in 24 hours. Shattered in one blow was the concept of total detachment from the home base and total immersion in an isolated place of service. More important has been the possibility of international meetings which occupy quite a small proportion of the annual diary. We can be there and back in a week or a fortnight. So we meet more often, but perhaps with less preparation and with less leisurely discussion than in the historic councils of the church.

The vivid immediacy of modern communication has also dismissed into the old nursery the typical missionary portrait of the world. When we see peoples' lives, their struggles and tears; when we see the omnipresent symbols of pop culture; when we meet the ministers of churches across the world; when we reflect on the tribalism of Europeans, then we know that the basics of human survival do not alter very much,

however energetic and faithful the Christian witness. We used to be impressed with the
utter strangeness of other cultures. The mud men of New Guinea were, so to say,
paraded before us as a sign of the gap to be bridged by missionaries. But beneath the
masks we find that they are people with whom we can relate because their fears of
death and love of life are like our own. So modern communication, while it
demonstrates the vivid diversity of habitat and appearance, also confirms the unity of
the human family. This awareness of one another is a permanent change in the way we
know the world, for we can no longer pretend that, when tragedy strikes, we did not
know. We knew, but shut our eyes. Priests and Levites is the name for most of us in
the West.

Number

The third permanent change in the human family is simply its number. Our period
covers an exceptional growth in world population, far beyond the steady growth of the
nineteenth and early twentieth centuries. We have to thank medical science for much
of this increase in life expectancy and decrease in infant mortality in nearly every
nation. There were grave warnings that the world food supply could not keep pace and
mass famine would result. There has, indeed, been famine in Africa but hardly on
account of the population. The green revolution with its scientifically developed
strains of seed and farm animals increased food supplies in many places. India, for
example, even with greatly increased population became fully self-sufficient in grain.
There are still grim warnings, however. Green revolutions do not occur every few
years and the soil of the planet is likely to be seriously threatened by over-cropping and
wood gathering. So we take the population graph as a serious limiting factor for the
future.

The Christian churches have been nervous about facing this. During this period
there were some harsh and probably corrupt government campaigns to limit the size of
families in India, China and Singapore. Churches did not wish to be involved with
such intrusion and enforcement. There was also a moral hesitation. The Roman
Catholic Church led the campaign against contraception on the grounds that it thwarted
the true purpose of sexual union. Other churches, far less sure of the "natural law",
sought a balance between parental responsibility and resources. It was a lukewarm
response to a major human issue which may yet prove to be the most inclusive crisis
facing us. It is difficult to understand why the churches have not regarded the welfare
of the human race and the quality of human life as so precious in God's purpose that
debate on the precise method of contraception fades into the distance. To plead for the
sanctity of life and also to plead for no limitation on family size is one of the grimmer
illogicalities of Christianity.

The pressure of population has created many social tensions. Since human
mobility has enabled rapid international travel we have witnessed constant attempts to
cross borders and resettle, with numbers far in excess of the capacity of states to
receive new people. The borders between Mexico and the USA, between China and
Hong Kong, between South Africa and its neighbours, between eastern and western
Germany were challenged repeatedly by those seeking a new home. Africa in the
1970s became the top continent for refugees. Britain received waves of immigrants,
first from the Caribbean, then from Pakistan, India and Bangladesh. Germany
discovered that the second language of the country was Turkish. Israel and Australia
continued to welcome large numbers of immigrants. Vietnamese fled to Hong Kong.

This displacement of so many thousands, the provision of reception centres, the building of new communities and the strengthening of border controls were eloquent signs of the times. But the result was for many nations a permanent change of the population mix with all the attendant possibilities of cultural exchange. For Europe, as for Canada and Australia, it brought into the neighbourhood all the theological questions about the Christian call to mission, the dangers of racism and the meeting with other living faiths.

Personal identity

Alongside this people-pressure in a finite world we saw increasing stress on personal identity, which developed in many ways. The most significant for our purpose were freedom of expression, feminism and local patriotism. The 1960s were a time for personal experiment in language, the arts, popular music, popular food, youth culture and also in morals, particularly sexual morals. Because of the speed of communication this mood, which originated in the USA and Europe, touched many other parts of the world so that a 1960s style could be seen in New Zealand and Brazil and even in Samoa and Zambia. The conviction was that personal choice was the great determining factor of life — a choice as to what I do with my life, what I look like, what I read, what I consider good. It was the overthrow of what has been called "prescriptive theology", reliance on the writings of others. In some of its phases this conviction led to excesses which reached the point of folly, as with pop art which exercised surprising influence on a gullible public. At its more serious the movement for freedom of expression was important and valuable, for it gradually penetrated our consciousness that we do not have to be imitations of anyone and that we can take responsibility for our own development. This severely limits the power of class which had been a serious social handicap in many countries. An Oxford college head once told me: "Class distinctions began to go when everybody started wearing blue jeans." So in one sense this was a fresh uniform; it was also a declaration of independence. The fall-out from this emphasis on personal freedom touched Christian life at many points, for example in the more relaxed approach to the liturgy and the teaching of situational ethics.

Even greater impact flowed from feminism. The release of women from the stereotype of mother and housewife has been a revolution in many societies. At this point we note that in most of the poorer, agricultural societies the changes are less, for the hard labour of women has been and remains critical for human survival. Where there was some freedom of choice the approach to family life has been shifted very considerably. There was a widespread expectation that women would seek the kind of employment for which they felt fit and that all occupations would be open to them. The implications for society go much farther, for the questions are asked whether the patriarchal and masculine patterns of our corporate life are fixed for ever, and whether that male emphasis in the history of Christian faith is required by God. This may prove to be one of the most radical developments in the second half of the twentieth century, as half of humanity becomes aware of the possibilities of life, of talent unused and of injustice long suffered. Secular bodies have generally dealt with it in more open, constructive ways than have churches.

Identity is also an emphasis in the growth of local and regional patriotism. In some circumstances we call this tribalism, but that has become a very negative word. It is the declaration: we know who we are, we will be respected for who we are and will not tamely accept that our future lies in the hands of others. The power engendered by this conviction has been amply shown all over the world — North American Indians and Australian Aboriginals, the Biafrans and the Basques, the Kurds and the Scots, the Matabele and the Armenians — the list goes on. In some cases violence has been used but in vain and we still await signs that the nation-states, as they were defined at the end of the second world war, can accept the degrees of local autonomy which now are demanded. To deny the sense of identity has proved impossible. To acknowledge it with gratitude and translate it into more acceptable political frameworks has been beyond us, so in most places there is at best an uneasy truce.

World division

It has been a generation of world division. For the inhabitants of Europe its sign was the wall between East and West, a split between systems and ideologies that brought constant tension, misunderstanding and a furious and futile arms race. For the great majority of the world's population it was a time of increasing divide from the world's wealth. There are many different estimates of poverty levels and the way they moved — some observers see a trickle-down effect, with wide access to basic commodities. This is most evident in East Asia where rapid industrialization and human adaptability have lifted the average income. But most see the wealth gap steadily increasing. Certainly the consumption of resources by the North has grown rapidly and there has developed a thin crust of affluence even in the South where the great majority continues to scramble, sweat, plead and labour for minimal living standards. In the light of this reality the nations of the tropical world watched the cold war with cynicism for it seemed to them an artificial game played by the arms industries. While the USSR and the USA were arguing about the number of nuclear warheads, far more people were facing large numbers of homeless refugees and of dying babies. It is this indefensible division of humanity which characterizes the life of this generation. The political call for justice and the human cry for food and shelter are one prayer that we may live together in this globe as children of one God.

The Christian response

It is against this background that we examine the record of one Protestant missionary organization, but before we turn to the details it is helpful to recollect the main strands of Christian thought and action which affected all the participants. Those who served through the London Missionary Society formed a small part of significant movements and were themselves sometimes significant forces within these movements.

Theology

To put theology first — and that itself betrays an author's upbringing — there was a major struggle, a creative struggle, between the liberal approaches of the interwar period, which continued after the second war, and the new orthodoxies which were labelled with the impressive name of Barth. This struggle reached its peak with the publication of *Honest to God* (1963) by Bishop John Robinson, of the later works of Bonhoeffer, the secularization writers of the USA and the published documents of the Second Vatican Council. There was a considerable theological divide. Those who were drawn to Barth — as he had been drawn to P.T. Forsyth — took as their starting point the otherness of God's revelation, the divine word, distinct from human thought, religion, searching and habit, a voice from the eternal into time, to be heard, obeyed and adored. In such a tradition the objective character of the revelation is assured by scripture. The whole world is addressed and is called to respond. The judgment of God is focused on how we respond. Therefore the preaching of that word is the primary calling of those who minister in the church of God. One aspect of this tradition was the missionary calling of the church, well described by Hendrick Kraemer in *The Christian Message in a Non-Christian World* (1938).

Those who developed the other track attempted to start from the actual experience of life itself. Outstanding was Paul Tillich, who probed the reality of divine influence and challenge in the deepest experiences we know, in suffering and despair, in fear and loneliness and in sexual love. For theologians of this tradition it was pointless to refer to the objective character of the word unless there was a reality in every human life through which the word was made subjective, an inner awareness formed out of the very stuff of human experience. Our very doubts are then seen to be pointers to the divine, the unsettling of our shallow confidence. God is no longer "out there", wholly other, but is seen in the splendour of human gifts, touched in human creativity and worshipped in human love.

Both views, when carried to extremes, are fatally flawed. If the neo-orthodoxy proclaims too insistently the otherness of the divine word then it gives but a poor account of the goodness, self-sacrifice, courage and generosity of very ordinary people who are not Christian and never will be. It devalues humanity. The liberalism of this period, when it shoots off to the circumference of Christian thought, fails to take seriously the incarnation in Christ and the centrality of the cross. But the tension between these directions of thought has been an energizing force, requiring all preachers and teachers of the churches to determine where they stand and what they can honestly preach. There can be no doubt that up to the first world war it was orthodoxy, centred on the gift of salvation in Christ, which was the mainspring of the world missionary movement. With the discussion of the new liberalism many questions were raised about the necessity of the missionary calling. If there is not "prescriptive theology", what are we sent out to teach? This questioning marked our period in all debates on mission, so that those who held strongly to the traditional understanding of the gospel call began to doubt the faith of the liberals. The theological divergence was to lead to division in mission organization.

Ecumenism

Mission organization was equally affected by the major movement of the century which we call ecumenism. It is very much the twentieth-century stirring of the Spirit in the churches, for it has created a wholly new relationship among them. In previous centuries, from the split of East and West, churches have stood in opposition to one another, with anathemas and exclusions, because each had believed that it stood for truths while others had drifted into error. There are places where this attitude continues to persist, right to the end of the century. It is a view through very narrow-focus lenses. It sees a definition of truth forming the title deeds of the church so that truth and error can be readily judged. It also looks at others in the most negative way possible, highlighting all the supposed errors and ignoring the agreements, even though they are very considerable. Many people have proclaimed that the virility of their church life is to be seen in the narrowness of its convictions, the total dedication to a single view of faith.

It has been an exciting process, though a slow one, to move out of that framework of church beliefs and structures. Tradition has acted as a brake. Gradually Christians have come to see that those in other churches also love and follow Jesus Christ, receive the Holy Spirit, serve the kingdom of God, pray for forgiveness and trust in eternal life. If then they are "in Christ" there cannot be a complete barrier between us. We have to work out on the ground just how we relate to one another and what progress we can make to overcome the serious differences that remain. This process has been a major concern of the churches through our period.

Immediately following the second world war the churches of those countries involved in the fighting faced enormous tasks of reconstruction and serving the needs of countless displaced persons. This was a spur towards mutual commitment. So the slow process from 1910 to 1940 in the areas of theology and discussion of social issues was accelerated by very practical necessities. For the North Atlantic area the imperative was plain; get together, work together, pray together, for the good of humanity. For churches in other parts of the world the ecumenical calling was fuelled more by their strange missionary history. This had exported denominational loyalties which were wholly unsuited to their experience and context. So one reaction was to seek fresh ways of relating to other churches locally and to parent churches across the world. The calling to witness faithfully in the countries with vast populations and powerful ancient faiths also brought Christians together in a common obedience. For many reasons, therefore, the commitment made in the formation of the World Council of Churches in 1948 was the signal that change had occurred and that greater change was due. The parallel with the founding of the United Nations is inescapable. Churches, like nations, were conscious of entering a new era of human history when the globe could be viewed as a whole. A formative influence was exercised by the international gatherings sponsored by the International Missionary Council and, from 1961, by the Commission on World Mission and Evangelism of the World Council of Churches.

Regional ecumenical bodies swiftly followed. Since most of these were in places where churches had very slender financial resources they depended on grants from overseas in a mirror image of the economic dependence of new nation-states. This was an ecumenical weak link. It enabled the regional ecumenical bodies to handle large budgets independent of the churches they claimed to represent. So they could, and did, adopt policies not wholly in line with the thinking of their members. The great gain was the stimulus to a regional consciousness of the churches. Certainly in the Pacific region the island churches had depended on strong associations with their parent churches and it was only the entry of the ecumenical agencies that introduced an equal sense of linkage between the groups of islands. Similarly the ecumenical groupings encouraged an Asian and an African awareness which could grow into mutual confidence and sharing.

In the following sections we shall see how the ecumenical impetus led to the formation of united churches in many places where the LMS was involved.

Service

The impetus was not only towards new church-to-church relationships, for ecumenism has always involved care for the wholeness of the human family. As the rescue of refugees from a life of hopelessness was a primary concern at the birth of the World Council of Churches, so the cooperative action of churches in every area has been directed towards the support of oppressed, starving, handicapped and homeless people. This direction of Christian service has been part of the western missionary movement from the end of the eighteenth century. From the abolition of the slave trade, to the care of Chinese concubines, to the deliverance of Indian widows and the uplift of outcastes, this was a familiar theme. The deliverance of the gospel applied to all. What was peculiar to our period and of significance for the whole story was the separation of the major social programmes from the traditional missionary agencies. This was partly due to the sheer volume of the work. Very large sums of money had to be raised and spent, first in shattered Europe and then in poverty-stricken areas of the world, in order to touch human disasters. A part of that money came directly from churches, but much had to be raised through public contribution and by government grant. In several European countries, most notably in Germany, the income of development organizations came largely from taxation. So specialized agencies were needed to ensure the proper use of the money and to organize a corps of trained people who could advise both donor and recipient agencies. The agencies were, in the main, ecumenical. It was an early test of how willing churches were to cede their authority to a body which represented them all.

For our purpose the significance was that the concept of mission was practically divided at that point. The new agencies, with larger resources, dealt with the enormous social problems that startled the Christian conscience. The churches and their mission boards, with smaller resources and longer histories, maintained the relationship with churches, supporting overseas training for ministry and similar work, church-related schools and hospitals, and the pastoral and evangelistic tasks of the local church. This division meant that for the many supporters of overseas mission there was often a choice as to which most needed enthusiasm, advocacy and resources. In Britain the claims of Christian Aid often appeared more urgent than those of any missionary society. Those claims were placed before all the churches and so were a spur to ecumenical engagement. Although in theory it all belonged together under the title of "mission" there was a tendency to develop diverging lines of thought and devotion. However necessary this was for practical reasons, the theology in western missionary policy suffered. The gain was that churches in the affluent countries developed a conscience about world poverty and so were able to act as a challenger to governments; the new specialized agencies did their educational work well.

Church independence

The new mood of independence from colonialism after the second world war stimulated the whole process of church independence which had begun long before and which forms a major theme in the Goodall volume of LMS history. Now it had greater urgency and a sharper tone, for in a newly independent state it was seen to be anomalous for the churches still to be dependent on a mission board far away. The task was to make the decisive break in authority structures while keeping the sense of unity and mutual care which is the quality of real church life. In many places it was a double transition. It touched the missionary agencies in the sending countries and also the church-to-church connections, for throughout the previous century mission boards had often acted as though they were the ecclesial entity directing operations. They now had to reconsider their position within the life of the church. Why is it, asked the bishops of Anglican dioceses in Africa, that when we visit England we have to deal with the office of the Church Missionary Society or the other societies and not with the General Synod of the Church of England? Why relate to the Methodist Missionary Society and not the Methodist Church? There was a strong challenge to European and North American structures, which, in the new era, were plainly one-sided, formed originally by enthusiasts, not by formal church bodies. The voluntary societies have put up a strong rearguard action, claiming that specialism is a fact of life, that without enthusiasm commitment withers, and that initiative is made more possible by independent boards. But the weight of argument has been on the other side. World church relationships are the framework within which international mission takes place and churches need to deal with one another as equally competent bodies. The agencies for any specialist part of mission therefore need to be held within the overall structures of the church. A failure at this point suggests that the missionary enterprise, however defined, is a voluntary addition to the life of a church when theologically it is the very reason for which the church is called into being.

The movement towards independence spurred the development of local, regional or ethnic theologies. This was partly the reaction of people living in poverty who needed to express the gospel in their own situation, and partly a longing to be no longer imitators of the West but creators of a new tradition. The appearance of such regional diversity frightened all centralizers in church life but gave great stimulus to all who realized that national and church independence needed each other.

The pressure also came with a touch of impatience concerning western influence on church life. This became much publicized under the heading of "moratorium". The word was used first, I believe, in East Africa but was quickly picked up in Asia. It was a suggestion that, if churches were to discover their own identity, fashion their own leadership and patterns of authority, and develop their own theological stance, then the sending churches should cease for a time to send any missionaries at all. This was a recognition that European and North American skill, influence and resources could be inhibiting factors, however well meant. The sending bodies reacted very guardedly. They saw this as the work of a few radical spirits which was not to be encouraged and not truly representative, so there were no mission boards which adopted moratorium as a policy. In some places, however, it became a de facto reality. Where a national government placed severe restrictions on the entry of expatriates the numbers of missionaries rapidly declined, for example in India. But the great experiment was China, where a moratorium was fully enforced by the communist government. A much smaller example was Burma. Looking back, it now appears that the moratorium was entirely beneficial. It did enable Christian people to identify entirely with their nation without reliance on external aid. It did enable Christians to forget the old denominations and come together in a single fellowship. It did produce new evangelical thinking and energy. And, during the Cultural Revolution, it revealed the true faithfulness and courage of a wholly indigenous church. It may well be said that the Chinese experience was exceptional. There are other places where local Christian leadership proved weak or corrupt and thus there was a loss of confidence in the gospel with regret that expatriates were not still there. On balance, however, I believe that the moratorium call should have evoked a more positive response than it did and was dismissed partly because the mission agencies were unaware of the effects of their dominant position.

The end of western dominance

This particular slogan was a part of the much broader change which took place quite abruptly during our period. It was signified at the Bangkok conference on world mission and evangelism, a major element of the World Council of Churches (1973). One of the thoughts that emerged from that conference was: "We are at the end of a missionary era; we are at the very beginning of the world mission" (Emilio Castro). This intentionally signalled that the period of western dominance in the international mission of Christianity was over. But what happened? Most of the major western agencies continued to fulfil their nineteenth-century mandate in good spirits, with skilled personnel and with socially conscious policies. It may have looked as though little had changed. As a missionary serving in the South Pacific during that period it did not seem to me that the LMS was finished. Yet the message was in a large measure true. Just as the colonial officers of the European powers were the last of their kind, so the great network of European missionaries was becoming thinner every year. It was not only visa problems that caused this. There were two further significant reasons.

The first was the availability of trained indigenous leadership throughout the world church. Through the work of many seminaries, universities and legal training schools, there was a growing supply of people just as well qualified as the Europeans who had been their teachers. The need for the expatriate, in however modest a role, could prove to be a stifling or depressing effect on local leadership. This is not to say that they were unloved or unrespected; but that very love and respect could inhibit a local person from speaking and acting in the freedom of the Spirit. As this became evident, fewer posts were filled by expatriates and the influence of the sending agencies diminished.

The second reason was even more basic to mission thinking. It was the realization that Europe, the USA and Australia were mission fields where the churches were dangerously weak. This fact was well known to such church leaders as William Temple in the 1930s. Yet the traditional portrait of Europe as the heartland of Christianity where churches exercised great influence was slow to fade. So it was a shock to many to discover in the horrors of the second world war how close to the surface of Europe were bestiality and barbarism. It was a potent sign of the weakness of traditional Christianity. In the rebuilding of Europe the churches took a courageous part, especially in the care of refugees, but the activity could not conceal how many people had rejected Christian faith. Millions found no strength in the traditional worship, no vision of what life could be, and often no love in the formality of chilly buildings. It was as though great numbers of young people throughout Europe and North America were looking for a "new thing", a way out of the power struggles which had produced death, and the churches offered a very old thing, a routine which was hugged by the membership like a hot water bottle in a frosty bedroom.

The weakness was also financial. After six years of war the churches in Europe had enormous tasks of reconstruction which absorbed much of their energy and their capital. In America there was still great wealth in churches and foundations which could finance considerable new enterprises. Major ecumenical initiatives, such as the Theological Education Fund, were largely financed from America. For British churches there could be no such open-handedness and some policy directions in missionary work were taken on financial grounds. This caused some dismay in other parts of the world where churches related to the USA received more generous aid while those related to Britain found their budgets being squeezed. Those mission agencies with large investments or properties maintained their income; the struggle was for those dependent on the people in the pew.

For not only were there fewer of them. They had to turn their first attention to the missionary tasks in the neighbourhood. It was often much easier to work for a distant mission. What was happening "over there" was seen in glimpses, it could be exotic, could touch the emotions and was always challenging. What was to happen in the next street was an alarming puzzle, for the average congregation was not trained to be a missionary to others. During the 1960s and 1970s it was this weakness as an evangelizing community that disheartened many Christians. It was as though the team was assembled, the pitch was ready but no one had been taught how to kick off. There were many alternative strategies attempted, for example in chaplaincy work in industry, hospitals and colleges, but to commend Jesus Christ in ways that were accessible to ordinary people was a tough commission. As ever greater attention had to be given to this area of weakness it was not surprising if the international mission slipped down the list of priorities.

To many Christians in Africa, Asia and the Pacific this was an almost unbelievable change. The image of Europe as the centre and soul of the great Christian enterprise had been woven into the fabric of history. When young students were sent on scholarships for advanced training in Europe it was often a profound shock when they saw the small, elderly congregation in the uninspiring chapel and the massive disinterest of the population. What they could learn in the European college then might be of value but it certainly would not inspire confidence in the style of church life and witness. For during this period many churches around the world were growing. Local leadership was often of high quality, young people (particularly in East Asia) were longing for a faith not dominated by ancestral voices; the support of the anti-apartheid movement gave the churches in Africa a radical voice; everywhere the discovery of local music translated the gospel into a recognizable sound. It must also be admitted that in certain places American money was a significant contribution, enabling educational facilities at a much higher standard than before the 1940s. So the imbalance between European weakness and third-world strength came as a shock. It did not bring to an end the European missionary tradition but it raised very important questions which every church had to handle in its own way. We shall see in the following chapters how the churches of the LMS group dealt with this.

Two movements

It was partly as a response to the placid quality of conventional Christianity that two movements across the churches became clearly evident. One was for a return to old certainties. When doubt was being aired and liberal values promoted it was easy to suggest that these were the very recipe for failure, a steady betrayal of true faith. In the mission discussions of the period the debate often focused on the dreaded word "syncretism". Are there possibilities that God has been active within Islam and Judaism? And if so should we be able to receive God's work there, not urging those believers to become like us? Could the approach to the divine mystery be equally valid whatever the name? To press those questions was very much the mood of the 1960s and 1970s and to enshrine them within church programmes called "dialogue with other faiths" was the ecumenical way forward. The conservative reaction was natural. The gospel is the good news for all humanity, not one option on the shelf, and Christ is the saviour of the world, not of one segment. The way of Christ has been clear through the centuries, so in place of doubts we proclaim our certainties. This mood was clearly evident in the Roman Catholic community when there were signs that Vatican II might have opened wide the door for major reform. It was evident also in the less thoughtful area of American popular religion, with a succession of conservative, popular preachers who drew many people who were loosely attached to the mainline churches. The most stable and effective was Billy Graham whose crusades (and that is a word that dates the programme) carried a clear message of personal repentance and rebirth through faith. In many parts of the world this was a refreshing breeze. There was a serious attempt to link the evangelistic special events to the regular life of local churches but this was always difficult; the gulf between the great throng in the stadium and the average Sunday congregation was not easily crossed. The theological question this posed was whether being "in Christ" itself means being part of the worshipping community of his people, or whether there can be an individual experience which is eternally valid even if we are part of no church at all. The debate continues, for it is an issue which has been pressed by the evangelical experience since the days of the pietists during the time of the Reformation.

The second widespread movement of the period is called charismatic, the rediscovery and re-emphasis of the gifts of the Holy Spirit. Movements of this sort have been sporadic throughout Christian history and can be seen as signs of God's disturbance of his church where it reduces faith to routine and convention. There is an assertion that the gifts which were noted in the apostolic church are intended for the whole church throughout history. Alongside this is a pattern of worship in which there is informality, congregational response, repetitive hymn singing, prayers for healing, and energetic preaching. Such an outburst of energy has occurred in all the main Christian communions during this period, so that charismatics recognize kinship across all the old divides. It is perhaps inevitable that new cracks in the fabric of Christian fellowship have also been a consequence. When the charismatic approach has been pressed very hard in a congregation and there is not total acceptance of it, then a split may occur which will be very difficult to heal. We learn from the New Testament that an explosion of gifts is not necessarily a positive indication of the health of the fellowship; it has to be so interpreted and so subordinated to love that all may be refreshed by the wind of the Spirit. In the circle of churches with which we are chiefly concerned this movement did not occupy a large place but it was present within nearly all of them.

Between 1940 and 1980 there was a major shift, a gale of wind, which took the historic missionary movement in new directions. Gone was the romantic picture of the pioneers. Gone was the Christendom model of the church. Yet all that was not loss. The reality of living churches around the world which were able to direct their own programmes and policies was a blessing. The loss, if we can speak in such terms, was the reduced place of European churches in their own countries. The combination of these facts indicated a shift in the overall balance of Christianity in the world. One visible sign of that shift is the make-up of the World Council of Churches. At first, in 1948, it was led very largely by western Christians of considerable experience, many of whom had graduated from the Student Christian Movement, but quite swiftly over the next forty years the weight of membership shifted to the churches of Africa, Asia, the Pacific and Latin America. The agenda shifted too, to the discomfort of many in the North. Much of the irritation evident in North American and European churches over the WCC is simply a reaction to an unwelcome agenda which no longer had the old flavour.

But there may be a much deeper concern arising from the shift in focus. It is the question of world evangelization. When the sending out was the visible evidence of commitment and obedience there could hardly be any question that the sharing of the gospel with the whole world was the proper objective. When the church is present within every nation there is some doubt as to whether each national church has a calling to evangelize in every other nation. Is this a universal duty laid on every church by the Lord of the church? Or is it not more likely for the basic calling to evangelize to be addressed to the Christians of each place within their own society? We can then be led to regard the world enterprise as mainly a matter of interchurch relations, churches facing churches rather than Christians facing non-believers. In our period this debate has separated people in the churches and in the whole world body of Christians. There are many of the traditional evangelicals who are firmly convinced that the preaching of the gospel to those who are not Christians is one of the most basic of all forms of obedience. Others are less convinced and would speak of the presence of a Christian community as the primary sign of what Christ has done for the world, regardless of its numbers. In all Christian communions there was need for rethinking in the light of what God had done through the missionary movement. It is significant that of all the Vatican II documents the one on missions *(Ad Gentes)* is very solidly traditional and barely mentions the emerging critical issues. But none of the major communions found it easy to look at the world dimension of Christianity in the new form demanded by a global community of faith.

The circle of churches linked to the LMS had to face these questions. In doing so it was challenged to align the fabric with the world church reality, the means with the ends of mission. For as we look back on the remarkable story of western missionary enterprise it is inescapable that the medium and the message, though not one, were very closely intertwined. If a mission board, sitting in London or New York or Hamburg, has a worldwide responsibility, has resources to send out, has to make decisions and in these respects has no parallel in the receiving areas, then the message is plain — the North is the donor of the gospel and the South is the recipient. The surprising element in recent mission history is that so few of the major agencies have dealt with this critical issue in any radical way. So the LMS development has been one of the few to face fundamental change. This particular slice of the whole story of mission is therefore significant — the period is one of very considerable change in the life of the human family, of change in the position of all the churches involved, of change in the views held about the calling of Christians, and of radical change in the way this part of the whole church of Christ came to terms with the new era of mission.

2. Water from the Rock

Joseph Wing

The world provides the agenda

"The world is the agenda"[1] is a slogan which has influenced the church's approach to mission in recent years and set the pattern for much of its missionary strategy. Like all slogans, it might have become a cliche were it not for the fact that it affirms a biblical understanding of the interplay of the gospel and the contemporary situation. For the past half-century, the witness of the church in Southern Africa has demonstrated convincingly that it had been conditioned and shaped by political, social and economic events and their direct impact on the lives of the people. In consequence, the effective communication of the gospel has required the recognition of Christ as the Lord of the world as well as the Saviour of the individual.

Following his first secretarial visit to Africa in 1947-48, Ronald Orchard devoted the first chapter of his report to the LMS directors[2] to the economic and social background to mission in Africa. He wrote:

> The economic and social environment in any country... constitutes both the setting in which the church must carry out its redemptive task and also part of its evangelistic responsibility.[3]

A year later, in a penetrating paper presented to the South African mission council of the LMS, A.J. Haile emphasized that "the church has to work and witness under prevailing conditions... our lives are politically, economically and socially conditioned".[4]

Rural to urban

The period with which we are concerned opened with a massive movement from the rural to the urban areas. This process began before the second world war, but in the immediate post-war period the steady flow became an avalanche. Orchard describes this trend as a transition from a pastoral to an industrialized life, from a subsistence to a cash economy, from a "small scale" to a "large scale" society. These trends resulted in the breakdown of tribal and family life and an increased disregard of their social and moral norms, as well as economic, religious and mental insecurity.[5]

In 1945, all the LMS head-stations were located in rural areas with enchanting names like Kuruman, Kanye, Molepolole, Serowe, Inyati, Hope Fountain and Dombodema, redolent of the pioneering era of missions in Southern Africa. Nearby urban areas were, at best, out-stations of an historic mission station. At an earlier stage, the LMS had actually relinquished responsibility for its members in developing urban areas, transferring them to any church or mission which was prepared to give them pastoral care. A policy of "abandonment" was no longer possible, however, when the numerical strength of the LMS church was beginning to shift from the rural mission stations to towns like Kimberley, Vryburg, Johannesburg, Lobatse, Francistown, Bulawayo and Kwe Kwe. Moreover, new industrial and mining developments had opened up in the Western Transvaal, the Orange Free State, the Northern Cape,

and at Orapa, Selibe-Pikwe and Jwaneng in the Bechuanaland Protectorate. Industrial development in Rhodesia was concentrated in the midlands, where the Rhodesian iron and steel corporation set up its plant, just sixty miles from Zinyangeni, the most remote LMS mission station in Matabeleland.

It was in the 1950s that the LMS church began to take seriously its pastoral responsibility for its urban members, largely as the result of increasing pressure from the people themselves. A church was finally established in Kimberley in 1951 when an ad-hoc arrangement with the Congregational Union of South Africa (CUSA) was formalized and a united church constituted, followed by the appointment of the first LMS minister, K. Petso, three years later.[6] The Witwatersrand Congregational Church, an amalgamation of the work of the LMS and the American Board Mission in the Transvaal, serving hundreds of migrant workers from the Bechuanaland Protectorate, Rhodesia and South Africa, received the pastoral oversight it merited when John F. White was placed in Johannesburg as the first resident minister in 1954.[7] For many years, the virile church in Bulawayo had been much larger than its mother church at Hope Fountain, but it was not until 1956 that Paul S. King and Phyllis Wenyon joined Aaron Mpofu, the evangelist serving Bulawayo, and the church and two mission houses were built at Mpopoma.[8] When Welkom, at the heart of the new Orange Free State goldfields, was developed in 1946, thousands of people from every part of Southern Africa came to work on the new mines. The challenge to the churches was without parallel as a ready-made mission field emerged virtually overnight. In the early stages much interest was shown in the possibility of joint action for mission, but the early hopes began to fade as most of the churches established their own work in the area. Four churches, however, did agree to work together — the Paris Evangelical Mission, the American Board Mission, the Congregational Union of South Africa and the LMS. Together they established the United Church of the Orange Free State Goldfields on 6 February 1955 at an impressive service at Welkom. The vision of John F. White, the secretary of the joint council of the United Church of the OFS Goldfields, that the united church would extend to include all the work of the cooperating churches in Southern African, was not to be fulfilled.[9]

Early industrial growth in Botswana was overtaken by the euphoria which accompanied independence in 1966 and the creation of a modern capital city out of the former village of Gaborone. The sudden emergence of Gaborone as a splendid city with modern buildings and its own infrastructure epitomizes the transforming effect of social and political self-determination. Prior to independence, the Bechuanaland Protectorate had been controlled by tribal-based structures, with a British colonial support system. The pattern of church government had also been closely related to tribal structures, the LMS district churches being based in the same tribal centres, from which the missionaries-in-charge operated, exercising ecclesiastical authority over the same territory as the chief of the tribe within whose bounds they worked.

The economy of the Bechuanaland Protectorate had also been rurally based, confined almost entirely to cattle ranching. The discovery of rich mineral deposits at Selibe-Pikwe, Orapa and Jwaneng expanded the range of the economy dramatically and accelerated the urbanization process as people left their villages to work in the new industrial and urban areas. The pastoral needs of the people who were converging on Gaborone and the mining towns provided a splendid opportunity for ecumenical cooperation. An encouraging start was made when a scheme was accepted for a united church in Gaborone. Derek Jones (LMS) and Alan Butler (Anglican) were appointed as joint incumbents of Trinity Church, in which Anglicans, Methodists, Presbyterians, Quakers and the LMS church were united in happy fellowship. When the Anglican church in Botswana became a diocese of the Church of the Province of Central Africa and an Anglican cathedral was built in Gaborone, Anglican participation was reduced to a nominal minimum. The Methodist church put up their own place of worship in Gaborone and withdrew from official participation in Trinity Church. The constitution

of Trinity Church continued to adhere to the ecumenical principle on which the church
was founded, but it became, in effect, a church of the LMS/UCCSA (United
Congregational Church of Southern Africa). [10] A similar combined mission thrust was
initiated at Selibe-Pikwe. A very promising community-based church was started with
support from the United Society for the Propagation of the Gospel and the Congregational Council for World Mission (CCWM). Once again, however, when the other
partners in the scheme withdrew, the UCCSA had to minister to its own people and
build its own church. [11]

Political transitions

Independence marked the end of the colonial era in Botswana. Although the
colonial administration in the former Bechuanaland Protectorate had, for the most
part, been benevolent, the British colonial secretary had on occasion exercised
extraordinary powers which ran contrary to the wishes and best interests of the people,
and South African racial norms, though officially discouraged, were widely practised.
In fact, the influence of South African attitudes was clearly evident in the manner in
which the British government interfered in the affairs of the Bamangwato tribe after
Seretse Khama married Ruth Williams in London in 1948. Political tensions in the
tribe were exacerbated by the colonial office's intransigence, which was encouraged
by members of the LMS staff in London, resulting in the devious manner in which
Seretse Khama was treated before and after his return to Serowe and the subsequent
self-imposed banishment of Tshekedi Khama and his supporters to Philikwe. [12]

With the advent of self-government in Botswana, Seretse Khama's conviction that
democratic structures based on universal franchise were the right form of government
for his country received full vindication. The people demonstrated their confidence in
his political philosophy by electing him the first president of the Republic of
Botswana, thereby refuting the unfounded fears of the British government regarding
his acceptability as a ruler of his own people, and confirming the suspicions of the
Batswana that colonial reservations regarding his marriage to a white woman were
based primarily on white prejudice in regard to mixed marriages and not on the alleged
unwillingness of the people of Botswana to receive a white consort.

Throughout the long association of the LMS with Botswana the missionaries had
shown a concern for the political and social development of the country and had
advised and assisted the chiefs in many ways, notably in the initiative which resulted
in Bechuanaland being proclaimed a Protectorate in 1895. This had resulted in respect
for human rights and a participatory pattern of government at all levels. Consequently
the transition from colonialism to independence was a gentle, evolutionary process
without coup or revolutionary reaction. It was also a process in which the missionaries
of the LMS and the United Free Church of Scotland were invited to participate and to
help facilitate the adaptation to constitutional forms of government. Alfred Merriweather, the respected doctor of Molepolole, was elected the first speaker of the
legislative assembly. He was succeeded by Albert Lock of Serowe. Derek Jones was
elected overwhelmingly as the first mayor of the new capital city, Gaborone.
Significant Christian influence was also present in the first and subsequent cabinets, a
majority of whose members, from the president downwards, had been nurtured in
LMS families and educated at the Tiger Kloof institution.

A very different political climate obtained to the north in neighbouring Rhodesia
which, immediately after the second world war, experienced a revival of some of the

worst features of colonialism. The expanding economy of the country and the need for technical skills to accelerate industrial growth brought a steady stream of British and South African white immigrants into the country. This reinforced the predilection towards racial separation which had been a feature of the social structures of the colony since the granting of the charter in Matabeleland to the British South Africa Company in 1889. In response to the mounting pressure for political independence throughout the British commonwealth, the Central African Federation was constituted, consisting of the contiguous colonies of Southern and Northern Rhodesia and the Nyasaland Protectorate. There were strong African objections to the scheme, which was seen as a threat to black political advancement. Blacks feared adverse land adjustments, increased white immigration and the entrenchment of racial attitudes similar to those prevailing in South Africa. The leadership of the Federation, notably Sir Roy Welensky and Garfield Todd, held out the promise of equal rights for black and white citizens, which most of the white Rhodesians at that time were not prepared to concede. Following the dissolution of the Federation, (the former Southern) Rhodesia became a self-governing dominion within the commonwealth, until Ian Smith led the country into a unilateral declaration of independence in 1965 with disastrous consequences. Articulate black leadership was suppressed. Joshua Nkomo, born on an LMS mission station, Robert Mugabe, who once taught at Hope Fountain, and Ndabaningi Sithole, a prominent minister of the American Board Mission, were placed in detention. When eventually they were released, they went into exile and continued the struggle for independence from neighbouring Zambia and Mozambique. Despite United Nations sanctions and a long and bitter civil war, it was 15 years before full independence was granted to Zimbabwe, as it is now known, in the terms of the Lancaster House agreement in 1980.

Throughout the years of the civil war, the people lived under constant threat, particularly in the rural areas. Regular worship had to be suspended in many village churches. Thousands of people fled from their homes in rural Matabeleland and swarmed into Bulawayo for protection, creating unprecedented social problems but resulting in phenomenal church growth in Bulawayo and its environs. Most of the places in Matabeleland where the LMS/UCCSA was located were in the direct line of fire between liberation and government forces. A battle was waged between the Rhodesian army and freedom fighters on the sportsfield at Inyati school, boys were abducted from Dombodema school and taken to Zambia for military training by ZAPU, whilst the people of Zinyangeni, Tshimali and Lupane lived in constant danger. Joshua Danisa, the indefatigable secretary of the UCCSA in Rhodesia, showed a pastoral concern for the church and its institutions which held them together "through cloud and sunshine" and prepared them to take their place in a new and free Zimbabwe. For twenty years, both during and immediately after the civil war, the cross cast its shadow over the country. Two missionaries of the LMS/CWM, Peggy Payne, who gave more than thirty years of her life to the church and people of Zimbabwe, and Jean Campbell, a former administrative secretary of the UCCSA in Zimbabwe, were murdered in tragic circumstances.

South Africa

The imperialism which had dominated Africa for most of the nineteenth century and the first forty years of the twentieth century began to yield in almost every part of the continent in response to the incessant demand for decolonization and desegregation. Even South Africa which, since the Act of Union of 1910, had had racism entrenched in its constitution, began to move fractionally in the mid-1940s. In a major policy speech in parliament, J.H. Hofmeyr, deputy prime minister and heir apparent to General Smuts, declared unequivocally: "I take my stand on the removal of the colour bar from our constitution."[13]

Z.K. Matthews, who came from an LMS family in Kimberley, with deep roots in Dikgatlong and Serowe, Albert Luthuli, president of the African National Congress and a leading Congregationalist in Natal, and other prominent black leaders were committed to working by peaceful means for a non-racial, democratic South Africa. Then Hofmeyr died suddenly and the Smuts government, now lacking the kind of leadership which was committed to full racial equality, foundered and in the absence of a clear policy on racial issues lost the 1948 election.[14]

The national party won the 1948 election on the basis of a racist policy. It lost no time in entrenching apartheid on the statute book, tampering with the rule of law and the jurisdiction of the courts to do so. There had always been racial separation in South Africa, but due to the untiring efforts of John Philip, the superintendent of the LMS in South Africa in the first half of the nineteenth century, there was equality before the law and "people of colour" in the Cape Province had a qualified franchise. With cold, calculating ruthlessness the national party legislated for total apartheid. Oppression was enforced by law, basic human rights were denied and the movements of black South Africans were controlled from the cradle to the grave. Within five years of coming to power, the national party had erected the five major pillars of apartheid with the passing of the prohibition of mixed marriages act (1949), the immorality act (1950), the population registration act (1950), the separate amenities act (1953) and the Bantu education act (1953).[15] The churches affiliated to the Christian Council of South Africa engaged in a relentless struggle against apartheid on theological, moral and legal grounds. The Council consistently and courageously defended the rights of the people who were the victims of apartheid, a majority of whom belonged to the churches and missions affiliated to the Council. Several LMS/UCCSA ministers and laypeople were in the forefront of what became an almost daily confrontation with the South African government. Basil Brown, minister of Union Church, Cape Town (of which John Philip had been minister) and grandson of John Tom Brown of Kuruman, was the convener of the action committee of the Christian Council in the 1950s. Because of his constant vigilance no repressive measure introduced by the government was left unchallenged. In 1961 Brown was appointed as the first full-time general secretary of the Christian Council. He not only paved the way for the Council to be reconstituted as the South African Council of Churches in 1968, but also equipped it for the intensification of the struggle against apartheid which was to dominate the Council's life and work for the next quarter of a century.[16]

Every black person in South Africa became a victim of apartheid, subjected to the indignity and the injustice of a system which, according to its perpetrators, was designed "to seek a solution which will ensure survival and full development — political and economic — to each of the racial groups".[17] The opposite proved to be the case as abject poverty and the deprivation of existing rights were inflicted on the majority of South Africans without their consent. Several million people lost their citizenship rights in the land of their birth, which was replaced by the counterfeit citizenship conferred by the puppet parliaments of the so-called independent homelands.

The LMS/UCCSA rejected the partition of South Africa into fragmented ethnic territories. When Bophuthatswana, in which most of the historic work of the LMS/UCCSA among the South African Tswana people was located, received its independence in 1977, the UCCSA addressed a letter to President Lucas Mangope protesting against the establishment of the homeland, but pledging itself to continuing pastoral care of the people, amongst whom the LMS/UCCSA had been working since 1816. The church's position in Bophuthatswana and the other homelands was an ambivalent one. The church had totally rejected the system, but the people had to come to terms with it in order to survive. Many of of the leading politicians, top-ranking civil servants and prominent educationalists came from an LMS background and continued to be active in the life of the church, whilst being an integral part of the homeland structure. It was a situation which produced tension and, at the same time, demonstrated the incarnational nature of the church's mission by being with the people where they were, under the conditions in which they were forced to live, thus making real the presence and power of Christ in every human circumstance.

In South Africa the wholesale uprooting of people and their resettlement in homelands or new areas designated for blacks impinged directly on the mission of the church. The Surplus People's Project estimated that 3,548,900 people were moved between 1960 and 1983.[18] When people were relocated on a piece of undeveloped, open veld, with no amenities, the desolate and inhospitable nature of their surroundings made them look back with longing to the strong stone churches, many of them built by pioneer missionaries, which like their own homes were being crushed by bulldozers.[19] As soon as they had erected temporary houses for themselves they began to plan the building of a church as a place of worship and a centre for community life. The LMS/UCCSA and the local churches responded magnificently to the challenge "to rise up and build". They did so with enormous enthusiasm and sacrificial devotion, generously assisted by LMS/CWM and partner churches in the United States of America.[20]

It was in 1976 that the disturbances in Soweto and other parts of South Africa began to reveal that the "cracks" in the apartheid system were a veritable chasm. The Black Consciousness movement had removed all fear of the oppressor from black children and young people; they were determined to dismantle Bantu education and with it the whole apartheid system. The government responded with strong-arm tactics, but the tide had turned and "states of emergency", bannings, detentions, torture and killings left the young people undaunted and unafraid. The 1976 assembly of the UCCSA suspended most of its normal business sessions to consider the crisis in the life of the nation. A former chairman of the church, some of its ministers and hundreds of its children and young people were languishing in detention as the assembly deliberated. The assembly addressed a letter to the prime minister, B.J. Vorster, demanding a national convention at which all parties, including those banned and in exile, would be represented, to prepare a new constitution for a non-racial democratic South Africa. The prime minister treated the church's submissions with contempt; he repeatedly told ministers to preach the gospel of love and not concern themselves with politics. The delegates came away from the 1976 assembly knowing that South Africa was approaching the end of an era; the chain of events which began on 16 June 1976 in Soweto were the birth pangs of a new order. The struggle intensified, and it was only on 2 February 1990 when political prisoners were released and the way was opened for exiles to return home that the convention to plan for a unified and democratic South Africa, which the UCCSA had requested in 1976, became a possibility.

Church government... agreeable to the word of God

Changes in the ordering of society impinge directly on the structures of the church which are shaped by sociological trends as well as by theological principles. Despite the LMS tradition of giving great freedom in matters of church government, the form of church government in Southern Africa was determined by the regulations of the LMS and the ecclesiastical background of the missionaries. For more than 140 years the mission maintained a pragmatic polity of church government in which the district committee was the highest court of the church, subject only to the veto of the LMS board of directors. In 1943 the district committee was replaced by a mission council; this still consisted of all the missionaries, but it made provision for three Africans to be appointed from each of the three regional councils, which were constituted simultane-ously with the mission council.[21] The regional councils comprised all missionaries, ministers and evangelists as personal members, together with lay delegates elected by the district churches on a proportional basis. Regional councils quickly became a forum in which the total life of the church at all levels was fully and freely discussed. The membership of the mission council in 1945 was 23 missionaries and nine Africans. With such disproportionate representation, effective control was where it had always been — in the hands of the missionaries.

For the next five years the mission council, the regional councils and the district churches gave careful consideration to the kind of structure needed to effect the transition from mission to church. In the southern regional council, where the traditional relationship between church and tribe had become little more than a perfunctory acknowledgment of each other's existence, the need for more participat-ory structures at local and regional levels tended to receive more detailed consideration than in the Bechuanaland Protectorate, where a semblance of the old solidarity between church and tribe persisted up until and, in some cases, beyond independence.

Predictably, the process of devolution started within the bounds of the southern regional council, when the Kuruman district church, with the approval of the mission council, released its southern section, centred on Danielskuil, so that it could be constituted as a local church, governed by its own constitution, controlling its own finances and owning its property. Shortly afterwards, the Taung district church was divided into four sub-districts (Taung, Mamutle, Manthe and the Western Transvaal) each with its own minister and deacons, its own church roll and full responsibility for the administration of local affairs. The new urban churches, which had never been part of an LMS district church, like Kimberley and the Witwatersrand Congregational Church, developed along constitutional lines from their inception. The same process of devolution had also begun in the northern region where the fast-growing Bulawayo church quickly assumed the responsibilities of a local church in an urban community.

In a paper presented to the Southern Africa committee of the World Alliance of Reformed Churches, Derek Jones maintained that the former LMS districts in Botswana "were natural units, with tribal, communication, economic and traditional cohesion".[22] The mission district remained the fulcrum of church life in Botswana until the formation of the UCCSA in 1967. It provided a pattern of church authority and administration which resembled the pattern of tribal authority, and with both having the same geographical areas of jurisdiction. Notwithstanding the absence of any clear theological principle underlying it, the LMS district in Botswana was perceived as a manifestation of "corporate personality", an integral dimension of African society and, in the light of biblical teaching on the "people of God", "agreeable to the word of God".

Despite initial reservations on the part of the LMS board regarding the new mission council designation, the LMS church council was the name chosen. The church council held its first meeting at Dombodema in 1954. The composition and role of the regional councils did not change, except that they now elected the full delegation to the church council, comprised of three African members and three missionaries from each region. The change of name and composition did little to alter the modus operandi of the church council, which never became an assembly of the whole church; it continued where the mission council had left off, the emphasis still being on matters of administration and finance rather than on the nature and mission of the church in a rapidly changing world. Several leading lay leaders felt that the church council could not speak with the "voice of the church". They also articulated their disappointment at the entrenchment of missionary representation on church council. This was seen as an attempt to maintain missionary domination. The LMS board and the Congregational Union of England and Wales, in an attempt to give content to the review process, prepared proposals for submission to the "sending" and "receiving" churches associated with the LMS. The LMS church council received these proposals in 1962 and in responding to them its secretary, J.K. Main, indicated the direction in which the LMS church hoped to move. In a letter to the general secretary of the LMS, he wrote:

> This church (LMS church) is not of course Congregational by any stretch of imagination, though the answer to this seems to be that Congregationalism can be stretched to cover anything. My own view is that in the setting in which we are here in Southern Africa, in 1962, the time for the minutiae of Congregational argument or any other denominational argument is past. The church has more vital and more urgent things to do. As far as we are concerned, we are engaged in conversations towards organic union between the LMS, the American Board Mission and the Congregational Union of South Africa and if that can be accomplished and the result known as the United Congregational Church of Southern Africa, then I think there is hope. [23]

Two initiatives for union

There was hope. Two initiatives regarding organic union occurred almost simultaneously. In the first place, the LMS church council and the Bantu Congregational Church of the American Board convened a joint consultation in 1960 to discuss the merging of the two bodies. Later that same year, the Congregational Union of South Africa (CUSA) at its centenary assembly in Port Elizabeth passed the following resolution:

> This assembly reaffirms its desire to explore further the possibility of organic union with the American Board Mission and the London Missionary Society in South Africa, and to this end invites these societies to appoint seven delegates to confer informally with seven appointed by this assembly to represent the Congregational Union of South Africa. [24]

On receipt of the CUSA invitation the LMS church council and the American Board Mission agreed to abandon their bilateral conversations and appoint representatives to the informal consultation proposed by CUSA. The consultation was held on 23-24

May 1961. Consensus was reached on the principles of union and a joint committee constituted. The need for a continuing relationship with the LMS and the United Church Board for World Ministries (UCBWM) was stressed and assurances from the two societies were sought and given in this regard. The principles of union[25] drafted at the consultation, including the name proposed for the merged church, the United Congregational Church of Southern Africa, were submitted to and approved by the negotiating bodies. The joint committee was thereupon directed to prepare a draft basis of union. This was accepted by the churches in 1962. The joint committee, with Basil Brown as chairman and Kenneth Main as secretary, was further commissioned to prepare a constitution for the UCCSA, together with schemes for the common accreditation of ministers, the ownership of property and the consolidation of finances and pension funds. The proposed date of union was set for October 1967. At its annual meeting in 1966, the LMS church council passed resolutions which would enable it to join the UCCSA, as did the assemblies of CUSA and the Bantu Congregational Church of the American Board (BCCAB) The scene was set for union. The embryonic regional councils of the church about to be constituted met in June-July 1967 to adopt their constitutions, elect their officers and committees and appoint delegates to the inaugural assembly.[26]

The UCCSA was inaugurated at a glorious covenant service in Durban on 3 October 1967, at which John Huxtable, the secretary of the Congregational Church in England and Wales, was the preacher. Representatives of the LMS, BCCAB and CUSA processed into the inaugural service as three separate churches. They came out as one people. Thus was born a church which acknowledged a common ancestry in the arrival of the first LMS missionaries at the Cape in 1799; a church spread over five countries of Southern Africa — Botswana, Mozambique, South West Africa, South Africa and Rhodesia. At the time of its inception UCCSA had a communicant membership of 192,556, 43,912 catechumens and adherents and almost 50,000 Sunday school scholars. This constituency was drawn from 251 local churches (with many times that number of out-stations), grouped together in six regional councils. The church had 164 ordained ministers, 92 evangelists and 40 church workers engaged in educational, medical and literature work. The inauguration of the UCCSA crowned with unity 168 years of LMS witness and service in Southern Africa.[27]

In appointing John Kenneth Main to be the first chairman of the UCCSA, the joint committee gave to the church a leader whose wisdom and long experience equipped him for the delicate task of presiding over the inaugural assembly. Main was appointed by the LMS to Southern Africa in 1935. After outstanding service at Tonota and Maun he was appointed in 1954 to succeed A.J. Haile as secretary/treasurer of the LMS church and as representative of the LMS board in Southern Africa. Over a period of thirty years Main guided the LMS church in the difficult transition from mission to church, finally leading it into the UCCSA. In an article in *The Congregationalist* giving an account of the inaugural assembly, Cyril Kemp described with feeling "the admiration evoked by the quiet, firm, gentle and patient way in which the new chairman handled every aspect of the assembly's deliberations".[28] The secretary of the church was the Rev. Joseph Wing who had come to South Africa as a missionary of the LMS.

One of the first acts of the inaugural assembly was to apply for membership of the Congregational Council for World Mission (CCWM).[29] This continued the commitment made by CUSA when CCWM was formed on 1 July 1966, and placed the

UCCSA in a unique relationship at that time as a constituent body of CCWM and also one of the major areas of its involvement in world mission. The combined effect of the inauguration of the UCCSA and the formation of CCWM broadened the horizons of the former LMS constituency in Southern Africa and transformed its understanding of partnership in mission, which now went beyond the earlier concept of receiving missionaries and financial aid from "the fathers and mothers in London". Prior to union, many people had been sceptical about the effect it would have on the LMS church in Botswana. Even the LMS annual report for 1964-65 inferred that the transition from the LMS to the UCCSA might pose an identity crisis for the church in Botswana. The report states:

> The church members are proud of the name (LMS church). They wear blue badges with the white dove of the Society and the letters LMS. They are aware that the name will change, but the majority do not know or understand what the point is of uniting with fellow Congregationalists in Southern Africa. [30]

Within three years of the publication of that report a new blue badge, still displaying the LMS dove as the central motif, against the background of the cross, the universal symbol of the church's faith and mission, but also dominant in the American Board Mission logo, was worn with obvious pride and prominently displayed on banners, pulpit falls and church stationery. The old identity had not been lost but had been immeasurably enriched by union.

Although most of the CCWM missionaries remained in the former LMS areas after union, the 1968 annual report of CCWM recognized the wider scope of its association with the UCCSA in the following statement:

> The council's relationship is with the church as a whole... The council must ensure that the special concern it may have for Botswana and Rhodesia is seen within the larger whole. [31]

Commitment to ecumenism

The unity experienced by the UCCSA at the time of its inauguration was not static. Within 24 hours of uniting the church committed itself to seek union with the Anglican, Methodist and Presbyterian churches, as founder members of the church unity commission. [32] Before the end of 1967 bilateral conversations with the Presbyterian Church of Southern Africa (PCSA) were revived after a lapse of many years. [33] Schemes for united congregations and the mutual eligibility of members and ministers were also initiated. The relatively small South African Association of the Disciples of Christ merged with the UCCSA in 1972. At the assembly in Pretoria at which the union was given effect, the Presbyterian fraternal delegate declared, amid shouts of acclamation: "You've done it again!" Two unions within the space of five years earned for the UCCSA the appellation of "trend-setters" in ecumenical affairs. It was a valid evaluation, not only in terms of the unions entered into, but also in regard to the pioneering role played by the LMS/UCCSA personnel in furthering the cause of ecumenism. Brian Bailey was the first general secretary of the Botswana Christian Council, who not only nursed it through its incubation period, but also made it into a significant agency for joint action for mission, service and development in a new nation. Felix Mokobi, Basil Manning and Derek Jones made a positive contribution to ecumenical schemes and projects in Botswana and Harsh Ramolefe was the general secretary of the Bible Society for many years. In South Africa John F. White, until his untimely death in 1960, was an ecumenical dynamo, active in the work of the Christian Council of South Africa and an enthusiastic promoter of united work, especially in new and developing areas. Congregationalists were secretaries of the church unity commission for the first 21 years of its life (1968-89). John Thorne, as president of the South African Council of Churches during the mid-1970s, led the church in South Africa prophetically and courageously during turbulent times, being detained and later tried and sentenced for his identification with the victims of apartheid and oppression. Bernard Spong made a unique contribution to Christian communication in Southern Africa through interchurch media programmes of which he was director. Christian cooperation in Zimbabwe was slow and often disappointing, but the joint schemes which succeeded owed much to the initiative and sustained persistence of Joshua Danisa, James Pelling and G. Owen Lloyd.

The designation "united" in the official title of the UCCSA represents a continuing commitment to the non-sectarian principle enshrined in the fundamental principle of the LMS, and also the acceptance of the challenge presented by John Huxtable in his sermon at the inaugural assembly:

> We are now more ready for unity, not less. The will of the great Head of the church has been made known in this matter. He wills the church to be one; that is not for us to argue or discuss. Our part is to understand how we can more perfectly express it, and what is the next step for us to take. [34]

Some of the "next steps" which the LMS/UCCSA took led the church into a cul-de-sac. The failure of the Presbyterian Church of Southern Africa to obtain the required vote in favour of union was an opportunity missed of uniting two churches in the Reformed tradition, which are complementary in so many ways. The repeated delays in the acceptance of the church unity commission's covenant for the reconciliation and mutual recognition of ministries, despite substantial theological agreement, resulted in increasing frustration and a diminished concern for church unity. The breakdown of the exciting ecumenical schemes in Gaborone and at Selibe-Pikwe placed a moratorium on other united projects in Botswana at a time when a united Christian witness would have made a more effective contribution to the life of a new nation. In a discerning welcome address to the assembly of the UCCSA in Gaborone in 1974 Seretse Khama challenged the church to give expression to its essential unity:

> In Africa generally and in Botswana as much as anywhere, we must work to remove the divisions which separate one region from another. The church could be doing much to abolish these barriers. First, however, it must abolish its own barriers and start to practise what it preaches. [35]

The inability of the church in Southern Africa to demonstrate its own unity during the four decades of apartheid in South Africa, throughout a 15-year civil war in Rhodesia (Zimbabwe), and in the prolonged struggles which preceded independence in Namibia and Mozambique, has been a serious indictment of the church's integrity. The churches' repeated advocacy of reconciliation between conflicting political interests in Southern Africa has not been matched by a marked willingness on the part of Christians to reconcile their own differences.

The failures and vacillations of the churches notwithstanding, the ecumenical movement in Southern Africa has made possible a new climate of relationships between the churches and an increasing willingness to cooperate, especially in matters of social concern. In its consistent commitment to the search for union and joint action for mission, the LMS/UCCSA has made a contribution to the cause of ecumenism in Southern Africa out of all proportion to its numerical strength.

Education

The school at Kuruman, started by Robert Moffat in 1829, is the mother of all the educational work of the LMS among the Batswana, Kalanga and Matabele peoples. There was still an LMS primary school on the mission station at Kuruman until 1956, when the implementation of the Bantu education act enforced closure. At the beginning of our period, however, the LMS was heavily involved in education, managing more than a hundred primary schools in Rhodesia and South Africa and controlling four institutions for higher education — Tiger Kloof, Inyati, Hope Fountain and Dombodema. Tiger Kloof, founded in 1904 as the successor to the Moffat institute at Kuruman, was unique in that it served the entire LMS constituency, approximately a third of the students coming from the Bechuanaland Protectorate where at that time there were limited facilities for higher education.

In 1945 A.J. Haile left Tiger Kloof to become the representative of the LMS board in Africa. His long experience, wisdom and statesmanlike qualities made him the right choice for such an important new post. But it is as *Sefako* ("hail" in Tswana), the beloved principal of Tiger Kloof for thirty years, that he was remembered by the old students of Tiger Kloof, whose lives he influenced for good. Many of them, like the first two presidents of Botswana, Seretse Khama and Quett Masire, rose to positions of consider-able eminence, not only in politics but also in education, commerce and the church. All of them remembered their alma mater with deep affection and held their beloved *Sefako* in the highest regard as father and friend. Aubrey Lewis, a young and energetic educationalist, succeeded Haile as principal. Compared with the benevolent despotism of W.C. Willoughby, and the strictly democratic and slightly legalistic approach of A.J. Haile, his predecessors, Lewis was described by one observer as "laissez-faire and socialistic in outlook". [36] His approach was shaped by, and appropriate to, the changing thought forms and social patterns of the post-war world. By the time Lewis assumed responsibility as principal, Tiger Kloof had grown from an elementary boarding school into a complex of schools and training institutions on the same campus. The high school prepared boys and girls for matriculation and junior certificate examinations. The teacher training school prepared teachers for certification at primary school level. The technical schools — carpentry, tannery, tailoring and building — had a reputation throughout Southern Africa for the excellent craftsmen and artisans they produced. Domestic science and needlework were available for girls and made them much sought-after as wives and home-makers. The day primary school was the practising school for teacher training. The Bible school trained ordinands and like the bookroom, which produced school and church books, served all the LMS stations in Southern Africa. While each school and department had its own head, the principal exercised oversight of the whole institution and administered its many-sided affairs.

In July 1955 about 18 months after the passing of the Bantu education act, the South African government intimated that Tiger Kloof would not be allowed to remain in the so-called "white area" of Vryburg and would ultimately be transferred else-where, when suitable facilities were available. This was followed by a letter from the department of native affairs announcing the intention of the department to assume control of the Tiger Kloof schools on 1 January 1956. The executive committee of church council gave careful consideration to these and earlier proposals in the light of its continuing concern for the students. It declined the offer to run hostels on the grounds that Tiger Kloof was a fully integrated institution and could function effectively only under unified control and that the preconditions imposed by the department of native affairs would lead only to a conflict of interests. It was with reluctance and regret, therefore, that the executive committee made the following decisions:

1) that the native affairs department assume control of the institution *as a whole* from 1 January 1956;
2) that the property (excluding the church and farm) be leased to the department for two to three years;
3) that the missionaries of the Society be advised not to accept teaching posts under the native affairs department;
4) that arrangements be made to continue pastoral care of pupils and residents at Tiger Kloof, the conduct of religious instruction in the schools, as allowed in the Bantu education act, and the care of the Tiger Kloof church.

In the same comprehensive minute, the executive committee gave reasons for the stance it had taken in this unequivocal statement:

1. Tiger Kloof was started as an institution for the higher education of the African people in the territories served by the Society in Southern Africa, particularly Bechuanaland. As a result of the ban on new entries from outside the Union of South Africa, the institution is now limited to a part of its former constituency.
2. The Bantu education act is part of the apartheid legislation of the Union government, and our Society cannot agree to be party to any legislation which places one section of the community in permanent subjection to another...
3. We further believe that Christian education is the fullest development of which the individual is capable, and not the training of the individual to fit into a particular place in a segregated society. [37]

The closing service of Tiger Kloof as an LMS institution, held in December 1955, was a deeply moving experience. The preacher was Cecil Northcott, home secretary of the LMS, who represented the board. The previous year, in September 1954, Tiger Kloof had celebrated its golden jubilee. B.C. Thema spoke for the hundreds of old Tiger Kloof students who were present at the celebrations when he paid tribute to the role that Tiger Kloof had played among the African people, especially the Batswana. In referring to Thema's speech, E.P. Lekhela, in his thesis on missionary institutions for the Africans of the North-Western Cape, writes:

The present writer came to much the same conclusions, namely that Tiger Kloof was like an oasis in the desert, a haven for those in Southern Africa who wished to avail themselves of a Christian education in the true sense of the word. Her products have been men and women who have striven to be good, complete men and women imbued with potentialities common to all people. But it did not end there because "Old Tigers" in their hundreds have shed their light around them and influenced to the good communities in the midst of which they worked and dedicated their lives to the service of their fellow men. [38]

An archway erected to commemorate the golden jubilee of Tiger Kloof still stands at the main entrance; it affirms a truth which was the secret of Tiger Kloof's success, and which even the injustice of the apartheid system could not undermine: "Other foundation can no one lay than has been laid, which is Jesus Christ."

In January 1956 Aubrey Lewis, who had raised the standards of the institution and enhanced its reputation, left Tiger Kloof for the last time. Janet Bryson, who had joined the staff in 1923, and who was a "mother" to the girls as well as their teacher, was transferred to Inyati school. So many people served Tiger Kloof over the years, but none better than those who took care of the pupils in the hostels, and who contributed so much to the Christian atmosphere which permeated the whole institution, among them Grace Matshane, Ellen Mangalaza, and James Mpotokwane who came to Tiger Kloof as a boy in 1912 and stayed there until his retirement in 1963. He served in many capacities, but it was as boarding master that he was best remembered, and with much affection. The LMS continued to exercise pastoral care until the institution was closed in 1963 and the staff and students were transferred to Mafikeng, leaving the splendid stone buildings to become a lonely ruin on the Vryburg veld.

Tiger Kloof was the fulfilment of a promise to the Batswana chiefs and had been aided by a grant from the government of the Bechuanaland Protectorate for most of its history. Its demise left a big gap in the provision of higher education there, which the LMS felt obliged to fill. A site for a new school was acquired at Ootse. The church council voted £45,000 from the proceeds of the sale of Tiger Kloof and a grant of £20,000 was also made by the Protectorate government for the building of the new school. Classrooms and hostels were erected and were ready for the commencement of classes on 2 March 1962. Graham Phipps Jones was appointed by the LMS to be the first principal of the school which was named Moeding College (*Moeding* being the Tswana name for the valley of Tiger Kloof). The school was officially opened by Sir John Maud, the high commissioner, on 24 March 1963, in the presence of Janet Bryson and many old Tiger Kloof staff and alumni. It was under the principalship of Kenneth Maltus Smith that Moeding College witnessed its most spectacular growth. The facilities, including the assembly hall, the library and the chapel, were either erected or extended. Academic standards were raised and the pupils developed a remarkable prowess in sport, especially athletics. The small church fellowship at the heart of the college has exercised a ministry of care and concern and has contributed to the tone of the institution. In more recent years, the increasing demand for higher education in Botswana, together with the greater measure of control exercised by the ministry of education, extended the enrolment of the school beyond its maximum capacity. This resulted in overcrowded hostels, classes which were too large for effective teaching, a drop in academic standards and a diminished church influence.

All the reports of LMS Africa secretaries visiting Rhodesia (now Zimbabwe) between 1948 and 1975 drew attention to the imbalance between the LMS involvement in education and the development of the church in that country. The board was also aware of the disparity. In response to substantial requests for new educational work in Rhodesia and the Bechuanaland Protectorate, the board passed the following resolution in May 1951:

> The directors recognize that in present conditions in Africa the progress of the church is linked with the availability of improved educational facilities… But they seriously question whether there is any real hope that the Society, in addition to its present commitments, will be able to staff and finance in an efficient manner all the projects envisaged. In the light of these considerations, it seems to the directors that educational advance in Africa will have to rely more on the availability of suitable African staff and local financial resources than on additional men and money from the mission. [39]

The directors' caution notwithstanding, the 1950s and 1960s were a period of considerable expansion in the mission's involvement in education in Rhodesia. In 1954 Dombodema was upgraded from a central primary school to a centre for secondary education and teacher training. Geoffrey Bending and later Christopher Wright were both dedicated headmasters who improved the facilities of the school and raised its educational levels. During the Rhodesian civil war, however, the activities of the school were disrupted by border raids and the abduction of pupils. It was reopened at the time of Zimbabwean independence as a school with an agricultural emphasis, suited to the rural conditions in which it is set and to which most of its pupils return.

Inyati school, the oldest in Zimbabwe, was raised to secondary status in 1953. In the years that followed an extensive building programme was undertaken to extend and upgrade the school's facilities. The entire process took more than thirty years and reached its zenith when the buildings erected with funds raised by the indefatigable Joshua Danisa, mostly in West Germany, came into use in the late 1970s and early 1980s. Kenneth Maltus Smith was appointed principal of Inyati in 1957 and he successfully consolidated the process of upgrading the school, raising the standard of teaching and improving student results. He also planned the Inyati centenary which was celebrated as a national as well as an LMS commemoration in 1959. On the morning of 24 October 1959, three ox-wagons which had trekked from Bulawayo arrived in Inyati. Among those who welcomed them were Sir Robert Tredgold, the chief justice of Rhodesia, and a direct descendant of Robert Moffat who had brought the first missionaries to settle at Mzilikazi's kraal in 1859 — the first Christian mission station to be established in Zimbabwe. Inyati was also in a very sensitive area throughout the civil war. The school community and residents on the farm were all caught up in the conflagration and several lost their lives in tragic and sometimes gruesome circumstances.

Hope Fountain was widely recognised as an innovative centre of African education, and during the principalship of W.McD. Partridge (1946-64) it had the reputation of being the finest training school for African teachers in Rhodesia, a fact given ample recognition when the Hope Fountain mission celebrated its centenary in 1970. Partridge was among the first to realize, however, that the small rural teacher-training institution run by the church lacked the staff, the resources, the buildings, the equipment and the expertise to be able to offer teachers an adequate training. Supported by LMS/UCCSA and the Methodist Church (British Conference) in the first instance, Partridge prepared plans for a United College of Education. Other churches were slow to latch onto the concept, but Partridge, in his own words, "clung doggedly to the idea until it became a reality".[40] By the end of 1963 the Anglican church, the Church of Christ (New Zealand), the LMS and the Methodist church were participants in the scheme and a governing council was constituted. Partridge went on a world tour in search of funds. Donations and grants came in from every part of the world, but mainly from German churches. Rhodesia's unilateral declaration of independence in 1965 resulted in the withdrawal of some promised support, but the project was already off the ground to the extent that a suitable site was acquired in Bulawayo and a handsome but functional complex of buildings was erected on the new campus. The United College of Education was opened in 1967 with Partridge as its first principal. Within a few years of its establishment the effect of its training methods, with their emphasis on the development of individual potential, was being felt in schools throughout Rhodesia. Although the United College was immensely successful as a teacher-training institution, it lacked the financial resources to make it viable. In 1981 the governing council had no option but to donate the college as a going concern to the government of Zimbabwe, now the people's government.

In the letter offering the college to the government the chairman of the governing council drew attention to the Christian foundation of the college. She wrote:

> I am requested by the council to remind the government that the United College came into being through the vision, faith and concerted efforts of Christian educationalists of many denominations... The council offers this gift, requesting in the strongest terms that the objects shall continue to be a Christian college engaged in the education of teachers, of practitioners in home economics and community development and in the promotion of cultural activities in the field of African art and music.[41]

In accepting the donation of the college the secretary of education and culture gave the assurance that the Christian tradition would be maintained.

When the UCCSA accepted responsibility for the former LMS schools in 1967, it did so in trust without making a study of existing commitments and potential developments. By 1971, with increasing requests for the expansion of existing schools and the constant clamour for new schools, the UCCSA assembly appointed a commission to undertake an in-depth survey of the schools under the control of the UCCSA in Botswana and Rhodesia. CCWM was invited to participate in the survey. The following year Joseph Wing, the secretary of the UCCSA, accompanied by E.J. Edwards, Africa secretary of CCWM, visited all the schools concerned and examined the potential for new schools. In his report to CCWM Edwards pointed out "that some restriction must be placed on institutional development with the recognition that an ever-increasing responsibility should be carried by government or local authorities until such time as they are able to accept full control".[42]

The dual control of schools in the face of increasing government subsidization has resulted inevitably in the schools concerned having to conform with official educational policy, the educational authority setting quotas for admission, often in excess of the physical capacity of the schools concerned, and a declining Christian influence in the overall life of the schools. The alternative for the church, faced with rising costs and inadequate or no subsidies, was to raise the school fees to a level which had the effect of making the schools elitist. In evaluating the work of the United College of Education and more than 35 years of service as an educational missionary, Partridge asks: Where did we go wrong? In an attempt to answer his own question, he makes several important observations regarding the church's continuing role in education. He writes:

> Christian service is to help the helpless, the ones no one else is looking after. We should have been educating more than we did the poor who wanted to become teachers, or the physically disabled or members of undeveloped groups... We catered mainly for the privileged and the relatively rich because our fees were high.[43]

Medical work

The Scottish Livingstone Hospital at Molepolole, staffed and maintained by the United Free Church of Scotland (UFCS) in association with the LMS/UCCSA, began a period of unprecedented expansion when its new maternity wing was opened in 1951. Under the superintendence of Alfred Merriweather, the hospital at Molepolole became a place of healing and evangelism renowned throughout Botswana, but with a special ministry among the Bakwena and the remote villages of the Kalahari. Merriweather became a legend in his own lifetime as *Ngaka,* the name given to David Livingstone, the missionary doctor who established the first mission station among the Bakwena at Kolobeng. In his foreword to Merriweather's book *Desert Doctor*, Seretse Khama pays tribute to *Ngaka,* the doctor:

> Dr Merriweather's long service in Botswana is well-known... We in Botswana value him for what he has done and is doing for our people. [44]

The Scottish Livingstone Hospital was subsequently transferred to the ministry of health of the Republic of Botswana, but the institution has retained some of the Christian atmosphere which was such a marked feature of its life and work.

The attempt to establish a clinic and later a hospital, also under the auspices of UFCS, at Kanye was a short-lived development in the late 1940s and early 1950s. Violet Taylor founded the Maun maternity centre and worked there until 1954, when she was succeeded by Audrey Wing, who was in charge for eight years. She was followed by Betty Metcalf and then Pat Hollamby. Sister Hollamby's dedicated service to the centre, the church and the Maun community continued until the centre was transferred to the Botswana government. Speaking at the handing-over ceremony on 26 April 1975, the minister of health, M.P.K. Nwako, said: "The foundations of this work laid over forty years ago have fostered a special relationship with you and a spirit of service which will continue to flourish for many years to come."

The clinics at Dombodema and Zinyangeni offered basic medical care to the people of very remote rural areas for many years until they were also handed over to the appropriate government authorities in Zimbabwe. The name of Gwen Bloomfield was closely associated with medical work in Zimbabwe, where she worked at different times at both Dombodema and Zinyangeni. Tough, direct and with a heart full of compassion, she was loved and respected by the people of the villages, who had complete faith in her medical and dental skills.

The place of women

Women have always constituted a two-thirds majority in the LMS/UCCSA. In many of the rural areas, the women are active as deacons and their leadership, pastoral concern and energetic enthusiasm have been the dynamic of local church life. Most of the women belong to the women's fellowship (Basadi ba Thapelo) a strong feature of all church work in Southern Africa. Clad in their black skirts, white hats and blouses, with the UCCSA badge proudly displayed on a blue rosette, the women bring an important indigenous dimension into the worship and the service of the entire church. Congregationalists in South Africa have been ordaining women since 1928. It is only in recent years, however, that women from the former LMS church in Botswana and Zimbabwe have been ordained. Marope Modukanele was the first woman minister to be president of the Botswana synod. A decade earlier she had been president of the UCCSA women's work committee and had given positive and persuasive leadership to the entire church. Joyce Childs, appointed by the LMS as a missionary teacher to Hope Fountain in 1949, was ordained following her retirement as an eminent educationalist in Zimbabwe, and was called to be the minister of the Harare Congregational Church. She was later elected to be the moderator of the Zimbabwe synod. The contribution of the women missionaries who served in Southern Africa enriched the whole church. They were women of character, with plenty of courage, tremendous faith and self-denying humility. In our period two such LMS missionaries exercised considerable influence in pastoral ministries — Phyllis Wenyon, in the western suburbs of Bulawayo, and Marion Ginger, who was transferred to Botswana from China in 1951. Her work, first in Serowe, and later in the urban township of Lobatse, where she lived in a room behind the church, always available when needed by her people, was marked by complete self-giving.

Barrie Scopes, the then Africa secretary of CWM, visited Southern Africa in 1975 and attended the assembly of the UCCSA in Cape Town. He had been impressed by women's involvement, especially at the local church level. At the assembly, however, he noted with concern the limited participation of women in the higher courts of the church and refers to it in his report to the CWM. It reads:

> Women are said to constitute two-thirds of the UCCSA's membership; only 33 of the delegates were women and few of them spoke. [45]

In more recent years the women of the UCCSA have made it clear that they are no longer content with the traditional role which women have played in the life of the church. Women's meetings, bazaars and cake sales, fund-raising and children's creches are not the only areas of women's service in the church. They also want a voice in the policy-making bodies of the church. They accept the validity of Barrie Scopes's comments on the 1975 assembly, because they had not been involved fully in the church's structures at other levels. The women are becoming more articulate as they acquaint themselves with church administration at all levels. They have insisted on the use of "inclusive" language in the courts of the church and in all official documentation issued by the church. The women believe that sexism is a denial of human dignity and freedom, as sinister as apartheid, and contrary to the gospel. Their plea for the recognition of the unity of humanity in the church and in African society has been heard and will be heard again.

Literature

The LMS has been in the book trade in Southern Africa ever since 1831 when Robert Moffat set up the printing press on which he would print the Tswana Bible. In 1956 the executive committee of the LMS church council decided to commemorate the centenary of Moffat's completion of the translation of the entire Bible into Tswana by publishing a centenary revision. Alexander Sandilands was asked to undertake this with the help of K. Petso. St Mark's gospel was issued in 1957, exactly one hundred years after Moffat's great achievement. Sandilands continued with the translation of the New Testament, ably assisted by Moabi Kitchin, the Tswana poet whose felicity of phrase enhanced the literary quality of the translation. The complete centenary New Testament was published in one volume in 1970. It is a fine example of sincere and meticulous translating. It is certainly not a light revision of the Wookey New Testament, as originally commissioned. Rather it is a fresh dynamic translation, pointing the way for the common-language Tswana Bible of the future.

At the beginning of our period the LMS bookroom was located at Tiger Kloof. It published a large range of church and school books in Tswana, including the *Padiso* series, which were used in primary schools wherever Tswana was spoken. Following the take-over of Tiger Kloof by the South African government in 1956 the bookroom was transferred to Lobatse. When the new capital of Botswana was established in Gaborone the bookroom moved to a central business site in the mall and assumed the name of the Botswana book centre. The range of its publications was extended and the growth of its retail operation was phenomenal. Visiting Southern Africa in his capacity as general secretary in 1973 Bernard Thorogood comments on this enterprise in his report to CCWM:

> Another project of the church has been the bookshop in Gaborone. The size and quality of the service are impressive... It is interesting to note how often the same questions arise whenever the church makes a success of a commercial venture. Should the book business be the servant of the church or its own master obeying the laws of business? Should its profits subsidize the needy aspects of church life or should they be ploughed back to ensure further development of the one concern? Having entered the field of book selling and made a success of it, should the church now cut the link and sell the enterprise to commerce?[46]

This dilemma was faced several times by the church and the book centre. A firm policy was adopted whereby the profits would be ploughed back into the publishing operation, thus making possible the production of Tswana literature of high quality for religious, educational and cultural purposes. For several years the Botswana book centre formed part of the Ecumenical Literature Distribution Trust — an amalgamation of the publishing departments of the UCCSA and the Church of the Province of Southern Africa (Anglican) — until the Botswana book centre trust was constituted in 1982 by the Botswana synod of the UCCSA and the diocese of Botswana of the Church of the Province of Central Africa. In the early days, the development of the centre owed much to the publishing and book-selling expertise of John Hagyard. It is to Derek Jones, however, who has been associated with it for most of its life and served as its general manager at various times over a long period, that the church is indebted, for his vision developed this into one of the most successful church-operated publishing and book-selling operations in Southern Africa.

Shortly after the second world war, on his return from chaplaincy service in the Middle East, Alexander Sandilands, an acknowledged authority on the Tswana language, was appointed LMS literature officer by the mission council. Within a relatively short space of time he had produced *Kobamelo* (a new Tswana worship book), *Tudetso,* a children's hymn book, and *Introduction to Tswana*, a definitive Tswana/English grammar. With the help of K. Petso, existing publications were revised and new materials were produced for the needs of the church. At a later stage Alan Seager prepared valuable materials for the use of the church and the Christian education committee. These included study guides and *Thuso ya Bareri* (Preachers' Help), containing biblical readings and a sermon outline based thereon for every Sunday of the year, an important resource for deacons and lay preachers in remote areas, rarely visited by an ordained minister.

The literature of the church in Rhodesia was supplied by the LMS/UCCSA bookroom in Bulawayo, which carried a wide range of church publications and prescribed school books. LMS missionaries were champions of the Ndebele language (originally a dialect of Zulu). Throughout our period, however, it was James Pelling who was the leading Ndebele scholar. After completing a full-scale revision of the Ndebele New Testament, he translated the whole of the Old Testament into Ndebele for the first time. In both projects he was supported by Amos Mzileti, the wise and respected minister of Inyati and later of Zinyangeni.

Training for the ministry

The demise of Tiger Kloof as an educational institution in 1953 coincided with the expropriation of Adams College in Natal, where the American Board Mission had its theological school. William Booth, the principal of the Adams United Theological School, had conceived a bold and imaginative plan for the establishment of a united seminary and ecumenical studies centre on the Adams campus. The South African government was not prepared to allow the American Board Mission to take charge of its own property and use it for *bona fide* missionary purposes. The expropriation order was served without delay. Adams United Theological School, of which the LMS and CUSA had become an integral part in 1956, was now looking for temporary accommodation. This was found at Modderpoort in the Orange Free State, another victim of Bantu education, where the Society of the Sacred Mission offered generous hospitality. The LMS appointed R.J. McKelvey to join Booth on the staff at Modderpoort in 1959. A year later the Anglican, Methodist and Presbyterian churches, as well as the churches in the Congregational family, found themselves stripped of nearly all their facilities for theological education as a result of the ruthless implementation of the Bantu education act or the group areas act. The affected churches, after much deliberation, decided to work together in the raising of standards for ministerial training and in acquiring shared facilities. They pooled their meagre resources and with the help of substantial grants from the theological education fund and overseas partners, including the LMS, the Federal Theological Seminary of Southern Africa was inaugurated in 1963 on a site generously donated by the Church of Scotland, at Alice in the eastern Cape Province in South Africa.

A federal model was adopted, with four autonomous colleges sharing the same campus, Adams United College (Congregational), John Wesley College (Methodist), St Columba's College (Presbyterian) and St Peter's College (Anglican). The seminary opened with 91 students and 14 lecturers, including R.J. McKelvey, seconded by the LMS, who later became the principal of Adams United College and president of the seminary. From the outset all students took lectures together and a shared faculty provided a broader training than any one church could give. Three levels of study were available — certificate, diploma and degree, the last leading to the Associateship of the Federal Theological Seminary (AFTS). The introduction of the AFTS was an attempt to circumvent the totally unacceptable edict of the South African government that degrees could only be taken by black people at one of the ethnic universities and also to affirm the principle that the church has the right to determine the content of the training given to its ministers. It was not long before the AFTS award obtained international recognition as a primary degree. In 1968 Basil Manning, a student at Adams United College, was accepted, on the basis of a first-class pass in the AFTS, for post-graduate studies in the University of London. The first students of the seminary came from every part of Southern Africa, including the Bechuanaland Protectorate. Government restrictions, however, made it increasingly difficult for students outside South Africa to obtain study permits. This limited the enrolment, thus restricting the vision of the founders of the seminary who had seen it as a major centre of theological education and dialogue for the whole of Southern Africa. [47]

By 1974 the seminary had consolidated its position and had proved that cooperation in the training of the ministry is both possible and desirable. Later that year, on 26 November, the South African government issued an expropriation order, giving the seminary three months to vacate the land and buildings. All attempts to obtain a reversal of the expropriation order were met with total intransigence. The seminary was handed over to the University of Fort Hare, in terms of the expropriation order, on 13 March 1975. The very same day the whole seminary community moved to Umtata to share the limited accommodation so generously made available by St Bede's College. The Transkei president, chief K.D. Matanzima, regarded the members of the seminary community as trouble-makers. He demanded that the intruders should leave the Transkei and within a year the seminary was on the road again. It found temporary accommodation at the Edendale lay ecumenical centre near Pietermaritzburg in Natal. At that time Christopher Wright, the principal of Inyati school, was forced out of Rhodesia because he refused to serve in the Rhodesian army. He was then seconded by CWM to be the registrar of the seminary. His contribution to its life while in exile was outstanding, as was his tireless energy in the planning and building of the new seminary in Imbali, above Edendale. The new seminary was built at a cost of R.3.6 million, only R.2 million of which was paid by the South African government as compensation. The churches in Southern Africa, with extremely generous help from churches and mission agencies throughout the world, contributed the balance outstanding. The seminary was opened in August 1980, Bishop Lesslie Newbigin preaching the sermon at the dedication service. A unified structure was later adopted, and it has recently become an integral part of the Pietermaritzburg cluster of theological institutions together with the department of theology of the University of Natal, St Joseph's Theological Institute (Catholic) and the Federal Theological Seminary. [48]

Until 1970 Meshack Serema had been the last candidate for the ministry from Botswana to be trained in South Africa. By the time he graduated in 1963 there was a serious shortage of ministers in Botswana, because of deaths and retirements. In 1970 Charles Mosimanegape was sent to United Theological College in Harare for training and subsequently, with a scholarship from CWM, to Rhodes University for post-graduate studies. Shortly after that Obed Kealotswe was sent to the University of Lesotho and he took the degree-level course in theological studies, but these well-educated ministers could only touch the fringe of the need. Other denominations in Botswana also faced an acute shortage of ministers, especially in the rural areas. The churches shared their problems through the Botswana Christian Council and identified the need for a theological training programme by extension. Richard Sales of Selibe-Pikwe, an experienced theological educator, who had made an in-depth study of a similar scheme in Zambia, spearheaded the preliminary work which was to result in the establishment of the Botswana Theological Training Programme (BTTP). It was both a lay training programme for lay leaders and a scheme for the theological education of non-stipendiary ministers, who would serve in the places where they lived whilst continuing in their secular occupations. In Barrie Scopes's 1975 report, following a visit to Africa, he describes BTTP "as one of the most exciting things I saw on my visit". Tutorials were held in every major centre of Botswana, which the tutors, Richard Sales and Zulile Mbali, visited regularly. By the end of the 1970s the new style of preparation for the ministry had been accepted. Local churches now had their own ministers. Pastoral care was being provided, the word preached and the sacraments administered on a regular basis, even in the remote deserts of the Kalahari. Basil Manning, a son of the UCCSA who was resident in the United Kingdom, succeeded Sales as principal of Kgolagano College (as BTTP was later designated in an attempt to stress its indigenous character). BTTP replenished the ranks of the

UCCSA ministry in Botswana. Several of the people trained through it took early retirement from their secular employment and became the acknowledged leaders of the synod of Botswana, among them Kgolo Felix Mokobi (at various times synod chairman, synod secretary and chairman of the UCCSA), J.I.B. Sekgwa and Marope Modukanele. BTTP-trained leadership helped to facilitate the transition from a missionary-dominated conciliar structure to one which was firmly rooted in the indigenous church. The fact that this coincided with a declining number of missionaries in Botswana underscores the urgent need for dynamic leadership training programmes.

No account of theological education in Botswana is complete without some reference to the Kanye Bible school, which takes us back to the beginning of our period. During the second world war large numbers of men from Bechuanaland Protectorate served with the allied forces, mainly in North Africa. Alexander Sandilands was their chaplain, together with Diaz Modukanele, Odirile Mogwe and Gerald Griffiths. The soldiers from the Bechuanaland Protectorate were scattered over a very wide area and received only occasional visits from the chaplains. Sandilands was quick to realize that this would not be enough to maintain the spiritual life of men who felt the need for a deeper experience of God. He embarked on a training programme for deacons and lay preachers which would enable them to lead groups of church members, catachumens and enquirers in a particular camp. The scheme worked well and resulted in the formation of lively fellowships in every camp. [49] On his return to Botswana, Sandilands believed that a similar pattern of leadership would work in the scattered villages and cattle posts, where there was little offered to sustain and deepen Christian fellowship. The Kanye Bible school inaugurated in 1947 was the result, and it sought to provide a leadership at grassroots level. The Bible school was not only a memorial to the men from the Bechuanaland Protectorate who were killed in the second world war, it was also an effort of the African church to meet local leadership needs in new ways. The Bible-oriented course designed by Sandilands was pragmatic rather than academic and adapted to the educational standards of the students, none of whom had passed more than standard VI. The course extended over three years and included some general education. K. Petso, an erudite and experienced minister, was appointed tutor. The first Tswana course had an enrolment of 14, all but one of them ex-servicemen. A second Tswana course attracted several men with better educational backgrounds, and included candidates from South Africa.

A similar course for Ndebele-speaking students was organized at Kanye for a time with Joshua Danisa as tutor. While this had a broadening effect on the Rhodesian students, it was out of context and far removed from the social and political patterns of Matabeleland.

The Kanye courses, which terminated at the end of 1953, served as a useful interim measure to provide an appropriate form of ministry in the post-war period. The LMS Board, however, warned against such an interim measure becoming permanent. Practical and economic necessity rather than a theological understanding of the nature of the ministry had prompted the launching of the evangelists' courses, which were seen by many as providing a second-class level of ministry at a lower stipend. Orchard points out in his 1948 secretarial report that any suggestion that pastoral work should in the main be the responsibility of an order of evangelists with a comparatively small number of fully trained, ordained ministers to supervise them, administer the affairs of the district church and be an itinerant dispenser of the sacraments, rests on a misunderstanding of the nature of the ministry. He writes:

> The function of the ministry... is in its essence the ministry of the word and sacraments and concerned with the worship, witness and pastoral work of the church and not primarily with administration. [50]

Throughout the 1950s and 1960s, when standards for ministerial education were constantly under debate, the LMS/UCCSA grappled with the nature of the pastoral office and the relationship of academic attainment to ordination. The UCCSA finally revealed its theological integrity in this matter when it resolved that all trained evangelists and candidates admitted to the self-supporting ministry should be ordained to the ministry of the word and sacraments, after they had complied with the requirements of the assembly. For more than thirty years ministers who had been trained as evangelists were pastors of the churches in most parts of Botswana, in many parts of Rhodesia and throughout Mozambique and the Orange Free State. One serious problem facing the church in Southern Africa during our period was the increasing difficulty of maintaining a stipendiary ministry amid conditions of third-world poverty. Stewardship campaigns have helped, especially in urban areas where members of the church are wage-earners. But there appears to be no permanent solution in a Southern Africa stalked by drought, unemployment, the population explosion, diminishing natural resources and social and political upheaval, unless the churches are prepared to take seriously the gospel imperative of unity and pool their total resources in people and money in joint action for mission and service.

As was mentioned earlier, candidates for ministry from Rhodesia were sent to Tiger Kloof and Kanye up until 1953. Thereafter several attempts were made to provide courses based in central Africa for ministerial training. One of the most successful of these was the Central African diploma in theology, which could be taken by extension, or at a theological institution in the countries which are now Zimbabwe, Malawi and Zambia. G. Owen Lloyd was the highly competent registrar of the ecumenically controlled governing body. Epworth Theological College in Harare (formerly Salisbury) had been a Methodist institution which had accepted students from other denominations for many years. In the process of upgrading standards, Epworth was reconstituted as the United Theological College with the Methodist Church in Zimbabwe, the United Methodist Church, the Evangelical Lutheran Church in Zimbabwe, the United Church of Christ in Zimbabwe and the LMS/UCCSA as partners. All LMS/UCCSA candidates designated for residential training in Zimbabwe have studied here. James Pelling was appointed a member of the teaching staff in 1979 and has made an important contribution in the field of biblical studies. A link has been created with the University of Zimbabwe and several students have enrolled for the degree programme and proceeded to post-graduate studies.

Despite the prominence given to black theology, liberation theology and the *Kairos* document in theological institutions, the ethos of much theological education has remained western and traditional. A lively group of UCCSA theologians, including Bonganjalo Goba, John de Gruchy, Steve Titus, Desmond van der Water and Robin Petersen have called for a "theology and ministry in conflict and crisis" and for "liberating reformed theology". James Cochrane, another Congregational theologian, has prepared an exciting "New Paradigm for Theological Education". [51] Much more needs to be done in developing a theology and a liturgy of Africa, born out of the existential realities of Southern Africa's tragedy and triumph. Theologians in Botswana have shown already that they have a distinctive contribution to make to African Christian theology and the research undertaken by Obed Kealotswe and others will interpret Christ and the church in terms of contemporary African culture as well as in the cultures of the Bible and traditional western society.

Mutuality in mission

The inauguration of CCWM/CWM revolutionized the UCCSA's corporate concept of mission. Mutuality took the place of dependence as the UCCSA shared in projects and programmes of CWM which enabled its members to discover that every partner church in CWM was both a giver and a receiver. The richness and the reality of the world church was made even more real for the UCCSA when the CWM executive committee met in Johannesburg and in Gaborone a few years later. The UCCSA was glad and grateful when John Thorne was elected as chairman of CWM in 1981, steering it through four of its most formative years and travelling extensively as an apostle for partnership in mission. It was also a thrilling moment for the UCCSA when its first four missionaries, Stanley and Ursula Green and Floris and Christine Jansen, were commissioned for service with the United Church of Jamaica and Grand Cayman. Mutuality in mission has made the UCCSA more responsive to the opportunities for mission within its own bounds. Mozambique has become a mission of the whole church. New initiatives in Namibia have been made possible with help from CWM. Long-neglected mission stations in Zululand were revived, and the Orange Free State has been designated by the assembly as an area which needs staff and support urgently if it is to respond to the challenges which confront it in the fast-growing communities in Botshabelo and Bloemfontein.

The strong call of the All Africa Conference of Churches for a moratorium on overseas mission personnel and funding was debated in special sessions of the 1975 UCCSA assembly. At that time there were 19 missionaries (CWM and UCBWM) — nine in Botswana, three in Rhodesia and seven in South Africa. The church was also in receipt of grants totalling R.160,000 per annum from its overseas partners, more than half of which were allocated to church-related educational institutions. Campaigning for and against moratorium took on a colourful form as delegates carried placards displaying the slogan "Missionary go home". Equally enthusiastic and vociferous were those who were against moratorium and who actually had the temerity to cross out "Go home" on the other side's posters and replace it with "Stick around". After a lively and, at times, hilarious discussion "Missionary stick around" represented a broader consensus than "Missionary go home". At the beginning of our period there were 22 missionaries of the LMS serving in Southern Africa.[52] At the advent of the UCCSA in 1967 there were thirty missionaries, 14 on short-term appointment and engaged in specialist jobs requested by the church.[53] Missionary leadership was much in evidence in the early years of the UCCSA and helped to effect the transition from mission to church in the former "mission" areas and the blending of centralized and "congregational" administrative procedures in the areas of overlapping. The first chairman, Ken Main, and the first secretary, Joseph Wing, of the UCCSA were both LMS/CWM missionaries. So were the secretaries of the Botswana, Central and Rhodesia regions. Norman Clarke, the financial secretary of the Rhodesia region, was also an LMS/CWM missionary to whom the region was deeply indebted for the manner in which he consolidated the finances of the church and the institutions in Rhodesia. Albert Lock fulfilled a similar role for the Botswana region in the years immediately following union. Within a decade the process of devolution was complete. John Thorne was appointed as joint secretary of the UCCSA in 1973, and Meshack Serema and Joshua Danisa were appointed secretaries of the Botswana and Rhodesia regions respectively, about the same time. Some missionaries who were elected to office by the church resigned as missionaries in order to identify more fully with the church they had been called to serve.

Transnational church

The establishment of the LMS church predates the arbitrary partitioning of Southern Africa and the delineation of the existing political boundaries. Although the three regions of the LMS church council were contiguous in 1945, the bounds of each were the political boundaries of the state concerned. There were close cultural, linguistic and social links however, and the Bechuanaland Protectorate, South Africa and Southern Rhodesia had a common economic, transport and fiscal infrastructure which made the entire subcontinent interdependent. Internally each country operated in terms of the requirements of its own constitution, which after 1948 became more widely divergent with the virtual erosion of the rule of law in South Africa. The LMS church council could make decisions on matters affecting the life, work and mission of the church. In the southern regional council, almost everything was evaluated and implemented, where possible, against the background of the repressive policy of South African apartheid. In the central regional council, the church operated within the political framework of an emerging fully participatory democracy. In Rhodesia, the devastating effects of the failure of the Central African Federation, in the first instance, followed by the bitter conflict between the liberation forces and an oppressive white regime, dominated every area of the church's thinking for a quarter of a century. In the LMS church council this led to increased tension between the representatives of the regions. Frequent accusations were made blaming a particular region for dominating the agenda of church council with its own special concerns, to the exclusion of those of the other regions.

Matters came to a head in a confrontation between the then Botswana regional council and the assembly ministerial committee regarding the ordination of BTTP trained, self-supporting ministers. Strong words were spoken at the final meeting of the Botswana regional council in 1980. Those who spoke for the synod made it clear that "either the delegates to assembly from Botswana were not giving expression to the views of the church in Botswana, or the UCCSA had decided to ignore these views. This did not reflect oneness in the UCCSA." At the first meeting of the synod of Botswana, held the next day, a memorandum was handed to the UCCSA secretary, for submission to the executive committee, calling for the removal of any constitutional provisions which might diminish the powers and status of synods. The UCCSA secretary gave the assurance that all anomalies would be either amended or removed from the constitution. In an address to the newly constituted synod of Botswana, its first chairman, Kgolo Felix Mokobi, closed the old era and opened the new by pointing out that "the UCCSA has not always handled Botswana seriously, but a new step was taken with the inauguration of the Botswana synod which called for new determination on the part of the church in Botswana". [54]

The constitutional provision for synods was a creative response to conflict. It was not surprising, therefore, that the inauguration of the synod of Botswana on Sunday, 26 August 1980, in Francistown, was such a joyous occasion, made all the more significant by the presence of the chairman of the UCCSA, Joshua Danisa, who constituted the synod. Highly respected and much loved throughout Botswana as a former minister of the Serowe church, Danisa demonstrated that there is a balm in Gilead (Jeremiah 8:22). Less than two years later the synod of Zimbabwe was constituted at a glorious celebration in Bulawayo. Subsequently the UCCSA in Mozambique was given synodical status.

The church is society in microcosm and although it is called to demonstrate a unity in Christ which transcends all human divisions, its members also reflect the attitudes and the cultures from which they come and with which they continue to identify. The euphoria which accompanied the inauguration of the UCCSA and the honeymoon period which followed was shattered when the World Council of Churches (WCC) launched its Programme to Combat Racism in 1970. The implications of the WCC's action were discussed by the 1970 UCCSA assembly at Paarl. Masks were ripped off in the debate and people's attitudes and prejudices were revealed. The majority of the UCCSA's members saw the programme as a gesture of support for the oppressed peoples of Southern Africa, a minority perceived it as the church supporting terrorism. The following resolution of the assembly was described by Dr Eugene Carson Blake, general secretary of the WCC at the time, "as being of a very high order of Christian statesmanship". [55]

The UCCSA remains a member of the World Council of Churches for the following reasons:
   i) because the WCC expresses the universality and catholicity of the Church of Christ;
   ii) because the WCC is the focus and the motivation of the movement towards Christian unity, to which the UCCSA is committed;
   iii) because it is essential that dialogue should continue between Christians in Southern Africa and the rest of the world.
The assembly affirms that the church is called to reconcile all people to God and one another by the cross. We abhor and therefore reject violence and terror as means to political change and also as methods of maintaining racially separated societies, believing that violence breeds violence and terror produces terror.

The assembly whilst viewing with concern the action of the World Council of Churches in granting financial assistance to liberation movements recognizes:
a) that the WCC is responding to a serious racial situation which calls for responsible Christian action;
b) that the desperate methods adopted by liberation movements are the products of a system in which men and women are denied effective participation in the state which governs every aspect of their lives;
c) that the action of the WCC is a judgment on the church's ineffectiveness in seeking justice, freedom and human dignity for all people;
d) that desperate people, even when they resort to violence, are still the concern of the Christian church.
The assembly therefore pledges itself to work by all means consistent with the gospel for justice, freedom and racial reconciliation in Southern Africa... wherever possible in cooperation with other churches. The assembly affirms the Lord Jesus Christ as the only King and Head of the church. The UCCSA is both inter-racial and international and operates in four separate countries of Southern Africa. As such, it witnesses to an allegiance and enjoys a fellowship which transcends race and political boundaries and in which loyalty to Jesus Christ is acknowledged as supreme. [56]

The tension over the Programme to Combat Racism continued throughout the 1970s, coming to a head in the 1978 UCCSA assembly in Port Elizabeth. The Rhodesian delegates gave first-hand evidence of the humanitarian purposes for which the WCC grants had been used at Dombodema by the liberation movements. Their courageous stand held the assembly together, but not before some delegates had walked out, one of them never to return. Following the assembly, Peter Schoonraad, the minister of Union Church, Cape Town, entered into a dialogue with the secretary of the UCCSA and inundated the whole church with his circulars setting out his views and campaigning for the immediate withdrawal of the UCCSA from membership of the WCC. [57] When he failed in this objective he campaigned for the withdrawal of his own congregation and other like-minded local churches from the UCCSA. Union Church, founded by the LMS and its headquarters in Southern Africa for many years, broke away from the UCCSA in January 1980. A few other congregations in the Cape Province followed them, including the Sea Point Church, another with strong LMS connections. The dissident group formed itself into the Evangelical Fellowship of Congregational Churches (EFCC). The EFCC has not grown significantly [58] and such growth as it has experienced has come about by exploiting dissensions in UCCSA congregations, disputes which are totally unrelated to the theological reasons for withdrawing from the UCCSA in the first instance. It is ironic that the strong evangelical preaching about God and humanity which John Philip proclaimed with such prophetic power from the pulpit of Union Church should be replaced with an other-worldly pietism, unrelated to the conditions and disabilities which are the daily lot of the common people. Fearing the Sovereign Lord alone and firm in the conviction that God conferred an inalienable dignity on each and every person when he made them in his own image, Philip refused to compromise when he was accused of being a political parson, as did the UCCSA when it was enjoined to withdraw from the WCC because of its political and social involvement. "If a minister is guilty of dereliction of his duty", wrote Philip, "in advocating the cause of the oppressed, or in relieving the necessities of the destitute, I plead guilty to the charge." The UCCSA lost the mother church of Congregationalism in Cape Town, but it retained the priceless heritage bequeathed by Philip as an integral part of its ongoing mission, in the context of *Kairos* which is *now*. Memorial tablets commemorating Philip's achievements still adorn the walls of Union Church. Their unequivocal challenge was repudiated by all but a few of Union Church's congregation, the small group which remained loyal to the UCCSA. The stark relevance of Philip's words and actions still have the power to challenge worshippers to discover that the advocacy of the civil rights of the poor is a Christian duty based on the second great commandment of loving your neighbour as yourself.

In summary

The UCCSA was inaugurated with a communicant membership of 102,556. Ten years later, in 1977, the membership had grown to 122,090; the total church community, including baptized adherents and children, was 214,378. These statistics reflect a significant but not spectacular growth rate. During our period the most spectacular church growth was that of independent African churches which appealed to local and kinship loyalties, and gained their following among the urban workers at a time when the mainline churches were still tied to traditional rural growth.

In 1976, towards the end of his active ministry, Humphrey Thompson wrote *Distant Horizons*, the story of one man's missionary service in and around Kuruman. Although written from a personal perspective, it is also a mirror of the times reflecting the rapid pace of social change and the transition from missionary paternalism to full partnership in the total mission of the church. Thompson's amazing versatility and his ability to adapt to every situation made him the right person to minister at Kuruman during the period of the overlap, as in Paul's phrase in 1 Corinthians 10:11. The many phases through which the missionary, the mission and the church passed during the period of overlap are summarized in the foreword:

> This book marks the end of the romantic era of missions and spans the whole period of devolution from "mission" to "church". The young Humphrey Thompson began his missionary service at Kuruman in 1932 as *mookamedi* — a junior patriarch set in the Moffat mould! By the time of his official retirement in 1972, he was the minister of one of the many local churches over which he had previously exercised oversight as an unconsecrated Congregational bishop. These far-reaching ecclesiastical developments are set against the background of rapid social change, the devastating effects of the policy of apartheid and the growth of black awareness. [59]

As the shadows of his earthly life began to lengthen for Thompson, so did his own concern for the future of the historic mission. He had seen and resisted the ravages of apartheid, the removal of the people into Bophuthatswana and the closure of the school founded by Robert Moffat in 1829, the mother of all the schools established among the Batswana. The historic buildings, without a worshipping congregation to care for them and funds to restore them, were deteriorating rapidly. Thompson, at the age of 78, felt that he lacked the springs of energy and enthusiasm to lead the Moffat mission into a new phase appropriate to the changed and changing circumstances of the closing decades of the twentieth century. The esteem in which the Moffat mission is held by all denominations as the "cradle of Christianity among the Batswana people" and the fountain of education, urged the UCCSA to approach Graham Chadwick, the then bishop of Kimberley and Kuruman, about the possibility of creating an ecumenical trust for the administration of the Kuruman property. The bishop responded positively and at the request of the UCCSA appointed Alan Butler to be the director of the Moffat mission. The Methodists and Presbyterians were approached and they agreed to serve on the Moffat mission trust, which was constituted in October 1981. CWM and the United Society for the Propagation of the Gospel gave generous grants. Within months of its inauguration, the trust had repaired and restored some of the derelict buildings and started work on converting the old school into the Maphakela conference centre, named after Maphakela Lelalake, the first Motswana to be ordained to the ministry of the word and sacraments, a ministry which continued right into our period until this veteran of the cross died in 1947.

We here return to the beginnings. The oldest mission station in the Tswana country, redolent in history, epitomizes the manner in which the church continues to build on the past, in the present, for the future. The church lives in the present tense. That is the incarnational process which began when God in Christ entered the context of human life. "The word became a human being and lived among us" (John 1:14). So as the church carries that mission it is set in a context, the context of Southern Africa, committed to its people, responding to the needy and seeking justice and peace. So it is a visible sign of the body of Christ. The founders of the LMS declared that "the union of Christians of various denominations in carrying on this great work is a most desirable object". [60] It was a splendid vision and remains the soundest principle on which to carry forward God's one mission in God's one world.

NOTES

[1] Walter Hollenweger, *The World Is the Agenda*, September 1966, pp.19-20.
[2] Ronald K. Orchard, *Report after a Secretarial Visit to Africa*, London, LMS report for directors, 1948, ch. 1.
[3] *Ibid.*, p.10.
[4] A.J. Haile, "What Lies Ahead?", May 1949, p.1.
[5] Orchard, *Report after a Secretarial Visit to Africa, op. cit.*
[6] Minutes, LMS council executive committee, 3 September 1952, p.71.
[7] *Ibid.*
[8] *Ibid.*, February 1956, p.173.
[9] J.F. White, annual report of the joint council, 1957.
[10] Minutes, LMS church council executive committee, 1966, pp.333,336,374-5,392-3.
[11] E.J. Edwards, "Report of a Secretarial Visit: Shashi Complex", May 1972, p.13.
[12] In A.E. Seager's as yet unpublished autobiography he gives details of these events. As resident missionary at Serowe at the time Seager had special knowledge of the people and the events as they impinged on the life of the church, the nation and the Bamangwato people.
[13] J.H. Hofmeyr, speech in parliament, quoted by Leonard Thompson in *A History of South Africa*, Wynberg & Stanton, RADIX, 1990, p.180.
[14] *Ibid.* Thompson makes a careful analysis of the segregation era and the apartheid era and the withdrawal of moderate blacks from non-racial politics, pp.154-187.
[15] *Ibid.*, p.150 gives a full list of disabilities and deprivations imposed by these repressive acts.
[16] B.H.M. Brown ed., *The New Dimensions of Mission for South Africa Today*, Cape Town, Christian Council of South Africa, 1964, gives a clear presentation of mid-term goals.
[17] "The Church and Social Responsibility in Southern Africa", a memorandum submitted to the World Alliance of Reformed Churches by the UCCSA task force on human relations, March 1979.
[18] Thompson, *op. cit.*, p.194, figures supplied by surplus people project in respect of removals.
[19] UCCSA secretarial bulletin, May 1975, reports how the church at Majeng founded by the saintly William Ashton in 1874 had been destroyed by the department of Bantu affairs, when the people who had lived there for more than a century were declared trespassers in their own homes.
[20] Joseph Wing, *As One People*, Broomfontein, South Africa, UCCSA, 1978, chapter on rebuilding, pp.21-25.
[21] Orchard, in *Report after a Secretarial Visit to Africa, op. cit.*, pp.40-41, outlines and evaluates the structures of the church during the mission council period.
[22] J.D. Jones, a presentation made to the Southern Africa committee of the WARC regarding the historical background to and the shape of the UCCSA in Botswana.
[23] J.K. Main, letter to the Rev. M.O. Janes, dated 7 February 1972, in response to proposals for a closer relationship between the Congregational Union of England and Wales and the LMS.
[24] D.R. Briggs & J. Wing, *The Harvest and the Hope*, Johannesburg, UCCSA, 1970, p.310, being the resolution of the centenary assembly of CUSA extracted from *The Proceedings of Assembly: 1960*, Cape Town, CUSA Year Book, 1961.
[25] *Ibid.*, pp.310-12.
[26] *Ibid.*, p.314.
[27] *Ibid.*, pp.314-18.
[28] Cyril Kemp, "Impressions of Assembly", *The Congregationalist*, December 1967, p.9.
[29] Resolution 67/A/20 of the inaugural assembly, October 1967, p.26.
[30] Annual report of the London Missionary Society for 1964-65.
[31] CCWM report for 1968, p.25.
[32] J. Wing, *The Search for Union*, published in *In Touch*, March 1991, Church Unity Commission, Johannesburg.
[33] Presbyterian/Congregational joint committee report to the inaugural assembly, 67/A/2, October 1967.

[34] John Huxtable, extract from sermon preached at the covenant service to inaugurate the UCCSA on 3 October 1967, as quoted in *The Harvest and the Hope, op. cit.*, p.316.

[35] Sir Seretse Khama, speech delivered at the 1974 UCCSA assembly, as recorded in *As One People,* p.67.

[36] E.P. Lekhela, in his D. Ed. thesis, *The Origin, Development and Role of Missionary Institutions for the Africans of the North-Western Cape*, University of South Africa, 1970, typescript.

[37] Minute 3 of the executive committee of the LMS church council, 24-26 August 1955, and Tiger Kloof newsletter, vol. 4, no. 14, 27 August 1955.

[38] Lekhela, *op. cit.*, p.619.

[39] Resolution of the board of directors of LMS, May 1951.

[40] W.G.McD. Partridge, *United College of Education, Bulawayo: 1967-1981*, Bulawayo, Louis Bolze, 1985.

[41] *Ibid.*

[42] E.J. Edwards, "Report of a Secretarial Visit to Africa", 1972, p.10.

[43] Partridge, *op. cit.*

[44] Alfred Merriweather, *Desert Doctor*, London, Lutterworth, 1969.

[45] B.D. Scopes, "Report of a Secretarial Visit to Southern Africa", 1975.

[46] B.G. Thorogood, "Notes on a Secretarial Visit", 1973.

[47] E.L. Cragg, *A Venture in Co-operation,* the story of the establishment of the Federal Theological Seminary of Southern Africa at Alice.

[48] Souvenir brochure, commemorating the silver jubilee of the Federal Theological Seminary, 1963-88.

[49] A. Sandilands, *Correspondence with Men in the Forces 1942-46,* a moving series of letters between the padre and his people, stored in the archives of the UCCSA in Johannesburg.

[50] Orchard, *Report after a Secretarial Visit to Africa, op. cit.*

[51] J. Cochrane, "A New Paradigm for Theological Education", 1988, a paper presented to the board of examiners for the joint diploma in theology.

[52] Statistics from the annual report of the directors of the LMS 1944-45.

[53] Statistics taken from the CCWM annual report for 1968.

[54] Proceedings of the final meeting of the Botswana regional council and the inaugural meeting of the synod of Botswana, August 1980.

[55] Letter from Eugene Carson Blake, general secretary of the WCC, to the secretary of the UCCSA, dated November 1970.

[56] Resolution of the fourth assembly of the UCCSA held in Paarl, October 1970. The reference to "four separate countries" reflected the historical situation at that time as South West Africa was still a mandated territory, not an independent state.

[57] Correspondence with churches and memoranda on the WCC, running into several volumes, in the archives of the UCCSA office in Johannesburg.

[58] The EFCC published a souvenir commemorating *Ten Years of the Restoration of Congregationalism*, Cape Town, 1990.

[59] H.C. Thompson, *Distant Horizons*, 1976, published privately in Kuruman, foreword.

[60] Quoted from J.C. Harris, *Couriers for Christ*, London, Livingstone, 1949.

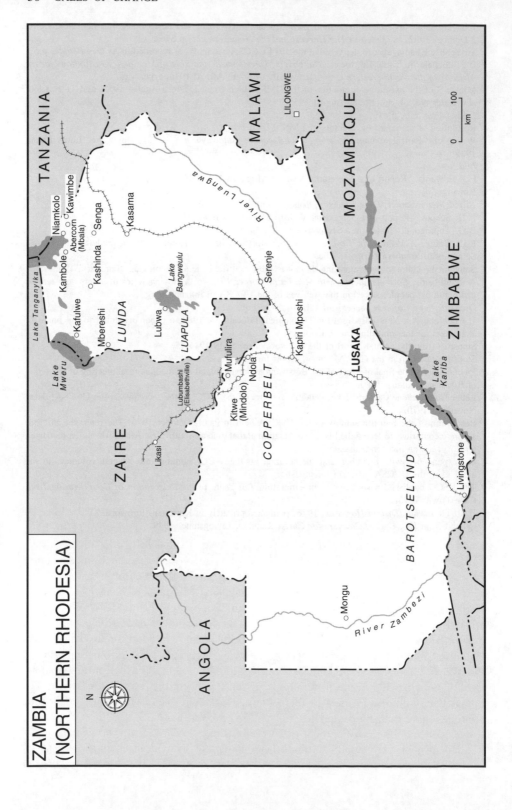

ZAMBIA
(NORTHERN RHODESIA)

3. All Things New

John Parry

The people and the church

Imiti ikula e mpanga. A Bemba proverb much loved by preachers tells us that the young trees are the forest of tomorrow. It was used to illustrate growth and the potential for growth in the family and tribe, and now, in the church. In 1945 the newly formed Church of Central Africa in Rhodesia (CCAR) was exhorted to nurture its young and secure a successful future.

Such a proverb was hardly applicable at that time to the conditions in the country. The end of the second world war found Northern Rhodesia a British colony with a degree of indirect rule through chiefs and traditional courts. It was not a nation, but a territory artificially constructed by a comity of empire builders with three to four million people scattered in an area almost as large as Europe, having to speak English instead of one of many indigenous languages. Moreover the countryside itself was undergoing rapid change; the whole land, covered with a canopy of forest undisturbed until the end of the nineteenth century, was being slashed. White settlers farmed huge clearings in the bush in the south and east of the country, whilst through the central copperbelt a great swathe was cut as the copper industry itself quickly became vital to the developing country's economy, drawing many able-bodied people from the country's villages.

The church was well into its second generation of Christian families. Protestants, following the comity of missions, were broadly tribal in their distribution. The LMS was working in the Mambwe and Bemba countries to the north and in the Lunda country in the Luapula valley. The Church of Scotland had entered Bemba country from the Livingstonia mission east in Nyasaland. The Plymouth Brethren were in the northwest and in Luapula and the Paris Evangelical Missionary Society were in the south and southeast in Barotseland. Anglican, Baptist and Methodist missions had some rural areas of influence, but were also in the two main areas where the population continued to explode, in the copperbelt and around the capital, Lusaka. The Roman Catholic Church had missions everywhere, increasingly related to administrative rural townships. Other Christian churches were settling in urban rather than rural localities, the copperbelt being home to hundreds of sects, especially from South Africa. The colour bar, the norm in most of the society where there were whites, affected urban churches more than rural ones.

Influence on the development of Northern Rhodesia came from the institutionally minded missions, especially through the schools that seemed an essential part in the spread of the gospel, and through medical and welfare work. These added to the basic gospel of salvation through a God seen in and through Jesus, a concern for the individual in society and the world that involved them in education and service. Not only was awareness of the value of each and every person realized which naturally led to ideas of political freedom, but also the country was given a growing sense of principle, purpose and nationhood based on scripture. On the question of colour it was largely the non-conformists who took the lead in breaking barriers.

Unlike colour, tribalism showed itself as a significant force in the nation, with most tribal hierarchies becoming local authorities dependent upon provincial or central government support. An event in the 1950s when a tribal chief encouraged witch-hunters (and in so doing had to receive a protesting church delegation) was a rare occurrence. (The chief gave in and banished the witch-hunters.)[1] It is significant that the emerging political parties bypassed the traditional chiefs, though they were not always successful in being non-tribalistic themselves in national politics. Tribalism never seemed to be disruptive in church affairs although squabbles could occur in the choice of the vernacular language to be used in urban church services. In later years theological students would show tribal loyalties, but only occasionally and with no lasting significance.

Progressive forces were naturally somewhat dormant during the war, and after-wards for a time, but with hindsight they were clearly inevitable. The proverb's analogy of the forest was significant — trees take time to grow. It is the certainty of the emerging forest that was implied.

LMS contribution

The LMS had a significant part in the emerging nation because of its fundamental belief that the mission should ensure that the growth of the church was of the people within their culture, i.e. truly indigenous. It was not that the emphasis, awareness and resolve to actualize this was always there or was seen to be there. Because of missionary dominance there might have been some paternalism in the 1945 decision which brought about the union of LMS congregations with about 5,000 members, the Church of Scotland's 6,000 members and the Union Church of the Copperbelt's 1,300 members, to form the Church of Central Africa in Rhodesia. However, it was the right move which was an example to the country that Christianity was serious about being one body as Jesus wished, and thus a moral force to be reckoned with. This development laid the foundations for the future when African church leaders would themselves preach against "religious tribalism" as they called denominationalism, and urge the missionaries to do "back home" what they had helped to do in their country. In the matter of training African leaders for its churches, Goodall had to point out how slow the LMS had initially been.[2] Later many evangelists and deacons were trained, but ordinands were few. Only three had been trained at Mbereshi by 1945. Others had trained in Southern Africa. Although few, they were influential in both church and society. One, Henry Kasokolo, became the first to sit as an African representative in the overwhelmingly white legislative council, though he had to resign as a minister of the church to do so.

Prominent in the life of the growing church was the fellowship of women (the KBBK: Kwafwana kwa Banamayo Bena Kristu, which means the fellowship of Christian women). Deriving in part from the experience of missionary wives and women missionaries in the organization of women in church life, and in part from matriarchal tribal society, the KBBK gave increasing strength to the church both locally and nationally. Their uniform of white cloths round their heads, red blouses with white collars and black skirts became standard throughout the United Church of Zambia.

In the sphere of education the LMS had a significant influence upon the emerging nation. The establishment of schools at Kawimbe, Niamkolo, Kambole and later of the model school for girls in the territory by Mabel Shaw (1915-45) at Mbereshi was followed by the establishment in Mbereshi of the Livingstone Memorial Training School for teachers. Using a curriculum which had been produced cooperatively by the government and all missions engaged in school management, men and women teachers were prepared for a unified service. In theory a teacher could be transferred anywhere in Northern Rhodesia. From 1945 onwards, the majority of rural schools were run by one mission or another. Apart from government institutions at Mazabuka, Ndola, Kasama, Barotse national school at Kanyonyo and Munali, all schools in the country were run by missions until the government take-over of schools in the 1960s. When Northern Rhodesia became Zambia in 1964 it was evident that every member of the new government had been educated in a mission school. The founding president, Kenneth Kaunda, had trained as a teacher at the Lubwa mission station of the Church of Scotland where his father had been minister of the church. Betty Kaunda, his wife, was trained at Mbereshi.

The LMS sent out missionaries as a team of educationalists, artisans, medical personnel and ministers. Thus through schools, hospitals and workshops as well as through churches they evangelized. In the process of building churches, schools, medical facilities and staff housing the LMS, like other missions, trained apprentices as builders and carpenters. By the 1950s this influence was noticeable. For example, in the long string of villages of the Luapula valley, rectangular dried brick buildings with windows were more common than in the small villages of the plateau bushlands. Mission-trained workers found employment in the copperbelt and the growing district and provincial townships. At Senga the LMS's desire to keep education close to the land led to the establishment of a unique agricultural teacher training school where, under the inspiration and energy of Norman Porritt, village teachers were trained in a down-to-earth way. After more than a decade of remarkable achievement the government closed it because it did not fit in with some officials' desire for a territory-wide pattern for teacher training.

In the medical service, training was directed to the provision of first-aid posts, dispensaries, leprosaria, maternity services and hospitals. During the 1950s and 1960s there were as many people being treated in rural areas by missions as by government institutions. Mission-trained personnel also entered the government and mine hospital service in increasing numbers.

The LMS participated with other missions not only in the bush but also in the tremendous development of the copperbelt during and after the second world war. The United Missions to the Copperbelt (UMCB), formed in 1935 through the able influence of the Rev. R.J.B. Moore, an LMS missionary to the copperbelt, was notable not only for its educational and welfare work but also for demonstrating ecumenism in action and in the lead it took in combatting the colour bar. Some missionaries were aware of the danger that the economy of Northern Rhodesia was too dominated by the copper industry, but the LMS along with other churches did not exercise a prophetic role to warn of the perils of this economic imbalance. However, it did back up its ecumenical vision in the whole copperbelt complex by taking a prominent part in the setting up of the Mindolo Ecumenical Foundation, which in 1958 received international recognition when it was adopted by the WCC as an independent foundation for ecumenical work worldwide.[3]

In the multiracial copperbelt the church needed varied expertise in its ministry. Congregations grew with the influx of workers and their families. A significant contribution was made by missionaries, including Dorothea Lehmann, who studied the sociology of the Christian community, and by Harold Cave, a minister whose skills in church design created good new worship centres, light, dignified and economic to maintain.

Independence

Though the LMS staff were hesitant in economic matters they were more forward-looking in the 1950s about national independence, as anxious for it as their African fellow church members and staffs of schools and hospitals. They gave a lead in exposing paternalism as a pernicious form of racism. For out of paternalism had developed that last-ditch stand of white dominance, the political doctrine known as partnership. The barely hidden rotting kernel of partnership was that it was grossly unequal. The proposal to form the federation of Northern Rhodesia, Southern Rhodesia and Nyasaland, a political expression of paternalism, led many missionaries to speak out against it. Whilst not denying that some material benefits from such a federation might ensue, they said that it was natural and right that Africans of equal attainments and qualifications should take part in the elections. They called upon Christians on both sides to come together in friendship, and gave this warning:

> To try and force through any scheme of federation against deliberately sought African opinion would involve a deterioration of race relationship that would far outweigh any economic advantages.[4]

Their letter to a national newspaper with these words was signed by nine LMS and six Church of Scotland missionaries, and included nine graduates, three medical doctors, a holder of a DFC (Distinguished Flying Cross) and a great-grandson of David Livingstone. In June 1953 the Christian Council of Northern Rhodesia warned the government how strongly Africans opposed federation, but nevertheless it was formed in September of that year.

The independence struggle that gradually intensified into unrest with the burning of schools, strikes, damage to roads and bridges and occasional death and injury on both sides, was never characterized by overt opposition or attacks on missions or churches.[5] On the copperbelt where racial tension was greatest the churches were divided politically and, it must be said, racially, but united in their commitment to non-violence. Missionaries of the LMS along with many other whites followed the lead of the Rev. Colin Morris, a Methodist member of the copperbelt team, who advertised his church as "colour-blind".

In 1963, shortly after the unrest started, Kenneth Kaunda, calling his political philosophy Zambian humanism, Christian in outlook, was elected prime minister. As Richard Hall wrote in his book *Zambia*: "Indeed the Federation died with a whimper."[6] On 24 October 1964, Zambia was born. Celebrations in all rural and many urban centres were conducted with prayers and church services. A deep sense of freedom and a desire for new development infused both nation and church. Despite the burden of refugees from the racial struggles to the south and the fluctuating international price of copper, independence was a time of hope.

The United Church of Zambia

Church action in the politics of the independence struggle was certainly significant because, at the same time, the church was putting its own house in order. There was constant appraisal of church organization so that it should increasingly reflect the Christian values of the status of the individual and the equality of all under God. In 1947 the LMS Africa secretary from London, the Rev. Ronald Orchard, said that he found the church was still almost entirely dependent upon the mission, in some ways perhaps more than it needed to be.[7] The few African ministers were at head stations under the guidance of missionaries. He felt that they should have more responsibility in stronger district churches. Three of the five African ministers of the Church of Central Africa in Rhodesia (CCAR) were therefore placed in the LMS area. One of these, the Rev. Wellington Mwanakube, was at Kafulwe during a long period without a missionary. The Rev. John Chifunda was also in charge at Kambole from 1947, the last year a resident missionary was there. The Rev. Joshua Nkole of Kasumpa was placed at Mbereshi.

With the opening of the Kashinda Bible school in 1949 the number of African ministers slowly rose. The Rev. Kenneth Francis was the first principal, and his wife Mildred used her nursing training to great effect running a dispensary and helping the students' families in a pattern of service common to many missionary wives. The Rev. Joel Chisanga, among the first to be trained there, was later to become principal of the United Church of Zambia ministerial training college at Mindolo. Another graduate of the Kashinda school, from the Mambwe country where the LMS first started, was sent to the Mbereshi district, where he and the missionary minister worked together, sharing responsibility as had been recommended in 1947.

The CCAR was formed in 1945 as a union of the LMS and Church of Scotland congregations in Northern Rhodesia together with the African congregations that had formed the Union Church of the Copperbelt. The LMS organization before this had been the Central African district committee, wholly missionary, and a general church council composed of African evangelists and deacons, one from each church, but the chairman and secretary were both missionaries. The Church of Scotland organization was presbyterian, also dominated by missionaries. On the copperbelt the UMCB congregations were of presbyterian polity. The CCAR had a presbytery, district church councils and churches with varying organizations. In the former LMS area church and deacons' meetings continued along congregational lines. In 1949 the Paris Evangelical Mission of Barotseland made a move to join the CCAR, but a visiting official from France counselled delay, which some said was because of missionary influence.

With the CCAR there was a steady move towards Africanization and a transfer of power from mission to church. Africans had been visitors to some sessions of the all-powerful district committee for some time; by 1953 some Africans were members. In 1954 the Central Africa district committee ceased and a mission council took over. In 1962 all the work of the mission came under the United Church of Central Africa in Rhodesia (UCCAR). This church had itself come into being through the union of the

CCAR and the Copperbelt Free Church Council (CFCC) in 1958. The latter council comprised English-speaking white congregations whose ministers were all missionaries, often with pastoral responsibilities in the black CCAR congregations as well.

There were African fears that the influx of Europeans into the church would stifle their increasing initiative. But some were realistic. Henry Makulu, a trained Christian education leader who subsequently worked full-time with the World Council of Christian Education, presented a memorandum on church union discussions to a retreat of African ministers of the CCAR and wrote:

> As more Europeans have come there has been a sense of stability in this community. Their churches have grown more financially powerful than the African community. These churches are still Free churches, i.e. a stage behind the African churches of the CCAR. For this reason there is no sense in talking about union between the CFCC and the CCAR. The obvious step should be for the European Free church council to come into the CCAR. The latter is not an African equivalent of the CFCC. It is one stage further in the ecumenical line. Thus CCAR would be better off as an African church and concentrate its efforts on finding means of self-support; it should not be tied to the apron strings of the European church because it has more money in the hope that ministers' salaries can be raised. Our churches in the copperbelt are capable of better financial support than they give now; our ministers could be paid twice as much as they are getting now.

But he concluded:

> The union if desirable should be both at the administrative and fellowship level. If not it must be rejected even if it will cause embarrassment. European churches and council should feel free and welcome to join the CCAR.[8]

At the following presbytery of the CCAR there was a heated debate. The Rev. Paul Mushindo, veteran minister of the Church of Scotland element of the CCAR, spoke trenchantly in favour of the union, hoping for inter-racial harmony, and ended:

> Finally we give thanks to God for the work which missionaries have done in Central Africa for bringing the gospel and building the church. We would like them to cooperate with us in every possible way until such time when we shall be able to stand on our own feet organizationally and financially.[9]

The presbytery agreed and on 26 July 1958 the United Church of Central Africa in Rhodesia (UCCAR), which was the union of the CCAR and CFCC, was consummated.

The formation of the UCCAR was a considerable achievement, six years before the federation ceased and the independent country of Zambia was born. There was also a great deal of experience in ecumenicity when the formation of the new state gave impetus to the feeling for a united church to bring together all like-minded mission churches. The LMS had in its fundamental principle the built-in freedom necessary for ecumenical moves. The Rev. Harold Barnes, a long-serving district missionary with very wide vision, had been tireless in all the stages of the negotiations. The Church of Scotland in Northern Rhodesia also had far-sighted missionaries with wider sympathies than some in Nyasaland, their historical base. On the copperbelt there were Christian expatriates, black as well as white, looking for worship and service with the faithful of similar and like-minded churchmanship. The United Church of Canada not only brought much-needed missionaries, but they also had an ecumenical ethos. Under the comity of missions the Methodists had a central area, a part of which became the capital city conurbation of Lusaka, but in the 1950s their missionaries soon noticed that 90 percent or more of their large urban congregations could be, as in one publicized example, from the LMS area in the north and Luapula areas. They, like the well-established Church of Barotseland, deriving from the Paris Evangelical Mission, had doubts about church order and training to resolve.

The problem as to where ministers of the united church should be trained was resolved in 1960 when Mindolo in Kitwe was chosen. On a site of the original LMS mission, at the centre of the copperbelt conurbation, itself central in Zambia, it had already seen the remarkable rise of the Mindolo Ecumenical Foundation, inspired by the World Council of Churches. The Foundation owed much to the Rev. Peter Matthews, an LMS appointee from Australia who mobilized church, government and industry to cooperate in a centre for the study of religion and life in Central and Southern Africa. To the centre was added the Dag Hammarskjold library, after his tragic death in an air crash near Ndola. Ministerial education was thus developed within the wider context of Christian education, and it embraced different tribal groups and denominational origins. The first principals were missionaries, but by 1970 the college had its first Zambian principal, the Rev. Joel Chisanga. After leaving the Kashinda Bible school and obtaining some pastoral experience he went for further theological training overseas. In January 1965, not many months after the state had become the Republic of Zambia, the United Church of Zambia (UCZ) was inaugurated with its headquarters in the capital, Lusaka.

Changing institutions

Whilst the status and power of the mission was by intention decreasing as the autonomy of the indigenous church became imperative, the teaching and healing ministries of the church's great commission were rapidly developing. Mbereshi, Kawimbe and Senga had upper schools; Kambole, Kashinda and Kafulwe had extensive station and district schools, all under LMS management. The Livingstone Memorial Teacher Training School at Mbereshi combined male and female teacher training by 1945, and this large and influential institution later became the major part of the Christian Council's Malcolm Moffat Teacher Training College which opened in 1960. This was established at Serenje, built and financed by the government. Missionary and African teachers from Mbereshi formed most of the staff of this northern college under co-principals Monica Wareham and Bevill Packer. Their rapport over many years with African teachers like Kosam Mfwika was largely responsible for the smooth transfer to Serenje (another teacher training college under the Christian Council was the David Livingstone College at Livingstone serving the south of the territory). There were further appointees by LMS/CCWM before the UCZ and the Christian Council of Zambia (CCZ) formally took over responsibility from the missionary societies in the 1970s.

Ordained missionaries had often been managers of village schools, but there were instances where lay specialists had been managers while being engaged in other work. At Mbereshi Frank Hodgson managed the schools along the Luapula Valley. At Kawimbe a many-talented missionary layman, Bert Holyday, had combined agricultural work with managing village schools, and in a decade had demonstrated with his African colleagues how the traditional hunger period before the rainy season could be avoided through appropriate crop rotation. Other laymen, including Frank Dobson, were architects and builders, mechanics and electricians as well as missionaries of the word. In the electrification by hydroelectric power and the building of a new hospital at Mbereshi, there was employment for mission-trained staff and apprentices. The management of village and station schools was also a sphere for the training of Africans to take over responsibility, and the integration of all the LMS, UCCAR and UCZ schools progressed into a national and unified educational system for the new nation.

In the medical world there was a similar pattern of development by mission and church where it was logical, necessary and right to hand over the institutions to the state, in the belief that governments could be instruments of God's purposes. At Kawimbe mission the leprosarium, the general dispensary and the wards under the management of a missionary nurse, Elsie Baker, continued to be satellites of the government hospital at Abercorn (Mbala), eventually to be taken over by the government. At Senga and Kashinda missionary wives ran small medical units for a time. The main outreach of the LMS in medical mission was at Mbereshi. The busy general wards that grew out of the sick bay of the girls' boarding school had been without a doctor from 1945, but their needs continued to be addressed by a full-time nurse.

Merlin Cole was sister-in-charge until Eileen Taylor was appointed to the hospital in 1948. Miss Cole was then appointed to "New Advance" women's work, a triple jubilee project of the LMS, and her gracious influence as district nurse, evangelist and friend touched many villages around Mbereshi. A similar widespread rural ministry was exercised by Barbara Lea at Kawimbe.

With the appointment of a doctor again to Mbereshi in 1949, the Rev. Dr John Parry, the LMS's commitment to the establishment and staffing of a district hospital was assured. The new hospital that opened in 1958 with a theatre and X-ray provision became a major health facility in the Luapula valley. Later a tuberculosis ward and classroom were added. The architect and principal builder was Owen Abel who, with this project, ended his long service in district evangelism and station development. After training medical assistants for a time, Mbereshi became a recognized enrolled nurses training school providing a two-year course. The curative services expanded into major surgery, ophthalmology, obstetrics and orthopaedics, which included locally-made appliances. Preventive medicine increased. The hospital and its clinics took part in the eradication of smallpox and the control of many infectious diseases. The nutrition centre which was opened was the first of its kind in Zambia, helping babies with protein-calorie malnutrition and malarial debility. [10]

An important feature at Mbereshi was respect for, but not necessarily agreement with, traditional medicine and its inherent belief in sorcery. There was a strong link with the local church, especially on hospital Sunday. The LMS/UCCAR/UCZ were active in the Christian Council and in the 1970s the Churches Medical Association of Zambia, representing all Christian agencies involved in medical work, was formed. Government grants at about 75 percent of the costs were adequate, but by the time control passed from the mission to the UCZ there was great pressure for medical work to be handed over to the government. This transfer was effected in 1969.

In 1968 the World Council of Churches sent two doctors to survey Christian medical work in Zambia. About Mbereshi hospital they wrote: "It was here that we found the greatest awareness of the healing ministry of the church in our journey through Zambia." [11]

The complex of schools and hospital at Mbereshi was the main centre of LMS missionary service throughout the period 1945-77. In 1957 there were 15 missionaries in the area. This was reduced to seven in 1965 and to three in 1971. In the annual report of 1965 it was stated with some confidence that, as regards the hospital, "it will be a long time before there are African doctors in charge", but events ran ahead of prophecy and Zambian staff were fully responsible for the work by the end of the period.

By 1977 the United Church of Zambia was well established as an autonomous church, being the largest Protestant denomination in the country. It was one of the 22 churches which became members of the international Council for World Mission, thus continuing from its mission roots an evangelical and ecumenical ethos in the world-wide church of Jesus Christ.

NOTES

[1] Personal communication, John Parry.

[2] Norman Goodall, *History of the LMS 1895-1945*, London, Oxford University Press, 1954, pp.296ff.

[3] Denis M'Passou, *Mindolo: A Story of the Ecumenical Movement in Africa*, Lusaka, Zambia Multimedia Publications, 1983, ch. 4.

[4] Letter written by Bevill Packer of Mbereshi.

[5] Cf. Richard Hall, *Zambia*, London, Pall Mall Press, 1965, in ch. 7 "The Creation of Zambia", p.208: "The Africans received powerful support from the churches."

[6] *Ibid.*, p.224.

[7] Ronald K. Orchard, *Report after a Secretarial Visit to Africa*, 1948, pp.35 and 59ff.

[8] Quoted by Eric Read in his projected *History of the United Church of Zambia*, as yet unpublished, m/s pp.400ff.

[9] *Ibid.*, pp.402ff.

[10] J.E. Parry, "Experience with a Nutrition Rehabilitation Unit in Rural Zambia", *Medical Journal of Zambia*, vol. 5, no. 4, 1971, pp.115-19.

[11] Report on survey of Christian medical work in Zambia, 11 September -17 October 1968, Geneva, WCC/CMC, p.48.

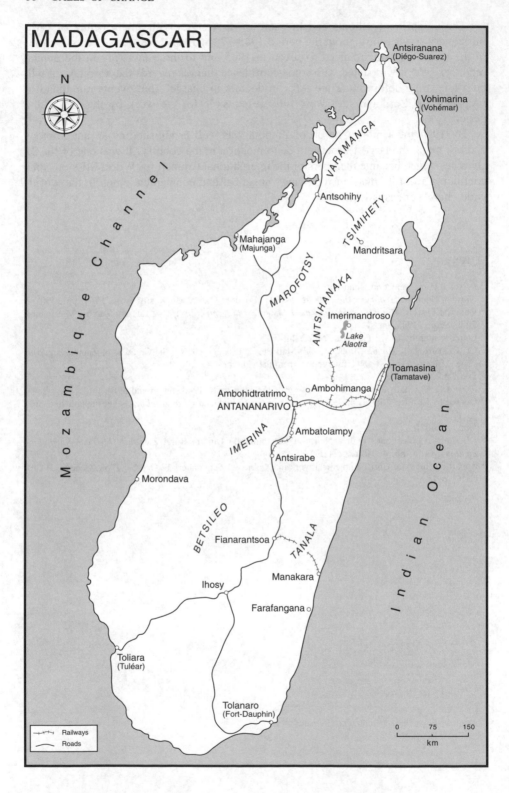

MADAGASCAR

N

Antsiranana
(Diégo-Suarez)

Vohimarina
(Vohémar)

Mozambique Channel

VARAMANGA

Antsohihy

TSIMIHETY

Mahajanga
(Majunga)

Mandritsara

MAROFOTSY

ANTSIHANAKA

Imerimandroso

Lake Alaotra

Toamasina
(Tamatave)

Ambohidtratrimo

Ambohimanga

ANTANANARIVO

IMERINA

Ambatolampy

Antsirabe

Morondava

Indian Ocean

BETSILEO

Fianarantsoa

TANALA

Manakara

Ihosy

Farafangana

Toliara
(Tuléar)

Tolanaro
(Fort-Dauphin)

| | Railways |
| | Roads |

0   75   150

km

4. Whose Kingdom?

Donald Schofield

The closing years of French rule (1945-60)

The royal palace on top of the highest hill in Antananarivo is a constant reminder that Madagascar was independent until it was annexed by France in 1896. At the end of the second world war, after fifty years of French colonization, folk memories of Merina sovereignty and Malagasy freedom from European rule were still very strong. Moreover, it had now been shown that France could be humiliated. It was the British army that had dislodged the Vichy régime and handed back the island to the Free French. In 1944 Général de Gaulle had made public his vision of setting the colonial peoples free and preparing them for self-government within a new French union.

By 1946, however, it became clear that the notion of self-government within the new French union fell far short of independence, although it was to give opportunities for more Malagasy to participate in government at different levels. The island was divided into five provinces. Two electoral colleges, one for French citizens of metropolitan status and the other for native-born Malagasy, chose their representatives for each provincial assembly, and they in their turn elected members of the representative assembly which met in Antananarivo to advise the governor-general. They also sent representatives to the French national assembly and senate and to the high council of the French union. In addition there were elections to municipal councils in twenty big towns. Voting was restricted to the more educated, property-owning and tax-paying members of society (just over a fifth of the population) but all these elections aroused great interest and excitement.

Political parties were legalized and these began to flourish. The strongest was the Mouvement Démocratique de la Rénovation Malgache (MDRM: Democratic movement for the renewal of Madagascar). Its leaders were two Merina Protestant doctors, Joseph Ravoahangy-Andrianavalona and Joseph Raseta, and a Betsimisaraka Catholic, the poet Jacques Rabemananjara. The MDRM campaigned for immediate independence within the French union. As a counterforce the Parti des Déshérités de Madagascar (PADESM: Party of the underprivileged of Madagascar) was created, with help and encouragement from the administration. PADESM rallied its Malagasy support mainly from the coastal populations and the underprivileged classes on the plateau, playing on their fears that the sort of independence the MDRM were seeking might mean a return to Merina domination.

The uprising which broke out in March 1947 brought Madagascar to the world's attention. The ferocity and fanaticism which fuelled it do not seem to have been the style of the political leaders, and who actually started it is still a matter of conjecture. Former soldiers who had been taught resistance tactics in Europe during the war played an important part. Atrocities were numerous and many old scores were settled during the months that followed. The French colonialists, some of whom lost a great deal, blamed their government and the new electoral policy for encouraging the nationalists. The administration blamed the MDRM and also suspected the Protestant churches of breeding political dissent. D.O. Jones wrote at the beginning of the troubles:

> One thing we can be certain of, it will make the government even more wide awake and watchful as to what goes on in our churches, and preachers will have to be very careful in what they say. [1]

Possibly as many as 80,000 Malagasy people died, some in the fighting and some from exposure or starvation after fleeing from their villages. Many buildings were destroyed, seven hundred of them belonging to the French Protestant Mission. On the other hand mission houses, schools and other buildings such as the hospital at Imerimandroso were used as refugee centres. Some British missionaries won the respect of both the French administration and the Malagasy population for their efforts in rescuing the vulnerable. They saw church life disrupted, members killed or arrested, and a widespread reversion to pagan practices. Yet on the whole congregations remained faithful, and at the end of the troubles more people than ever turned up at church services.

In March 1948 the new high commissioner, M. de Chevigné, opened the representative assembly by confirming that the administration would follow the principles laid down by the 1944 Brazzaville conference. Any idea of complete independence, even in the distant future, was ruled out. "In this territory," he said, "the only politics that will be engaged in are those of France and the French union." [2] To all except the highly educated and sophisticated Malagasy the concept of the French union meant little. The lives of the majority were affected less by the ideas of government than by the personalities of those who embodied it locally.

Reporting on his visit to Madagascar in 1948 as the responsible secretary of the LMS, Leonard Hurst outlined some of the difficulties of sending British missionaries to work in a French territory: "When a missionary of the LMS feels bound to stand with a Malagasy against an administrator, it is not merely a missionary, but a British missionary in most cases who is thus involved. There are obvious complications possible in such a situation..." But he came down decisively in favour of keeping an LMS presence in Madagascar for three reasons: (1) the fundamental principle of the LMS put it in a good position to help with the development of a truly indigenous church, (2) non-French missionaries might be strategically placed to facilitate moves towards the formation of a Malagasy Protestant church already spoken about and prefigured in the Malagasy Missionary Society (the Isan-Enim-Bolana), and (3) the LMS might be able to play an important part in promoting church union throughout Madagascar. [3] Commenting on this, an officer of the French administration first expressed some nervousness about the Isan-Enim-Bolana and its political aspirations, then added:

> A second point, which I can understand your not wanting to highlight perhaps out of discretion towards the French Protestant Mission, is the fundamental reason for the necessity of an LMS presence in Madagascar: it is precisely that you are British. The gospel which you preach does not have the same nationality as the government and cannot be suspected. This

reason appears to me to be paramount and in any case much more important than the other three you have expressed in your report. [4]

When French logic is less than clear one should read between the lines: in the period after the uprising the administration was looking to the missionary societies to assist them, in strictly non-political ways, to restore law and order in society.

During this time when political activity was banned, the churches came into their own as centres where Malagasy people could not only hear the gospel but freely share and exchange ideas. District church gatherings became opportunities for political activists to meet. There was much suspicion in the air and spies abounded.

Robert Bargues, who became high commissioner in 1950, launched an impressive development plan with funds from France. The provision of equipment and technical help for projects large and small gave a big boost to agriculture. With better food and health care there was a marked rise in the survival rate of infants. Generous subsidies for education were put to good use by the mission schools. *Fandrosoana* (progress) became the popular theme in church and politics. The colonial policy of assimilation remained unchanged, but sympathy for Malagasy nationalism was growing in France. In Madagascar press freedom was restored and trade-union activity recommenced with encouragement from the communists. In 1953 the Roman Catholic bishops declared Malagasy independence to be a legitimate aspiration.

A change of government in France in 1954 gave further encouragement to the independence movement. Under Mendès-France a deputy from Madagascar, Roger Duveau, became secretary of state for overseas. He secured an amnesty for those condemned in the aftermath of the 1947 uprising. A new socialist high commissioner, André Soucadaux, encouraged the development of political life. In 1956 Duveau became the Malagasy electoral college's deputy for the east coast, his colleague for the west coast being a Tsimihety teacher, Philibert Tsiranana, founder of the Social Democratic Party (PSD: Parti Social-Démocrate). That year Gaston Deferre introduced the *Loi cadre* (outline law), which provided for an elected executive to work alongside the representative assemblies at each level, a common electoral roll and universal suffrage. These reforms put the coastal peoples in the majority so that they no longer needed to fear Merina domination. Tsiranana, his party backed by the administration, declared: "Madagascar looks forward to an independence progressively acquired in a French association, the final objective being a status similar to that of a member of the British commonwealth." [5]

Pressure for independence of some sort was now intense. In May 1958 a strong left-wing Congress Party for the Independence of Madagascar (AKFM) was formed. In July a rival Party for the Defence of Madagascar by the Malagasy (MONIMA) was started in the south of the island. Meanwhile de Gaulle had returned to power. He proposed a new constitution allowing France's overseas territories to become independent whilst remaining partners in the French community. In the ensuing referendum 77 percent of Madagascar's votes were in favour of his proposals. On 14 October the Malagasy Republic came into being and the following day the law of annexation of 1896 was abrogated. The new white, red and green flag (the red and white of the former Merina monarchy, with the green added to represent the coastal regions) replaced the French tricolour, and the Marseillaise gave way to "Ry Tanindrazanay Malala O" ("Beloved land of our ancestors").

The new constitution of April 1959 began with an affirmation of belief in God, and went on to declare: "Liberty of thought, belief and the practice of religion are guaranteed to all, provided only that morality and public order are respected. The state protects the free exercise of worship."[6]

The PSD triumphed at the polls. Tsiranana became president and prime minister of the new republic. The three deputies who had been exiled were recalled, two of them joining the government. Negotiations between Tsiranana and the French premier Debré continued until 26 June 1960, when the independence of the Malagasy republic was proclaimed. Tsiranana reassured the French residents that they were still welcome, referring to them as the nineteenth tribe of Madagascar. *Malagasy daholo: tsy misy avakavaka* ("We are all Malagasy: there are no distinctions") was a slogan that appeared on many walls.[7] The situation now was very different from that which had existed before the French arrived. Madagascar had not only regained its independence; it had also discovered a new sense of unity.

Devolution and moves towards church union (1945-60)

At the beginning of our period the Christian population of Madagascar was approximately half Roman Catholic, half Protestant. Among the Protestants the LMS was the largest body, with its direct historical links to the pioneer Welsh missionaries, Bevan and Jones, who arrived in 1818. The LMS constituency was influential in national affairs. Among its members were many of the educated and professional people in Imerina, home of the largest ethnic group. The other main LMS fields were Betsileo and Antsihanaka, with outreach work among the Tsimihety, Marofotsy and Tanala. The French Protestant Mission (MPF) was working in parts of Imerina and Betsileo and in the coastal regions of the northwest and northeast. The Friends Foreign Mission Association (FFMA) had work in an area west of the capital. The Society for the Propagation of the Gospel (SPG) maintained an Anglican presence in Imerina, in the north and on the east coast. Three Lutheran societies were at work in the southern half of the island. All these missions were represented in the capital, Antananarivo.

Historically the impetus towards Protestant church union in Madagascar came from two movements.

The first began with the founding of the Isan-Enim-Bolana (six-monthly meeting) of the churches in Imerina in 1868 after the coronation of Queen Ranavalona II. Delegates from church and missionary society agreed to meet together regularly for prayer, to encourage the churches in mutual love so as to manifest the unity of their faith, and to consider what should be done to improve the life and witness of the churches for the sake of Christ's kingdom.[8]

The second followed on the 1910 world missionary conference in Edinburgh. At an intermissionary conference in Madagascar in 1913 the seven non-Catholic missions working there agreed on a combined strategy for evangelization. Each mission was allocated its own territory to avoid overlapping, and there was mutual agreement about availability of the sacraments and the transfer of members from one area to another. The Isan-Enim-Bolana of Imerina, by now representing churches of the FFMA and the MPF as well as those of the LMS, also played an influential role, spelling out its hope for "a united Malagasy church suitable to the genius of the Malagasy... one Malagasy church, not three denominational ones".[9]

In 1948 the LMS secretary for Madagascar attended the sixth intermissionary conference and twice met the committee of the Isan-Enim-Bolana. The Anglicans had left the intermissionary committee, but the representatives of the six other churches discussed moves to facilitate the formation of a united Protestant church for Madagascar. The Lutherans were not keen. The worldwide Lutheran church was their first concern and their membership of the intermissionary committee depended on an agreement not to discuss doctrinal matters. By contrast the French Reformed were eager to pursue moves towards unity but convinced at this stage that credal convergence was a priority in the process. The three churches which were members of both the intermissionary conference and the Isan-Enim-Bolana were left wondering which line to take. Some such title as "Protestant Church in Madagascar" was being used from time to time by both the Isan-Enim-Bolana and the intermissionary conference. The evangelizing spirit was strong in the Isan-Enim-Bolana, but so was the desire for a greater degree of independence from missionary control. To hand over the churches to Malagasy leadership was also the aim of the LMS, the FFMA and the MPF, but those who worked in the outlying areas were aware of the danger of confirming the impression, already gained by some from past experience, that Christianity was essentially a Merina religion.

The way ahead suggested in Leonard Hurst's report was that within each of the three denominations Malagasy leadership and responsibility should be increased, and that at the same time they should set up a joint committee to study the question of a truly united Malagasy church. But neither the directors of the LMS nor the church committees in Madagascar could have predicted the way that the situation would actually develop.

At the end of 1948 it became known that the Friends Service Council (FSC) was considering giving up work in Madagascar. Its missionary staff was down to five. It was very difficult to find more staff, controls on sterling aggravated the situation, and there was much questioning about the role of Friends in a situation where Quaker worship had lost so much of its character. "It is undesirable to strive to educate the Malagasy into the desire for Quaker ways... Christianity in Madagascar would be better served by union with other Protestant churches rather than laying emphasis on those things that may divide."[10] In Antananarivo an FFMA withdrawal would affect five churches, boys and girls schools and a printing press, and in the country to the west of the capital 259 churches, a training centre for church workers, and 86 schools with 3,500 pupils.[11] Faced with this crisis a conference in London in July 1949 representing the LMS, FSC and MPF recommended the setting up in Madagascar of a special advisory committee consisting of three representatives from each mission, "charged with the task of dealing with the difficulties in the FFMA field and the many far-reaching questions, involving wider cooperation between the missions and church union, that arise from it".[12] Each mission's field committee appointed its three delegates, but the FFMA Isan-Kerin-Taona (yearly meeting) protested strongly. It wanted a Malagasy district minister to be put in charge of its districts. At the request of the FFMA members the advisory committee was suspended, but at the same time two of their missionaries asked LMS colleagues to join them and the MPF in opening up the question of church union. All the LMS missionaries replied favourably, but events were speeded up by an unexpected letter to the FFMA from Major de Bary, government liaison officer for Protestant missions. He wrote:

> News has reached the governor-general that in certain areas of FFMA territory some political agitation in connection with propaganda in favour of the indigenous Tranozozoro church has been based on rumours about the possible departure of your mission. This leads me to set down clearly two points already mentioned in our previous conversation: (1) The

government only recognizes missionary activity insofar as religious communities are under definite direction and oversight and on condition that the local churches are not used for holding meetings in favour of sects or parties whose action is directed against the administration. (2) In the event of a reduction of your missionary activity leading to your leaving a certain number of your churches to their own devices, in which case they would easily become a hotbed of agitation in favour of an independent church, the government would be obliged, however reluctantly, to revise its present sympathetic attitude not only towards your own mission but also possibly to Protestant missions in general.

With this not inconsiderable push from behind, wrote LMS representative Eric Burton, "the advisory committee plucked up courage to resume its meetings". [13] In 1950 it became official and then it was joined by three Malagasy members from each denomination. This "comité mixte" aimed to study ways and means of helping the FFMA in the prevailing difficulties, to consider further cooperation among the three missions in northern Madagascar, and to prepare a working basis for the organic union of the churches connected with the three missions. "The union to be aimed at is the true union of the churches rather than the administrative union of the missions imposed from outside." [14] The MPF had secured an agreement that a common confession of faith should be at the basis of the united church of the future, but conceded that the task of formulating this could be entrusted to the church itself once it had been set up. The LMS churches were urged to speed up the formation of local synods (Isan-Efa-Bolana or four-monthly meetings) in each regional synod (Isan-Kerin-Taona or yearly meeting). The committee also studied the training and recognition of ministers, central funding, church discipline and the desirability of a common liturgy. These early stages were reported enthusiastically in the journals of the three missions, but the response of the local churches was cautious and there was some suspicion over the motives behind the report.

The Friends had found, when they were pondering whether or not to continue work in Madagascar, that an important factor in the situation was the strong feeling of loyalty towards the parent society, although after deciding not to withdraw they had been able to come to an amicable arrangement for an MPF missionary to work in their area. The LMS, with its deep roots in Malagasy society, was similarly regarded. A proposal made by the directors in London to hand over the work in Betsileo to the Lutherans had unsettled the LMS churches there and prompted them to make a big financial effort in order to remain part of the LMS field. [15] It was hardly surprising that church union with the MPF and the FFMA did not arouse enthusiasm in the south. But when the proposals of the union committee were published in May 1950 Malagasy reaction even in the centre was that this was an astute move to prepare for the departure of the British missions. It was suspected that once the union was set up the LMS and the FFMA would quietly withdraw, leaving the MPF in charge of the Malagasy church. [16] The news that four new missionary recruits were being sent out by the LMS in 1950 was welcomed by their colleagues in the field as a sign that might allay these suspicions, but the LMS was to be asked for repeated assurances for several years to come.

Church and mission relationships

Church and mission relationships were sometimes uncertain and uneasy because three processes were taking place at the same time: first, the setting up of a unified organization on the part of each denomination; second, devolution of responsibility from missionary society and missionary committees to indigenous church bodies; third, moves towards church union. Although the three processes were to some extent interdependent they did not always progress at the same pace.

In each of their regions the FFMA, LMS and MPF churches had yearly meetings (IKT) which exercised authority over the local churches. The MPF churches, modelling themselves on the Reformed Church of France, had had their general synod since 1937. Most of the authority of the MPF synod was vested in three standing committees whose chairmen had to be missionaries. When the LMS general synod met for the first time in April 1951 all the missionaries were automatically members, but Titus Rasendrahasina, who had been a district minister at Ambohimanga for two years, was elected chairman. For the LMS churches, brought up, like those of the FFMA, to regard the mind of Christ expressed in the local church meeting as their highest authority, the setting up of a general synod was a new departure. Even so it could be seen as a familiar pattern. The LMS churches were used to different levels of councils, from the monthly and four-monthly meetings (Lohavolana and Isan-Efa-Bolana) to the annual IKT. Government administration too was organized, with increasing Malagasy participation, on broadly similar lines: village councils, cantons, districts, provinces and national assembly. The prospect of having a say in affairs at the centre was very attractive to the churches in the outlying regions: they could only gain from a sharing of resources, and the new arrangement would demonstrate that, although the Protestant faith was stronger in Imerina than anywhere else, the responsibility for propagating it belonged to the whole church regardless of status or ethnic origin. In the larger churches of Imerina, while in theory it was the church meeting which made the decisions, the authority of the local minister was considerable. To many of these ministers another forum in which to exercise their influence was not unwelcome, particularly at a time when the comparative status of European missionaries and Malagasy church workers was being re-evaluated. But perhaps strongest of all the reasons for the coming together of the six LMS regions (still named after the predominant ethnic group in each area: Antsihanaka, Betsileo, Imerina, Marofotsy, Tanala, Tsimihety) was their common concern to strengthen and maintain what they saw to be the distinctive LMS witness to a gospel of freedom, in contrast, on the one hand, to the perceived authoritarianism of the French régime, the Roman Catholic and Lutheran churches and to a lesser extent the French Protestant Mission, and, on the other hand, to the stultifying or corrupting influences of deep-rooted traditional Malagasy paganism and modern western secularization.

Between 1945 and 1953 a significant number of LMS missionaries of long experience came to the end of their service in Madagascar. Harold Ridgwell, D.O. Jones and Eric Burton had played important parts in the church union negotiations as well as keeping up communication between Antananarivo and London. Others who had left were E.C. Baker, E.I. Groult, A.V. Hardyman, S.J. Hutchins, J.T. Jones, Elsie Sibree and J.N.B. Whitfield. They had all made important contributions to the work of the churches in town and country; they had inspired and trained new Malagasy leaders who, when the time came, proved ready to shoulder heavy responsibility in church and society. The departure of these long-serving missionaries and the increasing pace of change put a strain on those who remained. In Betsileo T.E. Buck and Katherine Ashwell were joined by Alfred Peyrot, Mair Griffiths and John Campbell. Jane Loughton went to Anjozorobe and Alec Walker began new work at Mandritsara, soon to be joined by Donald Schofield. Jim Hardyman at Imerimandroso was joined by Gwyneth Evans and Graeme Smith. In the capital Hilda Butter's grasp of the educational system and her firm and quiet counsel were a strengthening to younger colleagues. Many benefited too from Elsie Stark's skill in language teaching and Roland Leenhardt was shortly to bring his expertise to the aid of the Protestant schools. John Gilbey quickly gained the trust and respect of colleagues and churches with his clear-headedness in financial and property matters, as did Colin Carpenter in the field of church and mission relationships. Alan Paterson, sent out in later life to be mission representative, fostered understanding among the various missions and eased relationships between church and civil administration. John Grosvenor and Ray Arnold came in for some criticism for advocating congregationalist principles, but their new style of relating closely to their Malagasy contemporaries eventually proved to be significant in transferring the initiative for change from European to Malagasy and from mission to church.

By the fifth meeting of the general synod in April 1956, which was attended by LMS delegates Frances Bowers and Barnard Spaull, a new pattern was beginning to emerge. Although there had been little systematic visiting of one another's areas, representatives were becoming more familiar with the widely varying situations in which the church was working. The synod meetings were taking on some of the evangelistic concern and enthusiasm of the Isan-Enim-Bolana. Reports on conditions of church work in the outlying areas renewed a sense of the missionary task of the church among the representatives from the plateau, while the visitors from the less developed areas, lodging with ministers and active laypeople in and around Antananarivo, were learning from the experience of the influential and well-organized IKT of Imerina. At the same time there was a growing appreciation of the vast range of different beliefs, customs, dialects and economic and environmental circumstances which had to be taken into account in the work of evangelization. A district in the north might be concerned about the *tromba* (a widespread form of spirit possession), some on the plateau might want to examine attitudes towards the *famadihana* (the honouring of ancestors by rewrapping their remains in family tombs), while delegates from the Marofotsy or the Tanala might ask for advice about marriage customs or how to combat alcoholism. There was also a growing sense of responsibility towards the well-educated and sophisticated young people of the towns who needed pastors with the intellectual ability to share a faith that had meaning in a secular society. The old idea of the longer established churches sending out their own evangelists was gradually giving way to the newer one of recognizing the particular missionary work of the church in each region and providing mutual support and encouragement. It was in this context that official Malagasy leadership in the church was developing.

The number of churches in most of the LMS areas was growing slowly but steadily at this stage. Imerina had the most with 460, then Betsileo with 278. Antsihanaka had 146, the Tsimihety 119 (only 37 with church buildings), the Tanala 86 and the Marofotsy 70: a total of 1159 registered places of worship. [17]

New developments in the Tsimihety area centred on an integrated pattern of preparation for self-supporting lay ministry were arousing wide interest. Concern was being shown too for the Marofotsy, with students and staff from the Ambohipotsy Theological College making regular evangelistic visits. Plans to establish missionary centres in the Marofotsy and the Tanala were abandoned, largely on the grounds that anyone posted there would be too isolated. Later, however, John Kidd did manage to spend a few years based in Tsaratanàna.

External influences

As the national situation was about to be influenced by a change in French attitudes because of the Algerian war, so the church situation was being influenced by increasing knowledge of what was happening in the rest of the world church. Titus Rasendrahasina's report to the 1956 general synod on his visit to the Church of South India, the United Church of Northern India, and the United Kingdom gave impetus to the church-union process. The following year he represented Madagascar at meetings of the International Missionary Council and the All Africa Conference of Churches at Ibadan in Nigeria.

More church workers were training in Europe. In 1957 Joseph Ramambasoa returned from New College, London, to teach in Ambohipotsy Theological College, Antananarivo, later taking over from Ray Arnold as principal. He was to go on to become principal of the United College at Ivato before succeeding Rasendrahasina as president of the united Church of Jesus Christ in Madagascar.

In August 1958 the intermissionary conference was transformed into the Madagascar Council of Protestant Churches or FFPM (Fiombonan'ny Fiangonana Protestanta eto Madagasikara) and applied for membership of the International Missionary Council. At the time it was referred to as the national council of churches, but that term is now best reserved for the body which came into being in 1980 and included the Anglicans and the Roman Catholics. The FFPM's commission on political affairs played an important part in examining the constitution of the new Malagasy republic and making representations concerning religious liberty. The same year the LMS synod took over from the Madagascar field committee the responsibility for stationing missionaries.

"'Tis an ill wind that blows no good" is an apt comment on Madagascar's experience in 1959 when it was hit by five successive cyclones. The disaster was given prominent media coverage in the developed world. The French government felt compelled to be generous to the territory that had recently voted so handsomely to stay within the French community. The World Council of Churches and other church bodies, including the LMS and its associated churches, gave tangible proof of the reality of the world church; and the effort of distributing large amounts of relief aid reinvigorated the Council of Protestant Churches.

When Philibert Tsiranana became president of the Malagasy republic the Protestant church leaders presented him with two copies of the Bible, one for himself and one for his successor. Soon after independence day, Titus Rasendrahasina, chairman of the FFPM, made a statement to the new head of state:

> The Protestant churches have no one political objective on which they are united. The word of God alone is their foundation and it is that for which they stand and by which they are disciplined. The Protestant church gives complete freedom to every one of its members to participate in any political group which he or she considers serves the nation best... The church rejoices and gives thanks to God that full rights and sovereignty are restored to the Malagasy nation, enabling it to stand as an independent people. And the Protestant church trusts and expects that within that independent nation it will be free to serve God and to preach the gospel to all people. The church of Christ is conscious that God alone is author and perfecter of the life of the nations... Therefore the churches bring before God in prayer this new path which the nation is treading. [18]

The rise and fall of the Malagasy republic (1960-72)

On achieving independence there was no sudden change of regime as happened in some African states. France continued to control the important military bases and the Malagasy franc remained tied to the French franc. Some senior French civil servants remained in their posts, but the nationwide pattern was for former district officers to step down and become advisory assistants to their Malagasy successors before withdrawing completely. The medical services were gradually staffed by Malagasy personnel, although in some places Roman Catholic nursing sisters came in to help. In higher education the French presence persisted. At the same time an increasing number of technical experts from UNESCO, UNICEF, WHO, FAO and other agencies came to Madagascar to study the situation and advise on schemes for development. These were not always in tune with Malagasy thought and custom or with French ideas, particularly about education. But more and more Malagasy students were given scholarships to study abroad, a considerable number of young people from France opted to teach in Madagascar as part of their national service, and the number of UN and church volunteers increased. Dialogue was initiated. Old ideas were being called into question.

By 1962 Madagascar's population was roughly 5.5 million, an increase of 2 million over ten years. President Tsiranana was keen that it should increase still more rapidly, but in that year the health and hygiene classes at the Ambohipotsy Theological College started asking questions about family planning. So began the clandestine development of the "happy families" organization (Fianakaviana Sambatra) until it gained official government recognition in 1967. By 1977, despite some continued opposition, ten clinics had been established in different parts of the island. The traditional marriage blessing, "may you have seven sons and seven daughters", was heard less frequently.

In 1962 the proportion of the population under 15 years of age was about 45 percent and was rising. Even though the greater part of Malagasy society was still firmly rooted in the tradition that honoured the ancestors and hence also the older members of the family, the importance of the large new generation was not lost on the government. A form of national service called "service civique" was instituted, which helped to channel the energies of many young people into constructive activities after their two years' training. The government party (PSD) also had its own strong youth movement.

A seminar on development held in Antananarivo in 1962 brought together the "vital forces of the nation", numbering 10,000 people from all over the island. It was a notable success in popularizing the policies of the Tsiranana government. By 1965 French civil servants no longer held any important posts. In that year Tsiranana was re-elected president for a further term of seven years, backed by over 90 percent of the vote. Three hundred thousand transistor radios were imported and distributed at low prices throughout the population, greatly increasing the ability of the government to get across its point of view. But not all the government's initiatives were successful. Attempts to modernize the production and marketing of agricultural produce through large-scale "syndicats des communes" (associations of rural communes) eventually came up against all the problems of poor communications, falling world prices for basic export commodities, unavailability of spare parts for machinery, personal rivalries and dishonest dealings. Among the general population loyalty and affection were felt more strongly towards Tsiranana himself than towards the other members of his government, many of whom were reputed to have been feathering their own nests. After the independence day celebrations of June 1966 the president's health became a cause for concern, and from then on there were frequent reports and rumours of attempts to seize power and of ministers jockeying for position. Westernization was accelerating. Young people were looking for something better than the heavy-handed, paternalistic and self-satisfied style of the Tsiranana regime.

In 1971 there was a rebellion in the poor south of the island organized by Monja Jaona's party MONIMA. The head of the national gendarmerie directed operations on behalf of the government and the movement was vigorously repressed, leaving over 1,000 dead. In spite of attempts to hush it up, news of the death toll had a profound effect. There was a growing feeling that national unity was at stake and that the government was unable to deal constructively with the situation. In April that year the president closed Antananarivo University after a series of student strikes, and in June, convinced that André Resampa, the strong man of his regime, was plotting to supersede him, Tsiranana dismissed him from his posts of secretary-general of the PSD and vice-president of the republic. In January 1972 Tsiranana was declared re-elected with 99.87 percent of the votes cast, but in April there was a strike throughout the island's educational establishments, and in May there were uprisings in Antananarivo and Mahajanga led by students who quickly gained the support of most of the population. More strikes and violent confrontations between students and the security forces led to the declaration of a state of emergency. On 18 May president Tsiranana handed over full powers to general Gabriel Ramanantsoa.

From LMS to FJKM (1960-68)

During the first few years of the Malagasy republic, the authority of the LMS general synod became well established throughout the church. According to the constitution the general assembly, meeting every two years, became "the final authority in the LMS field in Madagascar".[19] Its decisions took effect immediately, except that "important questions concerning the nature of the church such as the sacraments, the statement of faith and matters which might give rise to differences of opinion in the general assembly" had to be referred to the regional synods before being decided on at the following meeting of the general assembly. The synod had a full-time president, an executive sub-committee and four advisory commissions. The commissions dealt with (1) the appointment and oversight of synod ministries, i.e. missionaries and district ministers, (2) church organization, the calling and oversight of local ministers, the oversight and inspection of ministerial training colleges and Bible schools, (3) organization and oversight of church schools, teacher training, church and school relationships, (4) finance. The size of the representation from each regional synod was determined by the number of its churches and communicant church members. There was nothing laid down about the proportion of ministerial and lay representatives, but from each IKT there had to be at least one layperson, someone engaged in school work and someone in theological training.

In 1961 the membership of the general synod was as follows: Imerina regional synod 42, Betsileo regional synod 15, Antsihanaka regional synod 10, Tanala regional synod 5, Tsimihety regional synod 5, Marofotsy regional synod 4.[20]

The Imerina regional synod had a clear majority in the general synod and there was a high proportion of Merina church members in the other regional synods. In some areas outside Imerina the figures of communicant membership were small compared with the numbers regularly attending church because of a traditional reluctance to get involved with officialdom by registering one's marriage (a prerequisite of full church membership). This affected mostly the non-Merina. Merina influence was strong in another respect too: the Imerina IKT was the richest (and, it must be said, financially the most generous) of the regional synods, and Merina settlers were often the most comfortably off members in congregations in the other areas. There was, then, a natural tendency for the Merina members of the FKM to call the tune, although this was offset by robust representations on the part of some of the other regions who could take heart from the new political situation, as well as by the wise counsels of some far-seeing members of the churches in Imerina. At the 1961 general synod an appeal was made for the abolition of the tribal names for the regions, but this was to take some time.

In 1961 the churches of Madagascar had five representatives at the World Council of Churches assembly in New Delhi, when the International Missionary Council was merged with the WCC, reflecting the growing conviction that church and mission must be one. It was in 1961 too that what had been known as the LMS general synod decided that "London Missionary Society" should cease to be part of its name. The LMS churches became the Church of Christ in Madagascar (Ny Fiangonan'i Kristy eto Madagasikara or FKM). In the same way the FFMA churches had become the Friends Malagasy Church (Ny Fiangonana Frenjy Malagasy or FFM) and the MPF churches the Evangelical Church of Madagascar (Ny Fiangonana Ara-Pilazantsara eto Madagasikara or FPM).

The London Missionary Society itself was at this time contemplating a closer identification with its associated Congregational churches, but the FKM decided not to apply for membership of the International Congregational Council for the moment. The church union negotiations involving the FKM, the FFM and the MPF were a more pressing priority, even though progress had been slow. The three churches were using the same hymn book, lectionary and service manual, and the three church journals had been united in the one *Fanavaozana* (Renewal). But the previous year had seen a last and rather desperate attempt on the part of the LMS churches in Imerina to assert their independency by insisting that "the particular contribution of the LMS churches to a united church" was the authority of the local church to call its own pastor, to pay its own pastor, to refuse to accept the transfer of its pastor to another church, and to refuse to accept the transfer of the church to another district.[21] Quaker susceptibilities had also been complicating the church union negotiations. Representatives of the WCC Faith and Order commission described a proposal that pastors might administer holy communion without themselves taking the elements as "a symbolic contradiction which raises pastoral as well as theological difficulties".[22]

More positive at this juncture was the increasing cooperation within the Council of Protestant Churches (FFPM). A new project for a rehabilitation centre for young women and girls was undertaken by the FFPM at Ambohidratrimo. A mammoth Christian youth congress held in the capital in 1962 with the theme "Who Is My Neighbour?" was further indication of a growing social consciousness. The inspired impatience of these young Christians with the denominational differences that divided them gave a much needed boost to the drive towards unity.

When the FKM synod budgeted for nine district ministers to be under its direct authority, it was a hopeful sign that the long-standing divergence on discipline between ministers of the FKM and the MPF might yet be resolved. The provision of transport for district ministers was a continual difficulty. Some of those in vast and remote country areas were obliged to walk or cycle or wait for lifts on lorries for days on end.

More projects were jointly funded. The LMS was paying 37 percent of the synod budget for district ministers. A new FFPM farm school at Andanona was opened with funds from Holland besides government and local resources. Rural training was beginning to take on an important part of the churches' witness. A number of new school buildings were put up with government and French development funds, and this included boarding homes which were still high priority in the church schools' strategy. The conditional offer of a grant of up to $100,000 from the theological education fund of the World Council of Churches for the development of a united theological college at Ivato helped to concentrate the minds of the three interested denominations.

The publication of Christian literature had always been an important part of the church's work. The LMS printing press dated back to 1822. From the beginning of our period, however, the experienced director, J.H. Conolly, was finding it more difficult to subsidize the production of Christian books by printing popular items cheaply and in quantity. Church presses found themselves competing with big commercial firms which had appreciable capital and large distribution networks and with a proliferation of small family businesses which ignored the regulations and were content with very low standards. A united Protestant printing press had been mooted for many years, but in 1954, after the closure of the FFMA press, the Madagascar field committee produced two strong reasons for keeping the LMS press going. One was Malagasy fears that the LMS was about to withdraw from the island; the other that "it is more than likely that the Lutheran press would regard itself bound to print only such publications as it felt did nothing to question Lutheran views and modes of thought and expression". The Lutheran press was quoted as saying that it would not print anything of a modernist theological nature and could not undertake to print periodicals. [23]

John Farmer became director of the FKM press in 1956 and more new machinery was installed. In 1959 the synod appointed John Grosvenor to be second missionary at the press in order to boost the production and distribution of Christian literature. It also proposed moving the press down from the historic site at Imarivolanitra into the commercial centre of Antananarivo, but failed to agree on a suitable alternative site. In 1964 the LMS in London, which was still financially responsible for the press, urged that serious consideration be given to setting up a scheme for contract publishing. The FKM finally agreed. Printing work at Imarivolanitra ended in 1965. George Andriamanantena became full-time FKM literature secretary, with responsibility for the Imarivolanitra publishing house which was independent of the Lutheran press.

The year 1966 saw the opening of the United Theological College at Ivato with Joseph Ramambasoa as its principal. Conditions were spartan and the financial situation was a matter for concern — the FKM was preparing to cut its overall budget by 30 percent — but the inauguration of the United College proved to be a most important step forward for the uniting churches.

The FKM continued to work on the implications of devolution and at the same time to plan for church union. Made wary by recent examples of misuse of church money, Rasendrahasina and others were questioning the wisdom of fully integrating synod and mission finances, fearing that funds paid in for missionaries' salaries might be syphoned off and used for other purposes. [24] The MPF had had integrated finances for some time, and such difficulties did not appear to have arisen, although the state of disrepair of that church's property gave rise to comment. This debate and the examination of other aspects of integration were cut short by the advent of church union. In November 1967 church bells were rung in Antananarivo as the synods of the three Protestant churches of the north voted in the constitution of the new united church. [25] They also agreed on the shape of the new regional synods (IKT), and decided that the inaugural meeting of the new body would be held at Toamasina (Tamatave) the following year. The date and place were chosen to coincide with the 150th anniversary of the arrival in Madagascar of David Jones and Thomas Bevan on 18 August 1818.

The triple jubilee celebrations took place first in Toamasina and then in Antananarivo, culminating in an assembly in the national stadium where 80,000 people heard president Tsiranana pay tribute to the contribution which the church and the Bible had made to the life of the nation. The name of the new church was Ny Fiangonan'i Jesosy Kristy eto Madagasikara or FJKM (Church of Jesus Christ in Madagascar). [26] The government official gazette of that year recorded its membership as 1.03 million out of a total Protestant population of nearly 1.5 million. The number of Christians of all denominations was estimated at 3.2 million out of a total population of 6.25 million. Predictably there were elements in the government who were unhappy with the size and influence of the new united church. Even during the celebrations there was a trial of strength when the church insisted on keeping the national flag out of its services, and the FJKM had to wait for the end of the Tsiranana regime before it could obtain full legal recognition.

Revolution and the second republic (1972-77)

After the events of May 1972 students and teaching staff continued their strike and organized seminars up and down the island. All ages and classes of society joined in, many local church leaders taking a prominent part in the process. Villagers studied together the main problems facing their country. Resolutions from these seminars were to form the agenda for a big national congress to be held in the capital in September. The FJKM national council backed the holding of the congress and encouraged all Christians to take part in the process. But just before the congress was due to start, the government announced its intention to hold a referendum on its own outline plan later in the year. This took some of the wind out of the sails of the popular movement. In addition doubts were thrown on the representative nature of the gathering, and unnamed sinister forces were accused of manipulating the participants. Despite these difficulties the congress went ahead. The 10,000 delegates from all parts of the island produced an 80-page report containing recommendations for the renewal of educational, social, political and economic structures. In general, although some of the proposals betrayed an unrealistic enthusiasm, they were the reflection of a movement that had already begun at the grassroots.

That October the government held the referendum seeking approval for its sketchy outline programme and for full powers of government to be exercised by General Ramanantsoa for a further five years. Pastor Andriamanjato's AKFM party, whose typical members were the parents of the students who had led the May protests, supported the proposals. The FJKM, the only church to take an official stance, threw its weight behind Ramanantsoa; 96 percent of the votes cast were in his favour.

The general appointed colonel Richard Ratsimandrava, a protégé of Tsiranana with close knowledge of the rural situation, as minister of the interior. Ratsimandrava had been head of the gendarmerie since 1969 and was in charge of the brutal "pacification" of the south in 1971, but he had refused to order his troops to fire on the Antananarivo protesters in May 1972. He was destined to be popularized as the champion of the ordinary people and even to be regarded as a martyr in their cause. Ratsimandrava was intent on a radical reform of the *fokonolona* (village council or community) which meant dismantling structures that had been in place since independence. His aim was to give the whole populace a hand in local affairs, and this included the election of local administrators. This emphasis made the bourgeois class feel threatened but won popular support among the rural majority. The old "tribal" divisions, which had played such an important part in colonial and post-colonial politics so far, were beginning to lose their prominence as more fundamental differences of class and culture came into the open, that between town and country, bourgeois and rural, the habitually powerful and the traditionally powerless.

In June 1973, 30,000 local councils (*fokonolona*) were elected by universal suffrage, and in October there were local elections for the 160-strong consultative development council to advise the government. Ratsimandrava's schemes for grass-roots participation caught the mood of the masses. Many instances were reported of people in town and country cooperating for the public good for the first time in a generation, and of hitherto disaffected young people setting to with pride and whitewashing every house in the village. This was a popular process to be remembered wistfully as events unrolled.

The development of the functions of the *fokonolona* led among other things to an increased demand for local schools. Between 1972 and 1974 the number of children in state secondary schools doubled. [27]

Meanwhile Didier Ratsiraka, a naval officer, former military attaché to the Malagasy embassy in Paris and now made minister for foreign affairs, had begun a series of travels abroad which were to take him to France, the People's Republic of China, North Korea, the Soviet Union, the United States, Japan, Romania, Tanzania, Cuba and Algeria. It was he who successfully negotiated new Franco-Malagasy cooperative agreements. He took Madagascar out of the franc zone and the last French troops departed from the island. He won widespread support, including the backing of the AKFM, for insisting on the need to cooperate with socialist countries "who provide the sort of aid to developing countries which respects their independence and sovereignty and excludes all interference in their internal affairs". [28]

In late 1974 and early 1975 personal and party rivalries were unsettling the government of Ramanantsoa. Coastal factions objected to the Merina influence at the centre of affairs and opposition grew. Despite efforts to cool the situation Ramanantsoa announced in February 1975 that he was handing over all his powers to Colonel Ratsimandrava. That raised fresh passions and a week later the colonel was assassinated by a hit squad. Who was behind it remained a mystery. The army leadership then took control and crushed overt dissent, appointing Didier Ratsiraka, with his socialist ideology, as head of state and of the government and president of the supreme council of the revolution (Conseil Suprême de la Révolution or CSR).

While this was happening, the British government announced that it was closing its embassy in Antananarivo as a result of overall budget cuts. In parliament Lord Merrivale and others pointed out that this was ill-timed, given the seriousness of the problems facing Madagascar, and that the financial saving might be less than the political loss when Madagascar was seeking to strengthen its commercial relations and cultural links with the United Kingdom. [29] The measure was generally interpreted in Madagascar as reflecting a lack of confidence in the new administration who reacted by closing the Malagasy embassy in London.

In a referendum on 21 December 1975 Ratsiraka obtained the endorsement, by 95 percent of the votes, of his Charter of the Malagasy Socialist Revolution, a new constitution and his nomination as president of the democratic republic of Madagascar. The revolutionary charter was printed in the official journal in a form that could be posted up, together with the president's photograph, on the walls of public buildings, and also as a little red book so that it could be studied at home and read out in *fokonolona* meetings. For the next ten years or more the word "revolution" was to be the theme and touchstone of every political pronouncement. The red book taught "there is no revolution without a revolutionary organization". At the end of 1976 the president announced the formation of a National Front for the Defence of the Revolution (FNDR) consisting of the five main political groups. All political activity was to be exercised exclusively within the Front. Those who had participated fully in the *fokonolona* but steered clear of political labels had now to decide to join the vanguard of the Malagasy revolution (Antoky ny Revolusiona Malagasy, AREMA) or else relinquish their responsibilities. Many good people were lost to the hopeful new development movement because of this.

In the elections for the legislature in June 1977 the FNDR gained a 96 percent victory. For the moment president Ratsiraka was content to reside in the centre of his capital and conduct from there the affairs of his new socialist state, assured of the agreement of the mass of the Malagasy population and the encouragement of his new friends abroad. Before very long, however, he was to be overwhelmed by events, not least by the rapid deterioration of Madagascar's economic circumstances and the consequent disillusionment of his former devotees. He then withdrew from the city to a stronghold built for him at Iavoloha by technicians from North Korea.

The Church of Jesus Christ in Madagascar (1968-77)

The FJKM came together without any formal statement of common faith. The service book and hymn book which all three uniting churches were already using helped to ensure a common approach, otherwise it was the preambles to the various sections of the new constitution that were the first indication of how the church was to express its faith. In the basic preamble the FJKM declared itself to be a part of the church universal, a member of the World Council of Churches and of the Madagascar Council of Protestant Churches (FFPM). It desired the union of all Protestant churches in Madagascar.

> The FJKM acknowledges Jesus Christ as Lord and Saviour of the world. It accepts the word of God, as revealed in the Bible and as interpreted by the Holy Spirit, as the source and

rule of its faith and life. It is the task of the FJKM, in its life, words and work, to serve and praise God in worship and in the preaching of the gospel of the Lord Jesus Christ to all. The FJKM works under the leadership of the Lord Jesus Christ. The authority for the conduct of the work rests with the meeting of the church members and the duly constituted courts of the church. [30]

For those who came from the FKM the biggest difference in the new organization was the appointment of a central committee to have "general oversight of the work of the church, with particular responsibility for the execution of synod decisions". This committee of twenty appointed and supervised synod workers and nominated the synod's president. Otherwise the levels of authority in the church were the familiar ones: district council (Isan-Efa-Bolana, meeting every four months), regional synod (Isan-Kerin-Taona, meeting annually) and general synod (Synoda Jeneraly, meeting every two years).

As in the former FPM there was now statutory *lay* representation on committees at all levels. The FKM had had quite a strong clericalist bias, especially since its Commission Ecclésiastique, the only committee meeting on a regular monthly basis, had consisted entirely of ministers. On ministry the FJKM was at pains to reject any ideas of sacerdotalism and to stress the importance of lay ministry. "All Christians are called to take part in God's work, and all are equal before God the Lord of the work. No person has any particular grace (or virtue) because of the work he/she is called to do." For the first five years after leaving college new pastors had to go where the synod placed them, but after that the way of calling pastors was what the FKM had been used to. [31]

The formation of the FJKM brought closer together the three supporting missionary organizations. An informal consultation of representatives of the Congregational Council for World Mission, the Friends Service Council and the Paris Evangelical Missionary Society was held in London in March 1968. A committee of the uniting synods in Madagascar had requested the three missionary societies to set up a joint committee to support the work of the united church, asking that all correspondence and requests should be channelled through the secretariat of such a committee. Instead of this the three societies decided that a purely advisory consultation would serve the need and that this should meet annually. [32]

Financial difficulties, not unfamiliar to any of the separate churches before union, soon became more serious in the new-born FJKM. The system of paying contributions into local and regional synod accounts before they reached the general synod treasurer led to delay and confusion. The increased size of the church, numerically and geographically, meant that not only was there an added load of administration which slowed things down at the centre, but the churches in the provinces began to feel even more isolated and distant from "headquarters" in Antananarivo. One of the biggest difficulties, however, was the reluctance of some of the bigger town churches to pay their contributions to general synod funds for joint work. On union it had been decided not to try to operate a central fund for paying church workers (as had been practised in the FPM) but instead to aim for a standard minimum salary. Even this was difficult to achieve. One might wonder what would have happened if in its infancy the FJKM had not had two experienced leaders who carried authority and commanded respect in all sectors of public life: its first president, Titus Rasendrahasina from the FKM, and its first general secretary, Victor Rakotoarimanana from the FPM. They both represented the FJKM at the 1970 assembly of the World Alliance of Reformed Churches in Nairobi, where Rakotoari-manana was elected a vice-president.

The general synod of that year illustrated the confidence of the united church in speaking out on national concerns:

> The FJKM declares that it holds no allegiance to any political party and refutes the opinion voiced by some that it is part of the opposition. And yet the word of God with which it has been entrusted will not allow it to be silent in the face of any situations which are at variance with love and justice. Therefore it deplores, opposes and condemns the many cases of injustice which took place during the elections of deputies and provincial councillors... The FJKM puts on record that the excessive gap between the few who have become rich and the masses, especially the country folk, who are becoming poorer and poorer, is continually widening. This does not square with the spirit of the gospel, and should be taboo in a country that calls itself socialist... Therefore the FJKM declares that it will make an effort to increase the part it is already playing in the development of the nation. [33]

This confidence was being reflected at the local level, with considerable church involvement in agricultural and community development schemes and a corresponding enthusiasm for more lay training. Pierre Ribereau, who first went to Mandritsara as a builder, was among those playing a leading part in agricultural development coupled with lay training, and Wim Brouwer succeeded him in this.

Whilst recognizing the need for developing Malagasy leadership the synod was keen to ask the mission boards to increase the dwindling number of missionaries from abroad. Peter Bellamy had begun with school work and then been ordained at Mandritsara. David Batchelor and Janet Rowlands had also worked there in both church and school. Jim Pottinger, having obtained his doctorate, taught in the United College at Ivato. Tony Ashcroft was in Fianarantsoa, working in the ministerial training college and visiting the Tanala. He was joined for a time by Ray Gaston. Eleri Edwards was soon to arrive to strengthen the unbroken Welsh connection, first teaching in the capital and then becoming communications secretary in the united church.

An important event in 1971 was the inauguration in Paris on 31 October of the Evangelical Community for Apostolic Action (Communauté Evangélique d'Action Apostolique or CEVAA), an organization with 25 member churches worldwide, mostly French-speaking. CEVAA had its offices in those formerly occupied by the Société des Missions Evangéliques de Paris. The FJKM was a founder member, and Victor Rakotoarimanana was called to be its first general secretary. He wrote of this new body:

> By its pioneering work CEVAA wishes to strive to create a new style of relationship between churches. It has put an end to the bilateral links which formerly united each church in Africa, Madagascar or the Pacific to missionary bodies in Europe. Now sharing is the order of the day for all. Resources of finance and personnel are pooled... People who are sent are placed under the responsibility of the welcoming church, of which they become members while at the same time retaining their status as foreigners. [34]

When CCWM delegate Colin Carpenter attended the inaugural meeting of this forerunner of the new CWM he was fascinated to hear the fundamental principle of the London Missionary Society quoted verbatim (but in French) as a basis for the new initiative. [35]

At the height of the student revolt in May 1972 the Roman Catholic cardinal bishop of Antananarivo, the delegate of the Anglican bishop of Antananarivo, the president of the FJKM and the general secretary of the Council of Protestant Churches came together and intervened. After meeting with the minister of the interior they made a broadcast announcing the immediate liberation of the students deported to Nosy Lava and reporting other government promises to heed popular complaints. This prevented further violence. From then on it was expected of the national church leaders that they would try to act together in times of national emergency.

Even during the colonial days the churches of Madagascar were keen that the Malagasy language should have a prominent part in their teaching, and this attitude now harmonized with the "malagasization" movement. Soon after president Ratsiraka took over, however, the church's influence through primary education began to wane. Many more government primary schools were built, and so church schools concentrated even more on secondary teaching. The churches and missions had regarded boarding homes as the best opportunity for training children in Christian ways, but now the deteriorating economic climate meant that fewer families could afford the fees, and most of the boarding homes were closed. Sunday school training was stepped up, while in the field of general education cooperation with the state in the development of the nation's rising generation was regarded as a legitimate practical expression of the gospel.

The concept of economic development which favoured the poor majority in town and country and stressed truth and justice in the face of corruption and oppression became a strong element in the exposition of the gospel in Madagascar. It did not always affect the more traditional theologies whose hopes were firmly fixed on a life beyond. In fact, the two theological attitudes were to be found coexisting quite happily among both Protestants and Catholics: a type of liberation theology that stressed the power of the Spirit in community and economic development, and a more conservative evangelism emphasizing the salvation of the individual soul.

Throughout our period the Christian revivalist movements (*fifohazana* or awakening) were growing in numbers. There was a constant and largely unrestrained enthusiasm which welled up from the grassroots, answering a need to express worship in Malagasy ways and with a particular emphasis on overcoming evil spirits. In the colonial period and under Tsiranana there was some strain between the revivalist movements and the official church authorities who were responsible for keeping good order. Quarrels between different revivalist movements only complicated the situation, until the synods demanded the registration of revivalist workers and advised the regions not to allow more than one sort of movement to operate in each area. But gradually, with the liberalization of the laws governing churches, the fear of sectarian breakaways gave way to a general recognition that the revivalists had a positive contribution to make to the work and witness of the churches. *Fifohazana* groups within the FJKM became responsible for valuable practical social work among deprived and disabled people, leading some to the conviction that the gospel can bring about a real meeting of minds between those who stress the importance of individual salvation and those whose horizon is development of the community.

In June 1974 the president of the FJKM wrote to CWM with the news that the United Theological College at Ivato had had to close temporarily because of lack of funds to pay the teachers' salaries and the grants of the 56 students:

> The present situation is due to the backwardness of the regional synods in paying their contributions to the general budget of the FJKM. The economic situation of the country, upset by the events of May 1972, is not yet back to normal. A certain stagnation is reigning

in the FJKM of which many parishes, especially those in the big towns, have not yet understood the theme of our 1972 Synod: "Living for others".[36]

The general synod which met in Antananarivo that July decided on a radical reorganization to take place the following year. The regional synods (IKT) were to be abolished, and in future the general synod would deal directly with 66 district synods *(synodam-paritany)*. Each district synod would send an equal number of ministers and laypeople, including women and young people, to represent its churches and organizations in the general synod. The number of central departments with full-time staff would be increased. All pastors were to be paid from the centre, and in this way it was hoped to be able to comply with the government's minimum wage legislation and to attract ordained ministers to the poorer country parishes as well as to the more wealthy town churches. Six hundred of the nine hundred ministers were currently working on the plateau, while the province of Mahajanga, three times the size of the plateau, had only 14. Rural training at Ambatolampy, Andranomadio and Mandritsara was a high priority, and the church was shortly to open a new development department.

In May 1975 the synod of the Malagasy Lutheran Church, celebrating its 25th year, achieved full self-government after consultations with Norway and America, and its head office was transferred from Fianarantsoa to Antananarivo. At a consultation of FJKM-related mission organizations the hope was expressed that these changes would improve the difficult relations between the FLM and the FJKM which had resulted in the non-appearance of the newspaper *Fanasina* over several months. That year CWM had four missionaries at work in Madagascar, FSC none and CEVAA 14. The reduction, due to a lack of candidates, was regretted. The Lutheran synod had said that the Malagasy church still wanted missionaries and was against the idea of a moratorium (as proposed at the Lusaka meeting of the All Africa Conference of Churches). The meeting of CEVAA which took place in Togo told its member churches: "The proposal for a 'moratorium'... is for us a stimulating challenge... But we do not think that (it) should be applied systematically."[37] The FJKM made no official pronouncement on this matter, but an unsigned article headed "The FJKM and help from outside" in the newsletter *Vaovao FJKM* of November 1977 said:

> The FJKM is not refusing all external aid, but all such help is by agreement. If there are any sent from abroad who do not do the work expected of them it is better that they should leave. They must be prepared also to go when the time comes for retirement, or if they can no longer work.[38]

The church decided to receive no more French national service volunteers, and the contracts of only a few missionaries were renewed on expiry. The Malagasy church was revaluing its native resources, which were "like the hedgehog's eye, small but enabling it to see clearly".[39]

Through the troubled times ahead the Christian church in Madagascar was determined to avoid both narrow dogmatism and easy accommodation with the powers that be, keeping its eyes fixed on the Lord Jesus. Our period concludes with the new central organization of the FJKM moving down from the heights of Imarivolanitra, the old site of the LMS printing press, to the busy centre of the city, into a spacious and prominent building called *ifanomezantsoa* (the good gift) obtained with the help of the German aid organization Brot für die Welt. To reach it one had to climb the stone staircase commemorating the notorious Queen Ranavalona I who persecuted the first Malagasy Christians. In these offices was now set up a new and dynamic department of evangelism, headed by a Tsimihety whose father was converted by an evangelist of the Isan-Enim-Bolana and who was himself brought up by a Merina pastor of aristocratic lineage who left his ancestral home to serve in the church in faraway Mandritsara. The old home missionary society, the Isan-Enim-Bolana, was no more, but what that mission body itself inherited from the early missionaries and the Malagasy martyrs lives on: a zeal for proclaiming in word and deed the glorious gospel of the blessed God, and a desire to share with all the world the unity which is in Christ.

NOTES

[1] Letter to H. Leonard Hurst 31 May 1947; CWM archives (CWMA), 1941-50, MA/16/37/A.
[2] Speech by M. Pierre de Chevigné, High Commissioner of the French republic in Madagascar and Dependencies, 31 March 1948, in Tananarive at the opening of the ordinary session of the representative assembly of Madagascar and Dependencies: Tananarive, Imprimerie Officielle, 1948; CWMA, 1941-50, MA/16/37/B.
[3] Report by the Rev. H. Leonard Hurst after secretarial visit to Madagascar, 3 May-25 August 1948, London, LMS, pp.32-33.
[4] Letter to H. Leonard Hurst from Commandant de Bary, government liaison officer for Protestant missions, Tananarive, 23 June 1949; CWMA, 1941-50, MA/17/41.
[5] At PSD congress, December 1957, quoted in Nigel Heseltine, *Madagascar*, London, Pall Mall Press, 1971, p.186.
[6] Constitution of 29 April 1959 of the Malagasy Republic, *Journal Officiel de la République Malgache*, no. 41, 29 April 1959; CWMA, 1951-60, MA/31/42/C.
[7] Heseltine, *op cit*, p.190.
[8] H. Rusillon, *Un Petit Continent, Madagascar*, Paris, Société des Missions Evangéliques, 1933, p.383; J.T. Hardyman, *Madagascar on the Move*, London, Livingstone Press, 1950, p.142.
[9] Report of deputation to Madagascar, London, 1913, p.163; quoted by Hardyman, *op. cit*, p.202.
[10] Friends Service Council, notes on the present situation in Madagascar, 29 October 1948; CWMA, 1941-50, MA/17/43, p.5.
[11] *The Future of Friends' Work in the Balance*, Friends Service Council (FSC), January 1949; *More about Madagascar*, FSC, March 1949.
[12] Report of proceedings at a conference of representatives of the LMS, the French Protestant Mission (MPF) and the FSC held on 12 July 1949; CWMA, 1941-50, MA/17/47.
[13] Report on the union negotiations between the LMS, FFMA and MPF, G.E. Burton, 1 August 1950; CWMA, 1941-50, MA/17/46.
[14] *Ibid*.
[15] Minutes of the Madagascar Field Committee, held in Fianarantsoa, 28-30 May 1950; CWMA 1941-50 MA/17/44/B.
[16] Letter from G.E. Burton to F.M. Bowers, 27 July 1950; CWMA, 1941-50, MA/17/46.
[17] Synod report, Antananarivo, 20-26 April 1956; CWMA, 1951-60, MA/24/13.
[18] LMS annual report, 1960-61, p.23.
[19] *Fitsipiky ny Firaisamben'ny Fiangonana Miray amin'ny LMS eto Madagasikara* (constitution of LMS general synod in Madagascar) 1960; CWMA, 1961-70, MA/15/36/A.
[20] Report by Rev A.F. Griffiths after a secretarial visit to Madagascar, 26 July-1 November 1961, London, LMS, 1961, p.7.
[21] Minutes of LMS general synod full committee, October 1960; CWMA, 1951-60, MA/19.
[22] Letter from Keith Bridston and Norman Goodall, WCC Commission on Faith and Order, to the church union committee, 28 January 1960; CWMA, 1951-60, MA/19.
[23] Madagascar field committee, April 1954; CWMA, 1951-60, MA/26/27/A.
[24] Letter from R.W. Arnold to A.F. Griffiths, 26 April 1967; CWMA, 1961-70, MA/15/3/C.
[25] Communiqué des Eglises FKM FFM FPM de Madagasikara, Antananarivo, 9 November 1967; CWMA, 1961-70, MA/17/39.
[26] In 1976 an agreed ecumenical form of the name Jesus, *Jesoa*, replaced *Jesosy*.

[27] Philippe Hugon, *Economie et Enseignement à Madagascar*, Paris, Institut International de Planification de l'Education, 1976, p.218.

[28] *Madagascar Matin*, 9 June 1973, quoted in P. Chaigneau, *Rivalités Politiques et Socialisme à Madagascar*, Paris, CHEAM, 1985, p.74.

[29] *Hansard*, Lords, 28 July 1975, pp.710-714; Commons, 31 July 1975, p.602.

[30] Extracts from the proposed united church constitution, translated by J.I. Pottinger, March 1968; CWMA, 1961-70, MA/17/39.

[31] *Ibid*.

[32] United Church in Madagascar consultation of related missions, meeting at Livingstone House, London, 15 March 1968; CWMA, MA/17/39/B.

[33] Annual report, 1970.

[34] *La CEVAA Pour Quoi Faire?*, Paris, CEVAA, September 1978, p.5.

[35] Report from F.C. Carpenter on a visit to Paris, 30 October-2 November 1971; CWMA, CEVAA, 1971-76.

[36] Letter from Joseph Ramambasoa to A.J. Todman, CWM, 13 June 1974; CWMA, FJKM, 1974-75.

[37] Message to the churches, CEVAA, Lomé, Togo, 1-10 September 1974; CWMA, CEVAA, 1971-76

[38] *Vaovao FJKM*, no. 4, 1977 (translated in *Madagascar News*, Friends Service Council, spring 1978).

[39] A Malagasy proverb.

5. The Struggle for Freedom: Adventure in Unity

Iorwerth Thomas

"A moment comes, which comes but rarely in history, when we step out from the old to the new."

Jawaharlal Nehru, 15 August 1947

At the outbreak of the first world war, the Indian national congress was maintaining its moderate, gradualist policy in the quest for reform and self-government. Other nationalist groups were forming — Hindu and Muslim, revivalist and secret extremist — whose policies were far less restrained. Hope revived and the congress and the Muslim league formed an alliance. However, the reluctance of the government to initiate reform fuelled increasing mistrust of both moderate leadership and policy.

In 1920 Mahatma Gandhi won control of the congress. Under his policy of non-violent non-cooperation the struggle intensified and his campaigns encouraged people to accept suffering, violent repression and imprisonment in the cause of freedom. Not all could follow his discipline; some chose the way of violence. The relationship between the government and the congress deteriorated and social unrest increased. Under the 1935 India act provincial elections were held which the congress won decisively. What had been clear was confirmed: the viceroy would not grant full political freedom, but only a limited measure of self-rule.

At the outbreak of the second world war, the viceroy, without reference to the provincial congress ministries, declared that India was at war. The ministries resigned in protest. Nonetheless the congress offered to cooperate with the government if a truly national assembly were formed at the centre. This was refused and the Quit India movement followed as a nation-wide campaign in 1942. Meanwhile the rift between the national congress and the Muslim league hardened beyond reconciliation, and further government initiatives broke down on this division. However, the labour party in Britain, on coming to power in 1945, authorized elections in India which the congress party won convincingly. The day of action launched by the Muslim league against the congress for its participation flared into brutal violence in the north. The partition of India became inevitable.

The British government appointed Lord Mountbatten as viceroy to carry through the transfer of power from Britain to India. This took place on 15 August 1947 and India became a dominion within the British commonwealth. Whilst terrifying violence broke out as Hindu refugees fled to India and Muslim refugees to Pakistan, India celebrated the achievement of independence and Swaraj (self-rule). The year 1947 will remain one of the most momentous years in Indian history and 15 August a day of dramatic and deep significance. Regret at the division of India could not rob the moment of its importance for India, Pakistan, Britain and, indeed, the world.

The task which faced Jawaharlal Nehru and his cabinet, made the more testing

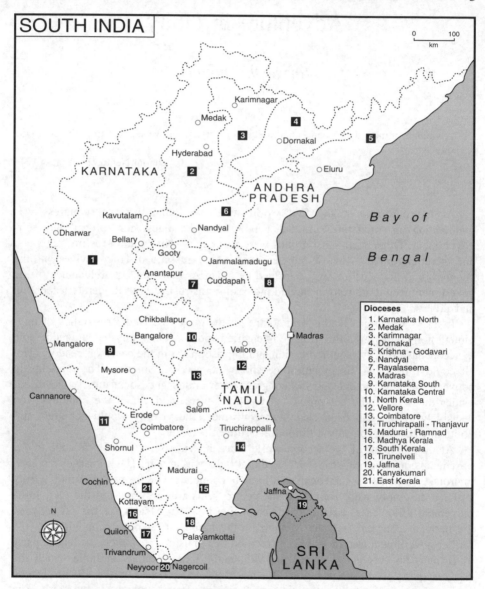

through the assassination of Mahatma Gandhi on 30 January 1948, was to lead into the unity of one nation peoples of many languages, fragmented by deep cultural, social, religious and historical divisions. These differences go far back into history and are still capable of creating mistrust and enmity. The sheer size and complexity of the internal problems were, and still remain, daunting.

The intention to proceed with rapid development, under the system of national plans adopted, was soon evident as projects relating to power, irrigation, industry, commerce and natural resources multiplied. Together with these there was a widespread extension of education at all levels and an advance in scientific, technological and nuclear research, as well as numerous programmes concerned with medical services and public health.

In significant ways, however, the stability needed for sustained progress was denied. The drift of people from the villages to new industrial areas, cities and towns accelerated, accentuating the grave problems of both rural and urban regions. Periods of severe famine and drought with the inevitable resulting malnutrition, suffering and social deprivation further decreased the quality of social life and the hardship endured in villages almost nationwide. The rising cost of living brought widespread unrest in the towns and the expected agricultural improvement was hampered. Throughout the period the voice of the people was increasingly heard: trade unions with their wage claims and the demands for better working conditions, the mobilization of depressed groups in villages and towns by activists seeking political change, and grassroots movements for rural improvement and justice.

There was international tension: first between India and Pakistan — both East and West — which flared into armed conflict at times. The unsettled state of Kashmir was a constant anxiety. When East Pakistan became a separate Muslim state (Bangladesh), a flood of refugees poured into West Bengal, causing serious social as well as political problems. The drawn-out dispute with China (1959-62) dominated political life and the issue of the Himalayan border came very near to open warfare before a compromise was reached. These conflicts and the need to strengthen and supply the armed forces weakened the execution of the national plans.

The congress party remained the major political force but the political climate was changing. The socialist members of the congress had resigned in the early years protesting against the inadequacies of the proposed reforms. The conservative Hindu wing became more influential and was increasingly in conflict with the prime minister. In the country, right-wing Hindu groups were being formed, some of which followed radical political policies in opposition to the secular provisions and safeguards of the constitution. The communist party made considerable progress for a time, forming governments in the state of Kerala and more continuously in the state of West Bengal.

National unity was threatened by the demand for the creation of linguistic states. Andhra Pradesh was the first to make this claim for its boundaries to be extended to incorporate all areas where Telugu speakers were in the majority. The national government was finally compelled to abandon its opposition to this movement and very soon this principle was adopted throughout the land.

In general, sectional and local interests began to subordinate national policies in state elections and so to entice new groups, especially the powerful in rural areas, to seek election to state legislatures. Submerged religious and other tensions — Hindu, Muslim and Sikh — broke through to the surface to inflame political and social issues beyond local to regional and, at times, national levels.

In the closing months of Pundit Nehru's life, before his death in May 1964, his daughter, Mrs Indira Gandhi, had become a leader in the congress power structure. When the new prime minister, Lal Bahadur Shastri, died after only a brief period in office, Indira Gandhi was chosen to succeed him.

The decline of the authority, power and unity of the congress party in the 1970s, increasing instability both at the centre and in the states, as well as increasing social unrest and violence in the country, led Mrs Gandhi to declare a national state of emergency in 1975. The prime minister then announced a 20-point programme for radical social and economic reform, a policy that called for social justice, development and integrity in daily life. For some this offered hope for a better life and it was welcomed. Others were doubtful and critical, suspecting that this was another promise to add to the many made in the nearly thirty years of congress rule. "Indian democracy", wrote Dr Russell Chandran in 1977, "has been incapable of bringing about the changes in economic structure to establish a just economic order. The real threat to democracy in India is the denial of basic conditions of human life to the vast majority of India's people."[1] Many became convinced that the promise was only evidence that the party was trying to stay in power.

In some areas the enforcement of the emergency became oppressive and confirmation of this was seen in the aggressive methods used by some of her followers, the arrest and imprisonment of individuals without charge or trial and the restraints put upon open and free discussion. A visitor to one of South India's largest cities in 1977 was struck by the number of people who spoke of the sense of freedom they experienced when the state of emergency was withdrawn. In the national election that followed a few months later the congress party was defeated for the first time.

The crisis had provided India's rulers with another opportunity to build a nation firmly founded on personal social and economic justice. This challenge was not accepted. The welfare, unity and freedom of India still depended upon confronting the challenge to achieve a just society.

South India: adventure in unity

Six weeks after India won her freedom and became an independent country, an event took place in Madras which marked the beginning of a new era in the history of the church and Christianity in India: the inauguration of the Church of South India (CSI).

On 27 September 1947 a large company of about 5,000 people gathered in and around St George's Cathedral to witness and share in the inauguration of the new united church. Among them were representatives of the dioceses soon to be formed, together with those representing the churches in India and overseas, and members of the uniting churches. After a brief act of worship the inauguration began with the congregation kneeling while a representative of each of the uniting churches read a resolution of his church accepting the scheme of union, and placed on the communion table a signed copy of the basis of union and the constitution together with a signed statement of the bishops and ministers of his church declaring their assent to these documents. After prayer all stood up to hear the presiding bishop, the Rt Rev. C.K. Jacob, read a solemn declaration which contained these words:

> I do hereby declare that these churches, namely the Madras, Travancore and Cochin, Tinnevelly and Dornakal dioceses of the Church of India, Burma and Ceylon; the Madras, Madura, Malabar, Jaffna, Kannada, Telugu and Travancore Church Councils of the South India United Church; the Methodist Church in South India, comprising the Madras, Trichinopoly, Hyderabad and Mysore districts are become one Church of South India.[2]

The congregation responded with the singing of the Te Deum. Then followed the commissioning of the six ex-Anglican bishops and the presbyters of the three uniting churches. The new bishops were consecrated at a service later in the morning which was followed with a communion service. In the evening a public meeting of thanksgiving at which greetings, congratulations and tributes were offered brought a memorable day to a close.

After 28 years of negotiation and prayer since the call to unity issued by those who met in Tranquebar in 1919, "the great adventure in obedience",[3] as Bishop Newbigin described it, had begun.

Six months later at the first meeting of the synod held in Madurai, Bishop Michael Hollis was elected the first moderator of the church and members ratified their commitment to the basic principles of the church, pledging themselves, an evangelistic community, always to seek further unity. Visitors attending the meeting remarked how quickly delegates spoke as members of the same church.

The moderator summed up their experience in these words:

> Things which had been called impossible have been done here. Barriers seemingly impassable have been passed. The Church of South India exists. The whole question of unity can never be the same again after what happened in Madras on 27 September 1947.[4]

Meanwhile, in each of the 14 dioceses work progressed towards the formation of a constitution, the erection of a framework for administration and the discovery of a way to create, out of the heritage and diversity each brought, a unity evident in their new life together. It was generally agreed that many of the dioceses were too large for the development of such unity, and by 1977, using the opportunities that occurred, the number had increased to twenty.

From the beginning, the synod exercised positive, forward-looking leadership and had understood its work not primarily in terms of organization but as a channel through which the whole church might hear God's message and be helped to act in obedience.[5] To this end, every meeting of the synod sought through the themes and speakers chosen, through the time given to worship and Bible study and through the discussions and resolutions adopted, to show the way forward.

The synod shared its work and responsibilities with commissions and boards appointed to coordinate and develop particular areas of its life, witness and service. These played an important part not only in carrying further the thinking and decisions of the synod but also in involving the dioceses with the concerns of the church. They not only covered all areas of its expanding life but also enabled the synod to take further advantage of new developments by appointing boards to provide the support needed by the dioceses. An example of this flexibility was seen in 1974 when the rise in unemployment called for a new pattern of education in South India. The synod appointed an industrial training and promotion board to make a positive response bearing in mind the special needs of rural areas. A decade earlier, a board of education and a central medical board had been formed to assist the diocesan boards with their problems and to advise on matters of policy. Throughout the years the committee whose work was much to the synod's advantage was the theological commission, "one of the most competent and active of the standing committees".[6] It was an indispensable guide for the church, drawing the attention of the synod to important issues for the life of the church as a whole as well as dealing with some of the problems that arose.

The church kept in mind its commitment, renewed at the first meeting of the synod,[7] to work towards the goal of wider union. However, there was disappointment that the interchurch committee working through most of the thirty years towards wider union failed to complete union with the South India branches of the Federation of Evangelical Lutheran Churches, though agreement on the major issues had been achieved. There was also hope that discussions with the Lutheran, the Baptist and the Methodist Episcopal churches in the Telugu area, revived in the 1970s, would enable a move towards union more quickly, but this did not happen.

Significant new developments

In spite of the pressures upon the CSI in the early years to focus attention upon setting in order its new life in districts, dioceses and the synod, the CSI demonstrated its freedom to initiate some significant new developments. Central to these was the renewed concern about the pastoral care available, in particular, for rural congregations. Bishop Michael Hollis, when he was moderator of the synod, stressed that the local congregation was the foundation on which the whole work of the church must be built, and that rural congregations were starved of the nurture they needed. It was recognized that the CSI was unable to support and provide a paid ministry for all. At that time each full-time presbyter had a minimum of 10-12 congregations in his pastorate. The inherited system for pastoral care was no longer adequate for the situation facing the church. A group led by Bishop Lesslie Newbigin prepared a report which gave this analysis: "The present system has the effect of destroying the congregation as a spiritual and ecclesiastical entity."[8] This report was studied by the dioceses and the synod. The new pattern that emerged required every diocese to set aside people to recruit and train voluntary lay workers who could be entrusted with the care of rural congregations under the guidance of the presbyter of each pastorate. They would be able to lead worship and serve as local resident pastors, preferably within their own home congregations. This would necessarily be a long-term programme but most dioceses quickly selected people to train volunteers and organize programmes to suit their needs. The synod also made provision for the ordinations of honorary presbyters — a programme that helped urban churches but, understandably, did not help where the need was greatest. Of the 62 honorary presbyters working in 1968 none was in a rural area.

The publication in 1946 of the Ranson report through the National Christian Council of India led churches in India to review their policy concerning ministerial training. In South India the CSI and other churches had already been moving along the lines proposed, and this was accelerated. Four ecumenical colleges were established and gradually were adequately equipped with new or improved accommodation and the other facilities needed. The teaching in each was through the regional language up to the bachelor of divinity level (Telugu in Hyderabad, Kannada in Mangalore, Tamil in Arasaradi near Madurai, and Malayalam in Trivandrum). Each developed a diversity of courses with the Tamilnadu college pioneering a wide-ranging contextual plan which influenced others. The United Theological College in Bangalore remained the centre for theological training through the medium of English with facilities for post-graduate and doctoral studies. During the principalship of Dr Russell Chandran the services of the college were strengthened with further courses, more accommodation and the provision of a growing archive library. Regular visits of theological teachers from overseas were maintained, and the college benefitted from the presence of the Christian Institute for the Study of Religion and Society adjoining it.

The CSI recognized and welcomed the increasing part that women played in church and society, and during the first thirty years of its life the momentum slowly quickened. In 1976 the synod, after a few years of study and discussion, passed by a very large majority a resolution which made it possible for women to become presbyters. Fourteen years earlier the synod had approved the formation of an order of sisters open to women in the full-time service of the church. The order was inaugurated in St Mark's Cathedral, Bangalore, at Pentecost in 1952 when 27 women were commissioned, of whom 17 were Indians and 10 were missionaries.[9] In 1970 there were 52 sisters in active service working either on their own or in pairs under the direction of their dioceses.

The women's fellowship emerged as one of the most remarkable developments in the first three decades. In 1947 the dioceses had inherited a mixture of women's groups, but within a few months women were calling for the creation of one fellowship for the one church. At the first meeting of the synod a scheme was welcomed and soon launched with Sister Carol Graham's help. In 1957 the women's fellowship already had a membership of 70,000 and was demonstrating its power to unite women across the barriers of language, education, traditions both religious and social, and between town and village. "This women's fellowship", said Graham, "has won for itself a place in the life of the church and in the hearts of its members."[10] The foundation had been laid for a strong and growing fellowship to enrich and challenge the CSI.

Regular assessment

Once in every decade a full meeting of the synod was devoted to an assessment of the CSI's achievements, progress and problems. The first was held around the tenth anniversary when the synod set the members three questions to answer: (1) How far have we grown in unity? (2) How far have we progressed towards becoming an Indian church? (3) How adequately have we discharged our evangelistic responsibilities?[11] By the end of the meeting the synod was left in no doubt as to where the church was making progress and where it was failing, and, through the resolutions passed, called the dioceses to action on a number of important issues. The review conducted in 1964 was prepared for in advance by a commission and their report *Renewal and Advance* was studied by the dioceses before the synod met. This was a detailed, radical and far-reaching examination of the church's life and witness.[12] The report included a section on the missionary societies and the need for an effective partnership between them and the synod. The third such exercise in self-examination was planned for the thirtieth anniversary in 1977 but the report *The CSI after Thirty Years* was not considered by the synod until 1979.

In 1958 the Rev. Paul and Mrs M. Manickam from the Tinnevelly diocese were commissioned for service as CSI missionaries within the Church of Christ in Thailand and they continued to work there beyond 1977. Behind this event lay a story with which the London Missionary Society (LMS) was directly involved. At the end of the second world war the Society launched a "New Advance" movement inviting all its partners to join in pledges to undertake new projects. The South India United Church (SIUC) at its assembly in 1944 expressed eagerness to take an active part in proclaiming the gospel outside India. The formation of its missionary society followed. Two years later in September 1946 the Rev. Sathya Joseph, a senior minister of the Telugu church council, and his wife were commissioned for service in Papua. The LMS had shared closely in this new venture. A part of the legacy of the SIUC to the Church of South India was its missionary society and the synod board of mission and evangelism accepted responsibility for stimulating interest and support. In 1952 when the Rev. Sathya Joseph and his wife were on leave the Most Rev. Michael Hollis as moderator commissioned them both as missionaries of the CSI at a special service held during the synod assembly meetings. Sathya Joseph died suddenly in Papua on the eve of retiring and the door for further participation within the church of Papua was closed by the Australian government. It was six years before the next CSI missionary for service overseas was commissioned for work in Thailand.

The link with Papua New Guinea was not completely broken. It continued through the Sathya Joseph memorial scholarship, created by the CSI and offered annually to assist a Papuan theological student studying for the ministry.

Integration

"There is a case for contending", wrote Dr Norman Goodall in the first chapter of his history of the London Missionary Society 1895-1945,

> that the history of a missionary society separated from the total and complete history of the church is something of an anachronism. In future it should be the history of the church that should be told — the story of that apostolic obedience which is fulfilled in younger and older churches alike. [13]

Ten years later in 1956 the Rev. Stuart Craig recorded in his report on his visit to South India: "We no longer have a mission in India. That belonged to former days. Our work is integrated with the church and our mission organization has been disbanded." [14]

The 14 new dioceses faced the task of integrating the work of the uniting churches and the 12 missionary societies supporting them so that they would truly be dioceses of the CSI. The process was worked through at four levels: (1) missionary societies to dioceses; (2) uniting churches within the diocese; (3) each diocese with the synod; and (4) the synod with the missionary societies.

1. The London Missionary Society (LMS) had close links with five dioceses. Kanyakumari diocese had links only with the LMS and was soon self-supporting. South Kerala diocese received support only from the LMS. Coimbatore diocese was receiving support from the LMS, the Methodist Missionary Society (MMS) and the Church Missionary Society (CMS). Mysore diocese (which later became three Karnataka dioceses) was supported by the LMS, MMS, CMS and the Basel Mission. The Rayalaseema diocese was helped by the LMS, the CMS aid fund (Society for the Propagation of the Gospel) and the Reformed Church of America. The process of integration took many years to complete as different missionary societies moved at different speeds.

In his report to the LMS Board after his visit to the CSI in 1956 the Rev. Stuart Craig saw the problem of transition in these terms:

> We are prepared for the diocesan council to have complete freedom in the use of our resources in personnel and money over the whole range of the council's work — that is to say in our case that they may be used in non-ex-LMS work. We need, however, to look at this freedom which the missions confer on the church... What we have handed over is a

complex bit of organization in which the funds which we say are freely at the church's disposal are, in fact, tied up in all their items and entirely to this or that institution and these and those persons. There are vested interests on every front. The situation is aggravated by the fact that the resources of the church have not kept pace with the rise in the cost of living. All this explains, at any rate in part, why the church has found it easier to make some redisposition of missionary personnel, though there has not been much of this, than to reallocate money... It is not too much to describe the challenge which confronts the church and the church's bondage to its present set up as a major crisis. It is fraught with deep spiritual consequences. Unless the church can break free, reshape its work, get some elbow room to do new things and address itself to its task in new ways and at the points which it knows to be significant, then there will be spiritual deterioration. [15]

From one point of view what could be considered a generous act of sharing was, from another point of view, an acutely testing challenge. In its specific recommendations on this matter *Renewal and Advance* urged the dioceses to take actions that would hasten the time when resources could be allocated to work in the diocese according to the policy decisions of the diocesan council, and missionary societies could act on the advice of the synod when requests for special grants were received from the dioceses.

By 1977 progress had been made and the *After Thirty Years* report was able to claim that "one of the achievements of the church union has been its more effective use of the resources in a wider area". [16] The debate moved beyond concerns about the integration of overseas grants to the kind of structure needed to manage and use the church's resources for the best ends at both diocesan and local level. "The old rigidity that had existed earlier has been broken." [17]

2. Dioceses in which two or more once-separated denominations had been brought together faced the challenge of integration at another level. Members of once-divided churches met initially as strangers. It required time and deliberate action to achieve such a measure of familiarity with, and openness to, each other, that new understanding, trust and appreciation could develop and lead to mutual enrichment and unity. The human desire to avoid being disturbed from familiar, especially religious, ways was at work. But the CSI maintained — and had soon discovered in some places and among some groups — that the churches united within the CSI had precious insights and traditions to share and possess in common. This proved easier to find in urban areas where members with different traditions had been living close to each other and where opportunities for sharing had been cultivated. Dr Rajaiah D. Paul, frustrated by the slowness in overcoming the barriers in this area, exclaimed in his book *The First Decade*, "conservatism has been the bane of our diocesan life". [18] Ten years later he was able to report that they had achieved a greater measure of integration, though there were still pockets of people who had not realized that there was no longer any Anglican, Methodist, Presbyterian or Congregational church in South India. A new generation had come which did not know the divisions of the past.

3. The relationship between the synod and the dioceses was laid down in the constitution. On the surface, therefore, the matter of integration did not arise. The CSI constitution was loose enough to allow for change and growth, but also to create problems. In *Renewal and Advance* the section on the unity of all the dioceses under the synod began with these words: "Though by intention and constitution we are one church, in practice, we still have the appearance of a collection of dioceses bound together in a loose federation rather than in organic unity." [19] And the editors went on to give evidence to support that. The problem was how to reconcile the position of the

synod as the supreme governing and legislative body of the church with the proper degree of autonomy that constitutionally belonged to the diocese. (Chapter IX:15 of the constitution states: "The synod shall deal with matters of common interest to the whole CSI and with those that affect the relations of the dioceses to one another and to the rest of the universal church, and shall leave the diocesan council to deal with the internal affairs of each diocese.") Uncertainty on both sides delayed the provision of a synod secretariat adequately equipped to meet the increasing demands placed upon it. The balance which preserves the synod as the organ through which the CSI's unity was expressed and the freedom of each diocese to deal with matters relating to its own life had yet to be fully understood, defined and established by the end of the third decade.

4. The remaining level of integration was that between the synod and the missionary societies. The societies promptly established links with "their" dioceses; their representatives visited them regularly and were soon involved in the process of integration. The concern to build relationships of like quality with the synod appeared later. It was, in fact, the synod which took the initiative to call the societies to relate to the CSI as a church through the synod. The slow pace at which this took place was frustrating to the synod. At its meeting in 1960 the question as to how the societies should relate to the synod was placed on the agenda. It became customary for mission secretaries to attend meetings of the synod and to participate in the special consultations at which synod officers and diocesan representatives were present. The consultation held in 1964 was of special significance for it dealt with the matters that had been raised in *Renewal and Advance* concerning the societies and their relationship with the church through the synod.[20] The situation thereafter was more clear.

Between 1947 and 1977 much was achieved regarding integration on these four levels. Though all the hopes were not realized, there was a fuller appreciation and an enriched experience of the role of the synod as the voice of the church and the new role of the societies as partners in mission with the CSI.

The changed setting for missionary service 1945-77

Two events between 1945 and 1977 greatly affected the environment of missionary service — the achievement of political freedom by India and the inauguration of the Church of South India.

Before 1947 missionaries had open access to India apart from involvement in political affairs. Their social status in the British hierarchy was a minor one. In their work they were, on the whole, little aware of any connection between their roles and those of the people of the Raj. From 1950 onwards a number of changes took place. An LMS missionary, who was a Swiss citizen, was refused re-entry after his first leave on the grounds that he was not a commonwealth citizen. Representations from the church and the LMS had no effect. Later, alone of commonwealth citizens working in India, missionaries were required to obtain entry and re-entry visas and to register with the head of police in the locality of their work. Provided the police in their area certified "good conduct", apart from the frustrations of bureaucratic delay, little difficulty was experienced once entry had been granted when first appointed. Missionaries working in politically sensitive areas were not so secure. They were, on occasion, forced to leave — a precaution not enforced against other commonwealth citizens in the area. Because of rising inter-religious tensions some Indian Christian leaders anticipated further restrictions being placed upon foreign missionaries.

Agreement was reached between the church and the missionary societies for the synod to deal with applications for the entry of new missionaries and the National Christian Council of India became the body to make representations to the government on behalf of the church. These were important changes making it clear that it was the CSI that was the body inviting support. In the past it had been the LMS that responded to the request of a diocese and had arranged the entry. Later it was the synod which not only negotiated the visa but received the offers of service from the missionary societies and dealt with the requests of the dioceses. This was a measure of centralization necessary to meet the regulations of the government, which had begun to limit the kinds of work for which missionaries would be admitted, provided that there were no Indians qualified to do the work. The CSI and the societies bore with the difficulties and the disappointments, sensitive to the attitudes of those who remembered past history and continued dependence upon foreign support, whilst firmly maintaining their witness to their membership of an international Christian community.

The LMS serving the CSI

Before briefly recording the story of those dioceses with which the LMS was closely associated, we refer to the events that took place in the first decade of the twentieth century — events which clearly, in retrospect, contributed to the formation of the Church of North India (CNI) and the CSI. The creation of the South India United Church (SIUC) in 1908, formed of church councils with Congregational and Presbyterian traditions, was the result of earlier movements which gathered together congregations in local unions in order to assume responsibility for the life and growth of the churches in the areas of these church councils. The purpose of the councils together within the SIUC was to develop a self-supporting, self-governing and self-propagating Indian church. Ultimately the SIUC included all the councils in the areas where the LMS had been at work — Telugu, Tamil, Kanarese and Malayalam (Travancore).

Throughout the history of the church in South India missionaries had played a large part in the creation and maintenance of social institutions, hospitals, schools, colleges, boarding homes and vocational training centres. During the second half of the period under review there was a marked increase in the number of institutions caring for the disadvantaged (especially children) and the disabled. The leadership of the various institutions was increasingly held by Indians but missionary service within them continued to be highly valued. It was the intention to bring institutions within the oversight of the church councils. They remained under joint mission and church council committees until integration within the CSI. The Travancore church council, however, had planned to complete integration in the early 1940s but decided to wait until the CSI was formed. The Telugu and Kanarese church councils had already indicated their support for union when in 1946 the SIUC at its assembly decided to unite with the other two churches to inaugurate the CSI. The North Tamil church council decided to defer a final vote.

Some years earlier cooperation between the LMS Telugu, Kanarese and Tamil areas had developed at another level when the LMS created the finance and reference committee to facilitate joint action. This new committee also had some consultative links with Travancore and Bengal. Fearing the imposition of an unnecessary increase in centralization, missionaries were uncertain as to the wisdom of this development. A new post of secretary-treasurer of the LMS mission committee had also been created. The warm acceptance and appreciation of the value of this new office, by both missionaries and Indian colleagues, was due largely to the grace and wisdom of the Rev. George Parker (1931-39) and the Rev. L.J. Thomas (1939-49) who held this office at the end of long and valued service. [21]

The LMS decided to continue this post under the new name of field representative in India to facilitate, amongst other things, integration within the CSI. The earlier misgivings over the secretary-treasurer were renewed but Dr Henry Lefever, the field representative, satisfied the critics of the new office that there would be no change in the nature of the post. Within five years the task was, in essentials, completed and in 1954 Dr Lefever, who had also served in Travancore where he was the first principal of the Kerala United Theological Seminary, left India to take up the chair of mission at the Selly Oak Colleges, Birmingham.

The shadows

The people in many dioceses live under the shadow of natural disasters. Storms of cyclonic force regularly sweep in from the Bay of Bengal across coastal areas destroying crops and homes and killing people and animals. Along that eastern coastline lie a number of CSI dioceses. Inland, in the Telugu dioceses, the rains frequently fail, drought hardens its grip and famine inexorably follows, threatening life and community. The dioceses of Rayalaseema, Coimbatore and the eastern side of North Karnataka lie within these age-old famine belts.

From Gooty, Ann Marsden described the situation in 1972 after some years of drought:

> A parched famine lies on the land. There is no strength to fight. Such rain as we have had has brought the beginnings of hope to those in whom hunger pangs had turned to numbness. Before the rain, the wells in the town were nearly dry and in the villages the people who had not emigrated in search of work were grubbing for their food in the earth. [22]

Witness to the gospel required a response to such disasters, driving many able Christians to give their service in social institutions and programmes where theology was interpreted as practical care, valuing every human life.

Rayalaseema diocese

No diocese of the CSI faced such difficulties at its inauguration as did Rayalaseema. Originally planned to become two dioceses, incorporating churches supported by the Reformed Church of America (RCA), the Society for the Propagation of the Gospel (SPG) and the LMS, they were faced at the outset by two disturbing challenges. First, the majority of the members of the Nandyal deanery (SPG) decided to withdraw from the CSI. For some years they were cared for by the Church of India, Pakistan, Burma and Ceylon, and then by the Church of North India (CNI) after its inauguration in November 1970. However, tension lingered on until 1975 when the situation was finally resolved by its transfer from the CNI to the CSI. Nandyal became a separate diocese with its own bishop.

Second, an even more threatening problem arose in the Telugu church council before union was completed. A separatist movement had been formed to keep that council outside the CSI. The ministers and congregations involved intended to continue as a Telugu church council and among the leaders of the group was an LMS missionary. The LMS conducted an enquiry which enabled the Society to assess the complexity of the problem, to realize the seriousness and width of the dispute and to acknowledge the personal antagonisms involved. The LMS recalled the missionary, and upheld the decision of the Telugu church council to enter the CSI. It was not able to prevent the division. The schism happened and throughout the following thirty years the dissident group maintained its separate existence alongside the CSI congregations. All attempts at reconciliation failed. The group took the diocese and the CSI to court to reclaim money and property and the cases dragged on through the years. The impact of the division upon the Christian community was grievous indeed, causing disruption, scandal, hostility (at times violence) and division between families, congregations and villages.

The Rayalaseema diocese was formed in 1950 in place of the two dioceses originally planned. It comprised the districts of Kurnool, Cuddapah, Anantapur and the major part of the Chittoor district, an area that still united congregations of the LMS, SPG and RCA traditions. Being a Telugu-speaking area it was soon transferred from the state of Madras to the linguistic state of Andhra Pradesh. The new diocese straddled the railway from Madras to Bombay in a corner of the great Deccan plain which is broken here and there by outcrops of solitary rocks and short ranges of low hills, cool above the heat. It was a land of many scattered villages of farmers and poorly paid labourers whose plight was made worse by long periods of drought. Rayalaseema in many ways was among the poorest of the dioceses.

Through these testing years the diocese became integrated, managing to sustain church life and its commitment to evangelism and service. The CSI community survived the rough passages of the years and was able to welcome back those who wanted to return and sometimes the pastor would lead the people back. [23]

Much of this was due to the leadership of the bishop in Rayalaseema, the Rt Rev. Hospet Sumitra, who was bishop from 1950 until his retirement in 1963. During this period he was also moderator of the general synod for eight years. He was widely respected, trusted and admired for his wisdom, patience and firmness. He was a pastor and a preacher whose message was both simple and profound.

Bishop Hollis stamped upon the agenda of the church the critical importance of the local congregation as the place where the church is and where the best possible nurture needs to be given. The diocese took seriously the call of the synod for all dioceses to engage in the special training and the use of lay leaders in pastoral care and introduced an effective scheme. This was one of the three aspects of the work of the Rayalaseema diocese commended in the *Renewal and Advance* report.

The lay training centre at Gooty served the whole diocese and arranged courses in a series of ten-day sessions to which those chosen were recalled until at least four sessions had been completed. The centre's programme was designed to provide a village congregation with a trained volunteer able to conduct worship in church and at home, to lead in prayer and to know something about the Bible and the essentials of Christian doctrine. The programme was also structured to teach supporting skills from drama to hygiene. The small full-time staff, led until 1956 by the Rev. Harry Wightman and after 1970 by the Rev. Geoffrey Marsden, faced an exacting task within the resources at their disposal as they sought to provide their volunteers with what they needed in order to exercise a pastoral ministry among their own people under the guidance of their presbyter. Few things were of greater importance for the care of congregational life than the supply of such support in rural areas where the majority of Christians lived.

Alongside this went the service of Bible-women which had for long been valued and the report acknowledged that women's work was still one of the major evangelistic activities in the diocese. For most of this thirty-year period five teams were at work and for much of the time four or five missionaries worked with them. The teams would spend up to 10 or 11 days at a time in a village concentrating on a wide range of activities for the care and instruction of women and young children and the support of the congregation. In some areas fruitful and lasting contacts were made and sustained with Hindu homes, where trust was developed and witness shared.

Research had led the writers of *Renewal and Advance* to believe that evangelism had gradually come to occupy a minor place in the programmes of the dioceses. [24] But they commended Rayalaseema because, in spite of its handicaps, it maintained its concern for evangelism. In the years before union some Sudhra (a farming caste) congregations had been gathered. In this work the preaching band, with music, mime and message, had played a significant part. Under the strain of the division in the Telugu church council the preaching band had broken up, but it was revived by the Rev. John Rolles on his return from medical study leave to form a medico-evangelistic centre in Kamalapuram. Provided with a building for the clinic and transport there was soon evidence that local needs were being met. With the preaching band's help renewed contact was made with the Sudhra people and the way opened for offering further support in evangelism. When the Rolles family returned to Britain in 1956 the band continued its witness under the leadership of the Rev. Devabushanam and the clinic became a small government hospital.

The Christian community in the Rayalaseema diocese had been mainly drawn from three groups — the Mala and Madiga people (with dalit backgrounds [25]) and the Sudhra community. A long history of hostility separated the Malas from the Madigas. Caste continued to stratify Indian society into the period of independence despite India's secular constitution and rules against discrimination on the basis of caste.

The Mala-Madiga tension had been brought into the church. A few years later, after he had been moved to lead another district, the Rev. Devabushanam called upon the preaching band to assist him in preaching the gospel within a Madiga community. When some of them seemed ready to join the church he gathered the people for a three-day conference. All the hospitality for those days was provided by members of the Mala congregation. Later on, a reciprocal visit took place when the Madigas welcomed the Malas. The gospel had been heard and bridges of reconciliation had been built.

Through the years a valuable ministry of healing continued, centred on the CSI hospital at Jammalamadugu, first under missionary doctors and then under Indian leadership. Important work was also done at the high school in Gooty where Frederick Maltus Smith gave dedicated leadership from 1923 until his retirement in 1959.

The increased concern for those in need which was expressed in many dioceses in the previous decade was also to be found in Rayalaseema where centres providing training for young unemployed people and for the care of children were started. The most striking example was a movement that showed an openness to the whole community beyond the confines of the church. The Society for the Promotion of Health, Education and Rural Economy (SPHERE), with which Mrs Ann Marsden was involved, united Hindus and Christians in a programme of rural development in villages around Gooty. Mainly by their own efforts people worked to improve their social and economic condition. It was not long before they met with the opposition and conflict inevitable in the struggle for justice.

Rayalaseema was among the poorest of the dioceses in property and land, the most acute in the poverty and oppression suffered by the people, and the most inadequate in its resources. It faced many crises and much frustration during the thirty years. In such situations the degree of cooperation and support between the dioceses was tested. The synod through its synod relief and development committee showed the way. The many intransigent problems in the dioceses called for special gifts of wisdom, grace and reconciliation.

The Mysore diocese and the dioceses of Karnataka

The diocese of Mysore formed in 1947 covered the area of the state of Mysore and brought together the Methodist church, the SIUC and the Anglican churches from the pre-1947 Madras diocese. These were supported by the MMS, the LMS and the CMS. In 1956 the state of Karnataka was created, incorporating the areas where Kannada (Kanarese) was the main language. The revision of the diocesan boundaries was made in 1972 when three dioceses were formed in place of the one, and included the Basel Mission churches and Anglican churches from the CNI.

The new state, encompassing 74,000 square miles, stretched from the Deccan in the east to the high, forested hills of the Western Ghats and onto the Indian Ocean. It is an area rich in natural resources, a potentially fertile and productive land and capable of industrial expansion. In Indian terms it enjoys a mild climate and adequate rainfall except along the harsh dry fringes of the Deccan.

Bishop Premaka Gurushanta, a distinguished Methodist minister, was the first bishop in the Mysore diocese. After his death in 1950 the Rev. Norman Sargant, a Methodist missionary, was consecrated bishop and led the diocese for 21 years through a period of rapid changes in the state and the church.

The congregations and ministers of the Kanarese church council of the SIUC became a part of the diocese in 1947 with one exception — the Rice Memorial Church in Bangalore, which withdrew with its minister from the CSI to become an independent church. The combined committee of the Kanarese church council supervised the integration until 1953 when it was dissolved at a special meeting with diocesan representatives and its authority and resources were finally merged with the diocese.

The Kanarese church council had existed in two geographically separated districts — Bangalore (with Chikkaballapur) and Bellary (with Kavutalam to the north). At the time Bangalore was the weaker both in leadership and in membership and it readily welcomed the wider unity within the CSI. The two secondary schools continued to serve the church and the city and, through their boarding homes, Christian boys and girls from further afield. The LMS primary schools in and around the city were gradually transferred to the government. The few congregations with their pastors in the nearby villages came under the pastoral oversight of the Bangalore district of the diocese. The growth of these churches remained slow — a rate of development similar to that of the Kanarese area in general, untouched as it was by the mass movements experienced in other dioceses.

Bangalore with its population of 2 million and more, the second largest city in South India, attracted many branches of the church and there was a comparatively strong Christian community. Good ecumenical relationships had been fostered over the years and particularly after Vatican II. As well as the United Theological College, Bangalore had two other institutions which served a wide ecumenical constituency. The Christian Institute for the Study of Religion and Society pioneered through its publications, conferences and research interfaith dialogue and the critical study of social, religious and national issues. The Ecumenical Christian Centre offered day and residential facilities for training courses and conferences for churches and other bodies for the study of the problems of life in a rapidly changing secular society.

A feature of this period was the remarkably swift growth of Bangalore, its cosmopolitan character, its commercial life and industrial expansion and its many educational and training institutions. There was inevitably a large movement of people into the city in search of work, and suburbs rapidly surrounded the old boundaries along with the spawning of slums. The CSI city mission attempted to find "lost" Christians and to link them with house congregations and churches while the establishing of worshipping communities in the new suburbs was a diocesan programme for the city.

Chikkaballapur (37 miles to the north of Bangalore) remained a rural town with a CSI community of some 2,500 people in the surrounding area. The two CSI congregations in the town were small; one in the centre depended upon the hospital whilst the other on the outskirts had a membership drawn from the dalit community and needed a strong and sustained period of pastoral care. In the nearby villages there were a number of congregations in difficult situations where progress was slow. There were, however, signs of awakening in a few and the most promising was the congregation, school and boarding home in Gangasandra though progress was hampered by frequent staff changes, limited finance and the need for more pastoral care.

The CSI hospital, known far beyond its immediate neighbourhood, continued to provide a valued medical service and witness to the ministry of healing. The appointment of the Rev. D.J. Elisha as the first full-time chaplain was warmly welcomed. During this period the hospital ceased training male nurses and later was recognized for the training of women nurses. Dr Cecil Cutting, a much loved superintendent and greatly respected in the town and the neighbourhood, resigned in 1961. He was followed by Dr Keith Graham and then by Dr Leslie Robinson in 1972.

Bellary and the district of which it was the centre remained unchanged in size within the diocese as a separate district. This could have resulted in a measure of isolation but over the years members brought up in the churches there contributed significantly to the diocese and to the CSI. Among them were Hospet Sumitra (bishop in Rayalaseema and a moderator of the synod), Luther Abraham (assistant bishop in Mysore and bishop of Medak), Albert Andrew (superintendent presbyter in Rayalaseema), E. Surappa and P.L. Samuel (secretaries of the diocesan council) and others who served on standing committees. During these three decades the town churches grew partly through natural development and partly by the immigration of Christians from other areas. The Wardlaw High School, under the principalship of J.P. Bhaskar, and the girls' boarding home sustained the quality of their service to the churches and the whole community

In 1949 the Rev. Cyril Firth, who had spent 19 years in the district exercising an influential ministry among the pastors and churches, became principal of the theological seminary of the diocese. It was a critical period for the seminary with fewer in training than were needed for ministry in the diocese. When he left Tumkur 15 years later the plan for the merger of the seminary with the theological college at Mangalore was all but complete. His concern for the quality of worship in the churches is reflected in his preparation of the *Book of Services and Prayers* in Kannada and the courses he ran for the ministers of the district, teaching afresh the importance of the sacraments and the essentials of the pastoral ministry. His parting legacy was *An Introduction to Indian Church History* for the Christian students library. Cyril Firth left India in 1965 to become Asia secretary of the Conference of British Missionary Societies in London.

The major new development of the period was the building of the hospital in Kavutalam in 1948. For a long time the district had known that the villages around Kavutalam were open to the gospel; congregations had been gathered from the dalit communities living in economic slavery. It had been proved that the area was in desperate need of medical help. E.D. Martin began his retirement from a distinguished principalship of Wardlaw High School in Bellary planning and supervising the construction of the small hospital. The five years Dr Rodney Todman spent there confirmed the value of the hospital as part of the church's witness and service, and Dr Gona Isaiah moved across from Jammalamadugu to take charge. Hazel Mickleburgh joined the pastoral team in 1952, living in the hospital grounds. Quickly accepted by the hospital workers, the pastors and congregations, she soon identified herself with the people. In 1963 serious illness interrupted her promising work. In 1964 she had to return to England where she died in January 1965.

The increasing difficulty in retaining medical workers and holding pastoral staff in that isolated area threatened the future of the hospital. Yet congregations were growing and villages were enquiring about Christianity. Meanwhile, in 1972, Bellary district became a part of the new diocese of North Karnataka. Dr Keith Graham moved from Chikkaballapur to spend his remaining three years service at the Gudag-Betgeri hospital, much nearer to Kavutalam.

In 1977 the diocese of North Karnataka sought the help of the Rev. Robin Sleigh who had served in Kavutalam from 1959 to 1961. He was invited to return to initiate and lead a rural community development programme.

There was a postscript to this record. After many years of isolation, misunderstanding, litigation and inner tension, the weakened congregation of the Rice Memorial Church in Bangalore, which had withdrawn from the CSI in 1947, sought help. A retired presbyter, Samuel Sadhu, responded and brought the church into the CSI through a memorable, if largely unnoticed, ministry of wisdom, patience and grace.

Coimbatore diocese

Much of the diocese lies in the plains in the state of Tamilnadu with the main railway line running through the towns of Salem and Erode and on to Coimbatore, where the diocese has its headquarters. Coimbatore is connected by mountain railway and road to the high hills (7,000 feet) of the Nilgiri range with their tribal groups, the holiday resorts and the schools. The plains, though still threatened by serious drought, are now somewhat protected by large irrigation projects. Coimbatore (the centre of the diocese) has been a fast-growing city with a few other large towns on the plains and in the hills and the many villages scattered around them where most of the people live.

Before the CSI was inaugurated the North Tamil Church Council (NTCC) had voted to remain outside the union. But after 1947 further thought was given in the council and in 1950 the NTCC adopted its executive resolution "that the council should enter into union with the CSI, being convinced that this step was in the true interests of the churches".[26] This decision was welcomed by the LMS which undertook to accept the diocesan council as the true successor of the NTCC and promised its continued support. The Rev. Arnold Todman was on leave at the time intending not to return, but the India secretary of the LMS persuaded him to return and to test the situation. "I never regretted that advice," Todman wrote. "I found that my fears of episcopacy were unfounded. The first two bishops were men of great wisdom."[27] He stayed on to exercise a very varied and valuable ministry, twice serving as bishop's commissary, and ending with a rewarding period, amidst many other duties, in charge of the boys hostel in Erode where he had begun his service.

The new diocese was inaugurated in 1950 with the Rt Rev. Dr A.J. Appasamy, a wise pastor and saintly scholar, as its first bishop. The diocese incorporated three traditions: the SIUC, the Methodist and the Anglican with the ex-North Tamil church council forming the largest group. The Methodist churches and work were in the Nilgiri hills and the Anglican churches mainly in the larger towns. Enshrined in the CSI constitution lies the conviction that the heritages of the uniting churches should be conserved "not only in their continuity of life but also in all that was distinctive of their life", enriched through their sharing with other traditions in unity.

In the 1940s the quality of life in the churches, notably in Salem and Erode, had seriously declined. Confidence in witnessing had waned, congregations were divided, and tensions, quarrels and rivalries marked their lives. Having become aware of this, the bishop in his inaugural sermon called the diocese to a two-year period of prayer and preparation for renewal. His message was heeded.

Some time later the evangelistic team from Ruanda visited the diocese, particularly the congregations in Salem and Erode. Later the Madras evangelist, N. Daniel, and his team came a number of times and also visited village congregations. Their message brought a challenge relevant to the situation of the people. Uncertainty and opposition from pastors were removed by the recognition of the evidence of "a power at work resolving their problems, healing broken relationships and enabling forgiveness to be received and shared".[28] The support from pastors removed doubt about the attitude of the church to the revival, and groups tempted to separate were kept within the fellowship. "This gracious movement of the Spirit in revival and new evangelism in many places",[29] as the Rev. Donald Collins described it, had a lasting influence not only upon individuals but also upon the life of congregations and institutions in the diocese.

The diocese made a positive response to the call of the synod for all dioceses to review their provision of pastoral care in village churches, and to undertake an adequate programme of training lay volunteers willing and able to offer this critically important service. Two presbyters were set aside to organize and lead courses for such training of lay pastors and to draw a steady stream of volunteers into such service. Instead of working from a single centre the leaders chose to move from district to district conducting brief and intensive courses, with regular refresher sessions for those already assisting congregations. This training was supplemented with longer summer conferences so that their basic studies might be extended. This allowed time to learn teaching skills, to experience evangelistic work and to receive guidance in personal devotion. The programme of training was a major attempt to meet the need of Christians in rural areas to become more effective as communities in their own villages.

Since independence, Coimbatore had grown steadily as an industrial city with a particular involvement in textiles and engineering. People from rural areas were attracted by the possibility of getting work. The Rev. Roy Martin was invited to initiate an enquiry into the task of the church in an industrial city and to explore the possibility of the CSI responding to the situation in the city. The group which he gathered together had access to two major sources of information and advice. First, they drew upon the experience of existing industrial missions in India, and especially those in Bangalore and Madras. This enabled them to study various aims and methods, and also the effectiveness of the missions in their contexts and their differences from the situation in Coimbatore. Second, they received valuable guidance and support from the mobile industrial team of the World Council of Churches then visiting India. The team spent a week with the group in Coimbatore visiting industries, industrial leaders and trade unions as well as meeting groups of pastors and concerned laypeople.

With the findings of this research group before it, the diocese encouraged the formation of a CSI industrial service unit for the city with four main aims: (1) to serve the needs of Christians working in industry, (2) to help the church understand its role in such a city, (3) to encourage pastors to think about their role in an industrial setting, and (4) to keep in touch with industry itself by study, contacts and visits to help the church be more informed about the kind of issues that constantly confront industrial workers at both management and employee levels. [30]

In 1974 the industrial service centre was established in the grounds of All Saints Church with the Rev. M. Gunabalan as its leader supported by a professional committee. The centre provided counselling, an employment exchange and some industrial training. Within two years a site in a large industrial area had been acquired, the foundations of a purpose-built centre had been laid and a bore well for the centre had been dug. A small beginning had been made in yet another part of South India by the church to meet the impact of industry upon individuals and communities in a fast developing city.

During this thirty-year period the diocese continued its work in secondary schools and at the hospital in Erode, which was developed from a women's hospital to a general hospital with a wholly Indian staff.

The last decade of the period revealed a widening concern among Christians and the church for the needs of unemployed young people and disabled children. This was expressed in the diocese, particularly through three pioneer projects. In the Nilgiri hills a professionally equipped and led creche training centre was established. With the help of some of those who had been trained there it was possible to open creches, one each in Salem, Erode and Coimbatore; a service for society in general. The formation of a secretarial centre in Coimbatore — the first of its kind in South India — enabled young women to prepare themselves for work in the city's industrial world. Also three technical and trade schools, one in Salem for thirty girls learning dress-making, and two at the diocesan press in Coimbatore training boys in printing and carpentry, provided opportunities for unemployed young people. In 1974 a school for mentally handicapped children was started in Coimbatore staffed by teachers trained in Madras. The demand for places soon exceeded the accommodation available.

The diocese of South Travancore

The diocese of South Travancore formed in 1947 covered the same area as the previous Travancore church council of the SIUC. None of the other uniting churches was represented in the new diocese, which had connections with only one missionary society — the LMS. This was the only monochrome diocese with which the LMS was associated, and it presented the diocese with some advantages such as the easing of the problems of integration. However, it also revealed some difficulties of integrating with the church as a whole and the possibility of isolation. The Rt Rev. Arnold Legg, a missionary of the LMS, was the first bishop of this large diocese.

The reorganization of the states on a linguistic basis led to the division of the diocese in 1959. The Tamil-speaking district of Travancore called Kanyakumari was transferred to the state of Tamilnadu (previously known as the state of Madras). This Tamil-speaking district of the diocese was formed into the new diocese of Kanyakumari with the same boundaries as the state district. The other two districts of the original diocese became the new diocese of South Kerala with the Rt Rev. Arnold Legg remaining as bishop.

One problem affecting both new dioceses should be mentioned briefly. In 1947 a group of some six congregations opposed to the CSI withdrew and sought recognition as an independent "LMS church", claiming the right to LMS property. The movement, given neither support nor credence by the LMS, received encouragement and finance from a few American churches. Throughout three and more decades the group maintained its pressure (including litigation) and was a troublesome distraction to both dioceses.

Kanyakumari diocese

Kanyakumari, which encompasses a densely populated area of some 8,000 square miles, lies at the southernmost part of India, and was the smallest diocese in the CSI. Its narrow, fertile coastal plain with villages of farmers and fisherfolk, is backed by the Cardamom hills with their villages of hill farmers. Cape Comorin, where the waters of the east and the west meet, is a holy place of pilgrimage for Hindus, and at Mylaudy not far away is the CSI church built on the site of the first church built by Ringletaube in 1806. So the church has a long and rich heritage here.

The diocese with its baptized membership of over 100,000 was a homogeneous, well-knit and, for the most part, well-educated and well-to-do community aware of the strength of its traditions. At its inception in 1959 it was almost self-supporting with a strong and competent lay leadership. Towards the end of the year the Rev. I.R.H. Gnanadason was elected and consecrated bishop in the diocese. He followed his father and grandfather in working for the church in Kanyakumari and after his first pastorate in a village among the paddy fields he was district minister in Neyyoor from where he was chosen to be bishop. He was elected moderator of the CSI in 1972, but within two months became seriously ill. A man of great qualities, both cultural and spiritual, his untimely death deprived the CSI of rare leadership.

Benefitting from the experience of older dioceses, the constitution of the diocese introduced a new structure, centralizing funds and responsibility for the ministry. Each congregation paid an agreed amount to the diocese for the support of the ministry together with a lesser amount towards diocesan administration. The diocesan ministerial committee with overall responsibility for the ministry drew the financial resources needed from the diocesan office. This was a reversal of the previous congregationalist practice but it succeeded in creating interdependence within the diocese.

In the 1970s the 322 congregations were organized into 83 pastorates each one of which was placed in one of the seven districts. Each of the 63 presbyters had a lay pastoral team to ensure that all the congregations received adequate care. A matter of concern, however, was the fact that two thirds of the adult baptized members were not confirmed. In this respect the diocese shared a problem common to many of the dioceses.

A distinctive and important feature of the life of the diocese was the evangelistic work undertaken by the home missionary society whose volunteer and trained members spearheaded evangelism in the area for nearly a century. They had been instrumental in gathering new congregations and continued to support them until they were ready to be transferred into the care of the diocese.

Neyyoor hospital, the first medical centre established in India by the LMS, once covered the area of the Travancore church council. It became the Kanyakumari medical mission with a sharpened commitment to the Kanyakumari district. In 1963 the hospital celebrated its 125th anniversary by the appointment of the first full-time hospital chaplain. Its five branch hospitals, including the two which offered specialist care for sufferers from leprosy and tuberculosis, and the others specializing in family health care, maintained their valued service to the community. The major development after the 1960s was the founding and building of the International Cancer Centre with its trained staff and specialized equipment. It was established under its own trust in order to facilitate the overseas support it needed. It was, however, integrated into the life and work of the hospital serving an area which has the highest incidence of mouth cancer in India.

Building on previous achievements, education had a special place in recent developments at both secondary and collegiate levels. The Martandam Christian College, which was started in 1964, made rapid progress and the Scott Christian College overcame the grave problems it faced in transferring successfully from Travancore University to Madras University. Plans were being discussed actively for the commencement of a women's college and university in Nagercoil. The necessary qualities of leadership, skill and energy were manifest in this area of diocesan life.

The centres for the embroidery and lace industries survived a testing period through fluctuating markets and competition to continue to provide centres of training and Christian fellowship, as well as additional income for the women and financial support for the diocese. This tradition of concern for others was extended in later years to include the provision of special schools for the deaf and blind as well as a home for the aged — all evidence of a growing movement among CSI communities.

The outgoing spirit of the diocese is reflected in the personal contribution made by individuals beyond the boundaries of the diocese both within and outside the church — in medicine, commerce, administration and much else. This is illustrated in the work and writing of the Rev. Dr Russell Chandran through his involvement in the synod, in theological education, within the committees and the councils of the World Council of Churches and in many political and social debates and discussions.

South Kerala diocese

This diocese, which contained the central and northern districts of the earlier diocese of South Travancore, stretches from Quilon in the north to Parassala in the south, with Trivandrum in the centre. The coastal plain is wider here than in Kanyakumari with its bamboo groves, inlets, waterways and river craft, and villages of fisherfolk and farmers. To the east the land rises to the Cardamom hills which reach 1,000 feet and are covered with scattered villages and plantations.

Bishop Legg remained in the diocese as bishop until his retirement in 1966. During his last three years he was also moderator of the synod, and earlier he had been chosen to preach the synod sermon at the meeting which marked the CSI's tenth anniversary. The theme of his message is summed up in these words: "I suggest that we have been more successful in learning to live together than in learning to live as children of God, more successful in becoming a family than in becoming a family of the children of God."[31] His searching analysis of the church's life was reflected in *Renewal and Advance* as he was a member of the commission that produced this report.

Adequate provision was made in the diocese for the pastoral care of the three hundred congregations, each of which was in a pastorate with its own presbyter and a full team of unordained workers. The 47 pastorates were gathered into 22 small districts with three superintendent ministers each exercising pastoral supervision over a few districts. It was a method that met the synod's appeal for better care of rural congregations. In the 1970s the diocese had 80,000 baptized members of the church but two thirds of the baptized adults were not yet communicants.

The reorganization of the diocese constrained the new diocesan medical council to develop the Kundara hospital as the main diocesan medical centre. Dr Geoffrey Milledge (one of the ex-China LMS missionaries who came to work in India) was transferred from Neyyoor, soon to be joined by Dr J.L. Bhanu as superintendent. Between them, and with the help of a special LMS grant, they achieved the necessary improvements in building and equipment. The mobile dispensary ensured contact with the two small branch hospitals and the needs of leprosy patients were met.

In the northern part of the diocese a large proportion of the CSI community had come from dalit groups. They were among the poorest and most socially depressed, and were denied the opportunity for progress. For years they had felt marginalized and neglected by the church and unsupported by the LMS. They had more recently been denied by the government the help awarded to "backward classes" because they were Christians. They could receive no justice until their poverty was assessed not on a caste basis but on need alone. As a result of this, leaders of the "Christian backward classes" (as they called themselves) appealed to the diocese. The Rev. N. Stephen gave leadership to their struggles. Bishop Legg's assessment of the seriousness of this appeal led him to gather representatives of the diocesan council together to discover ways of helping them "without destroying the measure of fellowship in the diocese".[32] A programme was formed through joint consultation to establish a number of rural industries for the community with the help of a welfare officer. The LMS assisted them with a grant and a number of cooperative societies were formed with membership limited to Christians. A beginning was made but the scheme failed to develop; the issues and problems were too complex to hope for a straightforward solution. The search for ways to heal and bring freedom continued, and the conviction that the church should be united in a common fellowship irrespective of communal and economic divisions held firm.

The involvement of the diocese in school education remained unchanged, but there was development at both the university and the social service level. A men's hostel for university students in Trivandrum met a need and provided opportunities for education. Also a Christian college in Kattakada was begun, which was still a junior college in 1977. Greater social commitment was apparent in the founding of a school for blind children and in 1965 an industrial training centre was started.

The motives for the creation of the lace and embroidery industries were twofold. First, there was concern for the welfare of women and their support through employment, together with their nurture within an environment of Christian fellowship at the work centre. The financial support given to the diocese through these industries was secondary, though valued. Second, a century-old heritage of service and witness, initiated by the wives of missionaries, was preserved, developed and, after the CSI was formed, led and staffed by Indian women. There was anxiety about their future because of trading difficulties, but they survived this thirty-year period pursuing their distinctive service.

The Attingal Bible centre for women, another inheritance from pre-union days, gave women the opportunity for Bible study, worship and the discussion of life-related issues within a Christian community of staff and students. The women returned to their homes and villages from these courses equipped to share more purposefully in the life of their congregations and communities. It was an institution of worth both for those trained there and also for the diocese, for some went further, taking advantage of the longer course to train as Bible women. The Kerala United Theological College, which served the three Malayalam-speaking dioceses, was in Trivandrum. Of equal impor- tance was the one-year course for laypeople in the Madhya Kerala diocese, available to members of all three Malayalam-speaking dioceses.

The synod gradually came to the consideration of youth work. There had, it seemed, been no plan to raise this matter from the centre. In 1970 the synod minutes make reference to "the role of youth in the church" and in 1972 a discussion took place which indicated concern at the neglect of this area of the church's life and the need for action to be taken by the dioceses. In 1960 Gabrial Robinson and the Rev. John Marshall Evans were set aside to organize a diocesan youth movement and to develop local branches. The secret of their success lay in the time given to associating existing local groups with the planning and to leadership training for which they prepared their own youth leaders guide. Finally a network of youth fellowships was formed into district units with a diocesan rally each year. This was taken a stage further when the diocese appointed a full-time youth worker.

Missionaries and the CSI

As the uniting churches moved closer to the inauguration of the CSI, missionaries working within them had to decide whether or not to join the new church. Some had no difficulty in coming to their decision; it had already been made during the years of negotiation. They would stay to serve within the CSI. Others were sure that they could not join. Their reasons were varied but for most of them it was their response to the statements about episcopacy in the scheme and basis of union that shaped their decision to leave.

There were some who wrestled with uncertainty to the end and then, still doubtful, decided to stay on to find their answers through the experience of living and working within the united church. Eber Priestley (bishop in Medak when he retired) went through this experience which he recorded in his booklet entitled *Church of South India: Adventure in Union*. He had been one of the leaders of the opposition to union in his own church and among his colleagues, believing "that by the adoption of the scheme a step was being taken away from the standards of the non-conformist conscience and the doctrines of the evangelical faith".[33] He wrote that it seemed to him "by union the church is being steered into dangerous waters".[34] After taking counsel with his friends he knew that if principles were in danger then the right course was not to run away, but to grasp firmly the liberty of conscience and mutual consideration for differences of opinion pledged in the scheme, trust the Lord and the brethren of other churches and join the CSI. This indeed he did and he ends the brief autobiographical introduction: "So began an exciting adventure in fellowship in which it is such a joy to have shared."[35]

It is necessary also to recognize that some missionaries with years of experience in South India resigned, being convinced that their continued presence hindered the development of Indian leadership.

All these differing responses to the establishment of the CSI were to be found among LMS missionaries serving in South India at the time. In 1945 there were 77 LMS missionaries working under the South India United Church. Between then and 1950 21 left either on retirement or resignation. Among them were a few who were conscientiously unable to accept the basis of union, and others who moved aside to give room to Indian leadership.

The arrival soon after 1950 of six missionaries from among those who had been forced to leave China was warmly welcomed and they did much to redress the losses sustained earlier. All but one of them went on to serve within the CSI until retirement. Two missionaries with serious reservations about episcopacy remained in service desiring to help the church in Rayalaseema during a particularly difficult period. Some ten years later they resigned. Service within the CSI had not changed their convictions about episcopacy nor were they able conscientiously to accept the conditions laid upon them to stay. It was their affection for the people and their zeal for missionary service which inspired them to stay on. In retrospect the parting of the ways seemed inevitable. The regret remained, however, that it was not managed with less scarring of relationships.

The number of LMS (later CCWM/CWM) missionaries continued to decline as people came to the end of their service and it became difficult, if not impossible, for new ones to be appointed. At the time that the Council for World Mission (CWM) became an international organization in 1977 there were only 17 left. The situation was similar for other mission organizations sending missionaries to be co-workers within the CSI.

NOTES

[1] J.R. Chandran, "The Emergency and Responsibility", *South India Churchman*, September 1975.
[2] Rajaiah D. Paul, *The First Decade*, Madras, CLS, 1958, pp.25-36.
[3] *Ibid.*, p.20, quoting L.E. Newbigin's *South India Diary*, London, SCM, 1951.
[4] Marcus Ward, *The Pilgrim Church*, London, Epworth, 1953, p.8.
[5] Paul, *The First Decade, op. cit.*, pp.46-47.
[6] Rajaiah D. Paul, *Ecumenism in Action*, Madras, Diocesan Press, 1972, p.173.
[7] *Ibid.*, pp.260-271.
[8] Paul, *The First Decade, op. cit.*, appendix iii, p.255.
[9] Paul, *Ecumenism in Action, op. cit.*, p.297.

[10] Paul, *The First Decade, op. cit.*, p.145.
[11] Paul, *Ecumenism in Action, op. cit.*, pp.51ff.
[12] *Ibid.*, p.112ff. and CSI report, *Renewal and Advance*, Madras, CLS, 1963.
[13] Norman Goodall, *History of the LMS*, London, OUP, 1954, p.14.
[14] Report of the Rev. C. Stuart Craig after his secretarial visit to the CSI in 1956.
[15] *Ibid.*
[16] Report of CSI synod special committee, *The Church of South India after Thirty Years*, Madras, Diocesan Press, 1978, p.57.
[17] *Ibid.*, p.3.
[18] Paul, *The First Decade, op. cit.*, p.233.
[19] *Renewal and Advance, op. cit.*, p.136.
[20] *Ibid.*, ch. VI, pp.91ff.
[21] Letter from H.C. Lefever to the Rev. I.L. Thomas, 1991.
[22] LMS annual report, 1973, pp.14-15.
[23] J.J. Pratt, *Outside the City*, London, Edinburgh House Press, 1967, pp.72-75.
[24] *Renewal and Advance, op. cit.*, p.70.
[25] Those concerned prefer the term dalit to the former term "outcaste".
[26] Minutes of the LMS board, 20 June 1950.
[27] Letter from the Rev. A.J. Todman to the Rev. I.L. Thomas, 1991.
[28] Personal records of the Rev. Donald Collins.
[29] *Ibid.*
[30] *South India Churchman*, April 1971, and CCWM, *Enterprise*, 1968, part 2, article by the Rev. Roy Martin.
[31] Paul, *Ecumenism in Action, op. cit.*, p.61.
[32] The statement prepared by Bishop Legg for the conference, 11 March 1961, of members of the executive committee and the action council of the backward class Christians.
[33] Bishop Eber Priestley, *The Church of South India: Adventure in Union*, London, CSI Council in Great Britain, 1970, p.4.
[34] *Ibid.*, p.5.
[35] *Ibid.*, p.6.

6. Mission with the Poor

José Robins

Introduction

By 1945 the London Missionary Society's work in North India was confined to Bengal and its capital, Calcutta. Other work started by LMS missionaries in the north had been handed over to other missions or churches over the years, the last being the work at Dudhi, near Mirzapur in Uttar Pradesh, which was handed over to the Churches of Christ.

In the national and international turmoil of the immediate post-war years, the life of the church in Bengal did not remain unchanged. An urgent spirit was abroad, seeking a new kind of world, and in India a way of life untrammelled by an alien — though much domesticated — rule. Things were changing inexorably and the church had to change, too. Indian independence in 1947 meant that the country and its leadership could develop in the direction that seemed good to them alone.

Parallel to what was happening in the wider context came the growing realization of the necessity for developing Indian leadership in the church. The National Christian Council of India had brought out an important statement on "The Life and Organization of the Church in India and Its Relations with the Church Abroad"; the document was to be taken into the thinking of the churches in both North and South India in the years to follow. The LMS churches in Bengal were to tread the road to church independence and church union in the three decades to come; they were to re-examine the life and witness of the church and of its institutions in changing India and to see themselves as integral to that change; they were to struggle with "the social gospel" to discover their call under God to make a positive contribution to social thought and action; they were to be encouraged in their mere nothingness to believe that the Lord had his hand upon them and sought to make them instruments of his glory in their own land.

The road to church union

In late 1944 the 22 churches associated with the London Missionary Society in Bengal, the majority small and rural, joined the United Church of Northern India (UCNI). A baptized community of under 5,000 persons, with 16 LMS missionaries and seven mission council workers, all Bengali, thus found themselves welcomed at the UCNI general assembly into a wider church fellowship of nearly 200,000 baptized persons. The LMS directors received this news in London "with great interest", noting that in an area stretching from Bombay to Assam the former LMS churches were now associated with churches of Presbyterian and Congregational origin within the UCNI. Further, they recalled "the part played by the Society in Surat from 1815 to 1847 and especially the translation of the Bible into Gujerati" and rejoiced at "these new bonds with an earlier field".[1] A momentous step had been taken on the road to union in North India.

The formation of the Church of South India (CSI) in 1947 brought new hope to the churches in North India. A definite negotiating committee was appointed and it met in Calcutta to draw up the first plan of church union in North India. The seven negotiating churches were the UCNI, the Church of India, Pakistan, Burma and

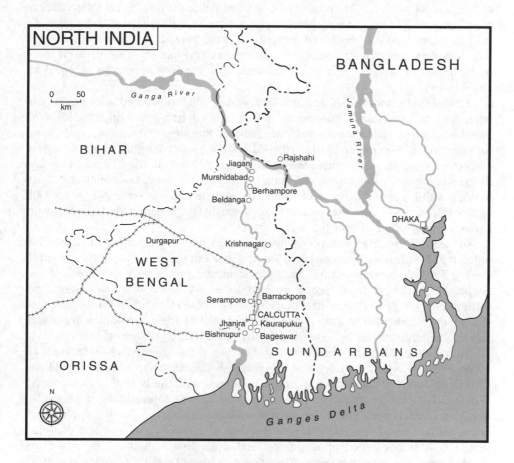

Ceylon (CIPBC — Anglican), the Methodist church (British and Australasian conferences), the episcopal Methodist Church in Southern Asia (MCSA), the Council of Baptist Churches in Northern India (CBCNI), the Church of the Brethren in India and the Disciples of Christ with a total membership of a little over a million people. After several revisions and a minority acceptance amongst the participating churches, the fourth and final edition of the plan was published in 1965.

Among churches of such varied traditions, with historical close links to churches in America, Canada, Britain, Australia and New Zealand, there were bound to be particular difficulties over the place of the episcopate, mutual acceptance of the ordained ministry, and the traditions of infant and believers' baptism. There were times of complete deadlock in negotiations, but "complete shipwreck" was averted "when time and again the Spirit of God moved those involved in the negotiations to an increase of charity and understanding".[2] Thus in the fourth revised plan these difficulties were overcome and the churches' decisions were made by March 1969. The episcopate of the Church of North India (CNI) would be both constitutional and historic. It would be constitutional because its bishops would be appointed and would perform their functions in accordance with the constitution of the church; historic because it would have historic continuity with the early church. However, the Church of North India would not be committed to any one particular theological interpretation of episcopacy. The negotiating churches practised episcopal ordination, ordination by the presbytery, and congregational ordination. These were all brought together in the intention of the representative act of the unification of the ministry by a mutual laying-on of hands. In the CNI both infant and believers' baptism were to be accepted as alternatives.

Though sadly the MCSA decided they were unable to proceed with union, the other six churches finally brought the riches of their traditions and their 550,000 members into the one Church of North India at the great service held in Nagpur cathedral on 30 November 1970. Ordained representatives recognized and accepted each other's ministry in a mutual laying-on of hands. The following Sunday in every diocese union was made visible and actual in a central service, again with that most moving act of mutual laying-on of hands, the ministers, pastors and clergy, now all called by the good New Testament title of presbyters, wearing the simple white cassock and crimson stole of the united church.

In the following five years a constitution for the CNI was drafted and finalized with much thought given to the question "How can structures aid renewal in the church?" During 1975 the church worked out its fundamental priorities, viz. witness to the gospel by word and social action as complementary forms of proclamation; the achievement of self-reliance in evangelistic and pastoral work by 1980; the re-examining of inherited structures and the discovery of fresh forms of witness and service, both relevant and within the capacity of the church to support.

How did all this affect the life of the churches at the grassroots? As far back as 1958, Frank Whyte had written that the bringing together of both the LMS and the Church of Scotland congregations and institutions within the Bengal church council had involved, and continued to require "a good deal of forbearance, accommodation and teachableness"; a wider church union would require "new disciplines of spirit, as well as of organization, new exercise of humility, patience and coopera-tion, and a further period of adjustment and unification".[3] It is a great cause for thanksgiving that, over the years of waiting and from the point of union onwards, this did happen.

In the 1960s, the UCNI appointed a stewardship director who travelled the country teaching and encouraging church councils. The Bengal church council took up the programme with some enthusiasm; as far as the remotest village church the idea of assessing and using "time, talents and treasure" for the Lord began to penetrate. The result was a certain increase in awareness of what it meant to be the church in Fulbari village or in the university area of North Calcutta. Visitation by members of the council, two by two, to all the congregations brought an appreciation of the wider church. Giving and pastoral concern increased.

Ties had been strong with the LMS and the Church of Scotland, but the churches were happily growing together within the UCNI Bengal church council. A greater adjustment was needed when those same churches found themselves in the CNI, divided between the largely urban diocese of Calcutta and the rural and smaller town diocese of Barrackpore. Former Anglican, Methodist and Baptist churches found themselves in the same situation; so, the common feeling of "bereavement" eventually helped to bring them closer together.

The youngest of the CNI bishops, the Rt Rev. Dinesh Gorai of Barrackpore, set about unifying the scattered churches of his diocese by introducing a programme of rural, social and economic development; by encouraging neighbouring churches of formerly different denominations to unite, as in Kaurapukur and Jhanjra; and by his own strenuous pattern of regular pastoral and teaching visits to all parts of the diocese. Though more compact, the Calcutta diocese was a more complicated affair. It inherited predominantly Bengali- or English-speaking congregations, but also a few whose language was Hindi, Tamil, Telugu or Nepali; it included many educational institutions from college to primary school; its local church traditions ranged from high-Anglican cathedral to poor, industrial-fringe Church of Scotland; its resources ranged accordingly. In such diversity and complexity, problems were legion and grumblings frequent. Yet, within a very few years the irreversible *fact* of the CNI, the challenge to live by its motto, "Unity-Witness-Service", within the late twentieth-century context of West Bengal, and the new energy born of the struggle under God to make the CNI "work" meant that the churches began to drop their ex-this and ex-that labels and even to enjoy being CNI, with a mission to work out together.

Leadership and lay training

The LMS "New Advance", initiated in 1945, placed emphasis on leadership from "the younger churches". In Bengal the churches formerly associated with the LMS, but now readjusting to being part of the United Church of Northern India, gave their support to a new ecumenical training institution, the United Theological College. The college trained, and still trains, ordinands through the medium of Bengali, supplementing the facilities already offered in English at Serampore College and at Bishop's College, Calcutta. Among Bengali-educated young men this widened the opportunities for ministerial service to the churches, particularly benefiting the rural churches, as the number of missionaries declined.

In the villages south of Calcutta, set amongst endless rice fields, were numerous small churches and several church primary schools. Missionaries and, here and there, teacher-pastors, had responsibility for oversight. By 1951 three teachers had been theologically trained and were settled in village pastorates. A few years later a grant from the LMS helped to send several village pastors to other parts of India for short study tours to experience church life in another setting. They looked at such things as youth work, Sunday schools and evangelistic work. The excursions proved a lasting inspiration to them.

Sermon classes, started by the Rev. Vaughan Rees, continued on the wide verandah of the bungalow at Bageswar well into the 1970s, attended by village pastors and teacher-pastors. Thus gradually their biblical knowledge and theological thinking were developed and through them the faith of church members was strengthened. Lay conferences also continued the process of Christian education for members of all the churches in the council area. These were often held in the beautiful, spacious setting of the boys' high school at Bishnupur or the more limited but welcoming premises of the girls' or boys' schools in Kaurapukur just south of Calcutta.

Annual youth camps particularly were times of inspiration and training, a challenge and the broadening of church experience for young men and women drawn from the whole Bengal church council area, from Jiaganj in Murshidabad in the north to the Sundarban villages in the south of the Ganges delta. Young people from urban, rural and metropolitan backgrounds — farmers, share-croppers, teachers, artisans, clerks, lecturers, nurses, peons — met to their mutual benefit and understanding. This was part of a wider awareness amongst churches in Bengal of the need to nurture and strengthen their young people in Christian faith and witness in a rapidly — often bewilderingly — changing India. In the 1960s the growing popularity of these camps and increasingly effective youth work in the churches led in 1967 to the formation of a central youth organization in the hands of capable and committed young people; this proved to be a valuable training ground for Christian leadership.

All this was happening at a time of considerable violence and political instability in Calcutta and West Bengal. Against this disturbed background, where youth were the initiators, the desire for a Christian youth movement throughout West Bengal increased and came to fruition in October 1970, a month before the inauguration of the Church of North India. The Christian youth movement incorporated Christians of many denominations and they were young people who were acutely aware of the problems and challenges of the period in which they lived and who wanted to learn how to relate faith to life. Some of the leaders in the youth movement have now become leaders in the wider work of the church.

Not only men, but Bengali women too, were being appointed to positions of leadership, replacing missionaries in schools, colleges and medical work, being invited as speakers for youth and lay conferences, and elected as elders in some churches. Mrs Kanak Das succeeded Olive Stillwell as principal of the United Missionary Girls High School, Calcutta, in 1952; Dhira Sinha followed Dorothy Taylor at Kaurapukur girls' school in 1960, and first Porimol Sarkar, briefly, then Juthika Halder for many years, served as principal of the United Missionary Training College when Mary Cumber left to become LMS candidates secretary in 1962. A few years later, Mrs Das and the principals of three other UCNI higher secondary schools in Calcutta were to receive the president of India's award for services to education. At Jiaganj hospital Dr Susama Mondol had become medical superintendent in place of Dr Honor Newell as far back as 1950, but the two worked together for a further twenty years.

It was during this period that the fine group of gifted, highly educated, deeply committed leaders in the church council's work were beginning to retire. The greatly esteemed and loved Dr Sudhir Chatterjee died in 1965, a loss not only to Bengal — where he was well known in the church, in the field of education and in sport — but to the whole UCNI, of which he had been the first Indian moderator for two consecutive three-year terms. Who would take the place of this group of leaders within the church, to whom everyone had so looked for strength and inspiration? "Successors of comparable gifts are not easy to find," was the understatement of the Congregational Council for World Mission (CCWM) report 1968-69.

A tribal Kond man in the Orissa hills said recently to his Christian anthropologist friend, Dr Barbara Boal: "A community is two annas spiritual people, fourteen annas ordinary people. The latter recognize the former and follow their lead." This ability to recognize and respond to "spiritual people" is deeply ingrained in the Indian soul, but it is being eroded in the more westernized elite, as they adopt secular, consumerist values and create an urban-oriented, technological society; as this needs a large, mobile work-force in the towns and cities, it leads to the disruption of traditional "community". The spread of formal education and the expansion of the media after independence has meant that many educated Christians are also drawn to the same secular goals, but God has not left the church "comfortless". In the 1970s with the pooling of resources within the new Church of North India dioceses of Calcutta and Barrackpore there came a new understanding of the wider church and a desire to identify and train future leaders.

Thus, young men and women were sent for training to the national Sunday school union of India, to the two-year laymen's theology course of evening classes at Bishop's College, to courses and experience in social and economic development in India and abroad, as well as to theological training for the ministry. Against a background of soaring aspirations, rising unemployment, rising prices and financial stringency, it is a cause for thanksgiving that any young people at all responded to the challenge to enter the still low-paid ministry of the church.

Christian action in society

In February 1975, the president of India, Fakrudin Ali Ahmed, said to the executive committee of the CNI in Delhi:

> The Christian community is an integral part of the variegated mosaic of the Indian nation. Their contribution for national welfare stands out as a shining example of how a community, though small in number, can do great and noble things, if only imbued with the ideals of service and sacrifice.

From the beginnings of the LMS missionary work in Bengal, mission and churches together had served the people of a wide area through educational and medical institutions. They had responded to need and suffering, especially at times of flood and famine. In the 1950s through the Churches' Auxiliary for Social Action (CASA), they had helped feed and rehabilitate East Pakistan refugees, who had temporarily camped near Sealdah station in Calcutta. They had worked with local Hindus in the villages south of the city on regular CASA-supplied food relief and food-for-work projects amongst the poorest people, especially in the lean times after floods.

Such programmes, however, though they keep hunger at bay, do not change people's hearts or basically affect the direction of their lives. A greater vision is needed for that to happen. This began to come in the late 1960s, both in political West Bengal and amongst some dynamic Christian thinkers scattered among the churches.

That was a time of chaos and regression in urban and rural life, particularly in industry and education. It was the period of *gheraos* (surrounding and applying pressure) by workers of their bosses and by students of their professors, until they yielded to demands; some of these were excessive, but the people's taste for power and the signs of what could be achieved by it were growing inexorably. Industry began to stagnate; factories were relocated in other states; some international airlines ceased to operate through Calcutta; revolutionary young Naxalites brought fear and violence to the state; schools and colleges saw examinations disrupted or postponed indefinitely.

The communist party (Marxist-Leninist), though still part of the united left front state government, was growing rapidly in influence and saw the possibility of the eventual control it still enjoys.

In the midst of all this the Ecumenical Social and Industrial Institute (ESII) was born in Durgapur. This is one of the steel towns with satellite industries created in India under the five-year plans; it is situated about a hundred miles northwest of Calcutta. The institute was part of a response by the churches in North India to the challenge of the new steel towns and all the problems as well as benefits that they had brought. The ESII was led by the Rev. Subir Biswas and a Methodist missionary, the Rev. Kenyon Wright. The institute, largely of their creation, provided courses for laypeople in the churches to help them to understand modern industrial society and make a significant Christian witness through their participation in it. It also provided a neutral ground for management and workers to reflect together on aspects of their new work situation and relationship, thus performing a function no other body could. The LMS, through the UCNI, supported this venture from its inception.

The ferment of that decade also saw the birth and growth of Calcutta Urban Service (CUS), an ecumenical Christian attempt to work alongside the poor of the city towards their own growth in social awareness and development action. This was pioneered by the Rev. Bilash Das and the Rev. John Hastings, another Methodist missionary. CUS also aimed to serve as a training ground for Christians to learn how to recognize the signs and help to bring in the kingdom of God in a city so maligned by the outside world, so hotly defended by its citizens, who both love and fight with it everyday. CUS lived by the belief that God also loved and grieved over the city; as our Lord said of Jerusalem, so he was saying to Calcutta: "How often have I longed to gather your children... but you would not let me."

The year 1971 saw the beginning of the great work done by Subir Biswas in Calcutta through the cathedral social and relief services. He was by then vicar of St Paul's Cathedral, which had a limited medical and education programme in a nearby slum or *bustee*. The endless stream of refugees from East Pakistan-Bangladesh into India that year evoked the compassion of everyone, rich and poor alike, to help make the refugees' camp life a little more bearable till the political tide should turn for them. Subir Biswas and Bilash Das used it as an appropriate opportunity to challenge the largely inward-looking Christian churches to meet Christ in the refugees and serve him by serving them in the vast camps round the city. Primary schools and a mobile medical service were started; local refugee talent was organized. The Cathedral Relief Service (CRS) grew out of this need; after Bangladesh had become independent later that year, the CRS continued the outgoing relief and imaginative development work in the Calcutta bustees with a large interfaith team of workers.

The most dynamic Christian leaders and thinkers of the time were searching, with great hope and conviction, for ways of making the Christian faith deeply relevant to fast-changing India. Continuing the CUS theme, Subir Biswas in Calcutta and George Ninan in Bombay, for example, both recalled the urban churches, particularly the cathedral in Calcutta, to God's mission among the poor, the despised, the outcaste, the slum- and squatter-communities. They particularly highlighted issues of justice to be faced. To do this in Calcutta, Subir Biswas called Anjali Sen, an experienced Hindu community organizer, to join the cathedral team and train social workers and bustee-dwellers in people's organization on specific local issues. This she did with considerable success in spite of inevitable opposition. The varied, far-reaching programme of

CUS and CRS and of the newly formed Europa-Calcutta consortium of Christian agencies, working for the development of slum people, continued right through to the end of the decade and beyond. The tragic death of Subir Biswas in 1977 was a great loss: the dynamic priest who saw Calcutta as "a city of God" and its slum and squatter people as millions of hopes in the life of that city had become an inspiration worldwide.

Meanwhile, in the rural diocese of Barrackpore, Bishop Gorai was strengthening the foundations of the diocesan Social and Economic Development Programme (SEDP) with its centre at Kaurapukur. Tapas Das, a young chemistry lecturer and a Kaurapukur boy himself, left his secure job to head and expand SEDP's thrust into the villages. Young Christian men and women from the villages were trained to live and work in teams, encouraging the local people to work together for the uplift of their villages: learning better use of land; growing hardier and more prolific strains of rice; digging common irrigation canals properly; starting small income-generating projects with loans from SEDP; discussing common problems and how to solve them. Through all these extensive, well-ordered programmes, Bishop Gorai was endeavouring to lead his people to a deeper experience of what it was to be the church — which exists not for itself, but for others and is to be salt and leaven in society — and to teach them that the grace and power to be the church came from God alone.

Christian institutions

It is fitting here to take a brief look at the two traditional means of Christian witness through service — education and medical work — as they had been established over many years in Bengal. The LMS, the Church of Scotland overseas mission and the English Presbyterian overseas mission had all been involved in such work.

Educational institutions
As far as schools and colleges were concerned, the period saw many changes. These were due mainly to the educational policies of the government at national and state level, the student political agitation and the social and economic climate, particularly in the 1960s and 1970s, rather than to church planning and policy. The UCNI Bengal church council was totally responsible, up to church union in 1970, for the running of two higher secondary schools, one basic school, four junior high schools and 13 primary schools; it also took a leading part in the administration of two other higher secondary schools and two teacher training colleges, one at post-graduate level.

In the 1950s and 1960s the role of the Christian institution — to what extent it could be called Christian, and what its place would be in independent India — was much discussed in the church in India at large and the Christian presence in all fields of life became a very important theme. Some schools, mainly primary, were staffed almost completely by Christians but, when secondary education expanded dramatically in the 1960s, and when the government curricula were fixed for a system of 11 years of school education before the final school leaving examination and when the degree and training levels required for principals and staff were raised, it became more difficult to recruit a sufficient number of qualified Christian teachers. In any case in the secular, competitive society of independent India, preference could no longer be given to applicants simply because they were Christian. "And a good thing, too," perhaps we might say with hindsight from a wider educational perspective in the late twentieth century, but this was not how it was felt at the time.

Promising young graduates were not attracted to the low, government-set remuneration levels of the teaching profession; rather, they turned to scientific research, medicine, banking, engineering, industry and the new technological world. The best students of the higher secondary schools were pressed into the science stream; better and expensive facilities for the study of science had to be provided. The Christian schools expanded; they continued high in public esteem; they maintained their standard of academic success, but the number of Christian staff and students declined considerably. In a Bengali-medium higher secondary school, a girl wrote in 1960 in her English essay: "School life is not the rose of beds"*(sic)*; it certainly was not for the managing committees in those days of educational ferment, experiment and increasing costs.

With the coming of the Church of North India in 1970, the former UCNI schools were incorporated either into the Calcutta diocese or into the Barrackpore diocese. For some years those in Calcutta considered themselves at a disadvantage compared with the English-medium, former Anglican schools; these, precisely because they were English-medium schools, were considered by the wider public to have more kudos and to lead pupils more easily into the westernized, middle-class world of employment opportunities. It would be a long time before diocesan education thinking really recognized and attempted to draw together the very different strands of educational history.

Medical work

Turning to the medical work of the church, we find Christiya Seva Sadan, the women and children's hospital in Jiaganj, 130 miles north of Calcutta, in good heart in 1945 with its first Indian permanent member of staff, Dr Susama Mondol, strengthening the missionary team. The story of the next three decades, however, is not a heartening one.

Founded in 1894, the hospital served a wide area. Its service to women and children of all communities had long been valued, but things were slowly changing, even in the Murshidabad district. It had always been a "frontier post" and, as such, miles from the city's life and facilities, it had not naturally attracted doctors to permanent work. In the year 1960-61 Dr Mondol, now superintendent, was reporting 2,144 in-patients, 9,817 new out-patients and 19,149 old out-patients. One can only imagine under what pressure she, Dr Newell and the staff worked.

Nurses had been trained in the Jiaganj hospital since 1908. Even after fifty years, Jiaganj, under nursing superintendent Ruth Scott, was the only Christian hospital in West Bengal providing a full nursing course, but this could continue only if the hospital facilities were extended to comply with government requirements. Hence, with LMS assistance, a male ward was built in 1963 and an assistant matron was appointed. There was still a problem; the hospital had not been able to recruit a sufficient number of qualified staff and too few trainee nurses with the right qualifications were applying for the course. Other hospitals in the city and larger towns were now providing training; why go so far as Jiaganj? Hence by 1964 the male ward was still not open.

In every annual report came an item stressing the urgent need for a doctor. Dr Mondol retired in 1969 and Dr Newell in 1970. No one expected that the next missionary doctor to arrive would be Dr Elizabeth Connan from Rajshahi Presbyterian hospital across the border in East Pakistan. In the spring of 1971 she and a considerable number of Christians from the Rajshahi hospital and church joined the 10 million people fleeing from the chaos and bloodshed that marked the birth of Bangladesh. The hospital became home to some of them for months.

By 1973 there was a very large modern government hospital in Berhampore, 14 miles south, and a government health clinic near the station at Jiaganj. Both offered free treatment. The number of patients in Jiaganj hospital had been falling very considerably for several years. A new Bengali doctor had come, but staff morale was at a low ebb. There was much discussion locally and in the CNI diocesan hospital management committee regarding the future of the hospital in these circumstances. It was decided to hand over the hospital to the government for specialist medical work, such as a tuberculosis sanatorium. However, resistance from hospital workers who were now unionized, and from power-seekers in the town, was making it difficult to carry this through effectively. The government declined to take over the hospital, but provided a monthly grant. The Council for World Mission (CWM) gave the usual grant for the year in 1973, plus Rs.10,000 for January expenses. This was the last CWM grant given; after this the CNI and the Barrackpore diocese took over responsibility, as far as they were able until a new direction could be found.

Spiritual life and outreach

The LMS churches in Bengal comprised urban congregations which were more educated, and rural congregations which included many illiterate people. Joining the UCNI in 1945, they received from the relationship a wider experience of Christ's church, a foretaste of the even greater fellowship of the Church of North India to come.

The LMS "New Advance" of 1945 has been mentioned. It was decided that in Bengal this should be expressed in outreach to the Santali tribal people at Itore, not far from Jiaganj. Lena Lewis was put in charge and the work made good progress, but by 1948 it had been handed over to the Santal mission of the northern churches (Scandinavian Lutheran), whose work in that area was recovering after the war. Financial resources were decreasing, costs were increasing, and the Murshidabad work was suffering drastic reductions. It was therefore decided to transfer the new evangelistic thrust to Jiaganj where the scope and opportunities were seen to be immense.

With the integration of the LMS and the Church of Scotland mission councils and their responsibilities into the UCNI Bengal church council in 1952, there came a new emphasis on evangelistic work, and congregation-based evangelistic committees were formed. Membership of UCNI was strengthening local understanding of witness and widening horizons of mission. In 1953, for example, at the UCNI general assembly held in Calcutta the Rev. Eliyah Pountsok arrived — in his red Tibetan robe — as a fraternal delegate from the small Moravian church in Ladakh, nearly two weeks' journey away. The Moravians were joyfully welcomed into membership two years later.

Even further away from Ladakh, the UCNI extended its outreach to Kenya, when in 1955 the Rev. Din Dayal and his wife, Rosie, were appointed to serve as missionaries amongst the Indians and the Pakistanis in Nairobi. The work of this gifted couple caught the imagination, touched the hearts and grew with the prayers of the whole UCNI, who were thus linked to the Presbyterian Church in East Africa. The churches of the Bengal church council strongly supported this work.

For many years the urban and rural churches had been celebrating the Christian home festival as part of the national Christian home movement. The festival, an annual local event in each church, ended with the threefold affirmation: "Christ is the Light of the world; Christ is the Light of our home; Christ is the Light of my life", and the symbolic lighting of candles in home and church. This was both a new act of commitment made by Christian families to Christ and a witness to surrounding families.

The constant background of life in Bengal villages was, and to a large extent still is, poverty, and all that goes with it. At a church council policy retreat in 1962, someone said: "Bengal villagers are hungry and have no mind for religion, and our advice about witnessing fails, because of their hunger." Yet, even in the midst of their apathy and unresponsiveness, there *was* amongst the people a hunger for life in its fullest sense in Christ and a desire to learn more of the gospel. The stewardship programme, carried to the remotest village church, helped this. Also the council set aside Stella Beare in the 1960s to stimulate in church members and adherents the thirst for biblical knowledge and understanding, and for a deeper relationship with Christ, through a programme of Bible study conferences and retreats. Many came to recognize that the mission of the church was largely to be fulfilled through the faithful witness of its members' everyday lives.

After 1970, the annual diocesan festival of the former Anglican diocese of Barrackpore continued in the new CNI diocese to draw hundreds of local people to listen to the open-air preaching and teaching, along with the Christians. In Calcutta the churches started united weekly services during Lent and an Easter day procession through the city to the Sahid Minar, the martyrs column, on the maidan, where a large, mixed-faith crowd would listen to the preaching of the Easter message.

Two of the good things which the former LMS churches helped to bring into the wider church were the tradition of Bengali hymn-writing set to Bengali music, and the *sankirtan* style of telling Bible stories. In the *sankirtan* the lead singer narrates the story, each line being repeated by a group of singers, accompanied by traditional drums and cymbals. These had for long been part of village teaching, witness and worship, but urban congregations tended to have a more westernized style of worship. In the early CNI days in Calcutta, Bishop's College, under the Rev. Pritam Santram, began to experiment with more naturally Indian styles of worship in their chapel, including sitting on the floor, lighting brass lamps for the dawn meditation time and using traditional musical instruments. At St Paul's Cathedral, the long years of English-speaking high-Anglicanism began to yield to the need to add a Bengali service on Sundays including the use of Bengali instruments, while at both services a brass lamp burned amongst flower petals on a brass tray.

The change in things was gathering momentum in the 1970s. With church union, it often appeared that there was a more generous spirit abroad, a greater openness to, and awareness of, others, a willingness to experiment, a certain release from fear. God's people were responding to the Holy Spirit moving in their hearts.

NOTES

[1] LMS board minutes, April 1945.
[2] *Forward to Union*, Church of North India handbook, ISPCK and LPH, 1968, p.4.
[3] LMS report, 1958, p.18.

7. Earthquake and Aftershocks

George Hood

Of all the post-war changes affecting the London Missionary Society (LMS) none was greater than those in China which brought missionary work to an end in that country. Within a period of five years, 1945 to 1950, not only had China become wholly detached from its wartime alliance with Britain and the United States, but it had brought under communist rule a further quarter of the world's population, and its forces in Korea were fighting its former allies.

The work of the LMS in Southeast Asia, that is in Hong Kong, Malaysia, Singapore and after 1972 in Taiwan, will be described in relation to what happened in China. First and most obviously, it was the withdrawal of missionaries from the mainland which provided the resources to support and extend work elsewhere in Southeast Asia. Second, at a deeper level, the China experience and the lessons to be learnt from it exercised a powerful influence on the thinking of the missionaries, the board and the secretaries alike. And third, there was the strong desire to maintain the tradition of working among the Chinese people which had a history nearly as long as the LMS itself. China's historical influence upon the whole area, and the fact that there were Chinese communities of varying proportions in each country, made it both a challenge and an opportunity. Although the nature of LMS involvement and contribution to the life of the church in the three areas of Southeast Asia was different in each case, the experience in China was their common starting point and that is where we must begin.

China

None of the LMS missionaries in China and Hong Kong had been left untouched by the war against Japan. Many had been working in areas of China previously occupied by the Japanese forces, and the attack on Pearl Harbour, followed by the allied declaration of war and the fall of Hong Kong, brought internment in north China, Shanghai or Hong Kong. A smaller number had been able to continue their work in the Christian institutions which had found refuge in free China. When the war came to its sudden end with the dropping of the atom bombs, the LMS along with all the other mission boards was faced with urgent tasks. Some of those interned had to be brought home as quickly as possible for health and family reasons, and some had to remain to cope with the aftermath of the Japanese occupation of church and mission property, to help with the return or reopening of Christian medical and educational institutions, and to share with their Chinese colleagues in the work of relief and rehabilitation. There were also new staff whose appointment and location had to be decided, and for whom passages, still severely restricted, had to be negotiated. All this had to be done in a continuing uncertainty of whether internal peace or war, and nationalist or communist rule would prevail.

During the war against Japan, mission boards in Britain had played a large part in popularizing China's long struggle, and in generating sympathy and support. The fact that general Chiang Kai Shek and his wife were Christians had been well publicized, and even those who were aware of the corruption in the nationalist government were usually ready to exonerate the Chiangs from personal involvement. In Britain the twenty-year-old struggle between the Guomindang (KMT) and the Chinese Commun-

ist Party (CCP) had been played down during the struggle against Japan, and at the end of the war there were high hopes that the need for national reconstruction would encourage a spirit of compromise on both sides. For two years these hopes fluctuated until the final failure of General Marshall's peace mission in 1947 led to the renewal of open civil war. In October 1949, Britain and the rest of the world had to face the fact that the People's Republic was now established with effective control over mainland China.

This rapid success was achieved in a country exhausted by 12 years of conflict. By the summer of 1948 inflation had reached the point where 3 million Chinese yuan were exchanged for one Hong Kong dollar. When the KMT government introduced a new currency and that had gone the same way, it finally destroyed any confidence in either the KMT's integrity or its ability to run the country. As the last of their troops crossed over to Taiwan there was a general sigh of relief and a mood of wary welcome to the new rulers. Both by its policies and the behaviour of its personnel the new government appeared to commend itself to the majority of the Chinese people who longed for peace and order. In the united front, there seemed to be a place for all who welcomed the creation of a new China and wished to play a positive part within it. The programme of land reform was popular among what had become an increasingly landless peasantry. In the industrial and commercial world, for all except the employees of foreign-controlled businesses there appeared to be opportunities as "national bourgeoisie". It had been a "made-in-China" revolution and it generated a strong sense of national pride that China had at last "stood up".

The first LMS missionaries to experience liberation were those in the north China field which included Beijing (Peking) and Tianjin (Tientsin). The countryside had been under communist control for many weeks before these two cities were occupied, in the case of Beijing quite peacefully, but Tianjin only after some bombardment. Like most other British mission boards, LMS policy was to continue its work as long as the church in China desired it. However, with the memory of recent internment of many missionaries during the second world war, and with warnings from the foreign office regarding the likelihood of food shortages and the lack of communication, mothers with children were advised to consider whether or not they should remain. Once the area of north China had been liberated the big question was their treatment by the new rulers.

Even within one area there were widely different reports. Ronald Orchard was Asia secretary of the LMS at that time and reported that the most encouraging were from Beijing and the least encouraging from Tianjin, less than a hundred miles apart. [1] While there was a general feeling of relief that the new rulers maintained good discipline, were not corrupt, and worked hard and effectively to establish the new order, the missionaries most enthusiastic for it were those who had closest contact with the students. They were impressed by their spirit of sacrificial commitment to the common good as they discerned it. But in Tianjin the more disruptive behaviour of younger students in the Anglo-Chinese College was criticized by the missionaries as the complete politicizing of secondary education under communist rule.

Within the next 12 months, as the whole of China came under the new regime, the LMS Board tried to come to terms with this entirely unprecedented situation. In Orchard it was guided by an Asia secretary who, unlike almost all of those holding similar appointments in the other mission boards, had never served in China nor anywhere else abroad. In spite of this he showed a deep understanding of both the issues and the feelings of those involved. He was unwilling just to follow a policy of "wait and see", believing, rather, that the times demanded a more positive effort to rethink and redefine mission policy. During the months of 1949 he discerned a "breathing space" following the advent of the new regime, and in it the opportunity to share thoughts with the home committee, the missionaries in China, and the officers of the Church of Christ in China (CCC). [2] The document he prepared set out the situation as clearly as it could be seen from the outside, and then focused on two perceived needs of the church in which the missionary might have a special role. The first was to help keep it within the universal tradition — the ecumenical dimension — and the second, to discover new ways of Christian witness and evangelism relevant to the new situation. Orchard contemplated for the future a smaller number of missionaries, no longer involved in the administration of institutions, in direct leadership and obvious evangelism, but working in more personal, less obtrusive ways for the deepening of the church's life. Not by virtue of offices held, but by the nature of their own faith and insight would they prove their value. In the light of the situation as it had been described and these suggestions, all the missionaries of the LMS in China and their district committees were asked to review their work, and to think along fresh lines rather than be discouraged by the frustrating of traditional methods of work. The same document was also sent to Dr H.H. Tsui, the general secretary of the Church of Christ in China, to seek his views and those of his colleagues in the central office.

During the early months of the new regime the missionaries chafed under the limitations of travel which were imposed, officially explained to be for their safety during the period when there was still apprehension of KMT-inspired subversion, and air raids from Taiwan were causing death and destruction in the coastal areas. (The new government certainly did not want the diplomatic complication of possible deaths among the foreign community.) Those involved in educational and medical work were generally able to continue, but those working alongside the pastoral ministry were more frustrated. In spite of the difficulties of travel most district committees continued to meet and were able to respond to Orchard's paper with their comments. But the big questions were still how long missionaries would be allowed to remain, whether or not missionaries on furlough would be able to return and whether new appointments should be made.

The answers to these and other questions came in the "Manifesto". During the early months of 1950, through teams organized by the National Christian Council (NCC), the Young Men's Christian Association (YMCA) and the Young Women's Christian Association (YWCA) and including Protestant representatives on the People's Political Consultative Conference (PPCC), efforts were being made to explain to the Christian community the new government's religious policy as to what was and what was not permitted. They also helped at the local level to establish relations with the newly-appointed and still inexperienced government cadres who were having to reconcile their own negative convictions about religion with the pragmatic policy of the government. When such a team visited north China it was seen as an opportunity to seek clarification of some issues at the highest level. The result was a series of meetings between the Chinese premier, Zhou Enlai, and an enlarged group of Christian leaders which included those like Y.T. Wu whom the government had nominated to represent the Protestants in the PPCC. While the Christian leaders were impressed with the attitude of the premier and his understanding of both Christianity and their problems, they were left in little doubt that, in his eyes, they must take steps to establish their reliability and the unambiguous loyalty of the Christian community in China. The onus was on the church to clarify its own position before it could rely on the protection of its religious freedom.

The final outcome of these discussions was the "Manifesto", the basis of which was agreed in May but the text variously amended before its publication in August. Its prime intention, it has been claimed, was to clarify the position of Chinese Christians before the Chinese people as a whole, and it was therefore more a political than a religious statement.[3] But, being issued in the name of Christian leaders, this was not fully appreciated by the mission boards abroad. There had been earlier statements in the name of the NCC which had referred to the past connections of missionary activity with the imperialist designs of the western powers, but in the "Manifesto", which all Protestant Christians were called upon to sign, there was a much more explicit statement of the imperialist connection, "consciously or unconsciously, directly or indirectly" and a warning that "the imperialist powers… may also make use of Christianity to forward their plot of stirring up internal dissension, and creating reactionary forces in this country". In order to rid itself of this imperialist legacy, Christians in China were called on to pursue much more vigorously the long professed policy of self-support, self-government and self-propagation. [4]

Towards LMS withdrawal from China

Originally it was expected that however vigorously pursued, the achievement of "three self" would be a gradual process, especially with regard to financial support. The Church of Christ in China contemplated a period of five years during which external support would be reduced step by step and finally eliminated. For most missionaries the completion of their current periods of service, which might be of five years, or the expiry of their passports was expected to be the cut-off point. Even then, those whose services, e.g. in education or health, were greatly desired, and who were able to adapt wholeheartedly to the new conditions might still hope to have a place. Regarding self-government it was made clear that so long as missionaries served in any "governing" capacity, not only of institutions but even in the courts of the church, that institution or church would not be recognized and enjoy the rights of a "people's organization".

While the various churches' leaders in China were wrestling with the issue of endorsing the "Manifesto" and later commending it to their members for signature, events outside China, especially the fighting which broke out on 25 June between the North and the South in Korea, radically changed the atmosphere, and even more so later that year after the Chinese forces became involved. The Three Self Patriotic Movement (TSPM) which had taken shape in the weeks following the meeting with Zhou Enlai became the Three Self Patriotic Resist America Aid Korea Movement. For Christians in China it became even more urgent to affirm their loyalty to their country and independence of foreign control or influence. Without the Korean factor the implementation of the three self principles might have been more gradual, but the "Manifesto" had made it quite clear what was required of the Christian community in China and the situation to which mission boards and missionaries had to respond.

Orchard's perception of conditions and trends in China owed much to Frank Short, the China Council secretary, who was working in Shanghai. Short's contacts and good relations with the CCC and the NCC officers enabled him to provide the overview to complement the varying information from the districts. While the crucial meetings were being held in Beijing, in May 1950, Orchard was already writing to Short sharing his thoughts about the possibility that at some future time the mission would have to withdraw. This was in spite of their determination to stay as long as possible and to adapt their methods to that end. In June the Board endorsed this forward planning in a series of resolutions which were communicated to the districts. Only a few days later, the outbreak of fighting in Korea and the United Nations' naming of North Korea as the aggressor raised the political and emotional temperature. In July Orchard wrote to Short enclosing a letter to district committees which was to be "used at the discretion of the council of officers". [5] It gave authority to each local group to decide whether, and when, to withdraw. The board did not wish any to remain who felt that he or she ought to withdraw.

The two most frequently quoted reasons for withdrawal were the restrictions now being experienced in doing their work, and the increasing sense of being an embarrassment to their Chinese colleagues. The first of these was more easily demonstrable than the second which required honesty and sensitivity on both sides. The possibility that the extension of the Korean conflict might lead to internment influenced some who felt that the contribution which the mission might be able to make by remaining was too small to justify running the risk of waste that repetition of the 1941-45 experience would cause.

By the middle of June the mission boards in London had a fair knowledge of the content of the "Manifesto" but were still wondering how much weight to attach to it. The delay in its publication raised doubts as to how much it expressed the views of those church leaders with whom the boards normally corresponded and whom they trusted, or how much it had been issued under duress. Dr Tsui had been one of those who had met with Premier Zhou Enlai in May, and by August when the "Manifesto" was published, Orchard was urgently seeking through Short to find out the attitude of the CCC. For him and the board that was of decisive importance, both for policy in China and for the way in which the situation of the church should be explained to the home constituency.

It was not until 27 October that the CCC standing committee, following similar action by the NCC, officially endorsed the "Manifesto" and commended it to all its members for signature. By then the LMS Board had approved Orchard's recommendation that the end of 1951 should be the date for the final withdrawal.

During this time the other British mission boards were reaching the same conclusions about the end of missionary service in China but Orchard and the LMS were the first to set a date. Orchard explained that the prospect of obtaining re-entry permits was slim, and that with normal furlough dates the staff would be reduced to 15 by the end of 1951. His reason, endorsed by the Board, for setting a specific date for completion of withdrawal was

> in order that it can be carried out in an orderly and dignified fashion, and in ways which cause the least possible disturbance to the life of the church.[6]

He stressed that grants to the church and associated institutions should continue as long as the church, through its synods and the general assembly, desired them. In the time available steps should be taken by the district committees and the council officers for the transfer of the remaining responsibilities to the church, and for the disposition of property.

In the event the rapid changes of the next 12 months, hastened by Chinese involvement in the Korean hostilities, overtook the board's decision. From July 1950 onwards, district committees and individual missionaries, in the light of local conditions, decided that the time had come to apply for permission to leave, and the board, sometimes reluctantly, honoured their decisions. Any hope of normal activity rapidly disappeared, and during the worsening conditions of 1951, attention in China was concentrated on the procedures for obtaining exit permits and the pain of separation, and in London on the deployment of this displaced staff. At the meeting of the board in December 1952, Orchard reported that the last LMS missionaries had left: the Lapwoods from Yanjing in October and John Barr, after a long wait for his visa, from Shanghai in November. Much has been written by individuals of their varied experiences during this time.

Regarding the Board's decision to set a date so far ahead, two comments may be made. First, it was not a decision which was favoured by other boards but, while it indicated the wish that the oldest Protestant mission body in China should not just gradually wither away without any recognized conclusion, it also implicitly recognized that, however long and illustrious its history, there was a time to accept its temporary nature and that an end had come. No mission board was so important that it should risk undermining the best interests of the church.

The second comment concerns the provision which was contemplated, even after the official end of the mission, for the continued service of individual missionaries. The Board had in mind the possibility that there were

> missionaries who feel called upon to do so, and whose continued service is desired by the church or an associated institution and who are prepared to do so and prepared to face the risks involved. [7]

Such would be considered as having been seconded to the church or institution at its request, and as working under its direction, but the Board would be willing to provide the salaries and allowances so long as that was permitted. By making such provision the Board was respecting the position of those who felt strongly their Christian commitment to new China and their wish to serve it; they were also pointing a way ahead in which future missionary service, not only in China but elsewhere, might continue without the traditional missionary structures.

Orchard originally intended to inform the general assembly of the CCC of the board's decision in the early part of 1951. But the official "Message" from the CCC to its associated missionary societies, received in the first week of December 1950, brought forward that date. The message was that church's response to the demands of new China and its determination to play a part within it. It was received as a "courageous and enheartening word which can well be made widely known in the churches here". [8] Because this "Message" was the last comprehensive official statement from the church to which the LMS and so many other mission boards, British and American, were related, and from which they were now withdrawing, its contents were examined with special attention.

> The church which you helped to establish is now coming into a new position, being recognized by the New People's government as a Chinese organization serving the Chinese people. [9]

It endorsed the common programme and supported the policy of opposition to imperialism, feudalism and bureaucratic capitalism. It admitted past connections with, and even the possibility of having been used by these forms of political and economic control. But it also expressed the belief that the mission boards shared its desire to see the church in China free from all suspicion of domination by foreign imperialism and capitalistic interests, and that it should become in reality an autonomous church, growing in Chinese soil, developing strong Chinese leadership and meeting the moral and spiritual needs of Chinese society.

The "Message" gave assurance that

> in taking this political stand the Chinese church is not breaking its ecumenical ties, its friendly relations with the older churches or its long and treasured associations with western missionary societies and missionaries. [10]

It acknowledged both the responsibility placed on the church and the trust reposed in it by the transfer of property, distribution of grants, and administration of all church work to the general assembly, synods and presbyteries, and to the institutional boards of the CCC. Plans to achieve complete self-support within a period of a few years were being made and, meanwhile, they hoped for a continuation of grants on a decreasing scale. Regarding future missionary service there was hope that the time would come when a limited number might return, with government approval, to serve in various types of work. It ended with a strong statement of its resolution to stand firm in the faith, to make no compromise on the basic beliefs and ethical standards of Christianity, and to maintain the spiritual liberty of the church.

In the response which the Board made on receipt of this letter, and throughout the much more painful experiences which followed in the next 12 months, and the complete silence of succeeding years, the Board chose to recognize this as the authentic voice of the church it had helped to establish and from which, sadly but with love and understanding, it was now withdrawing. The letter from the Board dated 13 December was the last official communication and a worthy statement to bring to an end the longest history of any mission board in China. Other boards in the British Isles related to the CCC had received the same message and in due course wrote their own letters expressing their feelings of sadness combined with understanding and trust. What perhaps marks out the letter from the LMS Board was the stress laid upon the board's need of the church in China's experience, not only in order to pray with understanding but more than that:

> We shall need your prayer that we may know how rightly we as a missionary agency of the church can best serve the world mission of the church in these days of fundamental and rapid social change. And above all we shall need your continuing partnership in the worldwide witness to the one Lord and Saviour of all men. [11]

The response this letter received, written some time in January, showed how much these words and the whole letter had been appreciated.

> It is no exaggeration to say that your message of Christian affection and encouragement is one of the most inspiring that we have ever received in the general assembly office of the CCC. It reveals such a true understanding of our situation and problems and such a far-sighted view of the future of missions and the church that we are deeply moved. Like St Paul when he was met by the Christians upon entering Rome, "We thank God and take courage." [12]

Adjusting to the new situation

The LMS Board was bringing to an end in the best way in which the times allowed its long involvement in China. But there were still two other major tasks to be faced, how to explain what was happening to its home constituency, both in Britain and beyond, and how to deal with the seventy missionaries who were now leaving much more rapidly than had originally been expected.

Following the establishing of the People's Republic there had at first been a cautious optimism expressed in the information conveyed through the board's publications, such as the *Outlook*, and the *Prayer Fellowship Handbook*. When, however, reports of the "Manifesto", first rumoured and then confirmed, were received, all the mission boards were alarmed at its possible repercussions on their supporters. It was kept under wraps as long as possible while fear grew that the religious press might publish it without the background, understanding and interpretation of the situation which the mission boards felt was necessary in fairness to Christians in China. In the political climate of the cold war, and the conflict in Korea, they were very aware that some traditional supporters of "China missions" would be outraged by what was stated so strongly about the relation of missions and imperialism, and regard any who were associated with such a statement as "having sold out to the communists". [13] It was in these circumstances that the "Message" from the CCC had been welcomed as a more acceptable expression of the responsible leadership in the CCC, but the underlying difficulties of helping the mission supporters to understand and to maintain their prayer, concern and support remained. If this could happen in China, regarded as a successful mission field in terms of church development, and in recent years especially the focus of so much concern and goodwill, what questions might it raise about the whole missionary enterprise?

Much responsibility rested on the returning missionaries for interpreting what was happening in China. It was a task made more difficult by the course of events in 1951. The war in Korea, the United Nations refusal to seat China, and its condemnation of her as an aggressor, heightened tension both internationally and within China itself. The Chinese churches' withdrawal from the World Council of Churches (WCC) in protest at the statements it had made about the Korean conflict, the increase of political education, the campaign of accusation and denunciation of Chinese Christians closely associated with missionaries, the abrupt termination of receiving foreign funds, including mission grants, in retaliation for the American freezing of Chinese assets abroad, the complete cessation of direct communication with the resultant suspicion engendered — these were some of the conditions which made their task so difficult.

During the years 1951-53 the LMS along with other British mission boards shared in a painful process of self-examination as it tried to come to terms with what had happened in China. The challenging criticism of the missionary movement there and elsewhere presented by David Paton, [14] expressed dramatically in terms of *debacle* and the *judgment of God*, and the views represented by Roland Allen [15] were debated by the LMS China committee and in the committees of the Conference of British Missionary Societies (CBMS). No final appraisal of the LMS's long involvement was attempted, because it was felt to be impossible at that stage to gather all the information on which any judgment could properly be made. The mission as the scaffolding for the church that was being built was a favourite image and now the scaffolding had been removed and the strength of the building was being tested. Only time would show how much was built on rock and how much on sand. Those with the longest and closest experience of the church in China were confident of its ability to survive, but in what form none dared predict.

Although within the LMS, as in other boards, there was some feeling that more should have been done to prepare for the challenge which had come, at least two principles had been recognized: one from the beginning, and the other at a later date with growing conviction. The first was the autonomy of the Chinese church, and its right to determine its own form. The second was the principle of unity which had been expressed in ringing terms by the Chinese attending the 1910 Edinburgh conference. Following that appeal the LMS had pursued with other mission boards the vision of a single Protestant church in China. The formation of the Church of Christ in China, representing 40 percent of the Protestants, had only partly fulfilled that hope. For most of its history prior to 1949 it had functioned with great difficulty, but not always unsuccessfully, in a China divided both by civil war and war against Japan. In the eyes of some Chinese Christians it was compromised, like all other mission-supported churches, by financial dependence, foreign associations and missionary power. In the case of the LMS the parallel existence of a mission structure, the China council and the district committees, and the power they exercised was not to be denied. Could more have been done, and done more quickly, to enable the church to be more truly a Chinese church? This was the question about which so much discussion revolved, but there was no questioning the right of the church to autonomy and unity.

The church in China continued to have a place in the *Prayer Fellowship Handbook* until 1959. But there was also another way in which the LMS played a significant role in relation to that church. This was through the Conference of British Missionary Societies and the efforts made to renew contact with Christians behind the bamboo curtain. In 1953 Frank Short became the Asia secretary of the CBMS, and in 1957 its general secretary. In 1956 Stuart Craig, formerly of the central China district and now Asia secretary of the LMS, was chairman of the CBMS Asia committee. That year was the most hopeful time for renewing contact with Christians in China. In the autumn of 1955 a group of six Quakers had visited and met both with leaders of the Three Self Patriotic Movement (TSPM) and with Premier Zhou Enlai. This had been followed by a visit to China of the Indian Lutheran bishop, the Rt Rev. Rajah Manickam, representing the East Asia Christian Conference. When it was known that Bishop K.H. Ting would be coming to London in July 1956 to attend the Lambeth conference preparatory committee, Short acted quickly to make sure that this long-desired opportunity would not be wasted. To avoid the risk of embarrassing Bishop Ting it was decided that any meeting would be informal in character. However, most of the CBMS Asia committee were present. In preparation for the meeting, and in consultation with Stuart Craig, Short prepared an aide-memoire which was circulated to those who planned to attend. [16] Although presented in the name of the CBMS it bore the mark of its authors and, through them, of their mission board background.

In its ten statements Short's aide-memoire echoed very much the feelings expressed five years earlier in the final LMS communication to the CCC but took that thinking a stage further. It referred to the continued reflection of the mission boards on their past service in China, what they had sought to learn from it of the purpose of God for the total mission of the church in the world and, in particular, guidance as to the relationships which ought to exist between mission and church at every stage of their common task. It gave assurance that the churches in China were regarded in the same sense as those in the UK and in no way different in nature and responsibility. And from this it followed on to make it equally clear that the mission bodies did not regard China as a "mission field" in the sense that the re-establishment of missionary organization was contemplated or desired. Only if the church in China considered that there was any service which they might render would that be made available. And they also hoped that the churches in China, so far as their own task and resources would allow, would accept responsibility for participation in the task of witness and proclamation of the gospel in the world, a task which rested without exception on all churches.

When reports were received of the strong leftward swing at the tenth plenum of the TSPM, meeting from October to December 1958, and of events in the following year, during which some of the former leaders of the TSPM were severely criticized by their colleagues, a majority of churches closed or amalgamated, and the national organizations of churches ceased to function, and all of this had been done in the name, and by the action, of the TSPM, the hopes of the LMS along with other mission bodies were at their lowest ebb. To Short it appeared that there was now a blanket condemnation of all past and present missionary activity as imperialist-inspired. In the light of this apparently drastic change of church conditions the standing committee of the CBMS took the unusual step of issuing a statement. As chairman of the Asia committee Craig had a major part in drawing it up, and as a result faced criticism from opposite wings, both in his own and other societies. In the eyes of some "it fell over backwards to avoid giving any offence to the Chinese government and therefore gave too gentle a picture". To others "it erred in the opposite direction and did not do justice to the government and its achievements". [17] When so much was unclear and direct communication impossible, prayer itself was no easy option. As David Paton wrote at the time: "It is possible to pray against them when one fancies one is praying for them." And with regard to trusting people he said it was "easy enough to have good feelings for those on the other side of the world who agree with our position and suffer for it, but what about trusting those who seem to us (as we seem to them) to be failing in Christian witness". [18]

For the next ten years there was little more than prayer and trust so far as relations between British and Chinese Christians were concerned. In the turmoil of the great proletarian cultural revolution, launched in 1966, all religions, along with intellectuals, bureaucracy and traditional culture, came under attack. This was a further period in which little could be seen clearly, but conflicting reports aroused renewed interest in what was happening in China. Some saw there possible models for other developing countries, and even claimed that a new kind of man and woman had been created, wholly committed to selfless service. Yet there were also reports that the attacks on open religious activities had not destroyed the church but only driven it underground. The China Study Project arose out of this renewed interest and its founding document, dated 1972, embraces both of these concerns:

> The object is to provide for the societies, and through them the churches, a source of information and interpretation of contemporary China which will help them to understand what is happening there, both because of its intrinsic importance in world affairs and the influence of Chinese ideas and examples in other developing countries, and in order to enable them to react responsibly whenever the opportunity of renewing Christian contact with China comes. [19]

From its beginning the LMS, and later the Council for World Mission (CWM), gave full support to the project, welcoming its ecumenical approach and seeing its object as consistent with its own previously declared policy. Changes in China's relations with the outside world, first heralded by president Nixon's visit there in 1972, rapidly developed from 1976 onwards. Amid those changes the project was to play a vital part in that renewal of contact with Christians in China which had been so long desired and prayed for.

Hong Kong

The most immediate impact of communist success and the establishing of the People's Republic of China in 1949 was felt in Hong Kong. In the years immediately following the end of the Pacific war, however, Hong Kong and its Christian community were also in a state of flux, striving to recover from the shattering experience of the Japanese conquest and three and a half years of occupation.

Throughout Southeast Asia there would never again be anything like the former confidence in British power. The CCC congregations and the institutions related to the LMS had each its own programme of recovery proceeding at different speeds. The three city congregations moved quickly and by 1951 had recovered their vigorous life under able ministerial leadership, but in the New Territories some churches had not yet fully recovered from the effects of the Japanese occupation. Several had not been restarted. The main concentration of missionaries was in the staffs of the Nethersole Hospital, the Ying Wa girls' school and the Ying Wa College, all three of which had recovered rapidly and were now trying to meet the increased demands being made on their services.

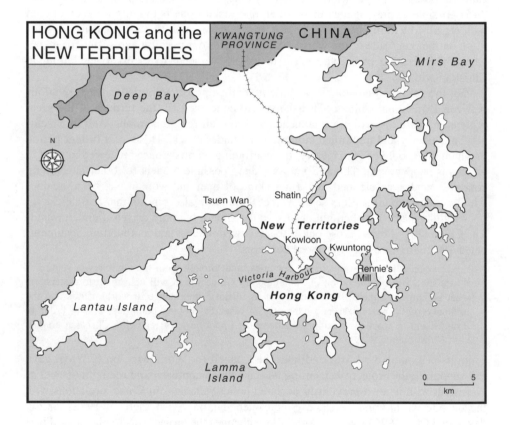

HONG KONG and the NEW TERRITORIES

The churches, institutions and missionaries watched the rapid decline of KMT fortunes and the rapid progress of the people's liberation army with apprehension, as did their fellow Christians across the border. By the time the whole of China had come under communist rule Hong Kong had already been engulfed by a flood of refugees, of all classes, estimated at over a million. Among them were some church workers, lay leaders in churches, and other members whose wealth and ownership of land or previous links with the KMT at varying levels made them fearful for the future. For those seeking to leave China there was a double uncertainty of whether they would be allowed out, and then whether they would be allowed into Hong Kong.

The CCC congregations in Hong Kong and the New Territories formed the sixth district of the Kwangtung (Guangdong) synod of the CCC, with its synod office in Canton (Guangzhou). The events of 1950 and 1951 brought the end of any official links between the synod and its sixth district, and the district was now faced with tasks and responsibilities which the synod had previously carried. Theological training, the ordination and appointment of ministers, the holding of property, the invitation and location of missionaries, and all the other relationships of the synod with mission boards now devolved upon the district.

When Ronald Orchard paid a secretarial visit to Hong Kong in April 1951, he first satisfied himself that in spite of all the accusations which had been made and were at that time, even more strongly, continuing to be made against missions and missionaries in China, and the full-scale withdrawal was in progress, there was still a welcome for their services in Hong Kong. [20] He perceived a growing recognition of the church's responsibility towards the total community, but perhaps there was an element of wishful thinking in this perception. He believed that missionaries could make a relevant contribution by transmitting the ideas and experience of western churches in the field of Christian social responsibility, and at the same time be a witness to the church's ecumenical character. There was also a role for them in the New Territories where he advocated a greater concentration of missionary service in a few selected centres rather than the itinerant work which had alone been possible with the very limited staff available. Through such concentration the great need for training at the local level would in part be met, but for this there was also need for a church training centre.

The need for more and better trained staff, both voluntary and paid, and for the church to be more deeply involved in the total community clearly echoed the discussions on the China experience which were on every mission board agenda at that time. The idea of a church training centre however also commended itself to the sixth district, and most fortuitously there was property for sale only a mile from Castle Peak which could be adapted to such a purpose. A major financial outlay recommended to the Board by Orchard was the purchase of this property at a price of HK $180,000 (£11,250). Because the sixth district was not an incorporated body able to hold property, what later became the Hoh Fuk Tong centre was registered in the name of the LMS.

One question mark hanging over all the thinking and planning of this time was whether or not the sixth district had the resources of personnel and leadership to sustain a large extension of its responsibilities. With some of the most able of its ministers and its laymen so deeply involved in the life of the three large city congregations, and with so much urgent action necessary to cope with the influx of mainland refugees, it was difficult to break new ground. Among the members the traditionally preached gospel of individual salvation, giving peace and assurance, was what most wanted to hear and inclined the church to be inward-looking. The decision taken to establish a Christian training centre was supported by the sixth district, and missionary staff were appointed to it, but the vision which Orchard outlined for its potential use was not achieved.

Two major issues

That vision did not exclude theological education for ordination as a possibility for the future, but at this time the LMS saw such training and the provision of Christian literature as two major issues which related to Southeast Asia as a whole. In Singapore the first steps had already been taken by Methodists (American), Anglicans and Presbyterians to establish Trinity Theological College, up to then only with part-time staff, and using English as the medium of instruction. For the Chinese-speaking churches in Singapore and Malaya, and even more if Trinity was to serve other Chinese churches throughout Southeast Asia, a Chinese-speaking stream was urgently needed. Until that came about it could not serve Hong Kong's need for ordination training.

In 1951 there were still some theological students from Hong Kong training in Canton but it was not yet known how long that would continue, nor whether or not they would be able to return to Hong Kong on graduation. As in the past the churches in Hong Kong might still be able to obtain ministers from mainland China and there had not yet been the kind of growth which made a large increase in their numbers either necessary or financially supportable.

The other major issue which was seen as part of the overall strategy for Southeast Asia was the provision of Christian literature. Traditionally the whole area had relied on agencies in China for the production of every form of Chinese Christian literature, and for distribution through such channels as the Bible, Book and Tract Depot in Hong Kong. By 1951 it was becoming increasingly clear that both the quantity and the variety were being reduced. To those outside China some publications appeared to be politically indoctrinated and unsuitable for their use. (To many of those within China there was a comparable criticism of what was produced outside and was seen as hostile to new China.) Ecumenical cooperation was a reasonable possibility in this field and discussions in Hong Kong and Singapore involved the Anglicans, the Methodists and the Presbyterians as well as the LMS in Hong Kong and Singapore. The outcome was the formation of a Council for Christian Literature for Overseas Chinese (CCLOC) with prime responsibility for planning and publication, and an expansion of the Bible, Book and Tract Depot for stocking and distribution, along with the printing and promotion of Chinese publications. In Orchard's view it was important to stress that the constituency for which this increased effort was intended was the Chinese Christian community *outside* China. At the same time he recognized that individual copies of books published might find their way into China, and that if contacts with the church in China became easier a comprehensive selection of Christian literature should be available for immediate use.

The withdrawal of LMS missionaries from the mainland did not mean an automatic increase of their number in Hong Kong. But it enabled the Nethersole Hospital to add to its staff Dr E.H. Paterson who had been working as a surgeon in the former LMS hospital in Tianjin. [21] A new stage in the Nethersole's development had begun in 1948 when the LMS agreed to transfer to the hospital two missionary residences in Bonham Road on condition that the hospital would resume full responsibility for housing its own missionary staff. After the demolition of the old houses, funds raised by the hospital provided a new five-storey building which was opened in February 1950. With these better facilities for the nurses training school, a chapel, nurses' rooms and two flats for married doctors, the Nethersole was still only at the beginning of its development into a modern and better equipped hospital. The previous imbalance of staff which had favoured gynaecology and obstetrics to the neglect of surgery and general medicine was rectified. Challenges presented by the great influx of refugees, their deplorable living conditions in those early years, and the resultant prevalence of tuberculosis, brought into existence a committee with Dr Frank Ashton as chairman and eventually, the Haven of Hope sanatorium in 1955 at a remote bay known as Rennie's Mill. Regular visits by the Nethersole surgeon to select cases for lung surgery who were transferred to the hospital and afterwards returned to the sanatorium to recuperate developed a close association between it and the Nethersole, and later with the United Christian Hospital, which has continued to the present day.

Recent events in China had led to some questioning by mission boards of the value of large medical and educational institutions in building up the church. LMS policy had favoured the creation of boards on which the church would only have its representatives rather than full control by people whose gifts and expertise were not necessarily in those fields. The need for the church to be involved in the local community should be qualified by the extent of its own resources, and some saw it necessary to distinguish between what the local Christian community was able to do in Christian service and what was dependent on mission, or sometimes the generous support of the benefiting community. Hong Kong was clearly different from the rest of China. The colonial government was generally well disposed, especially when church- and mission-related bodies, with appropriate financial aid from government and acting in line with its policies, were able to provide the necessary services. The local population at the receiving end demonstrated their appreciation of those services by responding generously to successive fund-raising medical and educational appeals.

Although there was no large-scale addition of staff the availability of both Cantonese- and Mandarin-speaking missionaries gave the Board, in association with the church, an unprecedented opportunity both to fill the normal vacancies and to appoint personnel to such new work as was planned. In addition to Ted Paterson, new arrivals in Hong Kong from work in China were:

> Anne Mackeith (till 1961), John and Ruth Barr (till 1966), Albert and Barbara Small (till 1961), Samuel and Ruth Withers Green (till 1960), Frank and Irene Short (till 1953), Dorothy Havergal Shaw (till 1952), Kathrine Brameld (till 1964), Edith Rawlings (till 1952) [22]

Along with those previously appointed to work in Hong Kong, these were the people who comprised what was now called the Hong Kong missionaries committee rather than the former south China district committee. With their varying backgrounds, the growth in strength and autonomy of the institutions, the somewhat ambiguous nature of the church's responsibilities, and in some cases the missionaries' own uncertainty about their role and the functions of the committee, it was a difficult period in which to achieve a deep sense of purpose and unity in a common task. In London the Board debated how far it should go in seeking to establish the same organizational pattern in Southeast Asia as had previously operated in China. Relations with the sixth district and other mission boards formerly related to the CCC throughout China, and also the close links being developed with the English Presbyterian mission, in London and in Malaya, created a very different situation. At a time in which many decisions were having to be made the Board felt the need of some organization or representation on which it could rely for guidance. On Orchard's recommendation it approved, for a three-year trial period, the formation of a Southeast Asia council, made up of a representative chosen by each of the committees in Hong Kong and Malaya, a chairman appointed by the Board, and as secretary the Rev. Frank Short who bore the title of representative of the Board in Southeast Asia. By the time of Short's appointment as CBMS Asia secretary in 1953, the growing integration of the LMS and English Presbyterian mission work in Singapore and Malaya, with the corresponding role of the joint Malaya group in London, and the different history of relations with the churches in Hong Kong and Malaya, such a council was seen to be unnecessary.

A modus vivendi with China

The next few years, until 1956, were a period of great uncertainty as Hong Kong adjusted itself to a modus vivendi with a different kind of China, whose impact beyond its boundaries extended from the initial flood of refugees to the policy of non-alignment, set out in the Bandung pact of 1955. For the sixth district it was a difficult period as it sought to come to terms with its new responsibilities. On the one hand there was the desperate need of many new arrivals from China, and on the other there were mission boards, mainly from the USA and Canada, who felt called to continue work among them. Having been related to the CCC throughout China these boards looked for some relationship with the CCC in Hong Kong, but not all saw that relationship in the same way or on the same terms as had been operating between the Kwangtung synod and its former mission partners, the LMS and the Presbyterian Church in New Zealand. From 1950 the sixth district had been independent of Canton and had had an office in the Hop Yat Church. In January 1954 it became the Hong Kong district association of the CCC, and the next year, with substantial financial help from the Presbyterian Church in the USA, it was able to have its own office, a secretary (Zheng Ke-lin) and a staff of seven. The same year it sent four students to study at Trinity Theological College in Singapore, and received a Hainanese congregation into membership of the association. It also took the first steps towards becoming a property-holding body by making application to the Hong Kong government. The educational needs among the new arrivals increased the pressure to open primary schools and kindergartens especially in the New Territories. Generous help was forthcoming from American churches for some church rebuilding, and in 1956 a family welfare centre was opened in a squatter refugee resettlement area in Kowloon. All this was evidence of growth and activity. But to the LMS, which had previously been the only mission board related to the CCC in Hong Kong, there was some anxiety lest the new relationships and the large resources which were now being made available to the district association might undermine the level of self-support and responsibility which had formerly been given high priority. It was a difficult situation and made more acute by recent experience in China where the church's dependence on foreign resources had been highlighted by its critics. On his visit to Hong Kong in 1956 Stuart Craig felt deeply the dilemma between the church accepting outside resources to meet desperate needs and immediate opportunities, and the long-term objective of self-support. He reflected:

> I think we shall still serve the church well by calling it to be related as intimately and sacrificially as possible to each new project, but we ought not to be unwelcoming to what other missions are doing to meet the unusual situation in Hong Kong.[23]

With hindsight it is not difficult to see that this was a situation crying out for strong leadership. With the arrival of Peter Wong from Canton the Hong Kong church received it.

Peter Wong had served as secretary of the Kwangtung synod both before and after liberation. He therefore brought to Hong Kong both experience of traditional church administration and also of the challenges to the Chinese church which had been presented by new China. Like all other Christian leaders he had been forced to recognize the compromised nature of Christian mission in China and the charges of imperialism which had been levelled at the missionary movement. He had also seen the positive achievements of the new order in its early years but by 1956, along with many intellectuals, he was critical of the direction in which it had moved. Such a background, added to his own strong and energetic personality, freed him from some of the constraints and deference which may have affected others in their relations with the mission and the missionaries. The steps which had been taken in China both before and after liberation to stress the centrality of the church and the ancillary function of the mission were never open to question in his mind. Early in 1957, soon after his arrival in Hong Kong, he was invited to serve as acting secretary of the district during the six months sick leave granted to Zheng Ke-Lin. When a special meeting of the district was held at the end of that period it was reorganized as the Hong Kong Council of the Church of Christ in China (HKCCCC), with full independence and exercising all the relevant authority and functions of a church. Congregations, schools, hospitals and any other related institutions were all to be represented. Secretaries were to be appointed with a general secretary exercising an overall executive authority. In August 1957, Peter Wong was appointed general secretary.

The missionaries were very conscious of the change. One of them wrote: "Under new leadership the old air of suspicion and cynicism and helplessness has gone, and a new atmosphere of trust and hope is growing."[24] Not for the first or last time in a Chinese church the celebration of a historical anniversary provided the opportunity to launch a major programme of advance. This time it was the triple jubilee of the arrival of Robert Morrison in Macao, celebrated as the establishing of Protestant Christianity in China. The church was called to promote four "movements": personal evangelism, the Christian home (literally, church members return home), the offering of youth to serve the church, and the sending of a missionary abroad. At the same time a capital fund of HK $1 million was launched for four construction projects, namely a Morrison Centre, including church offices, a church and school in an industrial zone, an agricultural region and a fishing area.

Education and welfare

The decisions in 1957 set a pattern for the programme which Peter Wong followed for the next twenty years. Its core was education, both for its own sake and as a means of church extension. By opening primary, secondary, and at a later stage vocational schools, strong forces of three kinds were harnessed together. First, there was the urgent desire of the rapidly-growing Chinese refugee population, now producing its own explosion of Hong-Kong born children of school age, for whom education was the key to their hopes for the future. Second, there was the need of the government to provide an education service, and through it the kind of work force which could add a strong industrial base to the colony's traditional commercial character. To provide educational opportunities, along with housing, employment and low taxation were the most popular actions by which an unelected colonial administration could satisfy the people of Hong Kong. The third force was the church's own concern to extend its work and witness. By accepting the challenges of the education department, and the grant-in-aid on offer, the church was not only seen to be concerned and involved in meeting the people's need, but was also able to create a base for Christian work within the schools and have a meeting place for congregations that might be gathered. In sharp contrast to conditions in China where the mission bodies had been in conflict with the Chinese tradition of keeping education and religion separate, the churches in Hong Kong had every encouragement to promote both together.

In 1958, when Hedley Bunton was invited to return to Hong Kong after seven years in Australia, there were five primary schools which had been started by the LMS, and four secondary schools. Fifteen years later, in 1973, there were over fifty CCC schools. This remarkable numerical growth must be attributed to the dynamic leadership which Peter Wong provided. He seized the unprecedented opportunity for extending the church's involvement in education and by so doing also maintained its place and future in Hong Kong's rapid development. It was the kind of situation more favourable to autocracy than democracy, one in which the committee method of decision-making was sometimes too slow to reap potential benefits. The appointment of Hedley Bunton as general supervisor of these schools and therefore the link person with the government both demonstrated Peter Wong's pragmatism and one kind of contribution which missionaries might still continue to make. Others served in institutions but there was no longer a missionary role in what might be regarded as purely church work.

During this period when the school programme was the most prominent feature of the new spirit at work in the church, much else was being done to consolidate its independent status. By 1958 the legal procedure for the recognition of the church was completed. This cleared the way for the transfer of various properties previously held under the incorporation of the senior missionary of the LMS. The fortieth anniversary of the CCC in Hong Kong was celebrated in 1959, and was an occasion for the promotion of a stewardship campaign. In the same year, and in accordance with its new constitution, the Council clarified the basis of its relationships not only with the LMS but with the several other mission bodies, American, Canadian and New Zealand, with which it was now associated. It also ordained its first two new ministers under the same constitution. In 1960 the Morrison Memorial Centre was opened, and used not only for offices of the Council and its committees, but as a centre for various training courses, conferences, language classes for missionaries and the regular monthly meetings of heads of schools. Theological training was based in Hok Fuk Tong where nine students were living, but some classes were taught at the Morrison Centre and the intention was ultimately to transfer this training to the Chung Chi campus at Shatin where the new university was being planned. Social welfare work and the family life centre were developed and, in part, sustained with capital grants from the government and North American sources, and these also contributed to the church and schools building programmes. To be able to accept help without becoming dependent, and to maintain freedom of action in both making plans and their execution, required the strong leadership provided by Wong and his colleagues.

The inauguration of a pension fund for church workers, a retirement home for its women workers, the graduation of the first class of theological students, and in 1966 the ordination of its first woman minister, the Rev. Lee Ching Chee, were all developments in the life of the church during the 1960s contemporaneous with the large-scale programme of church and school rebuilding and extension. The staffing of these schools and especially maintaining a high proportion of Christian teachers was always a major headache. There was still a place, it was argued, for missionary and other expatriate teachers, but by 1964, the councils of the Ying Wa college and the

Ying Wa girls' school which had long resisted the Society's urging at last agreed that the time had come for them to have Chinese principals, and began to take steps to find the right people. Even so, four years later, although missionaries no longer held these positions, they were still held by expatriates. In colonial Hong Kong there were, it appeared, some practical advantages in such an arrangement.

The extension of the Council's activities in both the educational and welfare fields gave it a new power and authority. Its importance was deliberately fostered by the promotion of an annual Council Sunday, and expressed in its being received into membership of the WCC. This took place in 1967, and it was the first Hong Kong church to be recognized in this way. Within its own membership the slow process of including non-Cantonese-speaking churches continued. By 1970 there were four of these, Hainanese, Mandarin, Amoy and Chao-zhou, but there still remained others, formerly with CCC links, which continued along the path of complete independence.

From time to time visits and reports of LMS secretaries combined admiration at the energy and growth of the church in Hong Kong, especially in its building, educational and welfare programmes, with expressions of concern regarding priorities. The mission of the church, the apparent lack of interest in ecumenism, the quality of worship, the relevance of the gospel to the new industrial areas were some of the concerns they felt had little opportunity to be studied in depth when everyone was so busy, ministers and laymen alike, with programmes, projects, ventures and their administration. This viewpoint reflected both the heart-searching which had followed the withdrawal from China and also the challenges which the churches were facing in other countries, especially in areas of rapid social change. Where the Hong Kong church was present in the new industrial areas, such as Tsuen Wan, its work and witness appeared to be along traditional lines of education and social welfare, but without coming to grips with the relevance of the gospel to industrial problems, and Christian witness within industry.

Because the LMS missionaries were almost all involved in institutions of one form or another, and there were none giving full time to working alongside the Chinese leadership in church life, these concerns could not be regularly expressed nor action promoted. When initiatives were taken in industrial mission it was through the Hong Kong Christian Council. As the ecumenical body it was appropriate that it should be so, but it was also the body which obtained resources from a number of mission bodies, making it less dependent on local support. Among many in the congregations there was reluctance to be involved in social issues, and the repercussions of the cultural revolution in Hong Kong, especially the violent disturbances of 1967, added fear and insecurity. As at other times and places the missionary society felt the tension between respecting the independence of the church and giving encouragement to the minority who seemed more aware of the new challenges facing it.

The development of the United Christian Hospital

The contribution which individual missionaries made by their work and life belongs to the history of the institutions in which they served. One field in which missionary initiative and leadership was able to make itself most clearly apparent was in the development of the Nethersole and later the United Christian Hospital.

The centenary history of the Alice Ho Miu Ling Nethersole Hospital provides the details of its developments in the 1950s and 1960s. By 1961, in the light of the large increase in government funding, two government representatives were included on its executive committee. In 1963 it resisted the transference of its property, and final control over its administration, to the newly incorporated Hong Kong Council of the CCC, preferring to relate to the Hong Kong Christian Council on which the Hong Kong Council of the CCC, along with other supporting bodies, was represented. The new constitution was finally registered in 1964. Such an ecumenical solution brought an extra bonus of adding significance to the Christian Council at a time when it was still a rather weak and unregarded body.

With the goodwill and support of the community it served, the hospital was able to carry out successive stages of development. But retaining the services of well-qualified and experienced staff in competition with the financial rewards of private practice and career opportunities elsewhere was always more difficult. The normal life commitment of missionary staff could not be assumed of all who were needed to maintain the work of the hospital. Some of those locally recruited gave long and faithful service at great personal sacrifice, but with others shorter periods for gaining experience was the norm. During the cultural revolution, when doctors in Hong Kong shared the feelings of insecurity among the professional classes and record numbers emigrated, recruitment of medical staff faced more than usual difficulties.

The Christian character of the hospital depended on the quality of the treatment given, and the personal contacts with the staff. The dedication of the nurses' Christian Fellowship, with the sympathetic support of other members of staff, achieved most in giving witness. Personal contact gave increased value to the other means involved, the paid church worker, the broadcast morning prayers, the ward filmstrips, copies of *A Little Hospital Prayer Book* given to every patient on admission, and the hundreds of copies of Bibles and gospels which were sold.

When Dr Frank Ashton retired in 1963, after long and distinguished service at the Nethersole, he had given the weight of his influence and authority to two new major developments. One of these, the new constitution and link with the Hong Kong Christian Council, has already been noted. The other was his support for the project of a United Christian Hospital (UCH), and, in particular, for the part which the Nethersole was asked to play in its launching.

The plan for the new 600-bed UCH went through several changes before its realization ten years later in the industrial zone of Kwuntong with its 300,000 population. Buildings and equipment totalled $47 million, of which $25.5 million was granted by the government. The committee which had been formed in 1963 by the Hong Kong Christian Council raised the balance from local and overseas sources, including $2.5 million from the Hong Kong churches, but the plan for the hospital had only become viable when the Nethersole gave its support and agreed to provide and train the initial staff. More than that, the basic ideas undergirding the new hospital, summed up in the slogans "To serve the health of the community" and "Hospital without walls", were ideas which had already been developing in the Nethersole. To break away from the idea of a hospital as only concerned with disease and to create an organization where health was the primary concern, both that of the individual and within the community, and to stress the wholeness of life, were central to the vision.

A community nursing service and the first training course for community nurses in Hong Kong began at the Nethersole in 1970. It paved the way for the Kwuntong community health project which was central to the role of the UCH in Kwuntong. It was a pioneering urban community health venture for which there were no models anywhere else in the world. Not surprisingly it took much time, effort and demonstration of its value to convince the government and obtain its recognition as a legitimate activity. When the government designated one of the units as a pilot model community health unit, the financial support was at last ensured.

The contribution which Dr Ashton made towards the future of both the Nethersole and the UCH before his retirement in 1963 has already been noted. In the realization of the vision of a United Christian Hospital, and throughout all its developments, it has been a remarkable story of united effort in which many people, too many to name, have greatly contributed. But the unique contribution of Dr Paterson, who succeeded Dr Ashton, and carried the chief responsibility for maintaining and realizing the vision during the next twenty years, must be recorded. It has been a most worthy finale to the long and distinguished history of LMS medical missionary work in China and Hong Kong.

The rapid growth both in Hong Kong's population and its industrial development, which required the building of the UCH and other hospitals, also increased the demand for more higher education and also for new classes at secondary level. By the 1970s Chung Chi College was well established as one of the three constituent bodies of Hong Kong's second university on the hills above Shatin. In its early days the LMS contribution to its staff had been through the services of John Barr in the English department, and later Ron Turner-Smith as head of the mathematics department. The Hong Kong Council looked to Chung Chi for theological training on an ecumenical basis of its would-be ordinands but there were also many other colleges, more conservative in character, which were competing for such students and whose graduates were being used by some of the CCC congregations.

At secondary level the Hong Kong Council under Peter Wong's dynamic leadership was quick to respond to the need for more vocational education. After the pioneering work done by its Kei Heep school the Council was asked by the government to provide three of the five schools for which funds were made available.

One hundred and thirty years of Christianity in Hong Kong were celebrated in 1973, and that same year marked the transfer to the Council of one of the most valuable LMS properties in Hong Kong, Morrison Hall.[25] At this time only three missionary families remained, the Buntons, the Patersons and the Turner-Smiths, each of them identified with a particular work and institution. Closely associated with them were Dennis Rogers, minister of Hong Kong Union Church, and his wife Joan, and at a weekly meeting for fellowship were also gathered the several LMS associates working in Hong Kong. By the transfer of property and the nature of their work the missionaries committee had ceased to exercise many of its former functions, and only met very occasionally. Without dramatizing the event the transfer of Morrison Hall can be seen as symbolizing the completion of a process of devolution which had been accepted in principle from the earliest days of the mission. The readiness to make this transfer was recognized by the church as an act of generosity and trust. It was also accepted as a spur to its own efforts and the same year brought plans to build five more middle schools with still more to come in succeeding years, as well as developments in their pastoral care. The income which was later to be derived from the sale of the former mission property, and the investment of the proceeds, has been used by the Council both within and beyond Hong Kong. The action of the LMS in divesting itself of the power inherent in property was a clear demonstration to the Hong Kong Council that the plans which were now being floated for a new CWM structure could mean a genuine and radical transfer of authority and responsibility to the indigenous churches, and a new form of partnership in mission.

As for many others attending the CWM Singapore consultation in 1975, it gave Peter Wong his first opportunity to see at first hand the breadth and variety of the LMS/CWM "family". Previous relationships in Hong Kong had all been with the various mission boards, the senders, and of varying duration. For nearly twenty years he had been building up the life of the church in Hong Kong and establishing the status of the Council, and in the process most characteristics of a "receiving" church had disappeared. The experience at Singapore was followed not only by his own further travels and contacts with sister churches but by his promotion of travel and arrangement of visits by church workers to Europe, America, and other parts of Asia. The Hong Kong Council of the CCC had outgrown an old relationship and was now being challenged to discover the obligations of a new one.

A life of its own

Looking back on this period, how then should we sum up the impact of the China experience on the history of the LMS/CWM in Hong Kong? In outlining the more significant developments of the church some reference in passing has been made to Hong Kong's colonial status. This of course provided the most complete contrast to what had been the situation in China. Moreover, unlike most other colonial territories, its status changed very little for thirty years. During that time, with the colonial administration so willing, on its own terms, to support the church and mission in educational, medical and social welfare concerns, did they become too dependent? While it was true that all of these were dependent on government funding, it could equally well be argued that by their own merits they qualified for public funding and so long as the public needed these services they were right to draw on public funds to provide them. Did it mean that the prophetic voice was smothered as much as it appeared to be silenced in China itself? It is true that the Hong Kong Council as a body kept itself at a distance from the Hong Kong Christian Council industrial committee when it became involved with workers' rights and labour legislation. Were members of the church, no more and no less than the rest of Hong Kong's population, caught up in frenetic activity, needing or choosing to concentrate on their immediate short-term well-being, material and spiritual, to the neglect or detriment of all else? Such criticisms have been made, sometimes accepted, sometimes resented. But what should also be said is that in one way or another the Hong Kong Council, its leaders and churches, have maintained both a Christian witness, congregational and individual, and a remarkable record of service out of all proportion to the size of its membership. When the LMS missionaries withdrew from China the emphasis was laid on the centrality and autonomy of the church, the importance of training, and the need to be more deeply involved in the life of the community. Perhaps at the time all three of these were perceived in western terms. But no serious attempt was made to rebuild in Hong Kong the mission structures which had been dismantled in China. And given time and space in which to operate, the Hong Kong Council discovered itself, adapted itself to the pace and pressures of Hong Kong life, worked out by design or default its own priorities and affirmed its place in the community. How well it is prepared to face new challenges in the future, and who will be there to provide leadership, time and only time will show.

Malaysia and Singapore

The "opening" of China in 1843 brought to an end the LMS Ultra Ganges Mission in Malaya and Singapore.[26] The end of its mission in China in 1950-51 opened up possibilities in reverse. But the decision to renew work there was taken in full awareness of what mission history of the past hundred years and the most recent experience in China demanded. Assurances had to be sought and principles of cooperation made clear.

The Chinese Presbyterian Church in Singapore and Malaya gave the assurance that it would welcome an increase of missionary staff from both the Presbyterian Church of England and the LMS. Being a church which had derived almost all its leadership and many of its members from the areas covered by the South Fukien (South Fujian) and Lingtung (Lingdong) synods of the Church of Christ in China, it shared both personal links and some common background with the two mission bodies. They, on their part, had not only worked together in China, particularly in South Fukien, but were also

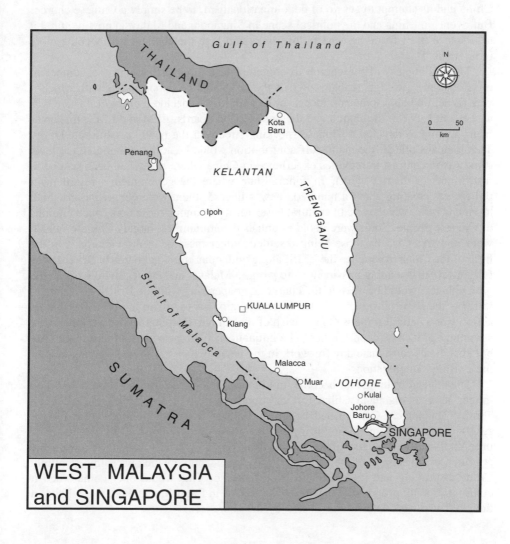

acting closely together in Britain. The cautious step by step approach adopted by the Board under the guidance of Ronald Orchard and Frank Short made sure that all was being done in agreement with both the Chinese Presbyterian Church and the English Presbyterian Mission (EPM) whose "field" this had been.

It was a critical time for that church of less than 3,000 members, 34 churches and preaching stations, and only seven ordained ministers. Throughout its history since 1881, missionary staff had rarely exceeded more than two or three at a time, and it had survived the Japanese occupation without help of either mission staff or grants. [27] That experience had encouraged its sense of independence and the spirit of self-support, but this hopeful development was overtaken by the "emergency" which both threatened its members' incomes and also cast suspicion on its traditionally close ties with China. Chinese throughout Singapore and Malaya were being faced with difficult questions about where they really belonged. Prior to the outbreak of violence in Malaya and the communist triumph in China, the church had already taken steps towards becoming an overseas synod of the CCC. It cherished the close personal links with the church in China and its attempt to get rid of denominationalism, to be simply a Chinese church. But events in China and the political scene in Singapore and Malaysia now required it to distance itself from these past close links and face the challenge to become more indigenous.

The willingness of the church to contemplate a large increase in the number of missionaries showed its realism towards the tasks and the opportunities with which it was faced, and also some confidence in its authority to decide their work. There was agreement between the church and the two mission boards, EPM and LMS, that apart from helping to develop a Chinese-speaking stream in the newly established Trinity Theological College, the main staff contribution would be at the congregational level (this was in contrast to previous experience in China where many had been related to institutions or district work). In Johore state where the government's resettlement policy was creating about a hundred "new villages", there were congregations, both town and rural, which were the natural bases for work among these new concentrations of Chinese people. Some were in old established communities, largely Chinese, which were now extended by those being resettled, either there or in the vicinity. [28] In the light of the China experience the LMS, along with other mission boards in Britain, was fully aware that sending missionaries to work in Malaya, and especially to work in the new villages, would be open to the charge of cooperating with the British government to serve the imperialist cause. It was therefore anxious to affirm the principle that its action was a natural response to the wish of the church to strengthen its work and take advantage of its new opportunities. The initial decision to provide six missionaries did not specifically designate any for work in the new villages but stressed giving help to the existing congregations.

Theological training had become an urgent problem because the church could no longer look to mainland China for its supply of pastors and preachers. Although Trinity Theological College had begun in 1948 as a united training centre for the Anglican, the Methodist (American) and the Presbyterian ministry, it only had part-time staff and its medium of instruction was English. Trinity had not yet won the confidence and support of the Chinese Presbyterian Church which was almost entirely Chinese-speaking and its leadership even more so. This would only come when it could offer a full programme in Chinese as well as in English, and there were those on the staff who were known and trusted by the churches.

The first LMS missionaries

The first LMS appointments, four in number, were all from South Fukien. Two were to be located in Malaya, the Neave family at Muar in Johore and the Legges at Kota Baru in Kelantan; and two in Singapore, both to be teaching at Trinity, Frank Balchin in the main theological training and Anne Stening in the training of kindergarten teachers which Trinity also provided at that time. Unfortunately the Legges were unable to accept appointment but Nan Lindsay, another ex-Fukien missionary who was well known and warmly welcomed by the church, took their place. By 1952 the appeal of working in the new villages had increased. Two Mandarin-speaking missionaries from north China, Irene Smith and Joyce Lovell, offered and were accepted specifically for this work in Johore. This brought the total number to six, the maximum at any time during the next twenty years.

In addition to working alongside their Chinese colleagues in strengthening the life of congregations and their outreach into neighbouring new villages, the missionaries discovered a growing desire for English-speaking work, especially among the young people. Within a predominantly Chinese-speaking church this raised some sensitive issues of authority and trust. These have continued long after English language services, youth fellowships, Sunday schools and well-trained pastoral oversight have become a recognized part of the church. The missionaries involved had to tread carefully as they tried to build bridges of trust with both the older leadership and with those of the younger generation, both Chinese and English educated, who might all belong to the same families. Moreover, prior to independence, English and Malay were the languages of government in Malaya, and English alone in Singapore, and this added a political dimension to the church's attitude to English language work.

The "emergency" coloured much of both church and mission life during those early years. Missionaries whose work took them to the new villages and even more those who lived in them were sharing some of the restrictions, such as the curfew and movement of food, which the regulations imposed. There was often some element of personal danger, and Johore state had more than its share of black spots, but there was even more appreciation of the pressures upon those among whom they lived. This brought them closer to their neighbours, and together with their simple living accommodation may have helped to exorcize the feelings of "mission compound" guilt which some missionaries had brought with them from China. In Singapore where the strength of anti-colonial feeling was no less present, the outward calm of control was at times shattered by strikes and violent rioting in the streets.

The LMS ex-China missionaries arrived in Singapore and Malaya at the end of 1951 and during 1952. This was also the period when the steps taken against the Malayan people's liberation army began to produce results. The death of Sir Henry Gurney in an ambush marked a climax of terror but it brought in his place Sir Gerald Templer. His strong measures combined with the positive results from the resettlement policy and the future assurance of independence gradually whittled away the armed resistance.

Templer was even more emphatic than Gurney about the contribution he wanted missionaries to make towards creating a better life in the new villages. He had appealed to Stanley Dixon of the Conference of British Missionary Societies to make this need known, and encouraged the various mission boards to undertake both health and education as well as evangelistic and pastoral work. Financial help was offered but the LMS and the EPM, acting together through their joint Malaya group, gave a very careful and cautious response. They minuted their appreciation of his concern for the religious needs of those living in the resettlement areas, their hope to make some appointments there, as determined by the requirements of the Malayan church's evangelistic and pastoral responsibilities, and then proceeded to say that

> if at any time medical or education work were undertaken by the mission in resettlement areas, the group would approve of government grants being accepted in respect of such work; but that church and evangelistic work was regarded as the responsibility of the church, and it would not be fitting that it should receive financial support from the government.[29]

This was in line with normal mission policy elsewhere, but in the particular circumstances of the emergency where so much depended on winning hearts and minds, those working in the new villages trod a difficult path, sometimes identified with the authorities but also valued as intermediaries.

Medical work, education and ecumenical cooperation

The China experience, involving the transfer to government control of all the educational and medical institutions founded and supported by mission boards, had aroused a major debate about their place in mission strategy. Regarding Malaya and Singapore, the LMS had not ruled out the possibility of at least some form of medical work, and during the 1950s the Malaya mission council on various occasions stressed the value of the traditional healing, teaching and preaching ministry to provide a Christian presence in the new villages. While the government's health service and the network of large hospitals ruled out the need or possibility of any comparable institutions, the Malayan government was encouraging the Red Cross and the mission bodies to provide rural clinics. Among the missionaries there was a positive desire to provide some form of diaconia. In these circumstances it seemed right to enable Joyce Lovell, a qualified midwife, and based at the biggest new village in Johore, to provide such a service. Having added a knowledge of the Hakka dialect[30] to her previous Mandarin she began a midwifery service in Kulai and the neighbouring rubber estates and villages. With financial help from the mission and the local community, this developed into the Kulai Maternity Home.

The church's involvement in education was very much at the congregational level. Apart from the two English medium schools at Katong in Singapore in which English Presbyterian missionaries had played a major role, and the English kindergarten at Prinsep Street Church, all the others were Chinese medium primary schools attached to individual congregations, the oldest of them, Pei Hwa, founded at Bukit Timah in 1889. They varied greatly in size and standards. As the government paid increasing attention to them, both for political and educational reasons, they became more dependent on government grant-in-aid to achieve the standards required for their continued registration. The result was that the stronger survived and the weaker went to the wall. There was still scope, however, to open kindergartens. The church had pioneered kindergarten teaching in Singapore fifty years earlier, building on the experience in South Fukien. In both Singapore and Malaya, in the town and country congregations, both Chinese and English medium, with, but more often without, any missionary assistance, kindergartens added to the widespread educational contribution being made through congregation-related primary schools. At the same time there was a strong desire on the part of the church as a whole to establish a Chinese middle school. Many plans were made during the 1950s but it was not until 1965 that these hopes were realized.

The joint mission organization between the LMS and the Presbyterian Church of England set up in London in December 1950, which soon became the Joint Malaya Group (JMG), and also the Malaya mission council, which was made up of both English Presbyterian and LMS missionaries, proved very successful as means of cooperation and integration of their work. In due course the Malaya mission council also included missionaries of the Presbyterian Church in Ireland, the Church of Scotland, the Reformed Church of America, and the Society of Friends.[31] Early ideas of maintaining separate EP and LMS committees in the field and for the LMS to be part of a wider regional structure faded away when it became clear that satisfactory relationships had developed with the Joint Malaya Group, irrespective of who was serving as secretary of the group or the council. The experience shared in China and serving the same church in Singapore and Malaya strengthened the fellowship among the missionaries so that differences of denominational background became wholly irrelevant.

By the year 1961 Malaya and Singapore had achieved their independence from British rule, and after a brief experiment of both being part of the federation of Malaysia, including Sabah and Sarawak, they had chosen to be independent of each other. Changes had also taken place in the church and among the missionaries. The particular challenge and opportunity presented by the new villages during the emergency had passed. There had not been any spectacular growth, and in almost all cases the congregations had grown out of a nucleus of Chinese Christians already existing and through the encouragement of stronger congregations in the neighbouring towns. But simple churches had been built, with some help through the JMG, regular church life was being maintained, and more pastoral oversight provided. The church had also made progress in the training of its own young people for the ministry, at Trinity Theological College in which Frank Balchin played a leading role, and in the Singapore Bible College supported by the Overseas Missionary Fellowship of the China Inland Mission.

During the previous decade the issue of ecumenical cooperation had caused tension within the church and between the church and the mission council. Supporters of the International Council of Christian Churches and the Bible Presbyterian Church associated with Carl MacIntyre had sufficient influence within the church to make it draw back from full cooperation within the Malaya Christian Council (MCC). The fear of dividing the church prevailed over its ecumenical concern. By 1961 a stalemate had been reached in which the church continued to share in the very active new village work and audiovisual aids committees but did not appoint official delegates to the Council itself. The fact that originally the MCC had been formed on the initiative of Anglican and American Methodist bishops and an English Presbyterian missionary, and that English had been the language mostly used, had always been a stumbling block to a church with a strong sense of independence and in which the leadership was Chinese-educated. During the emergency the MCC had played an important role both in coordinating the work of the various churches among the five hundred new villages throughout Malaya, and also in representing their concerns to the government. When the emergency ended the MCC continued to give support and stimulus to those working under what were often lonely and discouraging conditions. The church itself, following a pattern associated with South Fukien, and on the initiative of Dr Henry Poppen, a long-serving missionary of the Reformed Church of America, began a series of annual church-workers retreats *(Kek-le-thoan)* which were well attended and provided rest, recreation and spiritual renewal.

By 1961 there had also been a thinning out of the ex-China missionaries, and among the LMS staff only the Balchins and Joyce Lovell remained. But in 1960 the first of three new appointments, that of Frank Buxton, was made. Sadly his term of service, mostly in Kota Baru, was overshadowed by illness, and in 1964 he and his wife returned to England where he died on Whitsunday. The LMS continued its commitment to work in Singapore and Malaysia, and responded to the church's appeal with the appointment of three more missionaries, Derek Kingston and Clabon and Margaret Allen.

Link with Taiwan

Contemporaneous with a general thinning out of ex-China missionaries was a new development. This was the link with the Presbyterian Church in Taiwan (PCT) bringing new ministers and new ideas into the church's life. The PCT assembly was beginning to feel its way towards overseas mission, and the church in Singapore and Malaysia, still slow to ordain its own young people, welcomed this addition of experienced ministers to its strength.

In preparation for celebrating its centenary in 1965 the Presbyterian Church in Taiwan, from 1955 onwards, had committed itself to a doubling-the-church movement. Among the first ministers from Taiwan to serve in Singapore and Malaysia there was great enthusiasm for what was being done through this movement, and for sharing news of it. To the Rev. Yap Kok Hu, the synod's chairman in 1961 and minister of the oldest Chinese-speaking congregation in the synod, the Glory Church at Bukit Timah, it seemed the time was ripe for a comparable effort to galvanize the church in Singapore and Malaysia. The year 1961 was the eightieth anniversary of the founding of the church, and under his inspiration and leadership the church committed itself to a Five-Year Movement (FYM) for doubling its numbers. A second FYM followed in 1966, and the life of the church during the 1960s centred on these two successive movements.

From an early stage it was realized that a movement for membership growth must also be a movement for stimulating the whole life and witness of the church. The first of the annual mottoes, "Lord, revive thy church, beginning with me," echoed the church in China of the 1930s, but that was only the beginning of a widening movement of renewal. It involved in turn the Christian family, the life of the congregation and lay training, evangelism and church extension, and stewardship of the whole of life. The theme and its appropriate text and motto for each year were promoted throughout the church: on special days in congregations, through the women's work and Sunday school committees, training courses, women's and youth fellowships and their conferences, travelling bookstore, the church-workers retreats, outdoor film evangelism, in bilingual publications, posters and calendars for use in the home, special hymns written by the FYM chairman, Rev. Yap Kok Hu, and with the stimulus of gifted evangelists invited from abroad as well as the home-grown variety.

Alongside this programme of renewal went the establishing of new congregations. The past comity arrangement between the Methodists and the Presbyterians in Malaya, seen by some Chinese church leaders as a relic of missionary tutelage, had limited the synod's work to Johore and the northeast states of Kelantan and Trengganu. The growth of the towns and the mobility of the population increased the pressure to establish new congregations where it was known that Christians who had originally come from South Fukien and East Kwangtung were now living. Simultaneous with this desire for church growth was the changing condition within the four congregations of the Presbytery of Malaya. [32] Malayan political independence was steadily reducing the number of expatriate planters, miners, businessmen and government officers who had been the backbone of these English-speaking congregations. There was therefore more openness to the idea that the church buildings in Penang, Kuala Lumpur and Ipoh should be made available to the Chinese-speaking congregations that were being formed. By the end of the decade new congregations had been established in Penang, Kuala Lumpur, Ipoh, Klang, Malacca, and a Mandarin service in the Orchard Road Presbyterian Church, Singapore. During the first five years the total membership grew from 4,041 to 5,645, a 40 percent increase compared with 21 percent in the previous five-year period, and by the end of the decade the total increase was about 80 percent.

The influence of politics

During the same decade the synod had to face the new situation created by the separation between Singapore and Malaysia. A first step in 1962 was to divide into three presbyteries, Singapore, South Malaya and North Malaya. It increasingly felt the need to define itself in denominational terms and in 1968 took the decisive step of changing its name from the Malaysia synod of the Chinese Christian Church to the Presbyterian Church in Singapore and Malaysia. In the same year a new constitution saw the light of day, and this opened the way to union with the Presbytery of Malaya which was finally achieved in 1971.

After political independence, government immigration policy in both Singapore and Malaysia limited the number of new missionaries and their length of service. Those who obtained entry to Malaysia knew that they could only expect a maximum of ten years. This policy had stimulated the growth of indigenous leadership and during the 1970s those who had been born and trained in Singapore and Malaya at last took over leadership in the church. The long service which the last of the ex-China LMS missionaries, Frank and Ivy Balchin and Joyce Lovell, had given in their different spheres came to an end at their retirement. [33] Derek Kingston and the Allens, who had gone out in the middle of the 1960s, played a large part in the process of church extension in Malaya and integration between the synod and the Presbytery of Malaya. The CWM Singapore consultation in January 1975 coincided with the division of the church into the Presbyterian Church in Singapore and the Presbyterian Church in Malaysia. Soon immigration regulations would terminate the Allens' service but Derek Kingston, by transferring to Singapore, was able to continue his work in ministry to the rapidly-growing English-speaking congregations there.

In 1950 the situation in Singapore and Malaya had made a strong appeal to the LMS Board as it contemplated withdrawal of its missionaries from China. To work among the Chinese diaspora, so many of whom had links with South Fukien, to maintain the partnership it had enjoyed in the CCC, to contribute to an urgent need for theological education, to respond to the challenge of the new villages, and the strengthening of congregational life: all these had been part of the vision and expectation to which was later added the opportunities for church extension and English-speaking work. During the years that followed, in addition to personnel, the board made annual grants which were originally designated for work in the new villages and Trinity Theological College. Special grants were also made for missionary housing which in due course, both in rural and urban areas, has been handed over for the use of the local church. Both personnel and grants have been a valuable contribution, have built up a new relationship of trust and friendship, but have not radically affected the ways in which the church has developed. As far as human personalities are concerned those ways have continued to be, as they were in 1950, firmly in the hands of the Chinese leadership.

By the year 1977, when the Presbyterian churches in Singapore and in Malaysia became members of the new Council for World Mission, each had developed its own character. Both originated in a church of immigrants, cherishing the faith they had experienced in their homes in China, and constantly reinforced by new arrivals from the homeland. For seventy years very limited missionary help provided some pastoral care, challenged them to form new congregations, encouraged self-support, and brought them together in a church order which appeared presbyterian to congregationalists and congregational to presbyterians. Equally significant in shaping them was a succession of historical changes, the Japanese occupation, communist rule in China, and the emergence of two very different countries, Singapore and Malaysia. In one, the dramatic achievements, values and disciplines of the secular state, and in the other Malay interests and Islamic authority affected their development, spurred them to growth but also set limits to their outreach. In both countries one of the hopes expressed by the LMS in 1950 has remained unrealized, the same hope which detained Benjamin Keasberry in Singapore when all his colleagues left for China in 1843. Tradition says that his last words were a challenge to work among the Malays: "A time is coming when the Mohammedans will acknowledge and worship the Saviour." Historical changes have helped the church in Singapore and Malaysia to discover a role and mission, but they have also closed the door more firmly against sharing the gospel with the Malays.

Taiwan

The relationship formed between CCWM/CWM and the Presbyterian Church in Taiwan (PCT) in 1972 was a direct result of the union in Britain between the Congregational Church in England and Wales and the Presbyterian Church of England (PCE). Unlike the situation in Singapore and Malaysia there was no historical link which was being renewed. It was an entirely new relationship, and formed in such circumstances invites exploration of what it says about the selfhood of the bodies involved.

The Presbyterian Church in Taiwan, or Formosa as it was generally known, had a special place in the thoughts and affections of the Presbyterian Church of England. For many years it had been the "children's field", fulfilling for them the same role as the "John Williams" ship did for young supporters of the LMS. As an island, at least comparable in area to England, Taiwan could be more easily defined and comprehended than the vast expanses of mainland China. Its chequered history during the previous hundred years, briefly having provincial status in the Ching (Manchu) dynasty during the latter part of the nineteenth century, then for fifty years, 1895-1945, as a Japanese colony, and its subsequent development into the nationalist stronghold under an autocratic regime, supported by American military power and financial investment, all this had repercussions on the life and growth of the church. For the first eighty years of its history all Protestant missionary work had been

Presbyterian, Canadian in the north of the island and English in the south. When the deterioration in relations between Japan and the West in 1940 had brought danger to the church, by mutual agreement the missionaries had withdrawn. After the war ended they had only returned by invitation, and in small numbers. They found a church which had survived great trials but was also witnessing a remarkable opening up of the original population, the "mountain people", to the gospel.

In spite of the missionary withdrawal, the relationship with the church and the Taiwanese people had been maintained and personified during the second world war by Ng Chang-hui (Shoki Coe) who spent the years from 1937 to 1945 in Britain. He was to play a decisive role in the development of the church, especially in the field of

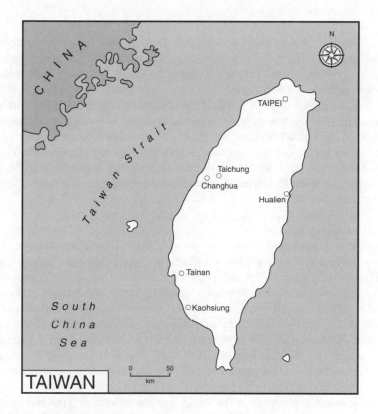

theological education, and in the church's struggle for both its own religious liberty and the rights of the Taiwanese people.

In the immediate post-war years the Taiwanese experienced some of the worst forms of KMT exploitation and misgovernment, and consequently viewed the nationalist withdrawal from the mainland and build-up on their island with grave apprehension. In these circumstances the southern synod invited the English Presbyterian mission to transfer a small number of its South Fukien missionaries, who spoke the same dialect[34] as the Taiwanese Chinese, to work in Taiwan. Their experience on the mainland of KMT corruption and incompetence made them all the more sympathetic towards Taiwanese resentment and suspicion of their new government. At the same time, the missionary withdrawal from the mainland and the end of all communication with the church there gave Taiwan, the remaining major "field" of the English Presbyterian mission, an added significance. The rapid development of the church under notable leadership and in difficult political circumstances made it a special focus of concern and support within the Presbyterian Church of England. By 1972 when the new relationship with CWM was formed the basic statistics were as follows:

churches	918
communicant members	64,767
enquirers	37,649
attending Sunday school	44,730
ministers/preachers	910
theological colleges	3
hospitals	2

There was also a variety of other educational, training and service institutions.

On the political front 1971 had marked the dramatic change of direction in America's policy towards the People's Republic of China, and from then onwards the KMT government on Taiwan rapidly lost much diplomatic recognition as well as its place in the United Nations. In contrast the church derived benefit from its international links with mission boards in America and Europe. Following nationalist China's exclusion from the United Nations, the PCT took the unprecedented and bold step of issuing a "statement on our national fate" which affirmed the rights of the Taiwanese people to have a say in their future. It was in such an atmosphere of heightened political tension that the Presbyterian Church found itself in a new relationship to the previously unknown CCWM.

The Presbyterians in Taiwan

From the very beginning of its overseas work the Presbyterian Church of England had valued the fact that such work was undertaken by a committee responsible to the whole church rather than by an independent missionary society. Consequently the churches overseas with which it related, even though their normal contacts were through the officers of the overseas missions committee, were encouraged to see themselves in a church-to-church relationship. As the negotiations towards church union in the UK proceeded it was necessary to assure the church in Taiwan that the former close ties with the church in the UK would remain. Fortunately the secretary of the PCE overseas missions committee was Boris Anderson, someone whom the church in Taiwan knew and trusted, and he was also to be the first secretary of the world church and mission department in the URC. For the church in Taiwan this personal rapport and mutual confidence probably counted more than the details and explanations of how they would correspond regarding missionary personnel, financial and other matters, with what was then the CCWM. So long as the old ties were not to be weakened the prospect of extending contacts with other churches had something to commend it.

The English Presbyterian missionaries, now reduced in numbers to ten, and only a fifth of all those serving the church, were more acutely aware of the changes taking place. They were concerned that they were losing a cherished relationship between the sending church and its missionaries whereby the latter, during their home leave, had a recognized place as elders and ministers in the assembly. In 1958 the assembly had endorsed the unique position of the missionary as a member of both the church in

England as well as the church in Taiwan. In the negotiations which led to the formation of the United Reformed Church they had been consulted, but they wondered whether in the future they would enjoy similar prerogatives. There was also some fear that the "family" character of the smaller church and its missionaries would be submerged in a much larger organization which had its own established traditions. Perhaps they were unaware of the leaven which had already been working for some years, changing the nature of the LMS and later of the CCWM, and ultimately helping to create the new CWM of 1977. When the 1973 oil crisis almost doubled the cost of living in Taiwan there was an additional anxiety that their financial plight might not be appreciated.

While much effort was made in the offices of CCWM to understand the history and character of the Presbyterian Church in Taiwan and to make it known to the enlarged body of mission supporters, it is unlikely that more than a very few in that church were aware of the new relationship. For them there were many more pressing issues on their agenda, both within the church and its institutions and in its dealings with the ruling body on Taiwan. By this time it was also in a relationship with six other mission boards, in Canada, the USA and Scotland. Their representatives, who now would include one from the CCWM, met yearly with those of the Taiwanese church on a consultative basis but without executive authority. At least a part of the value of such gatherings was to ensure that the rights of church and people were kept in view at a time when Taiwan was becoming more and more politically isolated.

From the end of the second world war Taiwan had come increasingly under American influence to which political, military and economic factors had all contributed. Although a number of those who proved to be the church's best leaders had opportunities to study in the UK, it was Canada, and even more the USA, which offered them the most. There was also a rapidly increasing number of Taiwanese, among them many Christians, who resented the position of being second-class citizens in their home country and sought to emigrate. In North America, in Brazil and in Europe were growing Taiwanese communities, and among many of them churches were formed. Many graduates from the theological colleges who had gone abroad for further study found a ministry awaiting them among their compatriots. Some took up other occupations rather than return to an uncertain future in Taiwan. For some ministers in Taiwan it was an alluring prospect which tempted them to join the large numbers of other Taiwanese seeking better opportunities for themselves and their families.

The new century mission movement which followed the celebration of the centenary in 1965 had included plans for extending overseas mission. We have already noted the presence in Malaysia and Singapore of those who were sent there from Taiwan. At that stage the PCT only contemplated sending abroad those who would minister to Chinese communities, speaking similar dialects to those of Taiwan. The receiving churches under which they served, or the Taiwanese Christian communities in America to whom they ministered, were expected to provide their salaries, but the church in Taiwan was challenged to raise funds for their travel and support during their home leave. Although there were mission organizations based in Taiwan which had American links and were involved in missionary work among races other than Chinese in Southeast Asia and Pacific areas, the PCT's practice of overseas mission was still predominantly of a "chaplaincy" character.

Between 1972 and 1977 within the church in Taiwan there was a growing self-assurance in its attitude towards the government. The re-election of Dr C.M. Kao as general secretary in 1973 and again, even more significantly, in 1978, was a clear indication that it was not going to be intimidated. The continued use of the romanized Taiwanese Bible, which had played such a large part in the church's growth and nurture, was an issue over which it resisted the regime's pressure. In a country where all other organizations were under strict government control it exercised its rights to religious freedom and in this way, both within and beyond Taiwan, it enhanced its reputation for defending human rights. Through its membership since 1951 in the World Council of Churches, the East Asia Christian Conference (later, the Christian Conference of Asia) and the World Alliance of Reformed Churches, its words and actions were widely publicized and received sympathetic support. [35]

The Presbyterian Church in Taiwan and the former English Presbyterian missionaries serving within it had scarcely become familiar with their new mission board relationship before they were drawn into the discussion of a new structure for CWM. Because the ideas which came out of the Singapore consultation affirmed church-to-church relationships, the principle of mutuality, and decision-making as a joint responsibility of all the member bodies, the new scheme for a restructured CWM had no difficulty in being commended to the general assembly. At its annual meeting in 1976 the PCT general assembly agreed to enter into membership, and the presence of the Taiwanese choir at the inaugural meeting of the new CWM in 1977 proved a fitting expression of that decision.

NOTES

[1] LMS board minutes, June 1949.

[2] CWM archive (CWMA) box CH/57, no. 106, and CBMS archive (CBMSA) box 333, Far East committee minutes, no. 1017.

[3] A full account and interpretation are found in P.L. Wickeri's *Seeking the Common Ground*, Maryknoll, NY, Orbis, 1988, pp.127-33.

[4] Donald E. MacInnis, *Religious Policy and Practice in Communist China*, London, Hodder & Stoughton, 1972, p.158.

[5] CWMA box CH/57, no. 106, notes on the future of the China mission, 20 June 1950, and text of letter "on Korean situation" with covering letter dated 28 July 1950.

[6] LMS board minutes, September 1950, p.12.

[7] *Ibid.*, p.13.

[8] LMS board minutes, December 1950, p.13, and letter of Orchard, 8 December 1950.

[9] *Ibid.* The "Message" is quoted in full, pp.13-14.

[10] *Ibid.*

[11] *Ibid.*, pp.17-18.

[12] LMS board minutes, April 1951, p.16.

[13] CBMSA box 334, China sub-committee minutes, 26 January 1951.

[14] David M. Paton, "First Thoughts on the Debacle of Christian Missions in China", *International Review of Missions*, vol. 40, October 1951, pp.411-20.

[15] Roland Allen, *Missionary Methods, St Paul's or Ours*, London, Robert Scott, 1912, and *The Spontaneous Expansion of the Church*, London, World Dominion Press, 1927.

[16] CBMSA box 338, papers circulated to the Asia committee, 28 June 1956.

[17] CBMSA box 392, file 35, letter dated 11 March 1959.

[18] David M. Paton, "On Understanding the Position of the Church in China", *East and West Review*, January 1960.

[19] Statement, dated 11 May 1972, circulated by D.M. Paton, chairman CBMS/DIA China group, and C.B. Firth, Asia secretary, CBMS.

[20] R.K. Orchard's report to the LMS board, May 1951, pp.1-2.

[21] For the history of the Nethersole Hospital see E.H. Paterson, *A Hospital for Hong Kong, 1887-1987*, published privately by the hospital in Hong Kong, 1987.

[22] Anne Mackeith, John and Ruth Barr, Albert and Barbara Small, Samuel and Ruth Withers Green, and Frank and Irene Short had worked in Shanghai; Dorothy Havergal Shaw, Kathrine Brameld and Edith Rawlings in Canton. Staff previously appointed to Hong Kong were Roland and Bessie Alderton, Frank and Elizabeth Ashton, William and May Chapman, Barbara Knight, Herbert and Ruth Noble, Dorothy Shilston, Vera Silcocks, Mary Smith, Annie Sydenham, and Alun and Elizabeth Lloyd Thomas.

[23] C.S. Craig's report to the LMS board, April 1956, pp.21-22.

[24] E.H. Paterson, letter dated October 1957.

[25] By this time the only properties held in the name of the LMS were holiday accommodation on Lantau and Cheung Chau islands, and some related to the Nethersole Hospital and mission houses in Robinson Road.

[26] Ultra Ganges Mission was the name used for LMS work in Malaya/Singapore until 1843.

[27] In the immediate post-war years, under the leadership of the Rev. Quek Keng Hun a large fund was raised and invested in a coconut estate to achieve self-support, and for several years no grant was received.

[28] Apart from six congregations in Kelantan and Trengganu all the other Malayan churches were in Johore state.

[29] CWMA box EA/4, Joint Malaya Group minutes, 26 March 1952, p.3.

[30] Both here and in the Taiwan section, "dialect" rather than "language" is used. Although the variations of the Chinese language, e.g. those spoken in Beijing, Canton, East Kwangtung, South Fukien and Taiwan, are so great as to be mutually unintelligible, their written form is the same. It is therefore a matter of opinion whether to refer to them as "dialects" or "languages".

[31] Ministers of the largely expatriate congregations in Penang, Singapore (Orchard Road), Selangor and Perak were also members of the Council.

[32] The four congregations named in note 31 originally formed a Malaya field committee of the London north presbytery. In 1958 they were given presbytery status, and this prepared the way for their integration in the Presbyterian Church in Singapore and Malaysia in 1971.

[33] In 1969 Balchin resigned from Trinity Theological College and gave full-time service in the church until 1979; Joyce Lovell completed her service at Kulai in 1977.

[34] See note 30 above.

[35] Under KMT government pressure the Presbyterian Church in Taiwan's membership of the WCC lapsed in 1971, but was reactivated in 1980.

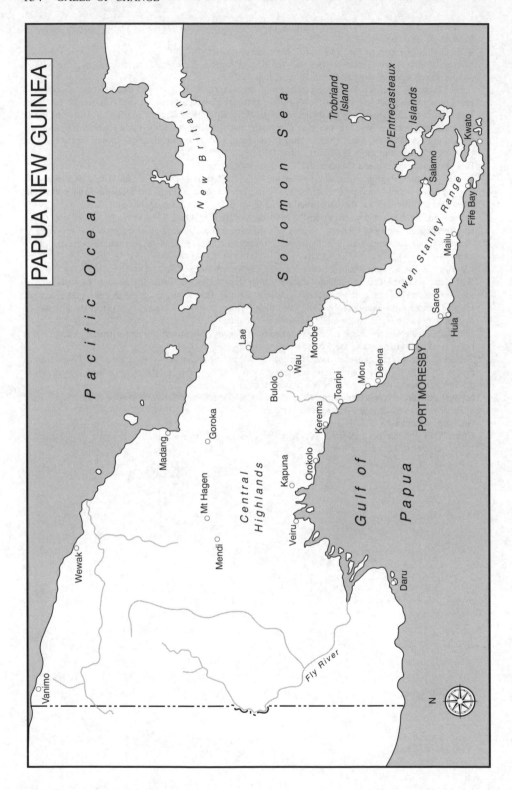

8. From Many, One People

Frank Butler

Papua after the war

The second world war saw much of the coastal fringe of Papua and New Guinea under Japanese military control. The Japanese army had come close to Port Moresby, and the Australian government had established a military administration. Its headquarters had taken over the LMS's Port Moresby head station. Female missionaries and the wives of the men had been evacuated in 1942 and began to return in 1944. Papuans from the villages near Port Moresby had been evacuated. Many Papuan men had worked in carrier lines and labour units serving the allied troops and returned home from new experiences to villages that would never be the same again.

It would be safe to say that until its troops were engaged in savage fighting in this rugged, inaccessible, hot and beautiful land, most Australians and the world at large had been ignorant of the large island on Australia's northern doorstep. Except for the few who had heard missionaries speak, or who were involved in government or commercial ventures there, they would have known little of its people of some seven hundred languages and a wide variety of cultures, its mountains and valleys, its few small towns and its many villages.

The war had wrought changes in this land that would be lasting, that would produce more change, that would open up new challenges to government, churches and missions, and that would radically alter the experiences, hopes and expectations of the indigenous people. Men of tribes with no previous contact had met and worked and worshipped together across differences of language, culture and mission influence. Some who had left home to work with the armed forces would not return on any permanent basis. They, and others who followed them, became permanent residents in places far from home, married and raised families there. A land that had been a closed book to the outside world beckoned to come, to live and work there.

In 1944 the Papua district committee's minutes show that it looked ahead to the return of civil administration, and was planning for the future. There was a long list of "New Advance" possibilities, but consolidation would also be needed, and the supply of pastors was small. The material infrastructure of the mission might need a lot of repair or replacement, to an extent not yet known. A reduction in the LMS financial

The assistance of the Mitchell library, Sydney, the library of the School of Oriental and African Studies in the University of London, and the archives of the NSW synod of the Uniting Church in Australia in making records available to the writer is gratefully acknowledged.

warrant to the field was anticipated, and there was encouragement for the local church to further support its own pastors. In education it was hoped that the government would train teachers, but if not, then the committee would look for LMS funding of a teacher trainer position. Syllabi should have a place for native arts and crafts and agricultural training, and village schools should be based mainly on the vernacular. There would need to be provision for education beyond primary levels. A lengthy minute set out medical policy decisions with proposals for midwifery and infant welfare work and moves for getting a nucleus of expatriate staff into the field. That a small group of remaining missionaries could, in the circumstances of 1944, address themselves thus to the future says much for their love of the people and their commitment to the task to which they were called.

As the LMS Board and the district committee with the Papuan pastors and members set out into the post-war years they were sailing into uncharted seas, so much had the land and its people to change. Planning ahead was going to be difficult, as is evidenced by the number of times during those early years the committee had to make provisional appointments of medical staff and so often not even contingency arrangements came to fruition.

The Board report in 1944 said that reconstruction must be thought of in terms of the best use of available resources, that future work should be built around the life of "younger churches" whose goals and welfare were to be the guiding principle, and that wherever possible there should be cooperation with other societies and churches.

Thirty years of change

Towards the end of our period, Mauri Kiki, a politician from the Gulf area of Papua, titled his autobiography *Ten Thousand Years in a Lifetime*. That was no exaggeration.

What were some of those rapid and dramatic changes? A brief outline now may be helpful, before looking at some of the ways in which the local church with the LMS and other related mission boards exercised ministry in this period of far-reaching social economic and cultural change.

In 1945 European penetration of Papua and New Guinea was confined mostly to the coastal fringe of the main land mass, and to the islands about it. There were very few roads. By the early 1950s administration patrols, missionaries and prospectors had moved deep into the highlands areas with their large tribal groups. By the early 1970s there was a road from Lae to Mount Hagen, and one could drive out of Port Moresby to some areas previously only accessible by foot or sea. The use of light aircraft, often into tiny difficult airstrips, increased greatly. The transistor radio age reached even quite remote villages. It had become possible for many people to travel and to communicate much more easily and rapidly than ever before.

Until the war the expatriate population had been very small. Ian Stuart says that in 1946 the European population of Port Moresby was about 600.[1] By 1970 there were over 10,000 expatriates in that town alone, and many in such places as Lae, Madang, Goroka and Rabaul. There was also a considerable drift of indigenous people from village to town. By way of illustration, in 1946 there were some 3,500 indigenous people in the Port Moresby area, and by 1970 this number was more like 40,000.[2] Towns had grown rapidly, and much of the increase was due to the movement of men, without their families, in search of work that often they did not find.

The shift of population contributed to social and economic change. In towns people who moved from villages lived often in poor unplanned and unserviced squatter settlements. They were usually settled in language groups, often unemployed, frequently unschooled. Their accustomed means of living from hunting and gardening was not possible. They were losing contact with their culture, and drinking and gambling were problems. In 1953 the administrator decided to combat lawlessness by increasing the number of European police in Port Moresby and legislating so that the administration could deal more quickly with vagrants, and remove migrants from outlying districts who were considered "undesirable".[3] By 1971 "rascal" gangs of unemployed disaffected youth were becoming a risk to property and to personal safety. In some villages the male work-force was depleted to a serious level, and social structures were so breaking down that the traditional norms and restraints that held society together in familiar ways were disappearing rapidly.

In the early post-war years education had been almost entirely a function of the missions, and that mostly in village schools, taught by pastors for whom school teaching was a secondary function, and to only a very elementary primary level. By 1975 there was a developed system of teacher education provided by both government and church. The churches were still heavily involved, but there were many government schools, including high schools. There were a university in Port Moresby which included a medical school, an institute of technology in Lae, and a number of technical colleges.

From 1946 Australia administered as one unit the Australian Territory of Papua and the (former German) Trust Territory of New Guinea through an administrator based in Port Moresby.[4] As late as 1955 the commonwealth statistician's population figures made no mention of indigenes, who in 1957 were still not recognized as citizens. But throughout the period there was a growing awareness among those same indigenous people of an identity as Papuans, as New Guineans, and a developing and openly-expressed determination to be the rulers in their own land. In November 1963 writs were issued for a general election of a house of assembly the majority of whom was elected. Self-government was achieved in 1973, and Papua New Guinea became an independent nation in 1975.

Within the lives of the missions and churches too there was much that changed during these thirty years or so. Increased awareness of a place generally known as New Guinea followed on the war, and brought with it a large number and variety of Christian missions. Many came without recognition of the work already well established by the mainline churches. In 1948 the district committee arranged for a meeting of Papuan leaders to prepare a constitution for a Papuan church assembly and make plans for the future. In 1962 the work of the LMS became an autonomous church named Papua Ekalesia. Relationships across the churches and missions developed so that in 1968 there was the first meeting of the assembly of the United Church in Papua New Guinea and the Solomon Islands, and by the end of the period it was a member church of a number of ecumenical bodies both within Papua New Guinea and worldwide.

Perusal of the secular press reveals marked shifts in attitudes and expectations. The first edition of the *South Pacific Post* was published in September 1950. At that time there was a strong emphasis on New Guinea as an element in Australia's defence. The administrator, in a message of welcome to the paper, wrote that he expected that

the editorial policies of this newspaper will take into consideration, as the government must, the interests of the whole of the inhabitants... It is my confident belief that a Christian long-range approach to the problems of our plural society will enable us to show to all that we are capable of keeping them tied to us in friendship.[5]

In 1950 the news was almost all about Australia and Australia's overseas interests.

By 1953 the content was largely local. In 1969 we had a paper in which local people, local news and local concerns predominated. In 1955 an editorial in the *South Pacific Post* had said: "We must treat New Guinea now, not so much as a trusteeship, but as the first bulwark of our defence against the growing menace of Asia."[6] That was a view sometimes expressed by expatriates living in the country in those early years, but which was virtually gone by the 1960s. By the late 1950s indigenous people were strongly pressing claims for their rightful place in the leadership of their country. In 1959 John Guise (later Sir John Guise and the first governor general of Papua New Guinea who, though an Anglican, consulted from time to time with LMS missionaries) was told by the district officer that he talked too much at meetings of the district advisory council.[7] In 1963 he was pressing for a

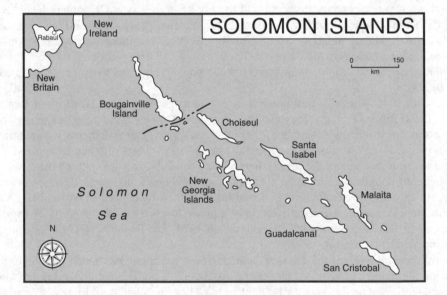

clear Australian statement about keeping the unity of PNG whilst moving towards self-government.[8] In May 1969 Mauri Kiki was reported as charging the Australian government with holding back self-government.[9] In 1974 a church high school teacher at Salamo wrote about a "heightening of nationalistic feeling among students". She said "it was a shock" (on return after a lengthy absence) "to be aware of racist sentiment albeit from only a very few students... I am sure it will pass when independence is granted".[10]

In the charge to ordinands in 1951 H.J.E. Short (then district minister at Hula) spoke words that held true throughout this period when he said:

During your ministry Papua will be changing more than other lands. Our government is doing much to help Papuans to share in the change, and Papuans must be willing to give their time, and even their lives, for their Lord. God's truth, his comfort and help, will be needed more in this special half-century than in simpler days. It is for you to show his mercy still in everything, and shining through all the mysteries.[11]

Growing a church

In 1943 an LMS Board report referred to the founding resolutions of the Board's "New Advance" programme. The younger churches should take the lead in evangelization of their own countries. Priorities included the training of leaders both lay and ordained, building up the Christian community and extension of existing work. Within these were included women in personal family and community life, and work in the hinterland of Papua.

Percy Chatterton (district minister, Delena) wrote of his experience on returning from leave in 1955:

> Fourteen years earlier I had been the big boss. Later I had become a kind of captain-coach. Now I found myself more a sort of ecclesiastical linesman, blowing the whistle when I deemed the ball had gone out of play.[12]

That is one measure of what happened as the work of the LMS in Papua (and later in New Guinea as well) grew from being a mission field to a local, self-governing, self-propagating and, at local levels, self-supporting church.

That the Christian faith had taken root in Papuan society was evident when, on a small coastal boat of a cooperative society, every evening the crew from Mailu gathered for prayers, and when in towns like Wewak and Madang people who were far from their homes in Papua and without benefit of pastor or missionary formed themselves into church communities — worshipping, witnessing and nurturing.

That these things happened was a result of careful planning by the district committee, because of support by the cooperating mission boards and, above all, because of the effective work being done in the districts and village churches by missionaries, pastors and deacons, which enabled Papuan people to be responsible for the work of Christ in their land at the points where it most counts, wherever people live and work. Chatterton suggests that the congregational pattern in which the LMS had developed its work made it easy for small ethnic groups around Port Moresby to organize for worship together on Sundays. Lay men and women in the villages had taken a big part in the work of the church and "a full-time pastor was regarded as a desirable but not an essential adjunct".[13] The same was true in many other places.

In 1945 Papuan pastors asked to be allowed to meet annually. The district committee did not find this possible because of difficulties in arranging transport. By 1948 arrangements were made for the first meeting which was to be held at Delena in 1950, of representatives of district church councils, "to prepare a constitution for a Papuan church assembly and make plans for annual meetings, including entire funding by the churches as far as possible".[14] In the event, 11 out of the 12 districts were represented and they talked about the establishment of a self-supporting church, Lawes College where pastors were trained, the LMS and Papuan finances, the "New Advance" programme and evangelism. Percy Chatterton suggested that the assembly must be given some authority.

In 1959 a draft constitution was referred to the district councils and a committee of a provisional assembly. In 1961 the LMS Australia and New Zealand committee reported to the board that it believed that what was reported was "agreeable to the word of God", and Norman Cocks (secretary in Australia and New Zealand) addressing the board spoke of Papua as "still a grim country... in its continuing battle with human nature".[15] He spoke of "signs of growing strength and deepening life in the Christian church, especially in the emergence of the Papua Ekalesia". In 1962 the first self-governing church in Papua and New Guinea, the Papua Ekalesia, was inaugurated. Overseas missionaries were advised that they should seek membership of the new church. The former LMS work at Kwato, which had been separated early in the century, became a part of the Papua Ekalesia at the end of 1964.

Behind these and other changes at the "central" levels of the church lay a steady and strong development at congregational and district levels. In village after village, as well as in towns, responsibility for the work locally resided with, and was accepted by, pastors, deacons and the members of the church. Meetings of the diaconate and of members were taken seriously and grew increasingly effective. At regional levels district church councils met, and progressively, though at varying rates, took responsibility for the life and work of the church in matters such as finance, evangelism, church extension and questions of social concern. Over the years the district executive committees became responsible for the appointment of pastors to village churches, a task which missionaries had in earlier years undertaken, and in which there were apt to be moments of considerable tension. A district minister in his 1959 report to the directors wrote of the district executive committee: "It has met both with wisdom and with firmness difficult questions of pastoral appointments and of ministerial discipline. It has shown a willingness to take responsibility..."[16]

Together with these developments a strong indigenous leadership, both lay and ordained, was growing. The need for progress in the training of ministers was clear in 1945 when, out of a total indigenous pastoral leadership of 204, there were only 68 trained pastors, with 25 evangelists and 111 lay readers. The Papua district committee minutes during the next years demonstrate that the struggle to provide improved training at Lawes College was not easy. The entrance standard was raised in 1951 to primary standard 4, and in 1959 to standard 6 English and arithmetic. The length of training was reduced to three years in 1954 because of staff retrenchment, and in 1960 more funding was still needed to increase it to four years. There was a long-lasting need for more staff, more buildings and more money if the church was to have the number and quality of ministers it needed. Lawes College would later be closed and the United Church's training for ordained ministry consolidated at Rarongo College (formerly Methodist) near Rabaul. By 1974 in a paper entitled "Hard Lessons from Abroad", Jack Newport, having visited Rarongo, cited the college for its educational method in which training was being contextualized "integrating in one theme study of the Bible, theology, ethics and contemporary issues", and said that "because it begins and ends with the latter, the study is always relevant". By 1975 graduates of Rarongo were studying towards masters degrees at Richmond, Virginia, USA, and at the University of PNG. They were part of an extensive programme of overseas training for ministers of the United Church. Meanwhile, in 1958, Chalmers College had been established at Veiru to meet the need that still existed for a place of training at a lower academic level for people who would become pastors and who would not be expected to proceed to ordination.

At both Lawes and Chalmers Colleges and later at Rarongo there was a significant programme of training for the wives of students. This included such matters as Sunday school, conduct of worship, women's and youth groups, handicraft and health. As these women went with their husbands to lead local churches they made significant contributions to church, family and community life.

Education

During the early 1950s it became increasingly clear that if on the one hand congregations were to be strengthened, and on the other hand church schools were to meet the rapidly growing need for higher standards, then ministers must be freed from school work, and the church must place adequately trained specialist teachers in its schools. In 1956 the LMS Board was at last able to provide a teacher trainer to be located at Lawes College. In 1957 the district committee decided that single men could be accepted for teacher training and in 1959 that teacher training for single women would be established on the Port Moresby head station, and that the programme in which theological students undertook a full year of teacher training would be terminated. In 1964 Ruatoka College (named after the pioneer Rarotongan missionary) was opened near Saroa to train men and women to be teachers. Within Papuan culture this decision to train single men and women in the one place was a significant step. The college was closed after the formation of the United Church so that all teacher training could be consolidated at Gaulim College in the former Methodist area in New Britain.

Papuan men and women were also being trained for medical work. In 1949 it was decided to train young women as infant and maternity welfare nurses at Fife Bay. Training was later extended to Kapuna and Orokolo and transferred from Fife Bay to Mailu. The pioneer work of the churches in this field was recognized by the *South Pacific Post* in an article published in 1954. In 1948 a doctor had been appointed to open a hospital at Kapuna, and the training of aid-post orderlies was undertaken there soon after a new doctor was appointed in 1954. At Gemo Island hospital orderlies became proficient in the care of tuberculosis and leprosy patients, while at Moru Anne Brown, the nurse-wife of the district missionary, provided less formal training for young women who assisted her in a significant medical ministry.

Yet another area of specialized training was opened up to what had been the Papua Ekalesia when church union brought with it access to the Christian education training centre at Malmaluan. At this centre near Rabaul men and women, mostly young, were equipped for ministry with youth and children, and some ministers did post-graduate training in these areas. The concentration of training institutions in New Britain was felt keenly by many Papuan folk as a loss to their own region.

Thus the capacity of the church to provide leadership to the church and service to the community was increased over the years as it appointed to work in villages and towns better trained ministers, school teachers, nurses, aid-post orderlies and Christian education workers. In many places the members of the church were taking an ever-increasing place in courses for deacons and youth leaders, in women's work, Sunday school teaching and church administration, and in Bible study groups. In at least one case a CWM minister was appointed full time for lay education and continuing education for ministers across three districts for a year or two.

During the early post-war years missionaries felt frustrated because of chronic shortages of staff as they faced the great needs of the people and the opportunities in Papua for outreach and evangelistic work. In a message to the directors the minutes of the 1951 district committee contain a strong complaint that Papua was "the cinderella of the LMS fields". They claimed negligible benefit from the Board's "New Advance" programme and compared this with the ability of other mission agencies to move into the newly opened up highlands regions. They called for a more enterprising policy "to enable us to win this country for Christ and his kingdom". In this connection it is interesting that in 1975 George Hood commented after a secretarial visit that 30 percent of CWM's overseas staff were serving with the United Church in Papua New Guinea and the Solomon Islands. [17] The following figures show this increase — in 1950 there were 19 overseas staff at the district committee; 26 were present in 1960 and in 1963 the minutes listed 41 overseas staff (some of whom were missionaries of Presbyterian churches in Australia and New Zealand). While missionary staffing in other areas of LMS work was being reduced the directors were responding positively to the opportunities for Christian service that presented themselves in this land that had more recently been opened to major contact with other cultures. Indigenous workers were being trained and were at work teaching and nurturing and reaching out, but the assistance of expatriate workers with a wide range of skills was still needed.

There was expansion as well as internal development. Within Papua new work was established in the hinterland of a number of districts, only some of which can be mentioned here. Inland from Moru the love of God known in Christ Jesus was proclaimed and the church was planted in the rugged Kunimaipa valley as Bert Brown (district minister at Moru) made his frequent and extraordinary footslogging journeys, taking love and practical help, and inspiring others with his enthusiasm and devotion to the people, and as pastors from the coast stayed to establish the work. Stan Dewdney (district minister, Orokolo) in a letter to the LMS general secretary, Stuart Craig, in 1956 wrote about an inland trip to the feared Kukukukus as a well worthwhile effort. Carriers were Torchbearers and young church members from coastal villages — "volunteers for a new beginning to the inland mission campaign". In the delta area medical patrols from Kapuna went hand in hand with the work of the minister at Aird Hill, and again there was evangelistic outreach and new work was established. Early travel was by canoe, but in 1973 Peter Calvert (doctor at Kapuna) reported that use of a float plane enabled contact with more villages and was less disruptive of the hospital's training programme. In the delta area there was also outreach by students and their wives from Chalmers College. Beyond Papua in towns like Lae, Goroka and Wewak, contacts were made, ministers appointed and church life developed. The bishop of the urban region was able to report to the assembly in 1976 that the region's evangelism programme was making an impact, but that expansion was limited by the availability of staff. Chaplains were appointed to the University of PNG and the police force, and ministry was extended to the growing number of tertiary educational institutions. The task of evangelism and service in the name of Christ had to be carried out to an increasingly wide range of people in an increasingly varied set of educational, social, economic and cultural circumstances.

Contribution of individuals

Mention has been made of the considerable contribution by the LMS to the growth of the church through its provision of missionary workers. What manner of people were these missionaries? They came from England, Scotland and Wales, from Australia, New Zealand and islands of the Pacific, from Switzerland and India. They were Congregationalists, Methodists, Anglicans, Presbyterians and members of the Society of Friends. They were artisans, ministers, nurses, educators, doctors, secretaries and accountants, and in many cases wives and families came with them. They were men and women with a remarkable range of experience, attitudes and skills. If some comments are made only about a few, that should be read as reflecting on the talents of all. There was Bert Brown, linguist and botanist, walker, practical man and visionary. There was his wife Anne, a nurse who like so many wives kept the home and the head station going while Bert was away. There was Bob Beavers, teacher and trainer of teachers, described by a colleague as having the most brilliant intellect of any he had ever worked with, sometimes fearsome in debate, gentle with children and practical with buildings and engines. There was Myra Kennedy, a nurse who had the attitudes, skill and personality to guide Gemo through a time of great change both medically and in relation to the department of public health. There was Stan Dewdney, fluent in the Orokolo language, close to the local people, who with his wife Maidie maintained a warm lasting relationship with expatriates in the area, such as traders and government workers. And many more who in their own ways encouraged and taught pastors and teachers, visited villages on mountains and in valleys, on coastal plains and river deltas, managed busy head stations, healed the sick and supported those whose spirits were low. Encouraged by the words in the front of the Bibles given to them by the LMS "go, live agreeably to this word, and publish the gospel of Jesus Christ according to your gifts, calling and abilities", they helped the church to grow as the body of Christ.

Increasingly complex interchurch relationships

The simple days when by and large the major non-Catholic missions worked in discrete areas and each related to one or two mission boards began to come to an end. There were a number of reasons for this.

The movement of indigenous people crossed the old boundaries of mission influence so that Methodists and Lutherans, Anglicans and LMS people worked together, lived in close proximity in strange towns, talked about their faith and sometimes worshipped together. They saw that they were of one faith, and began to ask why the churches and missions from other lands divided them.

The opening up of the more heavily populated highland areas in the 1950s led to an influx of missionaries from other parts of the church. There were Baptists and the Salvation Army, there were "faith-missions" of a variety of backgrounds and expressions, many of whom came without regard for the work already being done, even when it was well established.

The Second Vatican Council of the early 1960s contributed to radically changing relationships with the Roman Catholic Church. In 1948 the district committee had been concerned about what it called the "Roman Catholic menace" and was worried about the low standard of available anti-Catholic literature. It looked for a sounder approach to teaching about the differences.[18] Not long after Vatican II there was a healthy ministers' fraternal in Port Moresby that embraced a wide spectrum of Christian churches, including the Roman Catholics. In 1969 at Kerema there was a service for commonwealth youth Sunday led by the Roman Catholic priest and a CWM teacher, Jenny Young.

The ecumenical movement was influencing the understanding of mission and the relationships between what had traditionally been "sending" and "receiving" parts of the world Christian community. In 1959 the Presbyterian Church of New Zealand agreed to work in Papua, within the context of LMS work. Their first appointee arrived in 1962 and became the district minister at Saroa. The Presbyterian Church in Australia sent a youth worker to Port Moresby in 1960 who worked within the LMS district. Discussions with Methodists resulted in a Methodist minister being appointed to the Koke area of Port Moresby in 1960 working closely with the LMS minister there and in 1963 the Papua church assembly sought and received secondment of a Methodist minister to teach at Lawes College.

By the time the United Church in Papua New Guinea and the Solomon Islands was inaugurated in 1968 that new church related to no less than five cooperating mission boards in three countries. They were CCWM, Presbyterian churches in Australia and in New Zealand and Methodist churches in those two countries. This was a complex set of basic external relationships for a new church.

There were still further working relationships with churches in the Pacific. From the earliest days of LMS work in Papua workers from Pacific island churches had been in the forefront of the missionary endeavour. In 1955 the government limited the number of mission workers from the South Seas to 22. They then numbered 18 pastors and four nurses of whom 17 were from Samoa, one from Nauru, three from Niue and one from Tokelau. In 1960 the total was the same, all but one being from Samoa. In 1963 at the invitation of the church assembly the Cook Islands Church, after a gap of some forty years in its missionary service in Papua, sent a minister for extension work in the remote Morehead river area of the Daru district. There he joined Kwalahu Momoru and Mea Osea, two Motu ministers on whose good work Gordon Price (district minister, Daru) had commented in 1960. It was indicative of changing relationships that in 1949 the Samoan church proposed that there be a separate field of service for their missionaries. This was rejected by the district committee as being impractical. The committee proposed instead the possibility of Samoan-led sub-regions under white missionaries. In 1952 the committee rescinded its previous minute in the light of a growing sense of responsibility in the more advanced Papuan communities for the work in the more backward areas. It looked forward to continued Samoan participation in the work of the whole field. This did in fact happen, and in some districts Samoan and other Pacific island ministers took oversight of what might have been called sub-regions of districts. A perusal of minutes and correspondence in the early 1950s indicates that working relationships between the Samoan and some European missionaries were not always good. The reasons for this were complex. In Papua the pastor was not accorded the same high place in society that was given in Polynesia. There were sometimes differing attitudes to village people and the work. Some Europeans seem to have handled the three-way cultural mix better than others. But there were those who enjoyed happy and fruitful relationships with their South Seas colleagues, whose ministries as pastors, nurses and carpenters were greatly valued.

For a period of about eight years from 1946 the Church of South India (CSI) had a missionary working in Papua. This enterprise was fraught with a variety of obscure difficulties. Leonard Hurst, LMS secretary in Australia and New Zealand, in a letter in June 1947 said that it was clear that the CSI missionary would work under the "rules, procedures and practices of the PDC" (Papua district committee). It seems that there was a feeling that India wanted to "take over" the Gavuone part of the LMS field. But a minute of the board of mission of the CSI in January 1949 said that it desired "to participate in building up the church of Christ in Papua. We have no desire to initiate a separate church in Papua." It wished "to work in close cooperation with the LMS as a sister society... and... request LMS to allot us a field within their area as a base for our work". In the mind of the district committee it was clear that it controlled all the work in Papua. One suspects that the language used was not always understood by the other party. It seems also that there were interpersonal relationships which were less than could be desired and these led to things that were quite harsh being said, and the participation of the CSI in the work in Papua came to a sad end. It is a fact of life that sometimes the best intentions of the churches and their missionaries are subject to quirks of human nature and language difficulties, and that these are not confined to people of any one race.

Within Papua and New Guinea there were established the Melanesian Council of Churches (MCC) in 1965, the Christian broadcasting association in 1965 and a churches medical council in the early 1970s, to all of which the successor church to the LMS mission belonged. An Evangelical Alliance was also formed, and whilst the United Church did not become a member it was yet another body to which the church had to relate at times. In 1964 the Papua church assembly, preferring to use its limited resources through membership of the MCC, decided not to seek membership of the Pacific Conference of Churches or the World Council of Churches at that stage. By the end of our period the United Church was a member of, and active in, both. A Papua church assembly minute of 1966 refers to a conference on religious education in schools run by the MCC and the Evangelical Alliance, and to reciprocal arrangements with the Catholic bishops' conference for access to pupils in each other's schools. In 1969 the YMCA had established work in Port Moresby. It was based initially on the United Church's head station at Hanuabada and very close cooperative arrangements were enjoyed.

In 1974 the United Church's Christian education centre at Malmaluan was reported to have had students who were from the New Hebrides, the British Solomon Islands, West Irian as well as Papua New Guinea, and who included Anglicans and Presbyterians besides people from the United Church. [19]

These increasingly complex ecumenical relationships were not just difficult in terms of church structures. There lay behind them and across them a vast range of differences of culture and language, of traditions and understanding, of administrative practices and competences, and of material and people resources.

Church union

Mention has been made of the formation of the United Church in Papua New Guinea and the Solomon Islands which was inaugurated in Port Moresby in 1968. By almost any standards progress towards union was rapid. In 1958 the Papua district committee noted union negotiations in Australia and suggested there should be discussions with the Methodists in Papua and New Guinea to seek all possible ways of union and cooperation. Cecil Gribble, general secretary of the Methodist overseas mission in Australia, welcomed this initiative and it was supported by Norman Cocks, the LMS secretary in Australia and New Zealand. The district committee in 1959 noted meetings with Kwato and with the Methodist overseas missions about matters that included theological training, patterns of cooperation and integration in Rabaul and work at Koke, Port Moresby.

In a significant move for a newly independent church the first assembly of the Papua Ekalesia in 1962 decided to establish a church union committee with power to begin discussions with the Methodist church and Kwato, and with the Evangelical Lutheran Church of New Guinea and the Port Moresby United Church. This latter consisted of two congregations that had been pioneered by the LMS, ministered largely but not only to expatriates and had been linked into the United Church in North Australia, which was a cooperative venture of Australian Congregational, Methodist and Presbyterian churches. A minute of the assembly read:

> That believing that the union of the different churches is in accord with the revealed will of God, and with humility for our divisions in him, we hereby pledge ourselves to work and to pray for organic union with churches of other traditions which have been established in Papua.

Reatau Mea, the much-respected chairman of the assembly, is reported to have responded to some who were saying that the Papua Ekalesia should first become established more soundly by saying that movement towards union should go ahead "before we become too set in our ways".

In 1963 a standing committee on church union, consisting of representatives of the Papua Ekalesia, the Port Moresby United Church and the four Methodist districts (one of them in the Solomon Islands, relating to the Methodist Church in New Zealand), went quickly to work. It corresponded with the CWM and with the united churches and the churches negotiating towards union in a number of countries. The discussion papers and draft documents it produced were translated into many local languages. A broad range of comments on them were received from the participating bodies. It produced a statement of faith which, said its report of March 1965, "should have within it the elements to meet the challenges to the Christian faith in the modern world". It was "an attempt to set out the minimum basis for union... We now state the basic essentials of the faith, later the church in its life can make its own confession to meet particular needs." The report noted the strong impetus for union that came as people from widely separated areas met, and that for these people denominational differences became an embarrassment, and there grew a strong desire to be united. The report presented a statement for adoption which included these words: "We regard union not as a matter of expediency, but of obedience to Christ who is the Head of the church, and that this demands our response now." No obstacle was to be allowed to prevent union. It was important to establish a strong united Christian church to become an effective witness to Christ's reconciling power in the community.

To one who was involved in these negotiations this conviction that Christ wanted the churches to be united to achieve his reconciling purposes, and the determination that therefore union *must* happen, characterized the whole process. Several aspects of the government of the new church deserve mention. There were congregations with their church meeting and their leaders meeting. These were grouped in circuits with their circuit meeting, attended by representatives of the congregations and branches of the work, and led by a circuit minister. Regions were larger administrative units, each led by a bishop and having regional synods. The assembly was led by the moderator. It was the assembly that related directly with mission boards and overseas churches. Bishops were appointed by the assembly, on the nomination of synods, for periods of six years and were eligible for reappointment. Their work was to be primarily pastoral. Of the first six bishops two were Australians and four were indigenous people, whilst the first moderator was an Australian.

In the designation of regions there was one interesting departure from the norm of a geographic basis. An urban region was created with responsibility for the work in Port Moresby and those towns that were outside traditional areas of work of the church. These included places like Lae, Goroka, Wewak and Madang. It was an attempt to take seriously the fact that in these places where people from across the country lived, and where life was vastly different from that in the villages, ministry would face different demands and require different expressions.

For some who had lived and worked within the relatively small Papua Ekalesia the United Church was large and difficult to work in. Peter Calvert, a doctor working in Kapuna in the isolated delta area of Papua, put it this way: "The missionaries have given a cumbersome and efficient form of organization, with too much dependence on the clergy."[20] He saw weaknesses in the Papua Ekalesia and went on:

> Church union... emphasized and magnified these weaknesses, giving a more cumbersome, more expensive, more remote form of government.... Many ordinary church members, indigenous and expatriate, feel sad about the effect it has had. It has certainly weakened the work of our region at the district and circuit level.

Percy Chatterton, in a letter about the 1973 assembly, wrote:

> On the whole the United Church is progressing well. But as I see it, it is facing two problems. The first is to maintain adequate contact between the head and the hind legs — a problem the dinosaur died of... our average congregation is now less aware of, and less involved in, the life of the church as a whole, than it was when it was part of a much smaller body stretching along the southern coast of Papua. The second problem is cost....

The first assembly of the United Church met in 1968. At that assembly Leslie Boseto, the first bishop of the Solomon Islands region, is reported to have said:

> If you are planning for the immediate future, grow bananas, sweet potato... If you are planning for some years ahead, grow coconut, rubber... If you are planning for eternity, grow men. So the work of the church in this country is to help men and women to grow.[21]

The church in the world

What was seen by people both within and outside the church as being the church's role in a society of villages and towns, of races and cultures, business enterprises and government associations in which it was set? H.J.E. Short, in an undated paper from the period 1941-50, described it thus: "The purpose of Christian missions is to bring a Person to the people.... The word was made flesh and dwelt among us..." In 1973 in a paper on "Health in the Ministry of the Church" William to Kilala, then United Church chaplain to the university, stressed the total ministry of the church involved in body, mind and spirit. "The totality of man must be dealt with." He was critical of "narrow views of God's activities". George Hood commented on what he saw as a honeymoon relationship between church and government and said: "I felt that the church was aware of the dangers,... and the need to preserve its prophetic role."[22] A paper prepared by the assembly officers of the United Church for a consultation with cooperating churches in 1974 was titled "Life in All Its Fullness". It talked about development that is "mental, physical and social (Melanesian in community and spiritual relation with God and others)", i.e., "development to the fullest possible extent of the community and environment in which we live".[23] A report of an evangelism consultation in December 1975 saw the need for renewal of the church and evangelistic outreach to go along with help for the needy through social and economic action and political involvement. Paul Hasluck, then Australian minister for Territories, was reported in the *South Pacific Post* in 1959 as speaking about government funding of educational and medical work by missions and saying that "missions bring something else to medical and educational work... it had to do with leading a better life and learning to help other people". [24]

Any church which seeks to be engaged with society across the whole spectrum of daily life inevitably arouses opposition, and the United Church, as before it the LMS mission and the Papua Ekalesia, with its record of social service, found some vocal critics. An editorial in the *South Pacific Post* of 7 March 1952 claimed that some Territorians (a name given to expatriate residents) think "the missions have been allowed to get too strong a hold on the secular and religious education of the natives". They looked for some control of the missions and there was talk of "religious cranks" and the dangers of allowing such people to "roam at will among backward people", and of low educational standards. The editorial did, however, acknowledge that magnificent work had been done by some missionaries. In mid-1957 an editorial in the same paper suggested concern that in mission schools there was no way of knowing what they were leading young natives to think.

Mention has been made of the social and cultural effects of population movement into the towns. Creation of an urban region by the United Church followed earlier actions in which the LMS made possible the appointment in 1956 of Percy Chatterton to work with urban migrants at Koke, Port Moresby. He had working with him a Papuan pastor who had preceded him to Koke. Later the Koke missionary was to make contacts with migrants in other towns outside the traditional area of LMS activity, and care was taken in the selection of pastors likely to be able to minister in those situations, so different from the accustomed village context. The administration's endeavours to maintain order in Port Moresby, whilst having good reasons, ran the risk of summary denial of human rights, and on more than one occasion the church's ministers had cause to intervene and mediate. Ian Stuart makes reference [25] to the Port Moresby community development group that in the late 1960s worked with migrants living in squatter settlements to assist them in developing the ability to gain security and more acceptable living conditions. That group was largely the work of members of the United Church. George Hood noted that in response to urban drift and its attendant social evils there was a strong response by the church through evangelism, open-air meetings and hostels. [26]

Difficulties in the growing towns had, and still have, a particular visibility in Bougainville. In 1969 the *South Pacific Post* was reporting disputes over forced land resumptions in favour of the big copper mining project at Panguna. [27] Villagers had stormed the mining site. Later Hood said that the price of Panguna was "disintegration of the traditional community, despite efforts to avoid it,... the pollution of the river system,... the infection of rootlessness and loneliness, the problems of money and leisure." [28] The churches had responded with a shalom coffee bar, and there was joint use of a building provided by the Bougainville corporation. A church with meagre resources tried, but with hindsight its efforts did little to overcome the basic, deep human and material problems of Panguna, which were to lead to tragic violence by 1990. It is interesting, writing in 1992, to note that the moderator of the United Church is still making efforts to mediate in that situation.

Land disputes were a problem in a number of places. In the New Guinea islands region of the United Church, Bishop Saimon Gaius and the moderator wrote to the CCWM and the administrator protesting over the use of force to expel squatters at Mataungan, and putting forward the need to reallocate land to them. The writer recalls that Gaius placed himself physically between the angry contending parties at one stage. In 1974 he was to say in relation to the transfer of church land at Vunairima to village people: "It is the United Church's policy to relieve land shortage where possible by returning to village ownership land that is not being used by the church."

Towards autonomy

This was a period in which the old colonial system with its domination of indigenous people by white powers was rapidly disintegrating. The church was a part of the whole movement towards autonomy, independence and national dignity. It is arguable that the LMS's way of working through local meetings and leadership, to district councils and an assembly that crossed language barriers and cultural differences contributed to the people of Papua developing a sense of their identity as one people, and that the formation of the United Church crossing even greater distances of space and culture meant that here at least was one significant body of people growing towards a national identity and commitment. A reading of the *South Pacific Post* of the period reveals a succession of names of people who made their impact on political and social life and were prominent in the life of the Papua Ekalesia and the United Church; Oala Oala Rarua, Toua Kapena, Willie Gavera, Tau Boga are some; there were many others. Heather Boardman (CWM educator), in a circular written at Malmaluan in 1974, comments on visiting villages and being "asked to run studies on independence and self-government despite the fact that a government political education officer had been there". Percy Chatterton made a submission to the constitutional planning committee which reflected his long experience with, and understanding of, Papuan ways and style. He looked for a constitutional structure for Papua New Guinea that would "in the long run be productive of real and lasting unity". He wanted a decentralized system which would leave "touchy" issues to the provinces and a national "high council" with limited powers. In retirement he became a member of the first parliament of the independent nation, and was a confidant and counsellor to many of its members.

The period saw a vigorous development in the work of women in the church. In 1954 the district committee accepted "with great joy" the suggestion of the Papua church assembly that women be ordained. In 1956 the Saroa district had ten women deacons, and some were on the village council. A Papua Ekalesia women's fellowship had been formed. In 1960 there was strong participation in the Women's World Day of Prayer and the Fellowship of the Least Coin. There was an interesting Papuan angle to this last when some of the women said that you really could not pray about the needs of others and at the same time limit your giving to the least coin. In 1962 an annual Papua Ekalesia women's fellowship conference was held. In 1974 the assembly of the United Church decided that there would be a representative of the women's fellowship in its membership, and synods were to look to ways of including women and youth in their representation.

From the outset the women's fellowship was not seen as an auxiliary for raising funds and doing practical chores. It was a fellowship for study, worship and action. It provided serious consideration of issues that affected family and community. Once again, it crossed barriers and gave encouragement and strength. The LMS board in its survey for 1956 highlighted the significance of what was happening when it said: "In several areas women are playing an increasingly important part in the life of the church. To all who have been familiar in bygone days with the status of Papuan women, this can be no less than a miracle of grace."

For the youth too, life was changing rapidly and dramatically during our period. One early response to their needs was the formation of the Torchbearers organization. Bert Brown (Moru) had played a strong part in its formation, and Torchbearers had an important part in patrols to the inland areas of some districts. The Torchbearers' promise contained these words: "To carry the light, ever burning bright, by the power and might of Christ my Lord." Its aim, as expressed by district committee in 1958, was "to develop Christian character in our young people so that they may become worthwhile members of our church". In some of the towns there were hostels for young people studying at secondary or tertiary levels, and also for workers. They helped fill a social need, and in some cases were young people's first introduction to the gospel and a realization of their own worth in the sight of God.

The church had always, to some degree at least, tried to respond to the health needs of the people. Often this was through the limited efforts of missionaries who were ministers, and through their wives who may or may not have been nurses. Happily, during the post-war years the church took up the need to provide trained medical care. By early 1975 George Hood was able to report that in the Papua mainland region (the old LMS area) the church had seventy workers in aid posts, health centres and clinics, and that there was now little place for expatriate nurses. [29] During most of the period the work at Gemo Island hospital, which cared for patients with tuberculosis and Hansen's disease, grew. A physiotherapist was made available by the LMS, and specialist doctors, one doing corrective surgery, were provided by the administration. But by the end of the period the hospital was closed, because new treatments meant that these patients could be cared for at home. The church also had doctors at Kapuna and at Mailu, and at Kapuna in particular doctors Peter and Lyn Calvert strove to provide a service that was appropriate to the local culture and financial constraints. They, as others, saw the hospital as "a centre of Christian life and witness" with its first responsibility "to run an efficient medical service at Kapuna and in the delta villages". [30]

As the period progressed localization and indigenization became increasingly prominent matters, both in the church and in the wider community. Mention has been made of the increasing role of local people and the changing role of missionaries in the life of the church. There was an early tendency to place Papuans in positions formerly held by Europeans without special preparation for the task. In 1970, Frank Butler, who was to be replaced as bishop of the urban region by Riley Samson of Daru, wrote to Lindsay Lockley (CCWM secretary in Australia and New Zealand) about the "electrical political climate" and that there was a crucial need to implement plans for localization. In 1972 a meeting of Melanesian bishops was concerned that expatriate church workers should be seen as co-workers. By 1972 Leslie Boseto was saying that we had to talk not about localizing a position but indigenizing the church. At the same time Ian Fardon (then a minister in the Port Moresby circuit) in a paper for the same consultation wrote that "overseas standards do not mean perfection". The true nature of the church can be established "when locals take pastoral care of people from other lands". The *United Church News* in 1975 quoted Leslie Boseto (moderator):

> Our church has been struggling with the true meaning of localization which will eventually give shape to the truly indigenous church.... By an indigenous church we mean the church working and growing in a local place in a way that is natural to that place.

In 1973 Bernard Thorogood (general secretary of CWM), writing to London from Port Moresby, considered that "the fully indigenous aspect of the church seems to me to touch the local life of the church rather than its central organization. There the expatriate mould was fixed in the first few years of the union and naturally becomes very hard to break." He also wrote: "There have been expatriate personalities not always as sensitive as they might be to other points of view." Leslie Boseto, in a paper he presented to the board of ecumenical mission and relationships of the Presbyterian Church of Australia, talked about "a time for pulling down and destroying some unreal parts of the church's structure and organization". In retrospect these criticisms had some force, but then those structures and organizations were set up in the context of a land where no indigenous nationwide structure or way of acting and relating had previously existed, and at a time when there was a very strong expatriate influence.

Worship and culture

It might be expected that if Melanesian culture was being reflected in the life of the local church this would show in services of worship. Yet the *Book of Worship* of the United Church (published 1979) draws attention to "the fact that the order of service (for holy communion) contains very little to show that it is intended for use in Papua New Guinea and the Solomon Islands". The book encourages leaders to experiment in adapting the service to the Melanesian environment. The writer recalls that when that order of service was being written early in the life of the United Church, Reatau Mea, a leading ministerial member of the liturgy committee who was from Port Moresby, commented on the Methodist practice of going forward to receive the elements, that in his (Motu) culture that would be indicative of a greedy person. There is not one culture for all the people of the United Church. In some village churches there were indications of the influence of the local culture on worship and other aspects of church life. In many places men and women sat on opposite sides of the church. In a remote village in the southern highlands older women saw to it that all women removed their blouses before receiving the sacrament. Why? The *peroveta* songs introduced to the Motu people by Rarotongan missionaries strongly influenced worship. They were owned by many while western style hymns were not. In holy communion local food and drink were commonly used in place of bread and wine. These included baked yam or sweet potato, coconut water, clear fresh water. Dance became a joyous expression of worship on special occasions such as Easter and the bringing of the annual offering. Deacons exercised pastoral care and led prayers in their clan groups. There tended to be a style of preaching that was down to earth and practical, as the languages tend to be. Bernard Collins (CWM minister at Mendi) in a circular letter in 1976 wrote that "church leaders, equivalent of elders, did not need to be elected. They are those who are natural leaders amongst their *wantoks*, and keen to look after the people spiritually. They gather to visit lapsed members."

In a land of many languages it is not surprising to find that translation and the writing of texts in local languages received a lot of attention. In 1946 Percy Chatterton produced material in the Motu language for use in schools. It included Bible stories, Motu history and legends that contained a moral. In 1955 and 1958 the district committee listed an increasing number of texts being prepared, some in the vernacular. Translation of the scriptures was a strong element in the work of some missionaries. In

1967 Bert Brown reported to the LMS directors that translation would be the main task for his last three years in Papua. At one stage he was translating (and illustrating) the whole Bible into Toaripi, and was translating portions of scripture into another two languages never previously written. During our period at least six others were translating the Christian scriptures into Papuan languages, two of them full-time, and local people were working with them.

The world in which the mission and then the church lived and worked was a changing world, yet it was a world in which much of human nature and human ways continued as of old. The church continued to face that world and its challenges. Education had to be improved, and it was. Appropriate medical services were still needed, and to the extent possible were provided as a part of the church's Christian witness and service. Youth had their hopes and ambitions raised by the evidences of European wealth. They were often let down when schooling ended and there were no jobs. The church nurtured and taught and encouraged as best it could, in circumstances beyond its control. It proclaimed the gospel of Jesus Christ, it evangelized, and in the later years was enlivened by the Holy Spirit movement, and some were helped along the way.

We have seen the growth of talented, well trained, dedicated leadership. We have seen a church determined to act positively for the unity and health of its nation and its people. We have seen a church open to the moving of God's Spirit. The church was sometimes criticized for meddling in politics, sometimes sought out by politicians for counsel and advice.

We are reminded that in Papua New Guinea, as in other lands, the church which acknowledges Christ as its Head is a church of people with all the weaknesses and strengths and differences of race and language and culture that go with being human. And we have been reminded that as Christian men and women from different places and cultures work together under the Head of the church, lives are changed as God in his love moves in individuals and communities to achieve his own good purposes.

NOTES

[1] Ian Stuart, *Port Moresby — Yesterday and Today*.

[2] C.D. Rowley, *The New Guinea Villager*.

[3] *South Pacific Post*, 2 April 1955.

[4] In this text "Papua New Guinea" refers to the whole eastern part of the New Guinea mainland and its associated islands. "Papua" refers to the southern part of the whole. It is the former Australian Territory of Papua and the name familiar in LMS circles. "New Guinea" refers to the northern part of the whole. It is the former Trust Territory. This is the term which has been commonly used in Australia since the second world war for the whole. "Papua New Guinea" is the name of the independent nation and is so used, with PNG as its abbreviation.

[5] *South Pacific Post*, 26 September 1950.

[6] *South Pacific Post*, 2 April 1955.

[7] *South Pacific Post*, 6 February 1959.

[8] *South Pacific Post*, February 1963.

[9] *South Pacific Post*, 5 May 1969.

[10] Jenny Young, 1974 report to LMS directors.

[11] H.J.E. Short, unpublished document.

[12] P. Chatterton, *Day that I Have Loved*, Sydney, Pacific Publications, 1974, p.75.
[13] *Ibid.*
[14] Minutes of the Papua district committee, 1948.
[15] N.F. Cocks, unpublished document.
[16] Frank Butler, 1959 report to the LMS directors.
[17] George Hood, report on secretarial visit, 1974-75.
[18] Minutes of the Papua district committee, 1948.
[19] Circular letter from Heather Boardman, 1974.
[20] Peter Calvert, 1971 report to the CCWM.
[21] Myra Kennedy, circular letter.
[22] Hood, *op. cit.*
[23] Unpublished document.
[24] *South Pacific Post*, 6 November 1959.
[25] Stuart, *op. cit.*
[26] Hood, *op. cit.*
[27] *South Pacific Post*, 6 November 1969.
[28] Hood, *op. cit.*
[29] *Ibid.*
[30] Peter Calvert, 1971 report to the CCWM.

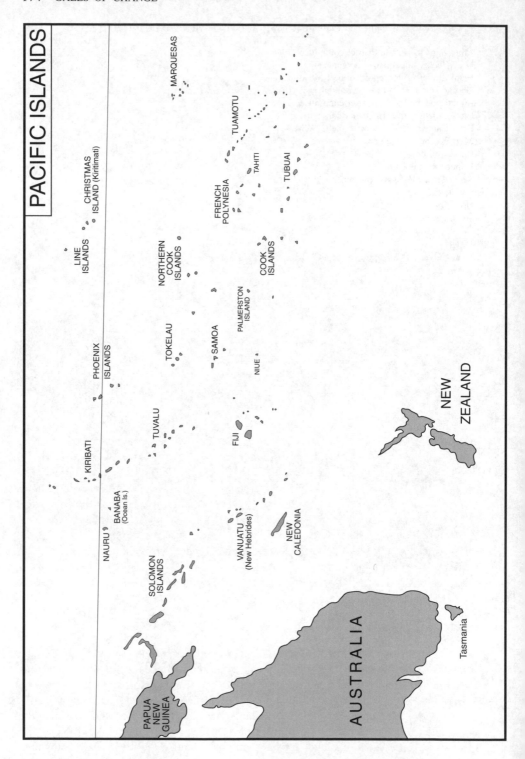

PACIFIC ISLANDS

9. Ways across the Ocean

John Garrett

Island churches of the South and Central Pacific

The London Missionary Society's (LMS) directors thought of the South Seas, their first mission field, with affection. The remote Pacific, like its name, was less tumultuous than Africa or Asia. The second world war shattered the stereotype. Between 1942 and 1945 the Japanese and Allied armies invaded tranquil lagoons and sleepy villages. Clashing colonial powers made many Islanders familiar with mechanized killing, military profanity, American black power, and Japanese offers of co-prosperity. In churches in the United Kingdom, Australia and New Zealand, colourful descriptions of the LMS's ship "John Williams", peacefully conveying the gospel among peoples depicted as "children", became more than ever inaccurate.

Administrators in London, Sydney and Auckland were obliged to adjust policies, budgets and programmes; leaders in the island churches shaped the government and interior life of their churches, using cultural forms of their own to incorporate missionary patterns of worship and church government. The result was mild culture strain and radical reassessment of the meaning of the fundamental principle of the LMS. Converts were expected to choose between presbytery, episcopacy and independency. But what if the form of the church included tenaciously preserved Polynesian or Micronesian customs, organization, and types of authority, such as the Samoans' respect for their many *matai* (village chiefs), or the protocol of the *maneaba* (community meeting house) in Kiribati (the former Gilbert Islands)? Such issues surfaced repeatedly; mission became church. Islanders, determined to conserve valued elements of custom and culture, established deliberate psychological distance, which had to be bridged as the LMS became the Congregational Council for World Mission (CCWM) and then the Council for World Mission (CWM).[1]

The Cook Islands

The expansion of the LMS from southeast to northwest Oceania was initiated in the Southern Cook Islands in 1821 by the young church on Raiatea in the Society Islands under the leadership of John Williams. Papeiha, the first missionary to land, spoke a form of the Polynesian language which links Tahiti and its surrounding Society Islands with the Cook Islands group and New Zealand (Aotearoa). New Zealand governed the Cook Islands as an overseas territory from 1901 to 1965, along with Niue and Tokelau. Before New Zealand appeared in the islands, the LMS had enjoyed a religious monopoly and moral authority among the *ariki*, the high chiefs. The "mission period"[2] had been marked by close relationships between chiefs and missionaries; the elegantly translated Bible paved the way to literacy. Pastor-teachers were trained in the South Pacific's longest continuing theological institution, Takamoa, at Avarua on Rarotonga. The paternal influence of the LMS declined under successive New Zealander resident commissioners. New Zealand introduced British statute law, reduced the power of the chiefs and gradually took over control of secondary education in schools at Tereora on Rarotonga and Araura on Aitutaki. Direct influence from Britain slackened, although New Zealand, a country of marked imperial sentiment, recruited Cook Islanders as soldiers in both world wars. During and after the second world war, Islanders met harsh and crude white people abroad; at the same time they consolidated a feeling of kinship with fellow Polynesians in New Zealand and Tahiti.

At a deeper level, the local culture and language, with attachment to many pre-Christian social structures and customs of the islands, persisted. Warlike drumming, dancing, feasting and sexual frolic were often frowned on by white LMS missionaries,

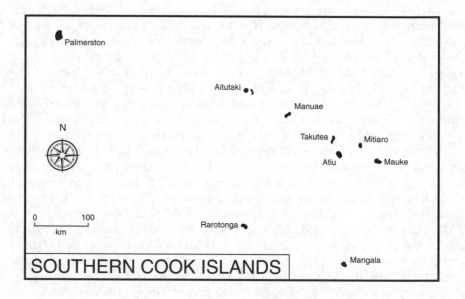

but were practised and preserved outside the church buildings. Prolonged community verbal jousting and Bible dramas derived from parent churches in Tahiti were encouraged by the LMS. The office of deacon, introduced from British Congregation-alism, provided status which would otherwise have been whittled down along with the traditional authority of the highest chiefs. Pastor teachers, as in many parts of Polynesia, were still widely credited with forms of holiness and judgmental sacred power formerly focused in priests *(ta'unga)* in the pre-Christian religion of ancestral and nature spirits. Moral behaviour, particularly illicit brewing of strong alcohol (bush beer) made from plentiful wild oranges and associated with adolescent premarital sexual adventure, was deplored and disciplined by LMS missionaries who came from a minority church background in the British Isles. In British Free churches, conformity to standards of monogamy and temperance was expected from members. In the Cook Islands, and elsewhere in the South Pacific under the LMS, genuine faith in Christ as Saviour and Lord often went along with more flexible moral standards often tolerated in majority churches. Missionaries from "gathered churches" presided over people's churches full of what they regarded as cheerful sinners. The experience gave the missionaries pain. Their complaints re-echo in reports of secretarial visits.[3] They also found themselves fighting a rearguard action against officers of the New Zealand administration, who introduced schooling in which the Bible was no longer central in the curriculum. Some chiefs, who traditionally had control over land which they had greatly increased during the mission period, took up commercial opportunities in the citrus and copra trades. The missionaries' discipline over alcohol abuse and sexual misdemeanours diminished as New Zealand court jurisdiction took over.

The ships "John Williams V, VI" and "VII" called less frequently than before. Communication by sea and increased travel between the Cook Islands and New Zealand led to missionaries taking furlough in Auckland and reinforcing connections with the Congregational Union of New Zealand and its office bearers, who also worked closely with the LMS's Australian and New Zealand Committee (ANZC) — later the Standing Committee for Australia and New Zealand (SCANZ) of the Congregational Council for World Mission.[4] New Zealand Congregationalists were directly interested in Cook Island affairs through the training of Islander troops in New Zealand during both wars and the gradual growth of migrant Islander churches in New Zealand.[5] R.L. Challis, who had been a missionary on Rarotonga in the 1940s, played a leading part in helping to gather Islander churches in New Zealand. As the need for ministers trained beyond standards hitherto set at Takamoa emerged in increasingly literate island societies, several Cook Islanders attended the Congregational Theological College in Auckland. The principal, Howel Nicholas, from the United Kingdom, reported on the progress of students from the LMS areas in the South Pacific.[6] The relationship with the small Congregational Union in New Zealand altered when a substantial section of Congregationalists united to become part of the larger and more influential Presbyterian Church of New Zealand.

The LMS missionaries in the Cook Islands after the second world war stayed for shorter periods than in the past, as in other parts of the Pacific. A walk-out by six of the ten students of Takamoa College in 1954 was a protest against the imperious regime of the then principal, W.G. Murphy, a former LMS missionary to India, who was described in confidence by the LMS foreign secretary Stuart Craig as "the last of our 'great' paternalists". The incident, preceding the arrival at Takamoa in 1955 of Murphy's more pastorally adaptable successor, Bernard Thorogood, revealed growing impulses towards self-government within the Cook Islands community and church.[7] Thorogood, the future general secretary of the CWM, had come to the Cook Islands in 1952. He began on the island of Aitutaki, but assumed Murphy's post on Rarotonga as Murphy reluctantly withdrew and finally retired in 1957. Thorogood strengthened training, youth work and general administration. He furthered the work of the Boys' Brigade which Challis had begun. Young men from the Cook Islands, dressed in Boys' Brigade blazers, visited the United Kingdom. The peaceful meetings and disciplined activities of the organization channelled marshal motives in what had been a warrior society, providing a peaceful alternative to the spirit of Islander army units in both world wars.

One of Bernard Thorogood's achievements was his upgrading of standards in English at the Takamoa Theological College, where he also supervised the opening of a newly designed chapel. During his stay, when he travelled extensively in the islands, including the northerly atolls, the earlier dominant role of the LMS was being challenged by Latter-day Saints (Mormon) missionaries and by the work of Roman Catholic teaching sisters with experience of the related culture and language of Tahiti. At the same time, Cook Islander leaders with LMS background and ancestry, bearing names widely known in Polynesia, the Marsters family of Palmerston Island and the Henry family on Rarotonga and Aitutaki, were taking positions of leadership in the church and an emerging island nation. William Marsters trained for the ministry at the New Zealand Congregational College and advocated continuing contact with New Zealand as preferable to wider contacts with other Pacific island churches. When the Cook Islands became an autonomous country, its citizens maintained full civil rights in New Zealand and continued to come and go freely. Bernard Thorogood, whose eyes were on future prospects of cooperation with other island churches within and beyond the LMS, led in helping the church to frame the constitution of the Cook Islands Christian Church as it became independent and began to reach out, in the 1950s and 1960s, towards participation in the emerging Pacific Conference of Churches and the Pacific Theological College.

When Thorogood left to go to Kiribati (the Gilbert Islands), the church nurtured under the LMS, still embracing a nominal 80 percent of a population of 12,000, faced a future which was potentially open both to New Zealand and other parts of the island Pacific.

Niue

The people of the small up-thrust coral island of Niue guarded their identity from pre-contact days against all intruders. They were converted to Christianity by Niueans and Samoans. Their remoteness and difficulty of access helped them to continue their isolation under the two first long-staying LMS white missionaries, the brothers W.G. and Frank Lawes. The culture of Niue absorbed and transmuted English Congregational independency in eight small districts with traditional chiefs. Before the coming of the gospel, the people feared and placated ancestral spirits. Local pre-Christian holy men had been guardians of customs and the land; their sacral authority and feared taboo systems united the warring districts within an overall system of belief. The Lawes brothers translated the Bible and introduced the training of pastors at Vailahi. Congregational forms of church order were instituted in each district and a fresh set of taboos clustered around observance of Sunday as the holy sabbath. Celebrations and gift exchanges commemorated the coming of Christianity and stimulated the collection of offerings for the new God and the LMS. Internal fighting ceased. Niue's people acquired a reputation for mildness, and even docility. The office of deacon devolved on those recognized as community elders.

By the end of the second world war, because a surplus of pastors had been trained at Vailahi, those not employed as appointed ministers in the settlements around the island nevertheless acted together, as appointed deacons, men of sacral significance, to exercise church discipline. Resident white missionaries between and after the two world wars strove to break down this new system, which they deplored as being legalism rather than grace. Visiting LMS secretaries Stuart Craig and Ernest Edwards held long talks with the island elders and the missionary. Youth work and programmes of direct Bible study in groups were designed to break down the influence of older deacons and encourage youth to know the gospel promise of new life. The missionaries also tried to revive the church meeting as a counterbalance to the negative rule of elders. Struggle against local misconceptions of the gospel, which reflected more of the Old Testament than the New, dominated this period in mission-church relations. [8]

Niue as a New Zealand protectorate remained abnormally sealed off from the outside world. Access by sea suffered from infrequent calls and lack of safe and easy moorings. The "John Williams", calling at least annually in its southern circuit, symbolized the fatherly oversight and care of the LMS and its directors, who were easily imagined on Niue as a distant but benign group of ministers and deacons with considerable holiness and power. Niuean missionaries travelled on the little ship; some crew members were from Niue. Worship in the district churches was marked by hearty hymn-singing and the use of simple forms of prolonged prayer. Preaching often deprecated breaches of Sunday observance. The authorities of the port area at Alofi, where the LMS missionary and the New Zealand administrators lived side by side, tended to be resented by deacons of other districts. English Congregational church order, which ceded power only on a consultative and limited basis from local church to Congregational unions, fitted neatly into the context of old rivalry between districts. Clan and congregational leaders clashed over land and prerogative. Visitors from London endeavoured, with several of the post-war missionaries on Niue, to hew out a new constitution for the church as a whole, making a theologically solid statement of faith the starting point. Stuart Craig's secretarial reports at this time spell the words "the Faith" with a capital, showing how, in the 1950s, 1960s and 1970s, British Congregationalism tended to rally to reaffirm a central core of credal orthodoxy, following a period of liberal modernism in the first half of the twentieth century.

Adolescent sexuality and breaches of marriage vows proved resistant to missionary discipline. The LMS missionaries frowned more gravely on sexual waywardness than on pride, greed or gluttony. On Niue, baptism and reception into full communicant membership tended to be postponed well past adolescence because pre-Christian norms of premarital behaviour among younger people continued under Christianity. A sense of shame did not prevent it. Missionaries tried to regulate marriage and deter sexual experiment by tightening island legislation governing marriage and divorce, but with no marked success. When New Zealand introduced improved health and child-care, population increase was relieved by emigration. Improved shipping, trade, and the building of an air strip led to an exodus. Niue's people retained the status and right of residence as New Zealand citizens. At the end of the period more of them lived in New Zealand than on Niue.

Two of the worst recorded Pacific hurricanes struck Niue in 1959 and 1960. Functional but flimsy traditional houses and churches were devastated. The disasters concentrated attention on a neglected speck in the ocean. In 1959, when patterns of mission assistance were yielding to new forms of interchurch aid coordinated through the World Council of Churches (WCC), the LMS was able to appeal through WCC headquarters in Geneva for relief and rebuilding. The director of interchurch aid in Geneva, Leslie Cooke, was aware of Niue's people and church; he had been general secretary of the Congregational Union of England and Wales and was in touch with the LMS. [9] The requirements of a small island after the disasters were relatively modest by comparison with the scale of relief needed after such events on greater land masses. The WCC's appeal brought funds and assistance to reconstruct housing and churches more durably. Rebuilding was not easy on account of local rivalries on Niue and the need to coordinate with the New Zealand administration's plans. The work went on for several years. When the first Pacific Conference of Churches and Missions met in May 1961 in Western Samoa, wider prospects of similar ecumenically administered aid opened up for many churches through the then projected Pacific Conference of Churches. [10]

In other ways also Niue glimpsed wider horizons. The LMS shared local concern about the coming of the Latter-day Saints (Mormons) to the island, complaining of their use of money and educational opportunities to proselytize. The Seventh-day Adventists also had a small church on Niue, led originally by Vai Kerisome Head, a woman converted to Adventism while a schoolgirl in the Papauta school of the LMS in Samoa. [11] The New Zealand authorities could hardly be asked to intervene to fend off the Mormons, or the Roman Catholics, who arrived later than the Adventists and built a pleasant church. In New Zealand Mormonism was strong and was growing among the Maori people. Some irony attended LMS pleas for regulation of the inroads. Where was the boundary to be fixed between desirable religious liberty and undesirable socially disintegrating proselytism?

Samoa

In the larger and culturally distinct Samoan islands the church founded and nurtured by the LMS was a source of mingled pride and concern. Norman Goodall, then of the London staff, had once referred to Samoans as "these baffling Polynesians". [12] The complex Samoan social system was difficult for Europeans to comprehend. It was known as the *fa'a Samoa*, the Samoan way, and had absorbed the introduced Congregational model of pastor, deacons and church meeting. Power in Samoa depended on contests between knowledgeable chiefly orators who assigned titles to the highest ruling chiefs, the *ali'i*. The LMS maintained social prestige through important orator groups on the island of Savai'i and in the neighbourhood of Leulumoega and Malua on the central island of Upolu. All Samoa's attractive villages were connected by family marriages, the custom of the *malaga* or group excursion, the accumulation and exchange of gifts, and ceremonial feasting. The *matai* system regulated social life. The *matai*, elected heads of extended families, had status and authority within each village. Under the old religion of ancestral and nature spirits, holy men with prophetic powers were allied with the *matai* in sharing wealth (crops, pigs, finely woven mats), and in policies pursued in peace or war. The system was held together by subtle etiquette and prerogative, which shaped the lives of men and women, young and old. The Samoans took pride in their melodious language and stylish public display.

Before the first world war, such experienced missionaries as William Clarke, John Marriott and James E. Newell were respected by Samoans. They understood many aspects of Samoan culture and leadership and stayed in Samoa for many years. [13] LMS missionaries between and after the wars stayed for shorter periods. They acquired a more limited understanding of the Samoan way. The council of elders, established in Newell's time, enabled Samoans to confer within the church and to evolve a nucleus for its future independence. The Samoa district committee of missionaries, which retained final authority, was often involved in wordy conflicts and stand-offs with the elders (the *toeaina*). In the period after the second world war the council of elders evolved further into the powerful financial and general purposes committee, in which a majority of Samoans could outvote the LMS missionaries on financial questions. This body's increased weight — and the relatively short periods of service of LMS missionaries — help to explain the processes by which the mission developed into the independent Samoan church.

In 1946, the anthropologist Derek Freeman was commended to A.M. Chirgwin, the then general secretary of the LMS in London, as a person who "will talk to you quite frankly about the past and present of our church here. He has great respect for the industry and integrity of the 'giants' in the history of our mission, and he realizes, as well, and even better than the present staff, that we aren't touching the roots of Samoan life at all."[14]

New Zealand administered Samoa during the interwar period under a League of Nations mandate, which passed to the United Nations after the second world war. Most of the LMS missionaries, however, still came from Britain. Between 1945 and 1960 problems of distance plagued the mission at a time when Samoans, having passed in 1930 through the experience of a threatened armed revolt, the Mau, were ready to take things into their own hands in the churches, especially the church of the LMS, which had contributed the most significant lay leadership to the Mau. The Society's schools, including the Malua Theological College and the nearby secondary

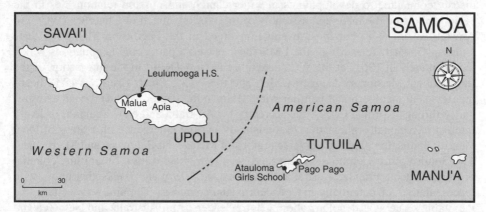

high school at Leulumocga, produced junior civil servants who worked within the New Zealand administration. This Malua-Leulumoega educational tradition provided many local villages, as well as church and government offices, with people whose English was adequate, but whose Samoan was impeccable.[15] In the church, as in the country, a nucleus of future local leadership was forming. Missionaries, except in American Samoa to the east and on the large island of Savai'i, tended to cluster at Malua, at Apia, the main port and capital, and (in the case of women missionaries) at the Papauta school for girls. The Papauta school ranked with Malua in educating an elite. Sometimes, to the chagrin of some male missionaries, its teaching staff included women who stayed longer than they did and excelled more rapidly in Samoan. The records of the district committee of the LMS showed traces of cantankerous personal relationships within the group as a whole.

Finance

Financial resources in London were severely limited after the second world war. Samoan local funds, largely collected by the system of thanksgiving offerings, increased at a time when London's capacity to support Samoa financially came under strain. Until 1970 LMS deficits recorded in London were always substantial. Between 1945 and 1965, overall South Seas recurring expenditure rose from £6,604 to £30,028; the cost of running the "John Williams" more than doubled in the same period from £7,079 to £15,384. [16] Malua, with its tradition of training Samoan pastor teachers to go to serve in Tuvalu, Kiribati and Papua, became a source of irritation to LMS staff, though they took pride in its record. Some of its students continued to go as missionaries to Papua, the point furthest afield, but by the 1950s the deployment and financial support of these missionaries was a source of contention. The general purposes and finance committee, run by predominantly Samoan votes, held local purse-strings. Since the missionaries went on the "John Williams V, VI" and "VII" to Papua, the Society bore the burden of transport there and back. The Papuan church provided support in Papua. London sought greater participation from the Samoan church in the cost of equipping and sending the missionaries. The Samoan church maintained that this should continue to be met from London funds to which Samoa contributed every year. The tension persisted until the cost of maintaining and running the "John Williams" became prohibitive and it was withdrawn from service in 1971.

Little direct reference was made by the preoccupied members of the Samoan district committee to developments in wider church and mission relationships in the period following the inaugural assembly of the World Council of Churches (WCC) in Amsterdam in 1948; but those events converged in the Pacific on Malua in 1961. Norman Goodall, formerly of the LMS staff, played a part in the negotiations which led eventually in 1961, at the WCC assembly in New Delhi, to the integration of the International Missionary Council (IMC) and the WCC. Stuart Craig, as LMS head-quarters staff member most familiar with affairs in the Pacific Islands, became aware, partly through Norman Cocks, the secretary for Australia and New Zealand, of lively interest in regional organization in the islands and the emergence of a sense of local identity uniting the otherwise diverse regions of Melanesia, Polynesia and Micronesia. The South Pacific Commission appeared — a new organization linking the colonial powers, Britain, France, Australia, New Zealand, USA and the Netherlands, with representatives of potentially independent island countries. The aim was welfare; the inevitable sequel was decolonization. Church leaders from Australia and New Zealand participated as consultants in the work of the commission. The importance of the churches, Protestant and Catholic, in a Christian majority area, was conceded. Governments were also generally willing to relieve the burden of unprofitable administrative investment in tiny colonies by granting independence and making way for multilateral aid through United Nations channels.

The churches in the United Kingdom, Australia and New Zealand, including those supporting the LMS, began to think in similar terms at a time when income was falling. The prospects of alternative funding for the small churches in the Pacific, using multilateral resources opened up through the WCC's division of interchurch aid, loomed larger after 1960. Prospects of more advanced training for the ministry in all the LMS churches in the South Pacific led to advocacy within the LMS early in the 1950s of a central theological college which could serve the needs of the Cook Islands, Niue and Kiribati (then still called the Gilbert Islands). The level of training at Takamoa in the Cook Islands was being raised by Bernard Thorogood, who shared Craig's interests and concerns. The World Council's New Delhi assembly enhanced the prospects of effective regional organization in each continent. Eyes turned towards the Pacific Islands, the cinderella of the third world, the last to be invited to the ball.

The idea of a central college was then expanded. Missionary administrators in Australia and New Zealand, particularly the LMS, the Methodists and Anglicans, conferred with each other, with London and Paris, and with the mission board of the United Church of Christ, the successor body to the American Board of Commissioners for Foreign Missions, which served churches in the Marshall and Caroline Islands. Could there be a regional council or conference of Pacific churches? Could a central college be ecumenical?

A crisis in relationships

Such questions, posed ahead of time, were among the most important confronting the first Pacific Conference of Churches and Missions, jointly sponsored in 1961 at Malua in Samoa by the WCC and its division of world mission (the former IMC). Malua's facilities and central situation commended its claims as the site for the meeting, which was attended and stimulated by the presence of leaders and speakers such as Lesslie Newbigin and Hans-Ruedi Weber. Pacific Islanders who emerged as a team of leaders for the future included Mila Sapolu and Vavae Toma of Samoa, Sione Amanaki Havea of Tonga (Methodist), and Setareki Tuilovoni of Fiji (Methodist). At the Malua conference the future Pacific Conference of Churches (PCC) and Pacific Theological College (PTC) were conceived, and born shortly after.

The meeting took place as Malua itself was passing through a crisis in relationships. In 1954, John Bradshaw, an able English theological teacher, went to Samoa to become the principal of Malua. He served the church in many ways. He drew up a new book of worship incorporating ideas from similar projects in the United Kingdom. Aware of current thought in ecumenical circles, he advised the church on the revision of its constitution, which was adopted when it became independent of mission control as the Congregational Christian Church of Samoa in 1962. He also cooperated closely with Samoans in raising standards at Malua and in looking for future candidates for the ministry who would be selected and sponsored on the basis of academic promise. In this way he aimed to keep future ministers abreast of well-trained laity prepared in government schools in Apia and elsewhere to serve the emerging state of Western Samoa. In 1959, when he was on leave in the United Kingdom, Kanape Falatoese acted as principal at Malua. Falatoese compiled in Samoan a history of the Samoan church, which was published in 1961. Vavae Toma became, at about this time, the general secretary of the church.

When John Bradshaw returned to Malua after furlough he requested the finance and general purposes committee of the church to provide scholarships for two candidates he marked out as promising students for Malua. The committee declined; such special sponsorship by the whole church would have created a precedent. Students at Malua were traditionally sponsored and supported by their extended families and home villages. The system followed established custom. It led in several directions. Pastors, though prestigious, could not be *matai*. Only those called to serve local churches could be ordained. The large surplus of trained but not ordained ministers entered into the life of the Samoan people and served their people and villages in other ways. Bradshaw's proposal was rejected because it was not the Samoan way, the *fa'a Samoa*. Ministers were part of a system which regarded them as being an offering for the church. Trainees were given by extended families, supported by extended families, and were at the disposal of their extended families and of the *matai* and the deacons, when their training was complete. The two views of human resources were not compatible. Dr Bradshaw resigned on principle, though in the end he stayed on to help the church transitionally until 1965, partly because he was involved in arrangements for setting up the Pacific Theological College in Suva, Fiji, following the Malua conference of 1961. The college offered an alternative route to a more academically advanced ministry for selected students who had already passed through Malua. Vavae Toma, as general secretary of the church, told Stuart Craig of the LMS that "while appreciating and trusting Dr Bradshaw, it is felt that there is not agreement with him when the unknown background of the Samoan people is involved".[17]

On another front, John Bradshaw participated in 1958 in negotiations over the alarm felt by the LMS, the Roman Catholics and the Methodists over an influx of large numbers of short-term Latter-day Saint (Mormon) missionaries into Samoa to pursue the building programme of their Utah-based church. Representatives of the three churches conferred with (Sir) Guy Powles, the New Zealand high commissioner, who was preparing the way for Western Samoa's political independence. They contended a ratio should be set in relation to the numbers already belonging to their three churches, with which Powles agreed. He was supported by Tamasese and Malietoa, two of the highest title-holders, who were partners with him in the transitional government. He fixed a ratio for Mormon entry of one in 200 relative to the 1956 census of the Samoan population, citing the need to avoid eventual "social disharmony". The controversy was made more intricate by the fact that American groups brought in money which assisted with the balance of payments in economically precarious island communities.[18]

Sensing coming changes in the Pacific, the LMS in 1955 appointed Richard Matanlé as its roving representative and intermediary among the churches. He made useful contacts with missionaries and the churches until 1959, when the LMS said he should settle more definitely in one place. His preference was for Auckland, where he would be near the Congregational Union of New Zealand. The Society decided he should instead be the minister of the small English-speaking Samoan Protestant church on the "beach" at Apia, continuing his wider advisory and "trouble-shooting" role while based in Samoa. He declined and resigned. The decision was based on a conviction that the work had to be done in the islands for the islands. In the transition from mission to church, the strategic central importance of populous Samoa had to be recognized.

Interchurch relationships

Relations between the two Samoas also demanded attention. American Samoa, a naval colony since the turn of the century, was nevertheless part of the single Samoan cultural system. There, as in Western Samoa, the church established by the LMS was a majority. Local extended family relationships reached across the border, but in 1950 the United States made its naval colony a dependent civil territory. A small Methodist church had seeped into American Samoa earlier in the twentieth century, not without protest and negotiations with the LMS. In 1949, following the change from naval government, American Methodists sounded out prospects of settling an American minister there to meet the needs of American households. The Australian Methodists were not enthusiastic about cooperating. Official Methodist-LMS relationships within Samoa were not cordial. The Australian Methodist Missionary Society was anxious not to sour things further; the ecumenical movement was influential on the missionary agenda in Australia. LMS resident missionaries on Tutuila, including the staff of the Atauloma school for girls and Hugh Neems, the resident missionary, who ran a bookshop for the LMS, watched over developments and affirmed the unity of the people of the LMS in the two Samoas. Some Samoans within the church, one congregation in particular, accepted oversight by a pastor of the Assemblies of God, who also made explanatory friendly approaches to LMS missionaries in the territory.

Administrators of the United Church of Christ in the USA, which had by then incorporated the American Board (Congregational) into its structures, were in contact at intervals with Stuart Craig. They discussed the possibility of sending a representative to work with the LMS, to meet the needs of Americans in the administrative and business community and keep a watching brief for emigrant Samoans in Hawaii and on the US mainland. By the late 1960s the new ties with the United States had become stronger. In 1970 Emerson Sanderson was sent by the United Church Board for World Ministries in the United States, with the assent of the CCWM, to care for the congregation of resident Americans and help with youth work and Christian Endeavour activities of the Congregational Christian Church in American Samoa as a whole. The scene was being set for later establishment of the separate Congregational Christian Church of American Samoa, with its own administration, external relations and theological college. Family and church connections to a large extent spanned the gap thus established, through the cohesive *matai* system. Colonial diversity was acknowledged, but an underlying unity, established by being Samoan and Congregational, was preserved.

Interchurch relationships in Samoa improved perceptibly after 1961. In that year the first sessions of the Second Vatican Council heralded a new openness alongside the impressive events of the Malua conference. In the 1960s, though more slowly later, ecumenical goodwill became the flavour of the decade in the churches. At the same time, internal constraints were imposed by long-standing groupings within the Samoan culture. Methodist-Congregational rivalries were associated with power exercised by important groups of orators, at Lufilufi to the east of Apia, where Methodism was strong, and Leulumoega (and in northern Savai'i) where the LMS was dominant. Roman Catholic associations with alternative high titles were also often in the back of the minds of the Catholic faithful. The London Missionary Society in Samoa was frequently in the grip of a seeming paradox; Congregationalists in England and Australia believed in a gathered church, a protesting and purifying force against compromise with a majority culture. In Samoa the church became itself a majority, defending the people's culture.

The 1970s brought many Samoan Congregationalists into prominent roles within the assemblies and staff of the PCC and the PTC. Fijian and Tongan Methodists also participated alongside them in wider ecumenical initiatives. As air transport and multilateral funding offered Samoans this new place in wider church life, they responded. In the many villages of Samoa "subsistence affluent" gift exchange and the influence of internal village journeying led to the building, near imposing churches, of substantial ministers' houses and stores, where prized fine mats, textiles and trade goods could be exchanged among Samoans with accepted ceremony. Competitive giving, as sponsored originally by the LMS in the month of May, ensured self-support for the church as a whole and for selective assistance to mission and interchurch aid beyond Samoa. The abundant collection and distribution of this internal system was at times disrupted by hurricanes or by delayed decision-making within the assembly, the *fono*, of the church. Among Polynesians, the Samoans are distinct and insist on their unique qualities. Women leaders among them, more especially those who are titled or pastors' wives and cooperate with each other, display a special style encouraged by the LMS in the girls' schools at Papauta and Atauloma, where the emphasis was on partnership between girls trained there and the pastors and *matai*. The fundamental principle of the LMS, that the people should themselves determine the form of the church, has been followed in both Samoas in a fashion not foreseen, but ultimately recognized and accepted, by the LMS, the CCWM and the CWM.

Tuvalu (the Ellice Islands)

The nine islands of Tuvalu are flat atolls. The British linked them administratively, as a protectorate, with Kiribati (the Gilbert Islands) to make a single convenient colony. The language spoken by the people of Tuvalu is Polynesian; in appearance and culture they are a Polynesian people, distinct from the Micronesians of Kiribati in language and physique. The LMS treated Tuvalu as an outstation of Samoa. The islands were converted mainly by the work of Samoan pastors trained in Samoa at Malua and serviced by visits of the successive "John Williams" ships. Between 1912 and 1920 two British missionaries served in Tuvalu as school teachers, one on Funafuti, the other on Vaitupu. Between 1920 and 1958 the islands were without a resident white missionary. Under Samoan care, the church language was Samoan and the Samoan Bible and hymns were used in worship. To the people, Samoan was the "holy" language; they understood it because it was like their own, but there was a gulf between the everyday language and the language of Sunday worship and the Bible.

After the second world war, when the atolls of Tuvalu experienced an influx of American troops, white and black, and bombing raids, the realization of the unity and identity of their islands expanded greatly among the population of between five and six thousand. They were virtually all by then Congregationalists. They felt drawn unnaturally in two directions. The British had linked them colonially with their Micronesian neighbours of Kiribati to the north; the work of the LMS had joined them in the church with Samoa. External connections were further complicated by the sending to Rongorongo, on Beru in the Gilbert Islands, of some Tuvaluan students, such as Pastor Lusia (Rusia), who served in both Kiribati and Tuvalu. In the post-war years to 1957, Tuvaluan laymen, some of whom were local civil servants in the unequally yoked together colony of the Gilbert and Ellice Islands, stressed the need for white resident missionaries to help them to stand on their own feet in this tangle of external relationships. [19]

In 1957 the plea was met. Brian Ranford was appointed and took up residence on Funafuti in 1958 with his wife Margaret (Peggy), a nursing sister. In the years before he eventually left the Pacific in 1970 he worked with the people of Tuvalu to achieve their aims for the church. He learned the language and helped to prepare a book of worship. He began, with local help, a translation of the Bible into the vernacular, beginning with Mark's gospel. Using the newly prepared constitution of the Cook Islands Christian Church as a preliminary model, he drafted a constitution for the future Church of Tuvalu, which was inaugurated in 1968. He assisted in sending Tuvaluan trainees to New Zealand, Malua in Samoa, and later the Pacific Theological College in Suva. They steadily replaced remaining Samoan missionaries. In a curious way his activities were supported by previous developments in education in Tuvalu.

The secondary school for boys at Motufoua on Vaitupu, once run by the LMS, had been resumed by the British colonial government in 1924. The "bluff" (and tough) New Zealand Scot in charge there until 1940, Donald G. Kennedy, established "secular" standards which influenced a generation of laymen who remained loyal to the church and were also involved in the movement for separation of Tuvalu from Kiribati as an independent island state. The influence of Lusia, who had originally been trained at Malua and had taught at the Rongorongo training institution on Beru in Kiribati, also remained strong. He had for a time edited a church paper in his own Tuvalu language — an earlier affirmation of separate identity. Brian Ranford was

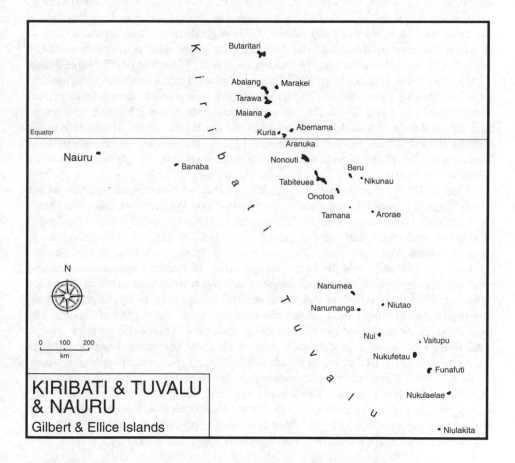

KIRIBATI & TUVALU
& NAURU
Gilbert & Ellice Islands

helped by Iosia Taomia, who was general secretary of the church and a member of the provisional legislature of the fledgling separated colony. In translation work, Alovaka Maui, who had been trained at the Pacific Theological College and in New Zealand and who died comparatively young, joined in translating the Tuvalu Bible. Kamoriki Taba and Kamuta Latasi were among laity active in the movement towards political independence. Officers of the LMS hoped, in the earlier years of Ranford's presence, that the churches of Kiribati and Tuvalu could form a single church structure — an aim which had earlier been part of the policy of George Eastman, who directed training from the institutions on Beru in Kiribati. In the sequel, politics and church life evolved in the inevitable direction — the formation of a small but ethnically distinct nation in which nearly all the people belonged to the same church.

From July 1967 Brian Ranford served as principal at Tangintebu Theological College on Tarawa in Kiribati, until November 1969, while continuing as a consultant to the Tuvalu church. The autonomy of the church in Tuvalu preceded national independence, which came only in 1978, a year before the independence of Kiribati, following protracted negotiations with the British government. In the intervening 1970s, the decade of national independence for many Pacific island countries, Edith Maxfield, who was proficient in Samoan, Gilbertese and the language of Tuvalu, was at the Motufoua school for girls on Vaitupu. She first went in the mid-1950s to Samoa, where she taught at the Atauloma school on Tutuila and came to know Tuvaluan students well. Between 1959 and 1969 she was in Kiribati, teaching on Beru, then on Tarawa. She came to Motufoua to help initiate Elize, a Tuvaluan teacher who had been with her in the teacher training institution on Beru. "Miss Maxfield", wrote Stuart Craig, "sees the possibility of fulfilling her earlier ambition of being a resident missionary in the Ellice Islands."[20] She worked with enthusiasm among both men and women until she left in 1977. "It's fun being here," she wrote. "I like it very much, and its good to be called 'Masefili' again in the old familiar way! The people in the village make me feel that I belong to *all* of them, and not just to the school as in Rongorongo."[21] She was one of a remarkable succession of women missionaries of the LMS in the Pacific.

Life in Tuvalu continued to be affected by the much-discussed itinerary of the ships "John Williams VI" and "VII". After 1948 "John Williams VI", a refitted ship, proved costly to run and maintain; she voyaged partly in the Cook Islands and Samoa and in the north to Kiribati and Tuvalu. In 1962 a smaller ship, the seventh and last to bear the name, was also based in Suva, Fiji, but spent much time in Kiribati and Tuvalu. Her captain at the end of her service, Richard Beadon, agreed with Ranford that the decisions about where the ship should travel were at times subject to sudden revision. Time had in the past been given to carrying ministers and missionaries internally around among the islands of Kiribati, rather to the neglect of Tuvalu. The coming of air routes and possibilities of using other vessels coincided with rising costs and limited funds for financing the "John Williams". The internal competition for using her between island missions meant that Tuvalu, as the smallest applicant, tended to be neglected. "The only people who seem to have any real concern for the needs of the Ellice church are Richard Beadon and myself," said Brian Ranford plaintively[22] during this last phase of the ship's life, when Norman Cocks, the LMS secretary in Australia, was winding down her operations and negotiating her sale in 1972. The LMS era of "sailing missionaries" had spanned almost 150 years.

Kiribati (the Gilbert Islands)

In the Micronesian atoll culture of Kiribati social life is regulated by the participation of the people in local corporate debate and decision-making in the *maneaba*, an open building where the elders, representing major extended families within a village, meet according to a clearly laid down pattern of balanced authority. The church, founded under the LMS, with its structure of pastors and deacons, has overlapped and supplemented the life of the community, particularly in the four southern islands of the group and in the central islands, where Protestantism has continued to be dominant. The Roman Catholic Sacred Heart Mission is stronger in the northern islands. Rivalry between the two missions has been strong — and has diminished gradually since the Second Vatican Council, especially since the Roman Catholic Church became a full member of the Pacific Conference of Churches in 1975. Some tension between Protestants and Catholics had been eased earlier when the high commissioner for the Western Pacific revoked the closed district order of 1936, which had barred Roman Catholic entry into some southern islands, an LMS preserve, to avoid social conflict. The World Council of Churches' general secretary, W.A. Visser 't Hooft, had conveyed the Roman Catholic protest. He voiced some uneasiness over the negotiations in correspondence with the International Missionary Council. What balance should be struck between resisting proselytism and permitting religious liberty, especially as minority Protestants were at that time being attacked for proselytizing among nominal Roman Catholics in South America? LMS headquarters secretaries were defensive on the issue but Emlyn Jones, of the LMS in Kiribati, had few regrets. He applauded the measure as welcome and inevitable and said "opposition from other denominations might have a bracing effect on our adherents". [23]

The progress of the Kiribati Protestant Church towards independence in the late 1960s reflected its will to localize leadership and take on a character derived from life on the scattered atolls. This desire was present already in the earlier community at Rongorongo on Beru, led by William Goward and his successor George Eastman. Goward worked in Samoa before coming to Kiribati. He worked through Samoan missionaries, including Pastor Iupeli, who was ordained in 1905, became the vice-principal of the Rongorongo training institution, and remained in Kiribati through the second world war. The many Gilbertese pastors trained before the war regarded their vocation in all the atolls where they were installed during voyages of the "John Williams" as nourishing a church close to their own customs and the *maneaba* — neither English nor Samoan. This sense of local custom and distinctiveness ensured the church's survival in the brutal conflict between the Japanese and the Americans during the war. [24]

The second world war and after

When Eastman, who did so much between the wars for the church, returned from a wartime stay in New Zealand, he was allowed to enter and make his survey in chaplain's uniform, "wearing six pips". He found that wartime destruction on Beru had not been a total disaster. He met his helper, Iupeli, noting with regret that he had not been as heroic in his relationship with the Japanese as Alfred Sadd, who had been executed by the Japanese after he remained at his post when the British colonial government required white Britishers to leave. Eastman incurred some displeasure in LMS circles by suggesting it would have been wiser for Sadd to have obeyed the orders of the administration and leave with the rest. He himself, as an expert on Kiribati, continued to advise and recommend on post-war policy, sometimes annoying his colleague John Spivey and his successor Emlyn Jones. He went to Suva, Fiji, with his senior Gilbertese friend and adviser Kaitara Metai, who later became secretary of the church in Kiribati. In Fiji he revised the translation of the Gilbertese Bible with Kaitara's help, then retired in England in 1947. [25]

Iupeli (spelt Jupeli by Eastman) was described by him as having suffered a breakdown under the Japanese after being "compelled to sign an undertaking to do nothing in any way hostile to Japan or his life would be forfeit". Eastman said "the subsequent visits and depredations of the Japanese so preyed on Iupeli's mind, that he suffered a physical, and partly a mental, breakdown and had to leave Rongorongo and vegetate in the villages throughout the year 1943". [26] Iupeli's own account of himself is apologetic. He said "there were many soldiers of the Japanese fleet landed at the LMS station and I welcomed them all". [27] He asked to be allowed to take a farewell cruise in the "John Williams" and did so in 1949 before retiring to Samoa. Local accounts on Beru report the courage and independence of his wife Nei Sera during the war and her solidarity with women at Rongorongo in their trials under the occupation.

Beru, until the second world war, had been the heart of the activity of the LMS in the central and southern islands. Its neatly laid out complex, with radio facilities, administrative centre, stores, schools and training institutions, had given justifiable pride to George Eastman and his wife Winifred, its guiding spirits. The LMS, however, was not the first missionary society to work in Kiribati. Hiram Bingham II of the American Board had been the first pioneer, on the island of Abaiang, further north, in the 1850s. The two missions met each other with goodwill and apportioned the field between them. After 1917 the American Board gradually handed over its work to the LMS. On Abaiang a second training centre took firmer shape at Morikao, as Hawaiian missionaries of the American Board gave place to Gilbertese pastors trained first by Americans on Kosrae in the Caroline Islands, and later on Ocean Island (Banaba), the one high island in Kiribati, which was also, early in the century, the administrative headquarters for the whole British colony. When the Japanese fortified the island of Tarawa during the second world war and were dislodged from its western tip and port area at Betio in the terrible battle of Tarawa, they drew attention to its central strategic location for administrative purposes. After the war, the British moved there. The post-war evolution of the pattern of work of the LMS tended to follow suit. John Spivey, with pre-war experience alongside Eastman, remained on Beru for much of his time until he left Kiribati in 1956. Rongorongo, once a significant central point for the "John Williams" and the whole group, became more detached from newly developing centres in the widely dispersed colony under conditions of new and faster communication. In the central islands, Emlyn Jones from Wales, a diligent and thoughtful missionary, lived for much of his time on Abaiang, recognizing its importance for the Protestants of the islands as the scene of "the coming of the light", which was celebrated on Abaiang in 1957, rather later than the real anniversary. The relative inaccessibility of Abaiang was highlighted at that time by the inability of the American Board to send its ship "Morning Star" to attend the commemorative singing and feasting on the occasion; but they sent a telegram. "The Rongorongo era ends. Tangintebu (the new theological college on Tarawa) begins a new chapter in Gilbertese church history," Emlyn Jones wrote in 1960, adding "Gloria in excelsis Deo". [28]

During the 1950s, in discussions about the future of Rongorongo and Morikao, eyes in London and Kiribati had turned towards Tarawa, where new colony administrative headquarters and a port town were emerging. Church administration against this background, when colonial servants were divesting an empire of one of its most distant and economically problematic colonies, called for a worker with patience and ability, who could, in the words of Bernard Thorogood "understand even the most convoluted Whitehall prose". [29] Eric Blacklock, who arrived in 1956 and remained until 1966, was the man for the task. His previous experience in local government in England made him familiar with procedure and protocol. He handled finance and delegated responsibility as he prepared local successors to take over his work. He had a sense of what was politically possible; at the same time he was a dedicated missionary, giving priority to the church. Colonial officials respected him. When the first meeting of the governor's advisory council was held, with the normal flourishes of vice-regal processions and plumes, he found himself installed as a council member in his own right. He was bothered by the fact that the Gilbertese members of the council, who were used to the *maneaba*, could not follow British rules of order and were bewildered by the way business was handled.

One of the main agenda items for the meeting concerned draft legislation to permit the import and sale of alcoholic drinks. Blacklock had ascertained that a recently arrived ship had allocated 29 percent of space in its hold to quantities of this favourite white man's drug, in anticipation of good business in the islands. The churches, including the Roman Catholics, were opposed to moving in one step from a permit system to free sale. Although Gilbertese Protestants and Catholics participated in the meeting, Blacklock's was the one contrary voice when the measure was put. Legislation was subject to the resident commissioner's final endorsement, which he was inclined to give so as not to discriminate against the rights of "the native population". Blacklock, knowing the church's opposition to consumption of sour toddy (fermented liquor of the coconut palm) and imported alcohol, especially on outer islands, drafted protests for the LMS in London, which led to negotiations with the colonial office and the eventual modification of the legislation to control sale and distribution outside major towns in the colony. [30]

Economics, land ownership, education

The episode characterizes one side of Eric Blacklock's work. In dealing with economic issues in the colony, which drew much of its income from an ailing copra industry and from the sale of almost depleted phosphate deposits on Ocean Island within the group, he was realistic and practical. He often advised the government as well as the church. He became familiar with vexed questions about land ownership on tiny atoll strips where every hectare was precious and contested. He saw that retention of the ship "John Williams" was uneconomic. Other ships — and aircraft — could in future do much of the work. He oversaw transfer of the church's main office to Tarawa, alongside government and port installations. He had to negotiate and persuade, dealing with old loyalties attached to Beru and Abaiang. When it was decided to build a new theological college to be called Tangintebu (the sound of the conch shell trumpet) on Tarawa, he superintended the allocation of funds and set up the accounting system for church headquarters. The leaders of the church and colonial servants who were sometimes out of their depth in the culture of Kiribati respected him and were glad of his help. He worked his way out from behind a desk as he handed over responsibility to local leaders of the Kiribati Protestant Church. In 1966 he was appointed as the first administrative secretary of the CCWM in London. In his six years of office at Livingstone House he was able to deal with problems involved in the transition from colony to independent country and from mission to church.

The other architect of the transition to Tarawa, Bernard Thorogood, had already served what he referred to as his apprenticeship, in the Cook Islands, consolidating administration and reviving at a higher level the work of the Takamoa Theological College. He was also a prominent participant in preparations for the founding of the Pacific Theological College, where he was a member of the council and the representative of the LMS. Coming from similar work beyond Kiribati, he was able to advise on framing a constitution for the Kiribati Protestant Church, which, in the event did not include the word Congregational in its name. Its ways reflected *maneaba* custom and gave powers to island councils which were not characteristic of the independency of an older Congregationalism. Thorogood became the principal of the newly built Tangintebu Theological College, where the memorial chapel was named for the affectionately remembered Alfred Sadd. The *maneaba* at Tangintebu showed the importance for the church of accepted local ways. Some of Thorogood's students went on to make their mark at the PTC and within the PCC. He completed tasks begun by Emlyn Jones and others, gathering up lessons learned on Beru and Abaiang and giving responsibility to local church leaders. Within the independent state of Kiribati, constituted in 1979, features derived from the LMS and from Britain survived. The word Kiribati is a local pronunciation of Gilberts; many politicians are church deacons.

Educational policy in post-war Kiribati led to dialogue with the government. On Beru, the high school named for Hiram Bingham fought to maintain standards alongside the work of the government-funded King George V Memorial School on Tarawa. Small subsidies for LMS primary schools in villages came from the government; the LMS said it was not enough and asked, without positive response, for more. Some of the most significant work was done at a less formal level among women. Nurses and health-care workers were trained on Beru. Women's groups learned to prize and pass on traditional skills of weaving, choral singing, local cuisine and to adapt various introduced art forms. The wives of pastors and the women's organizations they often led became a power in themselves in church and social life. Their dynamic singing and rediscovered dancing, with the humour of their speeches on social occasions in the *maneaba*, provided a counterbalance to the more solemn tone of male meetings. May Pateman, who spent many of her thirty years given to the Pacific in Kiribati, continued a tradition of work with women established earlier by Beatrice Simmons, Goward's niece, and by Winifred Eastman. Miss Pateman retired in 1953; her name and reputation live on in programmes she developed and sustained.

The Line Islands were included in the Gilbert and Ellice Islands colony though at a great distance from Tarawa. Subject to drought but rich in fisheries, the colonial power found their value first in telecommunications, with the trans-Pacific cable station being established at Fanning Island, and later in the military field, with Christmas Island becoming the major base for Britain's nuclear weapons testing programme. In the Phoenix Islands permanent Gilbertese settlements, begun in the 1930s, were abandoned in the 1960s and the people resettled, with LMS encouragement, in the Solomon Islands.

Mining

In Kiribati, for many reasons, Ocean Island (Banaba), the one high island in the group, was a special case. [31] When prospectors at the turn of the century discovered the island was mostly composed of calcium phosphate, a highly-prized fertilizer, its unquiet future was inaugurated. The boundaries of the Gilbert Islands colony were extended to include it, whereupon its exploitation as a mine by Arundel's Pacific Island Phosphate Company, later to become the British Phosphate Commission, commenced. At that stage its isolated people had accepted the gospel from missionaries of the American Board, who handed over responsibility to the LMS during the first world war. From then on, Gilbertese missionaries trained in Kiribati served the church, which expanded to include many workers from other parts of the colony who worked in the phosphate industry. John T. Arundel, whose company first exploited the resources, was a British Congregationalist, as were members of the Gaze family, his partners and successors in the British Phosphate Commission. A. Harold Gaze was for 24 years chairman of the Australian and New Zealand committee of the LMS. The Banaban people were deprived of their soil, under the terms of successive agreements to pay very small sums as compensation. A proportion of revenue from phosphate was allocated by agreement to meet administrative expenses in the Gilbert and Ellice Islands colony, which at one stage made Ocean Island its headquarters station. Many workers came from LMS Gilbert Islands churches. The Banaban people suffered grievously under the Japanese, some in forced exile, during the second world war.

After the war it was clear the phosphate deposits would be exhausted within thirty years; restoration of workable soil would be impossible. In 1945, the Banabans, with their own consent, were relocated as a community to a verdant alternative home on the island of Rabi in Fiji. The move was arranged between the British Phosphate Commission and the colonial governments in Kiribati and Fiji. Rabi, where Lever's Pacific plantations had a rather unprofitable copra operation, sold the island at a good price. The people were given civil rights in Fiji and authority to return and reside on Ocean Island if and when they wished. The London Missionary Society, as part of the overall solution, negotiated with the Banabans and agreed with them that they should gradually, over a ten-year period, be integrated into the Methodist Church in Fiji. Their leader, Tebuke Rotan, an ordained minister who had been trained originally at Rongorongo, took additional training in an Australian Methodist theological college. Future ministers were to be educated in the Methodist college in Fiji. LMS missionaries visited Fiji and conferred with representatives of the church and the Methodist Missionary Society of Australia to ease the transition, which was marked by ups and downs, but on the whole successful. Villages on Rabi were named for old home sites on Banaba; the church in one such village seceded at one stage out of nostalgia for the older Congregational system of having one minister to each gathered church; but in time the Methodist conference and circuit system, with stationing by conference, became accepted.

Complications gave persisting pastoral concern to the CCWM during the 1960s and 1970s, when the Methodist Church in Fiji and the Kiribati Protestant Church met with Banaban representatives to attempt conciliation. The Banaban community, convinced it had been defrauded of its land for a pittance and then attached to the Gilbert Islands by a trick, for reasons of avarice, made a claim for independence as a mini-state, contending that Banaba was distinct in language and culture from the rest of Kiribati. In 1975 a short-lived return was made to repossess and cultivate Banaba, where phosphate was then still being mined. Pleas for independence and compensation were made to the British government and courts. Tebuke Rotan, who was a member of one of the most prominent landholding families of the Banabans, led in presenting the submissions, which were disallowed, except for a substantial retrospective *ex gratia* payment. Eric Blacklock, in an unofficial statement he sent to the British government in 1968, after he had returned to London, commented that "there was little justice accorded to the Banabans by Britain in the early years", but also disparaged any attempts to establish "racial or cultural differences between a Banaban and any of the indigenous inhabitants of the islands of the main group". [32]

Nauru

The small island of Nauru is richer in phosphate than Ocean Island. Its people have a distinct language. They are settled in family groups around the circumference. Their life was deeply affected by conflicts among white settlers who jumped ship, married on Nauru and gave their names to families of local leaders in some of the main districts. The first missionary, Tabwia, came in 1887 from Kiribati under the American Board, which later sent Philip A. Delaporte, the pioneer white missionary and translator of the Bible. Descendants of Nauruans trained and sent to the United States by Delaporte were members of the families of Chief Timothy Detudamo and Jacob Aroi and have not forgotten these origins. After phosphate was found by the company of John Arundel, mining rights were transferred by the German Jaluit company to the British. The Protestants of Nauru were associated with Congregational executives of Arundel's Pacific Phosphate Company in Australia and New Zealand, but mainly Australia. The British Phosphate Commission and its executives based in Melbourne (some of whom were active in LMS affairs) provided religious and commercial support for Nauru. The beachcomber period, the original American mission period and the German period, together with the impact of Australia, Britain and New Zealand, were combined in the experience of the people. The Australian connection was severed in the second world war by the cruel interlude of the Japanese occupation. Many Nauruan leaders were deported to Chuuk (Truk) in the Japanese Micronesian empire. After the war, when leaders returned from exile, Nauru was administered by Australia under United Nations mandate until it eventually became an extremely small, but rich, independent microstate in 1968. The story of the LMS, CCWM and the Nauruan church during the post-war years emerged against this mixture of influences and pressures. [33]

After 1945 the church, badly bruised by the exile of its lay leadership and the devastation of buildings, plant and morale on the island, needed rebuilding. John Robinson from Australia, a minister and a trained carpenter, came as the LMS missionary for six years. He was followed by two other Australian missionaries. Between 1953 and 1968 Roy Foreman stayed for ten years, Rex Matthews for another three. During this period, Itubwa Amram, the first Nauruan to become a trained and ordained minister, was in college in Australia and later received a scholarship in New York City, where he renewed relationships with American Congregational churches. When he returned to Nauru in 1956 Foreman acted as his associate. In addition to the main Oro church on Nauru, which was rebuilt with help from the phosphate company after the war, centres for worship existed around the small island; an established tradition of lay preaching provided distinctively Nauruan leadership and helped to preserve the local language. Solidarity with LMS Islander tradition was also shown in missionary service abroad by James Aingimea, who went to work under the LMS at Daru in the Papuan gulf. Many Nauruans who, like Aingimea, later served on the staff of the Nauruan Phosphate Company, were educated in Geelong, Victoria, and knew the Congregational officials of the British Phosphate Commission in Melbourne. As landowners, Nauruans received royalties from phosphate. They did not normally work as labourers in the quarries. Most of the workers in the industry, Gilbertese and Chinese, were separately housed and had their own churches.

The United Nations Trusteeship Council and Committee on Decolonization reported regularly on Nauru's status and claims for independence. Should the island continue to be closely linked with the administering power? Should Nauruans become Australian citizens? Should they be resettled, for instance, on Curtis Island off the Queensland coast, which they inspected warily, gathering hints in the island's vicinity of pockets of Australian white racist feeling? As the questions were asked, the Nauru Protestant Church became a constituent member church within the Congregational Union of Australia and New Zealand from 1958 onward. Goodwill was expressed on both sides, with sympathetic visitation on Nauru by Norman Cocks, the LMS secretary in Australia, and by officers of the Australian Congregational Union. Harold Gaze of the phosphate commission, who had been a trusted figure as chairman of the LMS's Australian and New Zealand committee, died in 1954. The scene was by then already changing rapidly. Head Chief Hammer De Roburt, a deacon of the independently constituted Nauru Protestant Church, contended for the sovereign independence of Nauru and insisted on full ownership and management of the phosphate operations by his people. Independence came in 1968. The price of phosphate on the open market under the new management was more lucrative for Nauruans than the special prices negotiated since the first world war to help British and colonial farmers. Ironically, Japan, which had occupied Nauru in the second world war, became a prime customer.

As the Nauru Protestant Church entered this new era, Itubwa Amram, the solitary ordained full-time Nauruan minister, found his church surrounded by problems associated with suddenly increased affluence. Newly arriving small missions, conservative evangelicals and charismatics from North America, entered Nauru. An abundance of duty-free consumer goods brought problems, including alcoholism and endemic diabetes. A small sovereign state, 21 square kilometres in land area, with a Congregationalist majority within its population of about 9,000, faced attrition through materialism, which is also familiar within the numerically declining churches in Britain and its former colonies, where the LMS was formed to bring the gospel to the South Seas.

In CWM, the former sending and receiving partners now listen to each other and to Jesus Christ, who spoke of judgment, but also said: "Fear not, little flock, your Father's good pleasure is to give you the kingdom."

NOTES

[1] For these issues: Charles W. Forman, *The Island Churches of the South Pacific: Emergence in the Twentieth Century*, Maryknoll, NY, Orbis, 1982; John Garrett, *To Live Among the Stars: Christian Origins in Oceania*, Geneva and Suva, 1982, 1985; *A Way in the Sea*, Melbourne, 1982; and *Footsteps in the Sea: Christianity in Oceania to World War II*, Suva and Geneva, 1992.

[2] Richard Gilson, *The Cook Islands 1820-1950*, (ed. Ron Crocombe,) Wellington, Victoria University Press with the Institute of Pacific Studies, University of South Pacific, Suva, 1980.

[3] Confidential reports of Stuart Craig, 1952-53, 1961, and Ernest Edwards, 1965, 1971.

[4] See p.230, this volume.

[5] J.B. Chambers, *"A Peculiar People": Congregationalism in New Zealand 1840-1984*, Levin, CUNZ, 1984.

[6] "The glorious gospel, a called ministry and a true church in the newer world", comment in type by the Rev. H.G. Nicholas after four years' experience, 1956. LMS archives, SOAS.

[7] Ron Crocombe, "The Theological Students' Walk-Out, Rarotonga", *Journal of the Polynesian Society*, vol. 79, no. 1, March 1970, pp.6-21.

[8] S. Percy Smith, *Niue: The Island and Its People*, Suva, Institute of Pacific Studies and Niue Extension Centre, University of the South Pacific, 1983; J. Garrett, *To Live Among the Stars, op. cit.*, pp.135-38. Secretarial reports (confidential): Craig, 1952-53, 1960, 1963; Edwards, 1966, 1971.

[9] Personal observation, Geneva, 1959, 1960.

[10] Charles W. Forman, *The Voice of Many Waters*, Suva, Lotu Pasifika, 1986, pp.1-8.

[11] Garrett, *Footsteps in the Sea, op. cit.*, pp.210,221-22.

[12] Goodall to Copp, 17 December 1941.

[13] Garrett, *Footsteps in the Sea, op. cit.*, pp.189-202,399-407.

[14] Copp to Chirgwin, 5 August 1946.

[15] J.W. Davidson, *Samoa Mo Samoa; The Emergence of the Independent State of Western Samoa*, Melbourne, Oxford University Press, 1967, repeatedly makes this point.

[16] Information from CWM SOAS files compiled by Barrie Scopes.

[17] Toma to Craig, 12 February 1960.

[18] Details, with churches' submissions, in PAC/20, CWM, SOAS, 1958.

[19] On Tuvalu to 1941: John Garrett, *Footsteps in the Sea, op. cit.*, pp.216-20,410-12; Barrie Macdonald, *Cinderellas of the Empire: Towards a History of Kiribati and Tuvalu*, Canberra, Australian National University Press, 1982.

[20] Craig to Sykes, 6 August 1969, CWM archives.

[21] To Edwards, 29 March 1970, CWM archives.

[22] Ranford to Craig, 3 November 1968.

[23] Emlyn Jones to Craig, 15 March 1954; Ranson (IMC) to Craig.

[24] Garrett, *Footsteps in the Sea, op. cit.*, pp.260-69,428-37.

[25] Many of Eastman's papers are in the Pacific Theological College library in Suva.

[26] Eastman report to LMS for 1944; in CWM archives, School of Oriental and African Studies PAC/29.

[27] Iupeli to Hurst, 2 February 1947.

[28] Jones report to LMS for 1960.

[29] CCWM, *Enterprise*, part 2, 1972, p.32.

[30] Gilbert and Ellice Islands colony information notes no. 40/63, 3 October 1963; Blacklock to Craig, 19 October 1963.

[31] Garrett, *Footsteps in the Sea, op. cit.*, pp.267-68.

[32] E.H.G. Blacklock to Her Majesty's government ("personal views") 2,4.

[33] On Nauru church and people: Garrett, *Footsteps in the Sea, op. cit.*, pp.274-80 (and references) and *A Way in the Sea, op. cit.*, pp.43-47 (and references).

10. Liberation: Hope and Reality

Pearce Jones

Early in the twentieth century the London Missionary Society (LMS) passed responsibility for the Caribbean work to the Colonial Missionary Society (CMS) which gave encouragement and support to the Congregational Union of Jamaica and the British Guiana Congregational Union. After the second world war rapid political change affected all the Caribbean islands, with a passion for independence, an urge for education and pride in the local culture. The USA and Cuba were strong influences and there was much ideological debate. In this context the CMS itself was facing its own "gales of change". It had been founded in 1836 to provide a ministry for Congregationalists in British territories abroad as the empire expanded, and its monthly publication was called the *British Missionary*. In 1956, it changed its name to the Commonwealth Missionary Society, and the publication became the *Commonwealth News*. In noting the change of name, the annual report for 1956 stated:

> The term "colonial" has become increasingly inappropriate as former colonies served by the Society have become dominions within the commonwealth, while it seems certain that the West Indies will soon be accorded similar status.

Ten years later the CMS went out of existence as a separate organization. Together with the LMS it formed part of the Congregational Council for World Mission (CCWM). The 130th annual report presented in 1966 was the final one, and the CMS became the Caribbean and Pacific committee of the CCWM. Ralph Calder, secretary from 1948 to 1956, was succeeded that same year by Ernest J. Edwards, who continued after 1966 as an overseas secretary in the CCWM, and also later when CCWM became the Council for World Mission (CWM).

Guyana

The nation

During the eighteenth century, large-scale importation of slaves from Africa took place to man the highly labour-intensive sugar industry in Guyana. The original inhabitants, known as Amerindians, were pushed aside by the new arrivals. The Europeans were vastly out-numbered, and they feared slave uprisings. This fear increased during the period of the struggle for the abolition of the slave trade and of slavery itself from the 1780s to 1834. Missionaries were viewed with great suspicion, and John Smith, the LMS missionary in Demerara, died in prison in 1824 for his suspected participation in a slave rebellion.

After the abolition of slavery, the emancipated people deserted the sugar estates, and a system of indentured labour was devised. At first these labourers were of Portuguese origin, but they left the estates as soon as their period of indenture — usually five years — was over, to take part in retail trades. Some Chinese also came in the 1850s and 1860s, but the vast majority came from the subcontinent of India. The indenturing of East Indians, as they were called, continued from 1838 to 1917. By that time the size of the Indian population rivalled that of the people of African descent, and as the twentieth century advanced they became the majority ethnic group in the country. In 1970 the total population was 740,196, made up as follows:[1]

East Indians	377,256
Africans	227,091
Mixed or Coloured	84,077
Amerindians	32,794
Portuguese	9,668
Other Europeans	4,056
Chinese	4,678
Others	576

Following the second world war, the people began to express their desires for economic and social improvements. There had been a trade-union movement since 1919, and by 1947 there were some twenty unions joined together in a trades union council. There were also other movements and associations discussing and working towards self-government and adult suffrage, but there was no organized political party. Elected members of the legislative council, a part of the crown colony constitution, served as individuals. It was in 1950 that a mass-based party was launched, called the People's Progressive Party (PPP). There were two outstanding members: Cheddi Jagan, an East Indian and a dentist by profession, and Linden Forbes Sampson Burnham, an African, trained as a lawyer at London University. They were both committed socialists, and between them they dominated Guyanese politics from 1950 to the 1980s. The PPP was pledged to make the country

> a just socialist society in which the industries of the country shall be socially and democratically owned and managed for the common good, and a society in which security, plenty, peace and freedom shall be the heritage of all.[2]

The language in which these aspirations was expressed was of a Marxist nature, and admiration for the achievements of the Soviet Union was quite evident. This was the period when the cold war, which was to overshadow the world for almost forty years, had just begun. This meant that Guyana was not allowed to make a smooth transition to independence. The USA was to do all in its power to prevent the extension of communism in the western hemisphere, and the British government, although committed to independence for most of its colonies, would not allow a form of government of which it thoroughly disapproved.

Hence, when the PPP gained its first victory at the polls in 1953 and began to put in place the policies on which it had been elected, opposition forces mobilized to prevent communism from taking over. Within six months, during which time public disorder had erupted, the governor persuaded the colonial office to suspend the constitution and dismiss the elected government. British Guiana was now ruled directly by the governor.

It was this situation that produced the split between Jagan and Burnham, and resulted in the formation of the second mass party, the People's National Congress (PNC). For three years, 1955 to 1958, Jagan and Burnham struggled for supremacy within the PPP, while Burnham was being encouraged to break with Jagan by forces external to the party. When the constitution was resumed and elections were held in 1957, the two men fielded rival candidates under the banner of the PPP. Jagan's section proved victorious. Burnham then established the PNC in 1958. Jagan's success

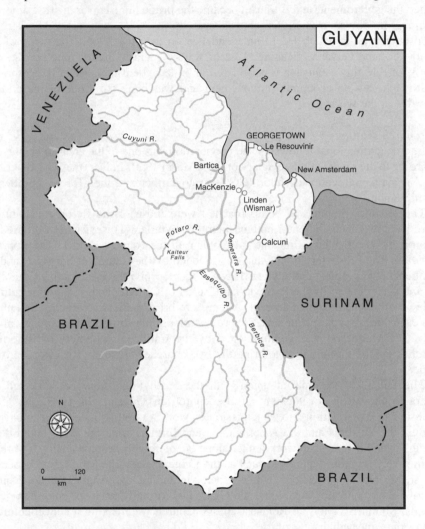

at the polls in 1957, and again in 1961 implied that he would be the one to lead the country to independence. However, from 1962 to 1964, his government was subjected to violent and sustained confrontation, with demonstrations, a general strike, and a sugar workers' strike during which racial violence erupted and nearly 150 people died, 800 were injured and much property destroyed. In Wismar, a village near MacKenzie, 200 homes were in ruins and 2,000 people made homeless. Once again the constitution was suspended. The colonial office in London now designed a new electoral system based on proportional representation with the entire nation regarded as a single constituency, and each party submitting lists of candidates from which members of parliament would be chosen according to the percentage of votes cast for each party. This was the system favoured by Burnham and his allies from a small but influential third party, the United Force (UF). [3]

In effect this meant that the PPP received 46 percent of the poll, the PNC 40.5 percent and the UF 12.4 percent. The coalition between the PNC and UF therefore formed the government, and Burnham became the prime minister for the first time. He remained in power from 1964 until his death in 1985, and presided over the constitutional talks which led to independence on 26 May 1966. The name of the country became Guyana, meaning "land of waters", and its motto "one people, one nation, one destiny". Guyana was declared an independent member of the common-wealth, but saw no economic improvement and was considered one of the poorest countries in the world.

Interchurch relations

Interdenominational fellowship and cooperation was one of the areas to be pursued according to the report of the secretary of the CMS in 1950. In fact, the Society wished the Guyana Congregational Union (GCU) to go further and look for possibilities of organic union.

The obvious churches to be approached were those of the Reformed tradition. There were two such churches, both of them Presbyterian. The existence of these two denominations reflected a fundamental problem of the country — racial division and suspicion. The Presbytery of Guyana was founded by the Church of Scotland, and its membership was almost entirely of African descent, while the Presbyterian Church of Guyana was founded by the Presbyterian Church of Canada, and was almost entirely made up of people of Indian descent. Attempts to bring these two churches into union with each other and then with the GCU proved impossible. In 1973 the secretary of the GCU, Pat Matthews, was commissioned by the Caribbean assembly of Reformed churches to take the initiative to bring the two churches together. His efforts proved fruitless.

The failure of attempts at union with the Presbyterian churches reflected the generally one-sided development of the church in Guyana. In 1967, the CMS requested an investigation into what missionary work was being undertaken among the Hindus, the Muslims and the Amerindians, and further, what the GCU could do to strengthen and extend such work, either alone or, preferably, ecumenically. The reply was not very hopeful. Churches, such as the Lutherans and the Moravians, generally had segregated congregations, while others, including the Anglicans, the Roman Catholics, the Salvation Army and the GCU, had virtually no work among the East Indians. Similarly, only the Roman Catholic Church was making a concerted effort among the Amerindians. [4]

The author of the reply, Arthur Thompson, had this to say on the prospects of the GCU undertaking work among the East Indians:

> I am regretfully of the opinion that there is nothing that the GCU can do to strengthen work of real missionary character among East Indians at all. Our denomination is almost wholly African, and even if willing — which it is not — is unlikely to meet with much success owing to the fact that both Africans and East Indians view each other with suspicion and distrust.

He also indicated that the Hindus and the Muslims were engaged in energetic missionary drives.

Regarding extension of work among the Amerindians, he was just as pessimistic; the only possibility was a united effort to provide resident ministers: "This may well come with time."[5]

The various denominations had always worked together under two separate entities: the Christian Social Council, which included the Roman Catholic churches, and the Evangelical Church Council, which excluded the Roman Catholics, but included the Pentecostal churches. In 1968, however, the Guyana Council of Churches was formed, consisting of 14 church bodies. Its aims were to promote cooperation and common action; to make representations to government on social issues; and to educate the public about the application of Christian principles to every aspect of human life. The Council was to function through ten commissions.

The Guyana Council of Churches came into being at a time when the churches were facing a major challenge. The government was committed to a policy of complete separation between church and state. Burnham was ready to assure the Council that he was not antagonistic to it, and was prepared to listen to it on matters concerning the welfare of the nation, but that the Christian religion was one among others practised by the citizens of Guyana. He established an advisory council on religious matters, but there were a number of areas of disagreement and conflict between the churches and the government.

Public education had been largely in the hands of the churches for many years; the Anglicans and the Roman Catholics had many schools of both primary and secondary grades. The GCU was responsible for 13 primary schools, serving an enrolment of 8,000 children. Ten years after independence the government took over responsibility for all education from nursery to university. All school property was taken over with no compensation to the owners despite protests.

In this educational measure, all education was to be free and co-educational; there would be no private or dual-controlled schools; no religious instruction of any kind would be given within the curriculum. Any worship or religious activity could be done only after school hours.

Guyana did not participate in the University of the West Indies (UWI) as it also did not join the federation of the West Indies, but established the University of Guyana in 1963. It was recognized as offering courses of international standard, and its degrees are accredited by universities overseas. However, it did not offer courses in theology, thus causing the churches to look to the United Theological College of the West Indies (UTCWI) in Jamaica and other overseas institutions for training.

Most, if not all, of the churches relied on personnel and money from foreign churches and agencies, but with the policy of Guyanization, the government imposed a ban on overseas personnel. A four-year period was given during which Guyanese citizens were to be trained. Following this period, expatriates would be forced to leave; the only exception being members of other Caribbean countries. This was a moratorium imposed by the government.

There is no doubt that churches benefitted from government support and projects, and the African background and numerical dominance of the churches made them instinctively reluctant to question the policies and practices of the Burnham government. They would criticize some who questioned those policies as becoming "involved in partisan politics". However, the questioning persisted, especially of the steps taken for constitutional change adopted in the 1970s which resulted in a presidential government. Side by side with these doubts over political actions was a growing unease about the economic situation of the country. Always a poor country, a rapid deterioration set in, with dependence on the International Monetary Fund, and the suspicious attitude of other countries and agencies. In 1982, the Guyana Council of Churches reacted to a collapse of domestic agriculture and cuts in food imports by convening a meeting of all interested bodies, political parties, trade unions, religious bodies, business groups and service clubs. Only the PNC, the governing party, failed to respond. As on previous occasions, the churches took responsibility for organizing foreign aid and the distribution of food, and other practical measures were adopted. It was further stated: "There is a need for a broad-based democratic government, no single party can effectively govern Guyana at this time."[6] This, of course, did not affect the presidential style of government now adopted by Burnham who some opined firmly controlled all the agencies of authority, including the judiciary, the police and the army, but it demonstrated the unease of the Guyana Council of Churches at the political and economic situation.

The Council established a community centre at Riumvelt, a Georgetown suburb, with medical and trade-training facilities. A significant event in interchurch relations took place when, for the first time ever, the annual Week of Prayer for Christian Unity was launched with a service in the Roman Catholic cathedral and a Protestant minister — Pat Matthews of GCU — delivered the sermon.

The Guyana Congregational Union (GCU)

The GCU has never been a numerically large denomination. Pat Matthews, its secretary for many years, reported in 1973 that there were 39 churches, divided into eight pastorates, with 3,500 members and a total community of 18,000. Its complement of ministers was eight, five Guyanese and three expatriates. It was the normal procedure of the CMS to maintain the supply of expatriate ministers, and this continued in the post-second world war period until Guyana achieved its independence in 1966. About that time, this policy was changed, and the Society decided to terminate the supply of pastoral ministers in a bid to encourage the GCU to produce its own.

The reaction of the GCU was to resist the change and to plead for continuing the long-standing system. When the Smith Memorial Church, Georgetown, became vacant in 1968, attempts were made by letter and by personal interview to persuade the CCWM to supply a minister.[7] In one letter the deacons suggested that "the objective of the church and the work of the CCWM was in jeopardy". In reply, Ernest Edwards stated that the committee had considered the position again "but could see no adequate ground for revising its policy not to send expatriate ministers for pastoral oversight in the Caribbean".[8] However, the problem persisted, and was raised forcefully when Edwards made a secretarial visit to Guyana in November 1973. By that time the ministerial strength had been reduced to four, three Guyanese and one Angolan. In his report he stated:

> I was left in no doubt during my stay in Guyana that help with the pastoral ministry was the crying need. By way of response I could only reaffirm our position that the day of sending expatriate ministers for the pastoral oversight of churches in Guyana was behind us; that the policy laid down eight years ago had been carefully explained to them during my last visit; that since then Mr Burnham had enunciated his policy of self-help and had stressed that Guyana must not look elsewhere for help when it was perfectly capable of helping itself.[9]

The CCWM continued to suggest ways forward for the GCU, especially in the field of training. The United Theological College of the West Indies had been founded in Jamaica, and the way was therefore open for ministerial training in the Caribbean. One Guyanese student at that institution was Prince Oscar Wharton who returned, subsequently to become minister of the Smith Memorial Church. It was felt that Jamaica was too far removed, and that some system of training based in Guyana was also needed on an interdenominational basis. Despite encouragement from the CCWM and other bodies, including UTCWI, discussions to this end in the late 1960s proved fruitless. If the CCWM was unwilling to supply pastoral ministers, it was willing to send specialists for specific schemes. In the secretary's report 1973 Ernest Edwards recommended a "missionary or expatriate presence" to be involved in training programmes of the church "to break their felt isolation from the church universal and to act as a link with the wider life of the world church in which we all share". [10]

Ministerial leadership was weakened by the migration of three Guyanese ministers to serve churches in the USA. This meant that the burden was borne mainly by ministers who continued to serve faithfully long after the usual age of retirement. These included Pat Matthews, Adam Johnson and Fitzroy Jackson, whose dedicated service was in the best tradition of Christian discipleship. A unique and memorable event in the history of the GCU was the ordination of its first woman minister, Una Matthews. Following her husband's death in 1979, she entered the New York theological seminary, and on completion of her studies was ordained and called to succeed her late husband in the Mission Chapel, New Amsterdam, and its outstations. Una Matthews gave outstanding service and genuine leadership, becoming chairman of the union in 1985.

In 1962, the CMS proposed a fraternal link between the GCU and the Congregational Union of Jamaica. This was agreed and representatives attended each other's assembly on alternate years. This continued after the formation of the United Church of Jamaica and Grand Cayman (UCJGC) and later closer links were established as the two churches became the Caribbean region of the CWM.

In 1943, a royal commission was sent from England to investigate the conditions of the "children of the forest", as the Amerindians were called. The commission recommended that the churches should give more attention to their welfare. The GCU responded by establishing a mission board as a separate and distinct entity within the union, and Pat Matthews was inducted as the first home missionary. He was to serve in the Calcuni mission 120 miles up the Berbice river and the Potaro and Bartica missions on the Essequibo river. To facilitate the work a motor launch was provided by the CMS, and named *Gem T* after Miss G.E.M. Tapp, secretary of the CMS, predecessor to Ralph Calder. Even so, travel was slow and arduous and the physical side of the work was very demanding. In later years, some improvements were made to land travel along the rivers, and the aeroplane came to speed up the time taken to reach the settlements far up the rivers. Pat Matthew's work was made possible by grants from the government as well as the CMS. He was appointed a sub-protector of the Amerindians, and this gave a social dimension to his mission.

The Calcuni mission had been long-established, but Pat Matthews was able to give time to the extension of the work. Sunday worship became regular; with the help of a teacher-catechist Sunday school and adult Bible classes were conducted, the Christian festivals observed, including the Easter sunrise service. At the same time educational, medical and welfare activities were undertaken, including a breakfast centre. From

Calcuni visits were paid to scattered Indian communities with a view to establishing more missions.

The home missionary also had responsibility for work at Bartica and Potaro on the Essequibo river. Bartica was described as the "pearl of the Essequibo", a lumber station of importance with a lively church community. Potaro, a hundred miles further up the river, was a gold-mining centre, and over the years a faithful group maintained their fellowship. Mine work was not confined to one place and as workers moved on to new areas, further mission effort was required. On one visit Pat Matthews discovered a settlement of Arawaks, seventy miles from Potaro, "having all the primitive tribal marks of their tribe on their faces… quite primitive and without religion or education". Unlike the Arawaks of Calcuni who were bilingual, Patamonias and Akawos had no knowledge of English, and without an interpreter he could not "make friends with them". He felt the need for more assistance and a resident catechist who could pursue the opportunities that were evident.[11]

A pioneer missionary enterprise was established at MacKenzie, 67 miles up the Demerara river. Here the Congregationalists, the Methodists and the Moravians combined to make the first united mission in Guyana. MacKenzie was a bauxite township built and owned by the Demerara bauxite company, and it had become the centre of a large community with two villages, Wismar and Christianburg, on the other side of the river. These three settlements were later combined and renamed Linden following the nationalization of the bauxite industry.[12] Reg Mitchell of the Methodist missionary society was the pioneer minister of the project who began his work in 1954. He also assumed responsibility for the work established by Pat Matthews at the gold-mining settlement of Mahdia.

In 1963, Gordon Smethurst, a theological student from Northern College, Manchester, England, went for 12 months to assist at the MacKenzie united mission. He was there during the vicious race riots of May 1964. The village of Wismar consisted mostly of East Indians, and they became prime targets for violence. Smethurst wrote of the effects on the mission which played a prominent part in rescuing the families, housing them temporarily on bauxite company premises and then transferring them to the safety of Georgetown. The mission workers and others who had in any way helped the Indians lived under threat. He sensed the deterioration of the moral fabric of the community:

> In recent sermons I have spoken about the lot of a community which sells itself to the extremist and criminal, and of the possibility of the church facing persecution, and called upon our people to draw closer to God, to be honest with themselves and quietly seek to maintain the moral standards they know to be right. I did not know how close to the truth I was: the houses burned in the last two weeks have been African houses; extortion is growing; decent people live in fear; and Christians must show courage to come to church — particularly the united mission.[13]

By 1973 the MacKenzie united mission had six centres of worship, and the area was developing fast with the opening of a new highway from Georgetown. Lay leadership was undertaken by three elders, one woman and two men, and their pastoral functions were clearly spelt out. A full-time youth organizer had also been appointed.

Pat Matthews maintained his mission work for 21 years, during which time he served also as secretary to the GCU. In 1964, he became minister at the Smith Memorial Church, and in 1968 moved to Mission Chapel, New Amsterdam, but he never gave up his interest and his care for the mission work, and it can be said that he served as a missionary pastor for 36 years. He was awarded the MBE for his services.

In spite of all the difficulties, the devotion of individual members for their churches has been great. It became increasingly difficult to repair buildings, replace cars, find fuel for transport, obtain paper, books, and educational aids — practical matters taken so often for granted. Congregations learnt to improvise and "make do". Special occasions were duly celebrated, including the 150th anniversary of the LMS in 1958, and the 125th anniversary of the Smith Memorial Church in 1967.

Una Matthews sums up the period as follows:

> Independence brought a great sense of pride to us. However, we tried to follow the socialist pathway and some of the dreams and promises for a better Guyana have remained unfulfilled... Guyana was ranked with Haiti as the world's poorest countries...
>
> Spiritually, however, I feel these strenuously difficult times have caused a spiritual awakening and a renewal of faith of Christians... the members of our churches have made great sacrifices to maintain the work. [14]

Jamaica

The nation

Nationally, the great event of this period, 1945-77, was the achievement of independence. The development of national self-consciousness was stimulated by dynamic leadership. Marcus Garvey pioneered the cause of cultural identity and Alexander Bustamante and Norman Manley gave political shape to the independence movement. A new constitution, which came into force on 20 November 1944, ended crown colony rule, provided a two-chamber legislature, an executive council, and full adult suffrage for all people 21 years of age and over, in spite of the usual fears of what this could mean. Amendments to this constitution were made in 1953, 1957 and 1958, by which time complete internal self-government had been achieved.

The next episode on the road to independence was the formation of the federation of the West Indies, a creation of the British government. It was felt at the time that the various territories of the Caribbean were not large enough nor prosperous enough to form viable economic and political units on their own, but that a federation would achieve this purpose. However, it did not take into account the separate development of these territories over a period of three hundred years, and the urge of the people to have full control over their own lands. Thus, it was doomed to failure. Federation was accepted at first as the way forward by both Jamaican political parties when it came into existence early in 1958 with the intention of becoming a dominion within five years. However, by 1960 the Jamaica Labour Party declared for the secession of Jamaica from the federation and began campaigning on this issue. A national referendum resulted in a clear majority for withdrawal, thus bringing about the dissolution of the federation in May 1962, and paving the way for the independence of Jamaica.

Discussions on the future of Jamaica came to a speedy conclusion; a constitution was drawn up and accepted, a general election held and a date for independence set — 6 August 1962, less than 12 months after the referendum. Jamaica became an independent nation with dominion status within the British commonwealth of nations.

Inevitably, the post-independence period, from 1962 to 1980, was characterized by a violent political struggle between the two main political parties, the Jamaica

Labour Party, which tended towards political pragmatism and the right, and the People's National Party, which was idealistic and followed the path of democratic socialism.[15] They were of equal strength, and both of them resorted to violence. The politics of confrontation dominated the scene, and the words "political tribalism" were used to describe the situation with attendant tribal warfare.[16] Providentially, neither party was able to dominate the political system for too long, and from 1944 to 1989 each party was elected for two consecutive parliamentary terms, and then was superseded by the other.

It was soon clear that Jamaica, though independent, was not to be allowed to follow its own pattern of social and economic development. Progress in health, education and social services over the first years of independence was halted as international agencies began increasingly to dictate what could and could not be done, and what social schemes had to be cut back or abandoned. Like other so-called third-world countries, Jamaica was subject to such agencies as the World Bank and the International Monetary Fund, bringing great hardship especially to the poor who formed the large majority of the population. Often there was the suspicion of covert

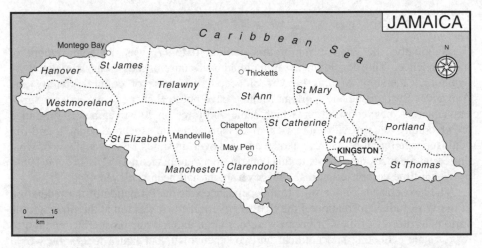

external interference in the political affairs of the country which fostered political tribalism.

Political independence brought great changes in the social and economic life of Jamaica. Free from colonial domination, Jamaica took its place as a member of the United Nations, and of regional groups and organizations. One factor making for change was the mass emigration triggered by the great hurricane "Charlie" of 1951. Emigration had traditionally been a safety valve in the history of Jamaica; from the 1950s onwards it began to affect all sections of the community. At first this emigration was economically based as the small farmers of rural communities and the unemployed of the towns sought an answer to poverty and lack of opportunity in a new life in the UK, Canada and the USA. Later, in the 1970s, this emigration also had a political dimension as wealthy professional and middle-class families fled in fear of communism. Either way, emigration brought its own stresses on the newly independent country and its institutions.

Another potent factor was the exposure of Jamaica to foreign ways and standards of living. In this, commercial radio and television had a part, together with other consumer-based goods introduced by Jamaicans living abroad. Jamaica became aware of the standard of living of countries such as the USA and Canada, and wanted to copy their life-style. This turn to consumerism divided the society radically into the "haves" and the "have-nots" and placed a heavy debt burden on the country as all had to be paid for in hard currency, mainly the US dollar. The strains were visible in the rising level of crime and violence. One hopeful feature in all this initial insecurity and violence was the absence of racially inspired hatred. Jamaica adopted the motto: "Out of many, one people". [17]

The Congregational Union of Jamaica (CUJ) and the
United Church of Jamaica and Grand Cayman (UCJGC)

The major development in the history of the Congregational Union of Jamaica was the merger with the Presbyterian Church of Jamaica and Grand Cayman. Talks of union between what are often called in Jamaica the "established churches", i.e. those formed as a result of the missionary endeavour of the British churches — Anglican, Church of Scotland, Baptist, Methodist and Congregational — emerged in the 1930s. These talks were not conclusive. Consideration of union resurfaced after the second world war, with the formation of the church union commission. Although tangible results arose from the work of the commission, e.g. the establishment of the union theological seminary in 1955, it became evident that little, if any, progress would be made towards organic union. However, two denominations, the Presbyterians and the Congregationalists, resolved to unite. Practical considerations helped the process: (1) They had a common history of belief and practice. (2) There was concern over the static condition of both denominations, the overlapping of congregations and the waste of manpower and scarce resources.

These factors in themselves were insufficient to produce organic union, but both churches were convinced that it was the will of the Holy Spirit that they should unite, thus strengthening their witness and making it more effective. Rapid progress was made. A basis of union was drawn up. It was a short document which did not try to solve all the practical obstacles and detailed matters of a constitutional nature, but kept to broad outlines. It had one very wise declaration which stated that neither church would be asked to give up any right or privilege which it had hitherto enjoyed. Thus, the Congregational churches could maintain their vision of the priesthood of all believers which allowed for lay administration of the sacraments, while the Presbyterian churches could continue with the supremacy of the eldership.

While the basis of union was the one "binding" document, it was agreed that the constitution of the Presbyterian church would be its practical working model over the first years of union as the Congregational Union had no written constitution. Over the next 10 to 14 years, a new constitution was drafted, section by section. Looking back one can say that over that period there were problems and heated debates both at synod and at council levels, and the ex-Congregational members longed for the cosy, family-type atmosphere of a church which consisted at the time of a union of 37 congregations and nine ministers, while the ex-Presbyterians found it difficult to accept the forthrightness and maybe the radicalism of the Congregational lay leaders. Much credit for the comparatively smooth transition to a united church can be given to Clement A. Thomas, the general secretary throughout the period 1965-77. His eirenic nature, patience and administrative gifts were a blessing. He was succeeded by Sam H. Smellie.

The UCJGC consisted of 140 congregations, 60 ministers and 16,500 members. There was no dissent to the union from either denomination and no subsequent breakaway. The momentous union took place on 1 December 1965. The new church geographically covered most of the island of Jamaica. In only the two eastern parishes (the equivalent of English counties) out of the total of 13 were there no congregations at all. The result of the union on Kingston, the capital city, was that UCJGC had more ministers there than any other denomination, thus allowing it to have greater influence at the heart of the nation. The fact that one of the five councils into which the church was divided was in Grand Cayman, a British colony, gave the church a supranational flavour.

Both the uniting churches had a history of overseas missionary involvement, the Presbyterian church in Calabar, West Africa, and the Congregational in present-day Zimbabwe. [18] Because of this, the UCJGC intended from the beginning to be involved in worldwide mission. Madge Saunders was commissioned at the inaugural synod to be its first missionary to Sheffield, England, as a member of a team ministry in the inner city, especially ministering to West Indian migrants, and a young minister went to Belize in Central America. Contacts were maintained or established with Presbyterian and Congregational churches in Europe and North America. Representatives were present at the 1975 CWM Singapore consultation, and they played a vital role in the formation of the restructured Council for World Mission.

Soon after union, the synod, which is the highest authority of the church, discussed and approved the ordination of women. [19]

Education

Public education: The London Missionary Society's mission to Jamaica resulted from an invitation sent by the government of Britain to missionary societies and agencies to share in the education of the people of those territories in which slavery had been abolished in 1834. Hence, the task of the first missionaries was to establish schools. This resulted in an ongoing concern for education and involvement in the educational process which has persisted until today.

Eventually many of the schools founded by the LMS became government-leased schools, a partnership between church and state. These were of course primary or all-age schools. This partnership involved the church providing the chairman and a certain number of members of each school board. In the 1970s, these boards were democratized, i.e. their composition was made up of representatives of the ministry of education, staff, parents, the community in general (and in the case of secondary schools, students), as well as those of the church itself. The church retained the right to appoint the chairman.

From 1838, the main thrust of education in Jamaica was on a primary and an all-age system with only a few secondary schools catering for an elite. However, as this century has progressed, gradually more and more secondary institutions have been created. In this move towards fuller education, the churches took their part. The Rev. Lester Davy, a Congregational minister, founded a secondary school in 1942; this was Clarendon College in the town of Chapelton. His aim was to provide the children of the small farmers of the parish of Clarendon with the opportunity of secondary education. The school was to be co-educational and include boarding facilities. He began with 15 students, but tragically he was killed in a railway accident one month after the inaugural service held at the Salem church in Chapelton. The Congregational

Union of Jamaica (CUJ), together with the Colonial Missionary Society, took over the venture and secured its continued existence. By 1950, the school had progressed to the point of being accepted by the ministry of education as a grant-aided secondary school. This meant that financial responsibility was undertaken by the ministry with the CUJ supervising the running of the school through the school board.

Clarendon College has had a distinguished history, surviving hurricane damage and the various crises of funding and staffing, to become one of the foremost rural secondary schools in Jamaica. It has grown in size to over 1,600 students and 80 staff members. It still maintains its boarding facility despite economic pressures.

In its early years the CMS played an important part in helping to purchase land and financing building projects as the school expanded. It also established a bursary fund for the support of students. Individuals, Sunday schools, and other church organizations in Britain contributed annually, and for twenty years or so personal contact was maintained between donors and bursary holders. This system was discontinued later, but the bursary fund itself has continued. Past students have gone on to play important roles in various professions, politics, commerce and finance, both in Jamaica and in many parts of the world.

With the formation of the UCJGC, the number of grant-aided secondary schools belonging to the church totalled five, with one private secondary school, Iona.

The public education committee of the UCJGC supervised the work of the church-related schools at all levels — infant, preparatory, primary, all-age and secondary, and the chaplaincy service extended beyond these to the training colleges and the university.

Theological education: Several attempts were made in the last century to establish a college for theological training by the LMS churches, but these did not take firm root. During this century, training was undertaken in the colleges of other denominations. However, the Methodist church offered its property at Caenwood, Kingston, to form an ecumenical college, and the CUJ (with support from the CMS) together with the Methodists, the Disciples of Christ, the Moravians and the Presbyterians established the Union Theological Seminary (UTS) in 1955.

As part of post-war development, university colleges affiliated to the University of London were founded in various colonies of the British empire. Included in this scheme was a University College of the West Indies with campuses in Trinidad, Barbados and Jamaica. In due time, the University College of the West Indies became a university in its own right, with a full range of faculties.

In 1959, discussions began to take place between the churches of the English-speaking Caribbean and the university. These led to the idea of a theological college affiliated to the university to be built on an adjacent site. Two years later the World Council of Churches, through its appropriate channels, conferred with the churches and offered substantial help from its theological education fund. This amounted to US$130,000 and was of considerable help, both in the purchase of land and the erection of buildings. There was already a history of cooperation among the churches which had brought the UTS into existence, and which had brought close association between it and two other denominational colleges — the Calabar Baptist and the St Peter's Anglican. Now these three Jamaican institutions were invited to think regionally, and to form a United Theological College of the West Indies (UTCWI). In 1964, ten communions, geographically spread throughout the Caribbean, signed the instrument of agreement. Included among the ten were the Guyana Congregational

Union, the Congregational Union of Jamaica and the Presbyterian Church of Jamaica. [20]

The UTCWI began its work as an institution in October 1966. Its first president was Wilfred Scopes who had spent a lifetime in theological education in India, having gone there in 1925 as an LMS missionary. He had participated in the 1961 consultation as secretary of the visiting survey team. Now he was entrusted with the task of establishing the new college. His term of office was for two years, 1966-68, after which he was succeeded by John Hoad, a Methodist minister and native of Barbados.

In the president's report for 1966-67, Wilfred Scopes stated: "I know of no institution of its kind, anywhere in the world, that is so broadly based."

Through its affiliation to the UWI, the college was able to offer an acknowledged university course for the licentiate in theology. Later this was followed by degree courses. [21] College staff members were given the opportunity to upgrade their academic qualifications and thus improve the standard of training for the ministry, and the churches of the Caribbean have benefitted greatly from this. Ministers of the UCJGC who have been trained at the UTCWI have proved their value and their high standard of ministry worldwide. Among them are Maitland Evans and Roderick Hewitt who have served the CWM, and Verna Cassells, tutor at St Andrew's College, Selly Oak, Birmingham, England.

During the second half of the twentieth century, a number of theologically-related issues have arisen which have influenced the churches of Jamaica including the UCJGC. The contextualization of the Christian faith has become increasingly important, i.e. the need to make it directly relevant to the ordinary people, their hopes, aspirations and experience of life. From this felt-need, liberation theology arose in Latin America, giving expression to the longing for economic and social justice. Use was made of the biblical experience of the Exodus (as it had been in the time of John Smith in 1823) and also a Christology which made Christ the "Sufferers' Friend", leading to the liberation of the people, the "Campesinos", from their economic, social, political and spiritual oppression. "Sufferers" was the term used by Jamaicans for that great majority of the population which faced many forms of deprivation. Specifically the gospel of Luke pointed to such a Christ. It cannot be said that liberation theology itself has had a profound effect on the church in Jamaica hitherto, but the processes of contextualization have become increasingly important.

The UCJGC from its inception considered the sacrament of baptism and the place of adult baptism in the life of the church. This subject had been of importance in Jamaica from the early days of the LMS, because the Baptist churches had been strong from the time of William Knibb. In recent discussions, the argument from tradition has not been persuasive, and the practice of adult baptism has increased among the congregations.

Another aspect of this process of contextualization was the need for what has become known as liturgical renewal. For many years, the Congregational and the Presbyterian churches had followed the Reformed tradition order of worship of the Westminster assembly, 1643. Now, the impetus was towards new forms of worship, greater participation by the congregation and a freer use of music. Verna Cassells wrote:

> ...the liturgy of many of the established churches in the Caribbean does not reflect the inherent culture of the members, but rather the cultures of the missionaries who brought them the gospel.

Liturgical renewal should not only lead to a richer and more meaningful cultic worship, but also, and more so, to the leading of a life that expounds a love for God. [22]

Rastafarianism made its mark on the social and spiritual life of Jamaica. At first, it was regarded with horror by the political and religious leaders of society, but its appeal could not be denied. It was attractive to young people as it offered a distinctive identity and a whole corpus of beliefs, goals, ethics and social behaviour. Rastafarian ideas could readily be expressed in language, dress and music, and in the 1970s Rastafarians gained access to the media and dominated the entertainment scene. Bob Marley's influence was extensive and powerful. [23] The church had to face the challenge of this movement, particularly as it related much of its beliefs and structures to the Bible. For instance, the equating of the biblical word "herb" with "ganja" (marihuana) gave mystical significance to the drug. A plentiful supply was available in Jamaica, and it became a prime, though illegal, export to the USA and elsewhere.

Christian education: The UCJGC through its two founding churches inherited a great respect for Christian education. Sunday or church schools were an important feature of the life of each congregation. At first, teaching material came from the USA or England, but attempts were made at producing Caribbean lesson handbooks for each age group from infants to adults, with material for a three-year cycle. Writers were drawn from all territories of the Caribbean; this produced a great variety of content, and also some criticism of doctrinal matters, as the books served not only a wide span of territories, but also of denominations. The UCJGC sought to deal with this by providing additional material to go with the books.

A number of organizations meeting on weekdays supplemented the teaching done on Sundays. These included girls' brigade, boys' brigade, women's guild and men's fellowship, each with programmes suitable for the groups they aimed to attract.

The most influential of these organizations was the United Church Young People's Association (UCYPA) which was formed in 1967 out of earlier movements. This association has had a profound influence on the church, and a steady stream of its members have entered the ministry, while others have become prominent lay leaders. From the UCYPA, which basically caters for the age group 16-21 years, the united church young adults action movement was formed for persons aged 21 to 39 years.

A special feature of Christian education activity has been the annual summer camp conferences arranged separately for each age group from 8 to 39. These have been an essential part of the church's calendar.

Each council of the church was responsible for its own programme of training for teachers, lay leadership, etc. Gradually it was realized that a concerted, unified programme of education was needed covering all aspects of church life. This was later put into effect. [24]

Congregational life

The period 1945-77 saw much activity among the individual churches of the CUJ and later the UCJGC throughout Jamaica. There was an ongoing building programme undertaken even by the smallest and poorest of congregations. This was necessary as ageing buildings had to be replaced, or as hurricanes damaged them. Churches and manses were rebuilt. Reports of the CMS frequently referred to such programmes and the help given by the Society. Some new causes were established; a highly effective one was formed in the expanding capital city, Kingston. This was St Stephen's Church, Cross Roads, established by J. Calvert Cariss, then minister of North Street, in 1954. In a very short time this church became one of the foremost in the denomination, and it founded its own mission also. Out in the country new causes were established at Thicketts by Trevor Hughes, while others were formed at Denbigh and Palmer's Cross on the outskirts of the quickly growing town of May Pen in Clarendon.

While there was a tendency to keep to the old ways, new forms of ministry began to emerge here and there. Shortly after the establishment of broadcasting in Jamaica, the St Stephen's Church began a weekly radio programme entitled "St Stephen's calling". This means of proclaiming the gospel was started by J. Calvert Cariss, and has continued unbroken for almost forty years by his two successors, Maurice Marks and Stanford Webley. The Mel Nathan Institute, the brainchild of Maitland Evans, at that time minister of St John's Church, Denham Town, Kingston, has proved how a church can serve its neighbourhood with a whole range of facilities, educational, vocational and commercial.

In the period 1945-65, the CUJ established an annual day of fellowship held on Ash Wednesday in Mandeville. Here the congregations gathered, arriving on trucks or in buses, and fellowship among the churches was renewed. This was the one "day out" in the year for many of those who attended. After union, this practice took some time to be re-established, but eventually all councils of the church held their own day of fellowship and regarded it as an essential feature of the church's calendar.

The large majority of the congregations are situated in rural areas, and have suffered the regular drain of young people to the towns of Jamaica as well as overseas. These congregations have faced hurricanes and many forms of deprivation, but their simple Christian faith, with strong emphasis on God's providence (often pronounced "provide-ance") and the comforting and close presence of Jesus, has given them a resilience and strength which humbles the observer.

NOTES

[1] E.J. Edwards, report of a secretarial visit to the Caribbean, 22 November 1973.

[2] Thomas J. Spinner Jr, *A Political and Social History of Guyana 1945-1983*, London, Westview Press, 1984, p.30, quotation from the Party's magazine *Thunder*.

[3] The United Force was formed in 1960 by Peter D'Aguiar to protect the interests of the middle class. The UF made a coalition government with the PNC in 1964, but it was not able to influence the government as it had hoped. Burnham had no need of the UF after the election.

[4] See further the work of Patrick Alleyne, Pat Matthews and the River Missions of the GCU. The Roman Catholics were systematic in their Amerindian mission, with resident priests and nuns in three areas. They also faced up to the language problem involved in working among different tribes.

[5] Correspondence between Ernest Edwards, dated 16 May 1967, and Arthur Thompson, 20 May 1967.

[6] Spinner, *op. cit.*, p.200.

[7] An eloquent letter from Judge J. Lyttleton Wills, prominent Guyanese layman, to C. Stuart Craig, 8 October 1969, pleads for a minister from England to go to Smith Memorial Church, Georgetown.

[8] Letter from E.J. Edwards to Pat Matthews, 7 March 1969.

[9] E.J. Edwards, secretarial report 1973.

[10] It was not until 1990 that Guto Rhys ap Gwynfor, minister of the Union of Welsh Independents, went from Wales through the CWM to establish such a programme.

[11] CMS annual report 1946, p.18. As Pat Matthews stated, many more resources of manpower and money were needed if his pioneer work was to have more than a limited sphere of influence.

[12] Re-named "Linden" after the prime minister, Linden Forbes Sampson Burnham.

[13] Article by Gordon Smethurst in *Commonwealth News*, December 1964-February 1965, vol. LIII, no. 4, p.75.

[14] Mss article, Una Matthews, "Congregationalism in Guyana: Some Highlights", 1991.

[15] There was also a communist party which made inroads into the trade-union situation, but it was unable to break the monopoly of power shared between the JLP and PNP.

[16] The politics of confrontation ceased after the 1980 election.

[17] While Jamaicans have their roots in many different parts of the world, including Europe, India, China and Syria, the vast majority are of African descent. It is claimed that concerted opposition to the introduction of indentured labourers from (East) India by the missionaries of the mid-nineteenth century prevented the huge inflow which occurred in Trinidad and Guyana.

[18] In appreciation of the work of J.H.E. Hemans, LMS missionary (1888-1906), native of Jamaica, Cecil Rhodes included Jamaica in the list of territories to be awarded the Rhodes scholarship. Earl Thames, twice elected moderator of UCJGC, is himself a Rhodes scholar.

[19] The first to be ordained was Adlyn White. By now there are seven, including Madge Saunders.

[20] That this was achieved in such a short period is a tribute to those who took part in the discussions, but they were greatly influenced by the support and practical financial help offered by the theological education fund and the overseas church bodies to which the local churches were affiliated.

[21] The degree courses now include BA (theol.), MA and M.Phil, and the most recent, doctor in ministry programme.

[22] Article in *International Review of Mission*, vol. LXXX, no. 317, January 1991, p.88.

[23] Bob Marley was a superstar performer in the 1970s, bringing the distinctively Jamaican Reggae style of music to international prominence. He was awarded the Jamaican Order of Merit.

[24] This programme, which included ministerial training, is now part of the institute for theological and leadership development which has overall responsibility for education.

Additional note: In 1977, operating completely apart from the churches of Guyana, and geographically remote from the inhabited area of the country, an American evangelist, Jim Jones, set up a community near the border with Venezuela. Subsequently, in November 1978, a mass suicide and killing, involving over nine hundred people, took place. Reports of this holocaust can be found in *Caribbean Contact*, the monthly newspaper of the Caribbean Conference of Churches, and in many books, including *Journey to Nowhere* by Shiva Naipaul (New York, 1981).

11. Patterns of the Spirit: Towards a Council

Robert Latham

Introduction — a personal note

My introduction to the London Missionary Society (LMS) was at the first conference to be held for final theological students from the Congregational colleges in England, Wales and Scotland. It was held in the Easter vacation of 1942 in Livingstone House. There were about thirty students attending, and we were provided with hospitality by friends of the LMS in the London area. The chair was taken by the Rev. Dr A.M. Chirgwin, the general secretary, and the presentations were made by him and by the secretaries of the Society: the Rev. Norman Goodall spoke on India, the Rev. Cocker Brown on China, and Dr Chirgwin on Madagascar and Africa which he had recently visited. The Rev. Ronald Orchard described the emerging pattern of policy which had come out of a recent Society-wide study entitled "New Advance", which had looked at every area of LMS work and made recommendations for the next stages. We were given a vivid picture of the church witnessing in many countries, supported by the LMS and other missionary societies, and moving in India towards a union of several churches which had been founded by the different societies. We met many of the missionaries who were home on furlough and who joined in the conference. I came away having been made aware of the extent of the work across the world and having felt for the first time something of the world dimension of the church. I was able to enter my first pastorate in Southampton well informed and able to lead the church there in its continuing study of the "New Advance" proposals. I was also impressed by the quality of the leadership of the LMS and of the missionaries we met. I felt we could trust them.

Some five years later, when the war was over, I was encouraged to apply for the post of education officer of the LMS. It was a new post created to follow up the insights gained by the "New Advance" study in the churches in the British Isles, and by correspondence with Australia and New Zealand. As a convinced Congregational minister I regarded the LMS and its Southampton auxiliary to be as much a valid agent of my local church for world mission, as the county union and the national union were valid agents for the wider fellowship of the church in Britain, with its reconstruction fund and home churches fund for ministers in the smaller churches. At that time there was no question that the national union, the union of England and Wales, regarded itself as a national church. It was a voluntary association of independent churches. In this dimension of church life great changes were to come, as we shall relate, but at the beginning of the post-war period they had not been formulated.

The post-war period

The LMS emerged from the devastation and deprivation of the second world war battered but not beaten, with its sights on the future, not on the past. The leadership was in the sure hands of capable men and women. The general secretary, Dr A.M. Chirgwin, referred to as "the general", evoked a style of leadership which integrated every section of the Society's work. He was well informed, he was interested in everybody and in every aspect of the work being done. He shared in all the important discussions, and frequently initiated them. The Rev. Norman Goodall was foreign secretary for India and the Pacific where he carried great responsibility and earned the deep respect and affection of the leaders of the churches and missionaries. The Rev. Ronald Orchard soon joined him as foreign secretary for China and Africa, two turbulent countries with emerging minority churches. His theological acumen and transparent friendliness helped the churches to face the increasing problems and see a future towards which they could work. On the home side the Rev. Cecil Northcott was home secretary and editor, supported by a gifted staff including Joyce Reason, who wrote for the children, and Dr Olga Pilpel who did the detailed editing of all publications and selected the pictures and illustrations. Northcott was essentially a writer and he produced a popular book each year on a missionary theme. He also travelled the British Isles year in year out, visiting the many auxiliaries and addressing rallies. He enjoyed fund-raising and on occasions when the income was not expected to be adequate to meet the year's expenditure, he would sally forth and call on the friends of the Society whom he knew had a good financial standing and ask them for an additional contribution. In this way he raised thousands of pounds, and usually balanced the books. The woman secretary was the Rev. Joyce Rutherford. She was responsible for the women's auxiliaries, women candidates, children's work and the educational project, "New Advance". She was regarded as the leaven in the lump of the otherwise all-male secretariat. She was followed at the beginning of this period by Frances Bowers, whose late husband had been a chairman of the board of directors. Eventually Mrs Bowers took over the whole candidature procedure, both men and women, and later became foreign secretary for Madagascar. These were the leaders of the LMS. They formed a secretaries' meeting, which met every week and reviewed the whole spectrum of the work. Each secretary raised whatever was the relevant or pressing issue in his or her field. They all discussed it thoroughly, and usually arrived at an agreed recommendation. These recommendations were then put to the committees, each made up of members of the Board of directors. Some of these committee members had served on their particular committee for many years and knew the situation and the personnel involved. The committee would then prepare a report to the full Board, which met three times a year. In an emergency, of course, action could be taken on the committee decision, or if necessary on the secretaries' meeting's decision, but always it had to be reported to the Board. This process meant that the agenda of the Board meetings was well prepared, that major decisions had been considered both by secretaries and appropriate committees, but the final decisions were always those of the Board.

One of the full secretaries of the Board was the secretary for Australia and New Zealand. At the beginning of this period he was the Rev. Leonard Hurst, who had formerly been a district secretary for the northeast of England. He was a full secretary of the Society, but was based in Sydney, Australia, and worked with the Australia and

New Zealand Committee (ANZC) supporting the auxiliaries in the two countries, carrying responsibility for Papua, and maintaining direct liaison with the London board. In April 1946 the Board adopted a new constitution for ANZC which gave to that body the normal responsibilities of an LMS committee and the power to carry out its decisions, subject to certain conditions.

In 1945 Leonard Hurst gave his final report to ANZC as he concluded ten years in the post and was called back to London to become the foreign secretary in succession to Norman Goodall. He had become a dynamic figure in Congregational church circles and in the Student Christian Movement and interdenominational missionary councils. After this further period as a foreign secretary Mr Hurst became home secretary in succession to the Rev. Cecil Northcott. In Australia he was followed by the Rev. Norman Cocks from 1945 to 1970. Norman played a leading role in fundamental changes which were to come about. He was in constant touch with Livingstone House. A letter from the Rev. Maxwell Janes, who succeeded Dr Chirgwin as general secretary in 1950, which I shall quote, illustrates this, but first a word about Maxwell Janes.

Maxwell Janes's appointment came as a surprise to many. He was moderator of the southern province of the Congregational Union of England and Wales (CUEW), and although a member of the Board, he had never taken a leading role. He was regarded as a "union" man. Several of the senior directors were convinced that the time was coming when the LMS and the Congregational Union should be brought into closer working contact. They used their powers of persuasion on Mr Janes and the board to secure his appointment as general secretary.

His letter to Norman Cocks dated 26 June 1950 in which he described his first Board meeting after his appointment and the retirement of Dr Chirgwin shows the intimate contact that was maintained with the ANZC secretary, as he tried to keep him in the picture in a way that the official minutes could not do. He commented that the speaking on the occasion reached an extraordinarily high level. I quote:

> The first to speak was the Rev. Stanley Herbert. He recalled the fact that he was one of the many whose term of service in the LMS had been under Dr Chirgwin's leadership, and he spoke of the way in which Dr Chirgwin had moulded and shaped many men, himself included, by making heavy demands on them, in meeting which they had grown in stature.

He used three phrases to describe Chirgwin: "his faith" which "has rebuked my own fear, his courage which has never been known to falter even in the darkest hours through which the Society has passed, and his courtesy which never snapped under provocation". He was followed by Mr Rider Smith who recalled Chirgwin's call to men and women in the "New Call" and then the "New Advance". In each case the gain to the missionary movement had been a gain to the churches. The Rev. Nelson Bitton, a former home secretary, then recalled inviting Chirgwin to become a junior secretary of the Society, and the trust and esteem he had developed, never treating the Society as a business organization, but as a fellowship. Reference was made by Howard Diamond, the assistant treasurer, to the fear expressed when twenty years earlier the Board decided to create the new office of general secretary, lest the new secretary should become a kind of general manager, to whom everyone else was an assistant. Instead he had been a leader and inspirer and friend to everyone. It was through him that the creative idea of celebrating the triple jubilee of the Society by a "New Advance" programme came. He was always forward-looking and constructive. Maxwell Janes added: "As you can imagine I myself am feeling far from adequate for my new responsibilities, but everyone is kind and sympathetic, and I am anxious to reach a stage of competence at which I can begin to give my best to the Society."[1]

Everyone who worked alongside Dr Chirgwin would endorse all that was said. One extraordinary gift he had was never to forget a person's name. He was renowned for that ability. When he retired, at his farewell party, someone commented on his remarkable memory for names. His answer was also never to be forgotten. He said:

> When I joined the LMS I had a very poor memory, especially for names, so I worked at it. I wrote down the names of everybody I met, and I referred to that record time and again before revisiting any town or attending any committee. Eventually I managed to remember names and it has been a great benefit to me.[2]

Dr Chirgwin would have been the first to recognize the value of the help he received from his personal secretary, Edna Cross. She joined the staff in 1938 and worked with Dr Chirgwin until his retirement in 1950. She continued to serve Maxwell Janes, and gave him the benefit of experience and wise counsel. She was efficient and friendly, accurate in detail and always willing to serve the best interests of the Society. She retired in 1967 after 29 years, never having missed a Board meeting.[3] The smooth and friendly working of the LMS owed much to the personal secretaries such as Miss Cross. They kept the wheels turning.

Howard Diamond as assistant treasurer served the Society for 24 years. He was a member of the Society of Friends, and so added to the earlier ecumenical mixture of the LMS headquarters team. He took a special interest in running the Society's line of "John Williams" ships, and was secretary of the ship committee. He nurtured the finances. He always urged caution on committees which wanted additional money. He maintained that the budget for expenditure, which he presented to the Board each year, was not a licence to spend that amount of money, but rather a guide to expenditure which could be up to that amount, and which preferably should be less. He was greatly respected and trusted. He retired in December 1952. The appointment of his successor, Austen Spearing, adds another link to the relationship of the LMS to CUEW, which Mr Spearing had served with distinction, as secretary of the home churches fund. He had travelled the country advocating the fund. He had consulted every county union every year about the collecting of the fund and its disbursement. He had worked out a clear and simple procedure which had been well received, and he appeared to be the embodiment of the home churches fund.

In some parts of the CUEW the LMS was regarded as a rival in its appeals for regular giving from the same churches, but this was never the view of Austen Spearing. He accepted the LMS post with alacrity, because he had been an ardent supporter and diligent director of the LMS for many years. He had been a member of the consultative and finance committee and understood the finances of the Society. He felt he could make a timely contribution in the role of financial secretary. He soon applied his procedures to the accounts of the LMS and set out each of the various accounts for Africa, India, etc., the ship and home expenditure, and the accounts for running Livingstone House, in a clear and logical manner, so that every director could see exactly what had been received, what had been spent, and what balances remained. He produced every detail in an annual book of accounts, from which it was possible to answer any question on the funds of the Society which anyone cared to ask anywhere in the country. The book was available to any church or county treasurer who asked for it. This procedure made advocacy a much pleasanter exercise because the answers were to hand. Mr Spearing shared in a major undertaking with Mr Rider

Smith, the honorary treasurer of the Society. Mr Rider Smith was well versed in property development and had an intimate knowledge of the financial world through his city of London contacts. The project was imaginative. Livingstone House itself could be developed into a modern office block in Westminster, so that it could become a source of considerable income for the Society. They waited until the time was right, and then proceeded to demolish the buildings the Society owned which surrounded the LMS offices on three sides. New offices to modern standards were erected with an imposing entrance on Broadway where the original entrance to Livingstone House had been. The new entrance to Livingstone House was sited in Carteret Street. This led to the old LMS offices being suitably refurbished, and made the new building, named St Andrew's House, available for letting. It has proved to be a major source of income for the Society and CWM. With the provision for periodic rent reviews it has provided income equal to, or sometimes more than, the contribution income from unions and churches.

A middle period

I would set this period in the 1950-60s. The post-war period was over. The Society operated through its normal channels, and a word needs to be said about these normal channels, both local and national.

From its origin the LMS had been supported by voluntary groups in churches where people had caught the same vision of worldwide mission and organized themselves as auxiliaries. Gradually the concept of these "auxiliary missionary societies" spread throughout the British Isles, all supporting and using the London Society, and sharing in the direction of it. They appointed officers and committees for the day-to-day work, but the final authority was vested in the LMS May meetings each year in London. This organization remained intact until the end of our period, although other missionary societies were subsequently formed by the Church of England and the Methodists, so the LMS was in the end supported almost entirely by Congregational-ists. One prominent and generous lay director of the LMS up to his death in the 1960s was a Presbyterian, Mr Highton of Reigate; he was conscious of maintaining an honoured tradition.

In Wales the auxiliary pattern evolved with a few mixed auxiliaries in South Wales of Welsh- and English-speaking churches, the English churches being originally offshoots from the Welsh, known as the "English cause". The relationship between the majority of the churches of the Union of Welsh Independents (UWI) and the Congregational Union of England and Wales was cordial. In 1925 the LMS council in Wales was established, which effectively coordinated the work of the LMS in Wales in both English- and Welsh-speaking churches. The council had its own LMS secretary, approved by the unions but appointed by and maintained by the LMS. The Welsh office was in Livingstone House, Westminster, and the office secretary was Nellie Deane, who learned the Welsh language and served three Welsh secretaries — the Rev. W.T. Morris (1938-49), the Rev. R.E. Edwards (1950-66) and the Rev. Ieuan Jones (from 1968). The location of the Welsh office was often on the agenda. The reasons for London were partly ease of communication. It was often simpler to travel to Cardiff or Llandudno from London than to travel the length of Wales. But the other factor was the importance of the Welsh secretary being at the headquarters of the LMS, and his being seen to be there. In June 1950 it was "unanimously agreed that the

Welsh office should remain in London at the HQ of LMS and that the matter should not come up for discussion again".

The auxiliary system was also developed in Australia and New Zealand. The 18 members of ANZC for which its new constitution provided were appointed by the auxiliaries in New Zealand and the six Australian states.[4] It was the custom for the auxiliaries to make reports to the Congregational unions in their own regions and the LMS was recognized as the channel through which the Congregational churches took their part in foreign mission, but the Society, with its auxiliaries, clearly operated as an autonomous body.

In Scotland the earliest record of an auxiliary is in a letter dated 4 May 1796 from the missionary society of Paisley pledging support for the LMS.[5] The interest in overseas mission spread to other Scottish cities as in England, and auxiliaries were formed — Glasgow 1796, Edinburgh 1797.... the Borders 1945, Dumfries 1953. A Scottish secretary was appointed by the LMS in consultation with the Scottish Congregational Union and was maintained by the LMS. At the beginning of our period he was the Rev. James Calder, who later became secretary of the Scottish union, and a chairman of the LMS Board. He was followed by the Rev. McMurray Adam 1951-57, and then by the Rev. James McEwan McKenzie Neave who served from 1957 to 1966 as LMS secretary for Scotland and Ireland, and then continued as world mission secretary of the Congregational Union of Scotland (CUS). The whole process, as with the other national unions, was one of consultation and negotiation. The Scottish members of the LMS Board played a full part in all the emerging policies both in the London committees in which some were leading members and in conversations and debates in Scotland at auxiliary and assembly levels. The Rev. James Proudfoot of Kirkcaldy was chairman of the consultative and finance committee, and later of the overseas committee. The Rev. Robert Waters, when he was the general secretary of the CUS, became an influential director. The Scottish secretaries appointed by the LMS were members of the funds and agency committee and answerable to that committee. They had a responsibility for the Scottish auxiliaries, and also for those in Northern Ireland, and the isolated Congregational churches in Dublin. From 1944 various attempts were made to set up a Scottish council of the LMS representing the auxiliaries, the CUS and the LMS directors with one representative from the United Free Church of Scotland. A constitution was approved in 1951 and the Scottish council set up. The LMS Scottish secretary acted as secretary and all travelling expenses were met by the LMS. This development marked both the separateness of the council from the union and also their close collaboration. The council's constitution was revised in 1956, but it was wound up in January 1963 when the LMS's work in Scotland together with that of the Scottish union's missionary committee was integrated within one CUS committee — its overseas mission committee.[6]

A similar arrangement operated in South Africa with the churches of the Congregational Union of South Africa. The auxiliaries functioned in support of the LMS with the blessing of the union. The situation was complicated by the fact that the LMS had missionary work among the black population out of which several Congregational churches evolved. They made a contribution according to their means and their sense of belonging to the LMS was vivid. Indeed some called themselves LMS churches, and continued to do so until the end of our period.

During the nineteenth century the Congregational churches, deeply influenced by the evangelical revival, attempted a variety of methods to expand their effective range of work. From this commitment to mission at home there grew mutual aid between independent congregations. County unions were formed so that the stronger could aid the weaker and by 1885 the county unions were instrumental in developing the national union, CUEW. By 1945 this national body had a major London office and a team of influential officers, comparable to those of other denominations.

Headquarters and board

The London Missionary Society had developed a similar structure with its headquarters in Livingstone House in Westminster, and with a parallel staff team. The auxiliaries in the UK related directly to Livingstone House where the Board of directors gathered three times a year. The directors were appointed by the auxiliaries, and also by county unions and the national union of England and Wales, the Scottish and Irish Congregational Unions, and the Union of Welsh Independents. The Congregational Unions of Australia and New Zealand and South Africa also appointed directors though, by the nature of things, it was only occasionally any of them could attend a board meeting. ANZC had its own full-time LMS Board-appointed secretary, as we have noted. The whole movement with which we are dealing, in Australia and New Zealand, and also its ramifications in Papua, was guided and helped forward in marked degree by Norman Cocks's convinced churchmanship, linked with his equally convinced understanding of the Society's fundamental principle as it applied to mission in an ecumenical age. As ANZC secretary Norman Cocks came to Britain at three-yearly intervals to share in the deliberations of the Board and secretaries' meeting, and to feed in the thinking of his committees. An Australian layman who made a notable contribution was Harold Gaze, CBE, chairman of ANZC from 1931 until his death in 1954. As general manager of British Phosphate he was frequently in London, and his intimate knowledge of the Pacific scene and his commitment to the Society's mission made for a distinctive contribution to the development of LMS strategy and advocacy.

The LMS Board comprised about three hundred members. They served on the various committees covering each of the areas overseas, Africa, India, Southeast Asia, South Seas, Papua New Guinea and Madagascar. The foreign secretaries, Norman Goodall and Ronald Orchard followed by Leonard Hurst, and then Stuart Craig and Frank Griffiths, worked through and to these committees. The committee members became well versed in the details of their fields and well acquainted with the missionary staff who reported directly to them when on furlough and regularly by correspondence. There was also a home committee with the strange title of "funds and agencies" covering not only fund-raising through the auxiliaries but also education, women's work, children and young people, and publishing. The senior committee was named "consultative and finance" on which all other committees were represented by their chairperson and secretary. Howard Diamond was secretary at the beginning of our period and he was succeeded by Austen Spearing. This was the executive committee with power to act in the name of the Board between meetings if necessary.

Throughout this period there were a number of organizations which carried the LMS label. They were significant for education and fund-raising, and each of them developed and adapted itself to the emerging pattern of church life which witnessed the gradual coming together of church and mission. First came the women's auxiliaries, which were a part of the local auxiliaries. They each had their own officers, raised their funds separately and held regular meetings. They were an influential force among the women of the Congregational churches. Some of the larger auxiliaries appointed their own directors to the London Board. They were led by the LMS woman secretary — the Rev. Joyce Rutherford at the beginning of the period, followed by Frances Bowers and then Mary Cumber. They travelled the country addressing women's rallies, which were often the largest missionary meetings anyone addressed. The local leaders were recognized as personalities to be reckoned with. For instance Mrs Rider Smith in London, for a time chairperson of the candidates committee, Mrs Chaffey of Weston Supermare, Miss C.M. Robertson of Glasgow, a former missionary in China, and Mrs C.B. Durrant of Edinburgh, also later a chairperson of the candidates committee. Mrs Morgan of Cardiff was another prominent leader in Wales. The Congregational unions also had their women's associations with similar rallies and conferences and fund-raising activities. The membership often overlapped and relationships were healthy. In Australia and New Zealand the post of honorary woman secretary was held by Kathleen Scott (1937-46) and then by Eleanor Rivett from 1949 for several years, following her very long and distinguished service in India.

Children's organization

The children's organization revealed an early and interesting development. The war years produced a working relationship of the CUEW children's section under the Rev. Bert Hamilton, and the LMS under the Rev. Joyce Rutherford and her assistant Frances Speakman. They launched a joint children's project for boys and girls from ages 6 to 12, based on the imagery of the "John Williams" ships. It was non-uniformed and was called "Pilots". The members, the pilots, trained to become ordinary seamen, able seamen, and midshipmen. They trained for various proficiency badges which they pasted into their "logbooks". They went on voyages of discovery through studying specially written books of stories. In the winter months they concentrated on overseas mission stories, not restricted to the Pacific but covering all areas of mission activity of all the major British missionary societies. It was truly ecumenical. In the summer the voyages were in the "home waters" and dealt with mission in Britain, Australia and New Zealand. The "Pilot" committee was appointed by the CUEW and the LMS and reported to both bodies. There was similar cooperation between the LMS and the Congregational unions in Australia and New Zealand. The nominal head was "the master pilot", the general secretary of the LMS, first Dr Chirgwin then Maxwell Janes. The "secretary" was known as the "cabin boy". Frances Speakman served in the first period. She was followed by Dorothy Biggs. They and their committees laid solid foundations. When Miss Biggs was called to the CUEW to be the youth secretary, "Pilots" was taken over by Elsie Jones. It became her life's work and the numbers increased. On the retirement of Maxwell Janes the role of master pilot was given to Sidney Stolton, a school master and deacon from Tunbridge Wells. He visited companies and camps and stimulated the whole movement. There has followed a succession of master pilots and cabin boys. "Pilots" has remained a lively organization, retaining its worldwide interest, and its links with churches of the Congregational Federation, the Congregational Union of Scotland,[7] and churches in Australia and New Zealand, though its main support is from the United Reformed Church (URC). More will be said about the URC and the LMS but in this context it is noted that "Pilots" is one organization which has retained its identity, and was a pioneer in the movement towards the integration of church and mission.

The interest in children was not confined to "Pilots". It ranged over the whole field of education, providing missionary lessons for Sunday schools, visual aids, and a special children's magazine entitled *News from Afar*. The editor was Dr Olga Pilpel and the chief writer Joyce Reason. Children collected each year for the line of "John Williams" ships, each being known in turn as "the children's ship". Raising money for the ship fund was also a very prominent feature in advocacy and fund-raising in Scotland, Australia and New Zealand, especially among and by children.

Publishing

The LMS had its own publishing department known as the Livingstone Press. The publications were not numerous. They covered the various fields where the Society was at work, for instance *Madagascar on the Move* by J.T. Hardyman, *The Cook Islands* by Bernard Thorogood and an early study on world poverty called *Hungry Men* by Leonard Hurst. Plays and pamphlets and an abundance of leaflets were regular features, as well as the monthly magazines, *News from Afar* and the *Chronicle*. The annual publication of the prayer handbook illustrates our theme. Originally it was a *Watchers Prayer Union Handbook* edited by Mary New. It covered all the areas where the Society was at work, with the names and birthdays of every missionary, a brief description of the work of each field and a prayer. Gradually the names of the church leaders in each overseas church were added, and when Janet Toms took over in 1950 the scope was widened further. Prayers for the Congregational unions associated with the Society, together with the names of their officers, and some material suitable for inclusion in Sunday worship were added. It became known as the *Prayer Fellowship Handbook*, and some churches used it as a regular element in their worship. Up to 30,000 copies were printed and distributed each year. Since 1986 the handbook has been produced by the URC in cooperation with CWM, the Congregational Federation, the Congregational Union of Scotland, the Presbyterian Church of Wales and the Union of Welsh Independents. It has become a resource book, an aid to prayer, without attempting to embrace the whole worldwide missionary enterprise. It is one of the treasures the LMS has bequeathed to our churches.

The work among young people as well as among children provided pointers to the future. After the war the girls auxiliary had a full-time secretary, Muriel Fairhall, who worked from Livingstone House. The young men's union had no full-time officer. Both organizations held annual conferences in local churches, but their memberships had naturally suffered because of the upheaval of war and military service. They decided, after full consultation with their members, to unite to form what they later called the Livingstone fellowship. The aims of the new organization were: (1) to build up the faith of its members; (2) to proclaim the gospel of Jesus Christ to all nations. To this end its members pledged themselves to study, prayer and service.

The study was usually a recent publication of the Livingstone Press or the Edinburgh House Press. Prayer was encouraged at every meeting so that members learned how to lead in prayer, and how to conduct meetings. Service took several forms. Some members offered for missionary service, others for the home ministry and others for social work. The local branches set up groups to care for the elderly, visiting them, shopping for them, writing letters, doing the garden, and reading to the blind or nearly blind. The first chairperson was the Rev. Philip Schofield, then a young Congregational minister. He was followed by Joseph Wing, who became a missionary in Southern Africa, and later the secretary of the United Congregational Church of Southern Africa. Joan Scales of Colchester followed him, and a new chairperson was appointed each year. Robert Latham, the writer of this section, was secretary as education officer of LMS; and the treasurer, Muriel Williams, went on to serve the World Council of Churches and then the churches in Zambia. She was followed as treasurer by Aubrey Curry, who became CWM's chairman of corporations in 1966 and financial secretary from 1982. They were a fellowship of dedicated young people, many of whom have served the churches with distinction. In 1958 the Livingstone fellowship, with the Rev. Stanley Wilton as its secretary, agreed to unite with the Congregational fellowship of youth, which embraced all young people in the Congregational churches in its membership, and was organized by the youth secretary of CUEW from Memorial Hall. The Rev. Stanley Wilton was appointed secretary of the joint youth and children's work of the CUEW and the LMS. The move was welcomed, for it was widely felt that we were all working towards the same end. This state of affairs remained until the youth and children's work of the Presbyterian Church in England was merged with that of the Congregational Church and the LMS. The Rev. Michael Davies, the Presbyterian youth secretary, was appointed secretary. These mergers reflected the mood of the times, and anticipated what was seen to be the next step. During that time, however, the nature of the impending union was not clear.

Throughout this period the LMS had received continual support from the boys' brigade and the life boys' companies in Congregational churches in Great Britain, Australia and New Zealand. Harold Osborne was boys' brigade secretary and Mr W.H. Allcock organized the life boys' annual Christmas appeal. The LMS hospital in Kundara, South India, was supported by the boys' brigade, and it carried an imposing archway declaring it was the boys' brigade hospital. The life boys embraced a variety of projects, including a Landrover for the hospital at Kowtalam, South India, sports equipment for the Cook Islands, and anchors for the "John Williams" ship. Mr Osborne served for 17 years until his death in 1951. He was succeeded by Mr R.H. Milne.

The financial situation

Throughout its history the LMS worked on a shoestring budget. This post-war period was no exception. After the flourish of the "New Advance" and the triple jubilee celebrations with the raising of the half million pounds over and above the regular giving, the rising costs of the work at home and overseas began to take effect. The decade from 1944 to 1954 shows a steady increase in costs which was not matched by increase in income.

The following table was published in the 1954 LMS annual report:

Year	No. of missionaries	Total expenditure £s	Total income £s	British Isles contributions £s	Surplus or deficit £s
1944-45	277	207,000	231,000	(160,000)	+ 24,000
1945-46	258	216,000	227,000	(156,000)	+ 11,000
1946-47	267	263,000	248,000	(148,000)	− 15,000
1947-48	253	273,000	243,000	(165,000)	− 30,000
1948-49	259	274,000	247,000	(166,000)	− 27,000
1949-50	254	304,000	279,000	(191,000)	− 25,000
1950-51	243	292,000	266,000	(180,000)	− 26,000
1951-52	222	298,000	276,000	(180,000)	− 22,000
1952-53	210	309,000	269,000	(172,000)	− 40,000
1953-54	190	298,000	295,000	(191,000)	− 3,000

In summary the situation was that the number of missionaries fell from 277 to 190 during this decade, and after 1945-46 there was a financial deficit in each of the next eight years. The annual report for 1954 sets out the problem in the following terms:

> During the year 1952-53 income fell and costs rose, with the result that a deficit was recorded of £40,000. By using up the last available reserves and by calling upon the churches for a special effort to clear the deficiency, this was reduced to £15,000 — which had to be carried forward. Since the budget for 1953-54 showed an anticipated deficit of £33,000 a budget adjustment commission was appointed. The September Board meeting accepted the proposals of the commission to reduce once more expenditure in India, East Asia, Malaya and Africa. The reduction in India amounted to £7,500. Madagascar, Papua and the South Seas were asked to raise more towards their costs. Home expenditure was reduced by £5,000. In most areas this meant reducing staff. The district secretarial system was discontinued and the directors and auxiliary officers were called upon for yet more intensive and sacrificial service. [8]

The response from the churches was wonderful. The auxiliaries in Great Britain raised their highest figure ever, £191,000. The overseas churches provided an additional £10,000, i.e. the "mission churches". Reductions in expenditure at home and abroad totalled £10,000. The result was that instead of the anticipated deficit of £33,000 the year ended with a deficit of only £3,000. This was serious enough but thanks to the efforts of so many people at home and abroad disaster had been staved off. The situation continued to improve and the next year showed that the deficit had been wiped out and there was a significant surplus of £25,000. The economies, however, had to remain in force. There were only 13 new missionaries appointed, which left twenty vacancies. This was not a planned economy, and may well have been the effect of the known deficit. There was a serious lack of missionary candidates.

One consequence of the shortage of missionary candidates was the timely introduction of the "Associates" scheme. This was also part of the changing pattern. Many members of our churches were taking up appointments overseas in their secular professions. They were challenged by the Society, through their local churches, to identify with and serve the churches in the countries to which they were going. There was a modest response. In 1954, 12 associates were recognized. The associates were interviewed in Livingstone House and briefed about the churches in the area to which they were going. Letters of introduction were sent ahead of them and a welcome was assured. They served according to their abilities — some as treasurers of local churches or districts; others, where the language was not a problem, shared in the leadership of worship. They also became friends of the missionaries and were a strength and support.

When they returned home they reported on what they had seen and done, and some undertook a modified form of "deputation". When a candidate for associate status was going to a part of the world where the LMS had no work, arrangements were made through the other missionary societies for a welcome and invitation to serve. The scheme pointed to the changing world situation, to easier travel, many overseas appointments, and the possibility of being a lay missionary, not dependent on the Society for travel or maintenance. Altogether over 230 men and women were recognized as associates between 1954 and 1977, the highest number at any one time being 90-95.

The ecumenical gale

In the opening chapter Bernard Thorogood writes: "The commitment made in the formation of the World Council of Churches in 1948 was the signal that change had occurred and that greater change was due."[9] In the story of the LMS the ecumenical movement, and the new approaches that were being made to mission, had a cathartic effect. It transformed the concept of foreign missions and inaugurated a period of reformation in the structures of the associated unions.

One of the powerful maxims emanating from Geneva was "the church is the mission". The underlying theology of churchmanship and missiology found ever wider advocates. In the LMS the Rev. Leonard Hurst, as home secretary, pressed for a commission to review the policy of the Society in this period of change. The commission reported that "the fresh understanding of the church which has been given to us during the last twenty-five years has convinced us that mission is an essential part of the work of the church, and that it needs to be seen as the responsibility of the whole church".[10] This emphasis was expressed in the policy statement issued by the LMS in 1952 in these words: "The total work of the church at home and abroad must be recognized as a unity... all possible steps should be taken in the direction of fuller cooperation between the Congregational unions and the LMS."[11] This report was distributed to all the constituent unions and local churches. It was considered at every level and in every church council. For instance the Scottish Congregational Union and the Scottish council of the LMS had several meetings, and in their report to the Scottish assembly in 1952 they gave "general approval" to the LMS policy report.

> It is in the sphere of the relationship of the LMS and the Congregational churches at home, and the national Congregational unions that there would appear to be need of better adjustment, if indeed complete fusion is considered not immediately practicable. For the enrichment of that relationship the Society, the unions and the churches must be prepared to make departures from their traditional practices and constitutions, bearing always in mind the over-riding obligation on all Christians to preach the gospel to every creature...

And further:

> Serious consideration (should be given) to changing the constitution of the Society in conformity with the situation, not as it was in 1795, but as it actually is in 1954. This may quite possibly lead to alterations in the constitutions of the national unions. The whole position should be examined fearlessly and imaginatively in the light of the existing ecumenical trends.[12]

In England and Wales the Rev. Leslie Cooke was general secretary of the CUEW and he was elected to the central committee of the World Council of Churches. He was a keen supporter of the LMS and an active director. In Geneva he met the leaders of the younger churches as his equals on various committees and was much impressed by their calibre, for example Dr D.T. Niles of Ceylon and Bishop Samuel of South India. He came to feel that the time was at hand when the churches from which these leaders came should be in direct contact with the churches of Europe and America rather than with the various missionary societies. He was just as frustrated by the constitution of the CUEW. As general secretary he had no authority to speak for British Congregationalism. The general assembly, the "May meetings" as they were known (reflecting the May meetings of the LMS since 1795), carried no churchly authority. They were consultative and advisory, and the member churches could ignore the resolutions passed if they so decided. These feelings of frustration he expressed in his own powerful fashion, and they reverberated through the following years. Leslie Cooke moved on to the staff of the World Council of Churches as secretary of the division of interchurch aid, refugee and world service.

The Rev. Howard Stanley followed as general secretary in 1960. He set up a series of commissions to examine in depth every aspect of the life and witness of the CUEW. Two of the commissions are relevant to our history.

> *Commission 1: Terms of reference.* (a) The relation of our Congregational churches to one another in council and assembly; (b) the nature of Christian unity and its challenge to our churches; the nature of Christian oversight (episcope).

The recommendation of this commission was that the churches should enter a covenanted relationship with one another, and that covenanted fellowship should become the Congregational Church in England and Wales. This reform gave to the assembly the authority that Leslie Cooke had sought.

> *Commission 5* was entitled the church's missionary obligation. Its terms of reference were: To advise the council and assembly (a) as to how the churches can most adequately discharge this obligation; (b) as to the changes which ought to be made in the relationship between the union and the London and Commonwealth Missionary Societies to this end.

Commission 5's findings were approved in 1961 as procedural notes, and were submitted to the LMS and the Commonwealth Missionary Society (CMS) with the understanding that both the union and the missionary societies would need to have ample opportunity for consultation with the other unions, and if possible these consultations should be made jointly.

The Rev. Dr Norman Goodall was chairman of commission 5, with Maxwell Janes of LMS and Ernest Edwards, secretary of CMS, among its members. Worldwide consultations followed with all the unions associated with the LMS and, because of the CMS, with the Congregational unions in the Caribbean. The LMS at the Board meeting on 13 September 1961 welcomed and approved the main finding of commission 5 that "the time has come when a serious attempt should be made to create a single organization responsible under God to the churches for work at home and overseas". [13] That resolution went on to add: "It does so recognizing that what is envisaged is the creation of a new churchly body, a covenanted fellowship committed to work both at home and overseas, and not an attempt to amalgamate the CUEW and the LMS as such." [14] The Society at that same Board meeting made the following pledge:

> to cooperate in the attempt, on the understanding that particular attention be given to the following points:
> a) The inclusion in the constitution of the proposed churchly body of the essential features of the fundamental principle of the Society. It is assumed that the new churchly body will enjoy the same freedom as the Society has done hitherto to appoint members of other denominations as missionaries.
> b) The provision for the fullest participation in the overseas mission of the proposed churchly body by the other Congregational unions with which the Society is at present associated.
> c) Assurance to the missionaries and the churches with which the Society is associated overseas that these developments are conceived as strengthening and extending concern and responsibility for missionary work.
> d) While the radical nature of the change will require the adoption from a fixed date of an entirely new constitution, replacing both the existing constitutions, the proposed

churchly body through its appointed organs of responsibility shall be left the freedom, under the guidance of the Holy Spirit, to devise the administrative consequence of the new constitution in such a manner and in such stages as shall best maintain unimpaired the continuity of the work for which the union and the Society are responsible. [15]

This was regarded as provisional approval and sufficient authority to consult with the other six Congregational unions, and indeed with the auxiliaries in each country. The unions were approached by both the LMS and the CUEW and relationship committees were set up in each area to give serious consideration to the far-reaching proposals.

The consultations

The consultations were taken up enthusiastically. In one sense they were a continuation of the process of reform which had begun with the LMS policy report, so that much of the ground work had been done. In Scotland, for example, a Scottish relationship committee had been set up in 1958. It comprised representatives of the Scottish Congregational Union, the Scottish council of the LMS, the LMS Scottish auxiliaries and the home secretary of the LMS. It had proposed already by 1960 to set up a new union missionary committee to replace the LMS Scottish council and the union missionary committee, and to retain the auxiliaries for the present but to encourage them to work more closely with the district councils and seek to become coterminous with them. It was this committee which entered into the new phase of negotiations. These took place in Glasgow and in London, and were stimulated by the regular reports from the other consultations.

In Australia and New Zealand the discussion was conducted jointly by ANZC and the Congregational unions. The situation had been simplified in 1960, just before the process of defining the new structure began, by the decision to separate the Congregational Union of Australia from that of New Zealand. This meant that each union was able to deal with the proposals from its own standpoint. When the Rev. Maxwell Janes reported to the Board in December 1962, following his visit to the two countries, he noted that in New Zealand the missionary auxiliary was already integrated into the Congregational Union (CUNZ), so that one session of the union assembly was given to consideration of missionary matters. For the small New Zealand union there was therefore no problem.

However in Australia there were complications, especially because, as Mr Janes observed, it was the various state unions which were strong, while the CUA (a union of unions) had only a part-time secretary and its assembly met only biennially. This posed some difficulty for the movement towards a missionary "churchly body", but Australian Congregationalists saw the necessity for the kind of closer integration which was being envisaged in the UK and, in the event, suitable means were devised. [16] At the same time, it has been observed that the structural alterations were achieved more speedily than was the understanding in the minds of many LMS supporters and ordinary church members of just what the change meant. [17] On the occasion referred to Mr Janes also visited Papua, for each of the overseas churches and all missionaries were included in this wide-ranging consultative exercise.

In the consultation with the Welsh council in December 1960 in Livingstone House Mr Janes reported on commission 5 of the CUEW. This was the first of many consultations describing the proposed new adaptations and responsibilities envisaged in the commission's report. Reports were sent down to the churches, articles appeared in *Y Tryst*, the weekly UWI paper, and the issues were carefully considered. The Rev. Ieuan Jones, missionary secretary of the UWI from 1968 commented on the discussions: "The problem that worried the UWI was concerned with the theology of the nature of the church which it put forward. This concern had its roots in its traditional emphasis upon independency." [18] The proposed title of the Council of Congregational Churches for World Mission was also unacceptable. After wider consultation the revised title Congregational Council for World Mission (CCWM) was proposed and accepted.

By 1964 the UWI annual assembly was able to say:

1) We confirm our belief that mission forms an integral part of the life and responsibilities of the churches.
2) We welcome the intention of the LMS and CMS to adopt the constitution of the new Council.
3) We pledge our full support through personal service, prayer and such financial support as lies within our power. [19]

Subsequent assemblies carried this approval further by amending the constitution of the UWI, setting up the missionary committee and council and by appointing 16 representatives to serve on the CCWM board.

The negotiations proceeded smoothly, but there was a real tension at the heart of them. The CUEW wanted to have responsibility for its world mission, and be seen to have it, but the existence and participation of the other unions made this appear to be impossible. The LMS, on the other hand, found it beyond acceptance to relinquish its role as the missionary agency for the other six unions, and as a "mother figure" of many overseas churches which had come into being under its witness. The Rev. Dr Norman Goodall and the Rev. Ronald Orchard, both former foreign secretaries of the LMS and both holding important ecumenical posts in the World Council of Churches and the British Council of Churches respectively, were the mediators. The Rev. Stuart Craig, foreign secretary for India and the South Pacific, staunchly upheld the unique position of the LMS and had the support of many of the directors, and the representatives of the other unions. After prolonged and detailed consideration a compromise agreement was reached in the form of a draft constitution, which having been submitted to all the constituent unions, was placed before the general assembly of the CUEW in 1963.

So the 1963 CUEW assembly had two draft constitutions to consider. The first provided for the Congregational churches of the CUEW to become a covenanted fellowship, with the title the Congregational Church in England and Wales (CCEW). The second was in the form of a report from the joint committee of the LMS, the CMS and the national Congregational unions related to the two societies.

This report contained a plan which would enable the CCEW and the other national unions "to share fully in the mission of the church so that the gospel is proclaimed to all men, and the church established in every place". [20] The details were worked out and agreed by all the participating bodies so that at the May assembly of 1966, the Congregational Church in England and Wales was brought into being, and in July of that same year the LMS and the CMS were transformed into the Congregational Council for World Mission. The societies, as such, ceased to exist. The charity commissioners approved the constitution of the new body, CCWM, the Congregational Council for World Mission.

The CCWM

The main features of the new Council were, first, that the fundamental principle of the LMS was retained in a slightly altered form. It read: "The Council shall encourage the churches with which it is associated to assume for themselves such form of church order as shall appear to them most agreeable to the word of God."[21] This meant that the Council retained its non-denominational stance despite being labelled Congregational. Second, the Congregational Church in England and Wales and the other Congregational unions would take full responsibility for appointing all directors to the board of CCWM which would be much smaller than the old LMS and CMS Boards. Third, the church and other unions would take full responsibility for all advocacy, money raising, education, recruitment of candidates and care of missionaries on furlough, including housing, deputation, and retirement. Fourth, the council of CCWM would be responsible for the overseas policy and for contacts with the overseas churches.

The arrangement was clearly a working compromise. It was not possible to go further at the time. The outworking, after some inevitable teething problems, was satisfactory. In effect, in England and Wales the home department of the LMS became part of the Congregational Church and moved over to Memorial Hall. It was integrated with the education department and the finance department. The finance department took over the raising of the funds from CUEW for CCWM. They agreed on a 50/50 proportion of the money raised from the churches, which was roughly equivalent to the amount that each had raised separately. A separate arrangement was made with each of the county unions. It was in this area that the most acute teething problems were experienced. The core of the problem, in each of the areas concerned, was that the LMS auxiliary system was disbanded, much to the dismay of many faithful workers who had served as missionary collectors, auxiliary treasurers and secretaries. They had become accustomed to working to the LMS annual budget, and to the several means of raising funds, including collecting boxes and cards, subscription lists, medical mission appeal and the special ship collections. The CCEW employed a different system. It was based on a budgeted triennium, so that the request to the churches was held steady for three years. At the end of the triennium normally all that had been budgeted was raised. Often in the first year there was a shortfall and this caused problems for CCWM. This is expressed by the Rev. Stuart Craig, who had succeeded the Rev. Maxwell Janes as general secretary in 1966 when CCWM came into being. He wrote in the first annual report of CCWM that its first financial year ended with a shortfall of £42,626; the board had received this more calmly than might have been the case because it recognized the serious difficulties which had to be met in changing patterns and procedures of giving, and in particular in securing a smooth flow of giving which was the aim of the CCEW. He wrote that this would take time, but that reiterated assurances had been given that what was lacking would be made up during the triennium.[22] This did take place, but the triennium concept meant that there could be no real increase in expenditure during the three years, which created problems for CCWM which was facing rising costs in many parts of the world.

Tom Chirnside of Lancaster had been appointed honorary treasurer of CCWM in 1966. He had rich experience in commerce and understood the delicacy of the situation. His wise counsel was of great value during these early years, and he was a welcome representative to the Scottish and Welsh unions, as well as to the CCEW.

The Rev. Stuart Craig paid tribute to Maxwell Janes for the 16 years of distinguished service he had given as general secretary of the LMS, and for all that had been achieved in church relationships during those years. During 1966-67 Mr Janes continued in a part-time capacity as an LMS consultant, while he also served as minister of the Congregational-Methodist Church in Crowborough.

The new board of CCWM elected by the constituent unions contained a blend of old and new faces. Some were former members of the LMS and the CMS Boards, whose experience was invaluable in that transitional phase. The secretariat was much the same, apart from the retirement of Maxwell Janes and the transfer of Stuart Craig from the India and Pacific desk to be general secretary. The Rev. Ernest Edwards, secretary of CMS, took over the Africa, Pacific and Caribbean desk. He had served as a missionary for over twenty years in Samoa, and as secretary of CMS had travelled widely in the Caribbean and South Africa. Mary Cumber continued as the woman secretary, which post she had taken up in 1962 as successor to Mrs Bowers. Miss Cumber also came with a rich experience, having served for 23 years in Bengal, where she had been principal of the United Missionary Training College, Calcutta, which provided teachers for schools throughout Bengal. In CCWM she took on the responsibility for candidate selection, and for the personal and domestic affairs of missionaries. She served on the Selly Oak Colleges committee where missionaries received their final UK training. At the other end of the scale she took care of the administration of Lomas House for retired missionaries. The CCWM team was experienced and capable and was felt to be in safe hands.

In Australia and New Zealand the anchor man was the Rev. Norman Cocks who had been serving as LMS secretary for both countries since 1945. He was in close contact with Livingstone House and was the LMS spokesman "down under". The CCWM committee, known as the Standing Committee for Australia and New Zealand (SCANZ), was smaller than its predecessor, and was fully nominated by the Congregational unions of the two countries. The old auxiliaries ceased to exist, and as in the British Isles, the responsibilities for fund-raising, deputations and promotional planning were passed over to the two national unions, CUA and CUNZ. [23] The new form of integration introduced by the formation of CCWM stimulated a further form of integration within the CUA, with its appointment of a council for mission which embraced world mission, home mission and concerns for aboriginal and social welfare. The standing committee was "to conduct (CCWM's) work in Papua and Nauru, to deal with candidates and to provide advocacy service in relation to CUA and CUNZ". [24] There were continuing peculiarities in the nature and responsibilities of SCANZ which were outlined by its chairman, Stuart Ennor, in his report on discussions he had held in London with officers of the board. He said:

> There was general coverage of the progress of development of CCWM and particular attention was given to the function of SCANZ, which is in special relationship to the council in that, whilst it is the only geographically decentralized committee, it is nevertheless an integral part of CCWM. It has a special relationship also to CUA and CUNZ. One of its main functions is as the representative of the seven constituent member bodies of CCWM in its relationship with the Papua Ekalesia. SCANZ also channels the interest and concern of CCWM as a whole towards the home constituency in Australia and New Zealand. It could be said that SCANZ is in fact more closely tied to CCWM as a whole than it is to the two unions by whom members are appointed to the board and nominated for committee membership. [25]

It was also noted that the CMS, now part of CCWM, had been a great support to Congregationalism in Australia and New Zealand, notably by helping to find UK ministers who felt called to serve in those countries. Despite this, the CMS had a much lower profile than the LMS, more so in Australia than in New Zealand. The formation of CCWM gave occasion for grateful acknowledgment of its valuable contribution. [26]

The Rev. Stuart Craig acted as secretary to the joint committee which brought about CCWM and he was the natural successor as general secretary. He brought a wealth of experience to his new office. He had served as a missionary of the Society in China. He had been interned by the Japanese. On his return to Britain he was appointed foreign secretary for India and the South Pacific, which he visited intensively and gained the trust and respect of the leaders of the churches and the missionary personnel. He was well equipped theologically and able to give sound and firm advice in his consultations, as well as in the negotiations with the Congregational unions leading up to CCWM. He saw CCWM as the overseas arm of the CCEW and the six Congregational unions which had been related to the LMS. He was careful and firm in maintaining this balanced view. He fully accepted the basis for CCWM and welcomed the advent of the Congregational Church in England and Wales, and the reforms it had inaugurated. He approved of the take-over of the home department of the LMS and the limitations so imposed on fund-raising. But he was insistent that the overseas policy was the proper responsibility of the CCWM Board, of which the CCEW nominated a part, but not the whole. He felt deeply that the relationships with the overseas churches were the prerogative of CCWM as the heir of the LMS, which had conducted them with care from the earliest days and knew them and their leaders personally. He worked unceasingly to make the new arrangements work and to keep all parties fully involved.

Constitution and policy

There were several modifications of policy. The changing pattern of missionary service, and the continued fall in the number of missionary candidates were perhaps the most crucial reasons for this. In June 1967 a new policy statement was issued by the board and the candidates committee.

> Missionaries are men and women appointed by CCWM and subject to its regulations. In most cases they are appointed to a council of the church overseas which decides where and in what work they shall be engaged. Those going to the Caribbean are called to a local pastorate on the recommendation of CCWM. It is expected that missionaries will give many years of service to the church with which they work as experience and a good knowledge of the language are essential to effective missionary service; but candidates are not expected to offer for life, rather they are expected to say that they believe it right to become missionaries and that they intend to serve as such until convinced that they should do otherwise. This kind of open-ended offer would indicate commitment in depth to the church and people to whom they go, with at the same time an openness to any new leading of the Spirit that might later be given. [27]

This policy statement was an important new development. It had come about partly from the process of winding up the mission administration overseas whereby CCWM now dealt directly with the church authorities in the different countries and no longer with board representatives, appointed by the Board as their agent in the country, and responsible for missionary personnel. When such arrangements were made with a united church, for example in South India, Papua New Guinea and Madagascar, the relationship was with the church as a whole, and not merely with one diocese or region where the missionaries worked. The new phase of mission which these developments represent came under the policy of "partners in mission". Stuart Craig saw the danger that this emphasis "could easily slip into a form of 'church aid' which was not what the Council existed for".[28] He saw that the situation required a close fellowship which, in his own words, "allows participation in the church thinking and planning" and "a readiness to operate in new ways". He was conscious that the relationship was fluid and he sought to emphasize the mission of the church as paramount, and the primary concern of CCWM.

The new constitution of CCWM contained a vital clause. It was that the total policy and operation should be radically reviewed every five years. The first five years were hectic as we have indicated, with new patterns and relationships and responsibilities. The number of missionaries had fallen to 137 by 1969, and there were urgent requests from the churches overseas for more missionaries. The number of associates rose to 87, men and women working overseas in industry and commerce and the professions. The financial position had improved. The constituent church and the unions had met their agreed targets by December 1969. The inflation factor had increased some overseas expenditure, but at the end of the year there was a small overplus on the accounts. The five-year review was undertaken with secretarial visits overseas and consultations with the church leaders in every area, at home and overseas.

The work of the first five years was deemed to have been satisfactory. The transition had been achieved smoothly and the main lines of CCWM policy were confirmed. The following priorities were listed with the need to ensure that increased resources were devoted to them:
— theological education and ministerial training;
— further experience and training for ministers (this group were ministers and others who had been given fresh and wider responsibilities for whom a study visit overseas would be helpful);
— training the laity for participation and witness in both rural and urban developments;
— religious education programmes and leadership for them;
— Christian literature;
— Christian broadcasting.[29]
These categories varied in importance in different areas. The council was actively engaged in consultation on these points with the churches overseas and other bodies.

The policy statement embracing the five-year review and its recommendations was widely distributed through the member churches to their ministers and members, and they were asked to respond. The response of the Union of Welsh Independents given to the Board in October 1968 is typical of the general reaction. It reads:

> The missionary board asks the Union of Welsh Independents to accept the policy statement of CCWM for the next five years, containing particular emphasis upon theological education and ministerial training, thereby providing further instruction and wider experience, the training of the laity for greater participation and witness... etc. as set out above.

The report goes on:

> We regret however that on account of the prevailing situation in which many of our churches find themselves, we cannot promise to raise more money than the £17,000 annually but will try to improve this figure.[30]

The Board, having received the various responses, still requested additional income for the five years from 1970 to enable the council to fulfil the programme outlined in the report. It reminded the constituent bodies of the declared intention "to extend" the work that had been taken over from the LMS and the CMS, and estimated that an additional £30,000 per annum of contributions income was needed. [31]

This was no declaration of failure; rather it reflected the normal procedure which had been very familiar in both the LMS and the CMS, namely that the needs and opportunities overseas always outstripped the expected income, but as we have already seen, over the years a healthy working arrangement emerged.

The Rev. Stuart Craig retired in 1971 after almost 34 years in the service of the LMS/CCWM. He wrote in his newsletter of May of that year: "I can conceive of no more satisfying and rewarding way of spending one's life than overseas mission with the kind of opportunities that have come my way." [32] The Board paid a warm tribute to him in the following terms:

> The Board records its deep appreciation of his long varied and devoted service to the work of the Christian mission through the LMS and the Congregational Council for World Mission... In his work as general secretary since 1966, these years of thought and experience in the missionary enterprise as a whole, his skill in the elucidation and presentation of issues of policy and his acumen in regard to theological and ecclesiological issues have enabled him to give valuable leadership in the period of adjustment to the new relationships resulting from the formation of CCWM... The Board recognizes it has been a costly strain on physical health and in mental and spiritual resources, and it expresses its deep gratitude. [33]

Towards further reform

Stuart Craig's retirement marked the end of an era. Changes had been wrought; the LMS had been superseded by CCWM. The national unions and the Congregational Church in England and Wales had taken over direct financial responsibility for overseas mission, but the overseas contact and administration had remained intact. This was a tribute to Stuart Craig's care and conservatism, and his concern for the overseas churches. The first steps had been taken, as many steps as could have been taken at that time. There was no division in the Board of CCWM and the gradual changes had been well received.

The Rev. Bernard Thorogood was appointed the next general secretary. He had served as a missionary in the Cook Islands and also in the Gilbert Islands. He was the senior missionary in the Pacific area and he had been invited to return to London to understudy Stuart Craig in 1970-71, so he entered his work well versed in the trends and movements in world mission.

The winds of change which were blowing through the churches throughout the world had been greatly strengthened by developments in the World Council of Churches and its associated national Christian councils. In 1961 the third assembly of the WCC meeting in New Delhi witnessed the integration of the International Missionary Council in the World Council of Churches, becoming its Division of World Mission and Evangelism. This integration brought into one world organization the national Protestant and Orthodox churches of the world and the traditional missionary societies. The principal tasks which the division accepted indicate the direction of change which was implicit in its formation. They were:

To assist churches, missions, and other Christian bodies to recognize and draw the practical conclusions from the fact that:

1. The Christian mission is one of salvation throughout the world, for the gospel is the same and the need of salvation is the same for all men.

2. This world mission has a base which is world wide and is not confined to areas regarded once as constituting "Western Christendom".

3. The mission implies a reaching out both to one's own neighbourhood and to the ends of the earth. [34]

From this basis there emerged a series of studies and action programmes. "Joint action for mission" set up three situation conferences in various parts of the world and they were instructed to examine the church's work and witness to discover on the one hand where there was growth and where new tasks needed to be undertaken, and on the other hand what was out of date and unproductive, or could properly be handed over to other agencies. Then to discover whether the total mission in a given area could be carried out by the total people of God, and what this would mean in terms of denominational loyalties and administrative structures. As the studies proceeded the inevitable question arose: "Is joint action for mission really possible without having achieved actual church union?" It was also clearly seen that joint action for mission was as important in the West as elsewhere in the world, and the slogan "Mission in six continents" was born. The Rev. Dr D.T. Niles of Ceylon summed up the conviction lying within these proposals when he said: "It is the privilege of the church everywhere to be involved in mission, not only at its own doorstep but also to some part of the worldwide task. To say that the 'home base' of mission is everywhere is not the obliteration of foreign missions but the universalizing of them." [35]

Arising out of these studies a further study was set up on "The missionary structure of the congregation". Working groups were gathered in Europe, America, Asia and Latin America. Dr Hans Margull coordinated the study and he reported to the division's conference in Mexico City in 1963. [36] He described the present structures as based on the principle that Christians come for worship and instruction, and they saw mission in terms of getting people to come to church. Faced with the necessity of going into the human sectors of today's industrial and pluralistic society, the very intimacy of the parish system emerges as the primary problem, as "parish paralysis". This prevents the presence of Christians in a world where being present means something quite different from the presence ensured in medieval Europe by the parish system. He emphasized that this paralysis is common to the Episcopal, the Presbyterian and the Congregational forms of church order in every continent. He asked: "How can the whole congregation be asked to receive the gift of spiritual renewal when certain structures make it impossible for them to extend their hands?"

Following the Mexico call for "Mission in six continents", the Conference of British Missionary Societies and the British Council of Churches launched a nationwide programme of education and mission in 1966. This included the Roman Catholic Church for the first time, and every mainline church and missionary society. The programme was called "The people next door". Study kits were prepared, training sessions for leaders were arranged throughout the British Isles, and groups of about 12 people were gathered from different denominations in towns and villages all over the country. The groups studied Bible passages, visited one another's churches for worship and called on neighbours in the street to listen, to learn and to share their concern and faith. It was an ecumenical breakthrough. One commentator wrote:

This marks the beginning of a new era in missionary strategy in every country in the world. It is too early to know what forms it will take, but it will be the furthering of the church's mission and the promoting of the cause of unity... there is no knowing where in the world or with whom in the world the Spirit will take us as He recreates his church for all men.[37]

Towards church union

Other movements were making an impact. Delays in achieving wider church union in New Zealand were a factor leading to a major part of the CUNZ constituency deciding to join the Presbyterian Church of New Zealand (PCNZ). When this took place, in October 1969, the PCNZ entered into a "special extra-constitutional relationship" with CCWM and, with CUNZ, continued to take its part, financially and in other ways, as CCWM went through its further changes. Both PCNZ and CUNZ were represented on SCANZ.[38]

Moves towards church union in Australia led to SCANZ, from 1970 onwards, holding its annual meetings simultaneously with those of the Australian Presbyterian and Methodist mission boards. Increasingly, the three bodies discussed matters and made decisions jointly and also coordinated other aspects of their work. During these years, and following the retirement of the Rev. Norman Cocks, the LMS Board had as its secretary in Australia and New Zealand the Rev. Dr G.L. Lockley (1970-74), the Rev. H.P. Bunton (1974-76) and the Rev. H.T. Wells (1976-77).

The newly formed Congregational Church in England and Wales (CCEW) reopened talks with the Presbyterian Church of England (PCE). The earlier talks had led to the CUEW and the PCE entering a covenanted relationship in 1950, celebrated in a special communion service in Westminster chapel in May 1951. The two bodies agreed to work more closely, but they could not agree to unite. The Rev. Howard Stanley, then chairman of the Congregational Union, led the service with the moderator of the Presbyterian church, Dr J.C. Bacon. Now ten years later Howard Stanley was secretary of the Congregational Union and the commission he had set up resulted in the formation of the Congregational Church in England and Wales in 1966. He was convinced that the time was now ripe to reopen the negotiations which should lead to the union of the two churches. The talks progressed positively and by 1972 both churches had agreed to unite, and agreed that the name of the new church should be the United Reformed Church in England and Wales (URC). For the purpose of this history of the LMS/CCWM, it is important to record that one of the major questions, and the most difficult to resolve, was the missionary responsibilities of the proposed new church. The PCE had conducted its overseas mission through its assembly missionary committee, and was directly answerable to the assembly. They had work in Taiwan, Malaya, Singapore and Bangladesh with missionaries serving in each field. The missionary secretary, the Rev. Boris Anderson, a former missionary in Taiwan, was appointed by the assembly and acted always on behalf of the assembly. CCWM did not appear to them to be an acceptable or even appropriate body, in so far as it was not answerable to an assembly of the church. The outcome was another compromise. The Council would drop its Congregational title, and would be known as the Council for World Mission (Congregational and Reformed) from 1973. It would continue for the time being with the URC appointing directors as the CCEW had done. In the process of achieving this agreement there had been full consultation with the other six Congregational unions, and they had agreed.

... and on to the CWM

In 1964 Howard Stanley decided that he would retire from his office as general secretary. He had suffered considerably from ill health in previous years and he felt that a younger man should take over. His successor was the Rev. Dr John Huxtable, then principal of New College, London, a Congregational theological college. John Huxtable had been an outstanding theologian and leader in the Congregational church. He had been a founding member of the church order group which over the years prepared Congregationalism for both reform and renewal. He had also been chairman of commission 1 and took a leading role in all the conversations leading to the formation of the URC. He was clearly the man to lead the URC forward, and his concern about world mission was manifest. In a Board meeting debate in April 1962 he said: "We have long given lip-service to the notion that mission and church belong together. We are now asked to put it into practice. Let us deal with the main principle and leave the details till later."[39] He was prominent in his advocacy of church union, and he used his influence to bring about the union with the Presbyterian church, and the arrangement made concerning CCWM. In recognition of all he did he was nominated the first moderator of the United Reformed Church in 1972.

The CCWM five-yearly review of 1971 had surveyed the proposed merger of missionary activity of the two bodies, and agreed for the time being to accept the arrangements made previously with the Congregational church. This meant that the income was assured, that deputation, advocacy and education were satisfactory. The overseas churches had all accepted the new set-up, but it was understood that the next review due in 1976 would be required to take a radical approach. The preparation for this review became the major task of the Rev. Bernard Thorogood. It was decided that every facet of the life of the Council, in every area, should be reviewed and reappraised. To achieve this it was necessary to involve all the member churches, that is the six Congregational unions and the URC, and the 16 associated overseas churches, together with a strong representation of the London Board and an ecumenical observer. The meeting place selected was Singapore, not London. Delegates were asked to be given authority to present the views of their churches, for the review to be undertaken was of the total operation in each area in the light of the current ecumenical thinking: joint action for mission, the church is the mission, missionary structures, fund-raising, advocacy, education, and sharing in the total world mission. There were to be no "no-go" areas. The review had to be open to the guidance of the Spirit.

The results were startling and well formulated. The overseas churches admitted that they had felt inhibited from mission because every initiative had come from London together with the personnel and the funds required. They felt, they said, they were second-class partners, without an effective voice in the Council where policy regarding mission was determined. The time had come for change. As one South African delegate, the Rev. John Thorne, expressed it: "The fruit is ripe; now is the time to pick it." The report also asserted that every church had the right and privilege to give to mission, as well as receive, both in people and in money, each according to its ability. Moreover the receiving church, wherever it is, should be fully responsible for the missionaries whom it invites to serve, and further every church should be represented on the board of CWM.

Within a very short period the proposals made at the Singapore consultation were given a shape which was accepted by the participating churches, so that on 18 July 1977 the restructured Council for World Mission was inaugurated at a service in the

City Temple, London, with representatives present from its 22 constituent bodies (member churches).

At that point of change one of the Congregational unions was no longer a participant, for in Australia Congregationalists were uniting with Methodists and Presbyterians to form the Uniting Church in Australia (UCA). In negotiations before union it was widely agreed that such a broad church would have its own overseas mission responsibility, quite distinct from the LMS/CWM links, and this was agreed by the Board in London. Although there were some regrets that one tradition had ended, the conviction that mission and church belong together was carried faithfully into the vision and the structures of the UCA.

So in 1977 the movement towards unity and the imperative of mission were expressed in new forms in the family of churches which had been nourished by the LMS.

NOTES

1 Letter from Maxwell Janes to Norman Cocks, 26 June 1950.
2 Words of A.M. Chirgwin recalled by R.O. Latham.
3 LMS board minutes 67 Bd 150, 19 July 1967.
4 Appendix of LMS board minutes, 25 April 1946.
5 Ibid.
6 LMS board minutes, 67 Bd 150, 19 July 1967.
7 Rev. J.M.M. Neave reported (letter dated 6 January 1993) that at its peak the CUS had 15 "Pilot" companies; from the late 1950s numbers fell to five, and then to one in 1993.
8 LMS 1954 survey report, pp.23-24.
9 See p.12 of this volume.
10 LMS commission, June 1952.
11 LMS policy statement, adopted 25 June 1952.
12 Report of ad-hoc committee to 1954 CUS assembly, para. 9.
13 CUEW commission 5 report, 1961.
14 LMS board minute, 61 Bd 98 (c), para. 1, p.33.
15 Ibid., para. 2, p.33.
16 LMS board report, 12 December 1962.
17 Letter from F.W. Whyte, dated 4 April 1992 (who was involved in the negotiations).
18 Letter from I.S. Jones to R.O. Latham.
19 UWI annual assembly minute, 2 June 1964, translated from Welsh.
20 Report to CCEW, 1963 assembly.
21 CCWM charity scheme (constitution) para. 4(2), 14 June 1966.
22 CCWM 1967 report, Discerning the Signs, p.8.
23 CUA minutes, 22-27 May 1967.
24 ANZC executive committee minute A6006(vii), 23 March 1966.
25 SCANZ minutes, 20-21 February 1967.
26 CUA minutes, 25 May 1966 to 1 June 1966.
27 CCWM general secretary's newsletter, no. 228, July 1967, p.3.
28 CCWM general secretary's newsletter, no. 235, May 1969, p.2.
29 CCWM board minutes, 16 October 1968, 68 Bd 174, para. 5, p.59.
30 Resolution of mission board, adopted by assembly of the UWI, 9-11 June 1969.
31 CCWM board minutes, 16 October 1968, 68 Bd 174, para. 10, p.61.
32 CCWM general secretary's newsletter, no. 240, May 1971, p.4.
33 CCWM board minute, 22 April 1971, 71 Bd 54, p.21.
34 R.O. Latham, God for All Men, Edinburgh, Edinburgh House Press, 1964, p.77.
35 Author's recollection of a speech by D.T. Niles.
36 Latham, op. cit., p.45.
37 Ibid., pp.57-59.
38 CCWM minutes, 70 Bd 13, 14 January 1970 and SCANZ minute, SC0021, 20-22 February 1970.
39 Notes on discussion at LMS board, 25 April 1962, Item 62 Bd1.

12. Whom God May Call

Bernard Thorogood

In this volume we have been telling the story of the LMS in the last period of its life as an independent society. Now we can reflect on the whole narrative, from 1795 to 1977, for there is a continuity of motive and method across the years. For all those personally involved the London Missionary Society (LMS) formed a distinctive and crucial element of their obedience to Christ. It carried more than pragmatic importance. There is about the story a resonance with the Acts of the Apostles, a sign of the continuing power of the Holy Spirit as well as a demonstration of the fallibility of all disciples. For many who observed the work of the Society from outside it appeared as a vigorous, committed and courageous body of people who were steadfast even if misguided. Now that the LMS has been reborn in quite a new form as the Council for World Mission (CWM) we can reflect on the remarkable two centuries of service. What was the essential character and gift of the Society?

A pioneering society

From 1795 the leaders of the LMS were conscious of a pioneering role as they endeavoured to spread the gospel. They had no hesitation in declaring this commitment to provide messengers who would speak the word of grace in every part of the world. It is a record of astounding audacity. That a group of non-conformist ministers and businessmen should steadily plan the evangelization of continents, looking at their half-empty world maps, pondering the choice of ships, selecting very varied companies of the faithful, accepting heavy losses and pleading for support, is a tribute to spiritually-based confidence of a high order. They began with the South Seas mission, following the travels of Captain Cook, encompassing great distances, impossible communications and small fragile human societies. Across the southern Pacific the LMS was a pioneer of the gospel, touching island after island. In South Africa and India, in Malaya and China and in Madagascar the pioneering continued, with quite small missionary groups entering these vast populations, their hopes high, patience strained and illness prevalent. The great names among those pioneers are well known in Christian history — John Williams, Robert Morrison, Robert Moffat, David Livingstone, James Chalmers and John Philip. And once read, there is an unforgettable tale of Edward Stallybrass who was despatched to Russia, had an audience with the czar, received a permit to proceed and spent months on a sledge in winter making his way to Irkutsk on Lake Baikal, where he learnt the Mongolian language and began translating the New Testament. Sanctified audacity must be the word for the board of directors who called people to such enterprise.

But the great names cannot occupy the whole stage. The company of pioneers includes the uncelebrated missionaries, the wives and children of missionaries and the great number of indigenous pastors, colporteurs, teachers and evangelists who often had the hardest tasks. They had negligible equipment and financial backing. Frequently they were cut off from family roots by both faith and geography. We know that, in some areas, many gave their lives through illness and ill treatment. But it was by the self-offering of these locally-recruited people that pioneering on a broad scale was made possible. An honour roll in the Pacific Theological College in Fiji tells of frequent sacrifice and adventurous service by a host of Islanders.

This dimension of pioneering was an outstanding quality of the first century of the LMS. What were the factors which enabled such an emphasis? First was the fact that in the period 1795 to 1850 the LMS was the first Protestant society to be engaged in many places. The Baptist missionary society had the honour of an earlier starting date (1792) and also pioneered, with signal achievements, in India, and the early locations for LMS work avoided overlap. So this was a fresh style, a fresh Christian voice on the world scene, gathering all the energy, enthusiasm, sacrifice, hope and determination of those who launch a great enterprise. Second, the early directors of the Society were not conditioned by the establishment of the Church of England and were not constrained by the responsibility of chaplaincies to settlers. They were free to consider human need across the globe. So to them Tahiti, Madagascar, Russia and China were equally valid places of service, as the British colonies were for the Church of England. Third, those members of the Board were able to give very considerable freedom to the individualistic enterprising people who operated on the frontiers of faith. In reading old minutes the impression conveyed is that sometimes such freedom was granted because communication was so slow. In other cases the directors urged restraint while the man on the spot was already away on trek. This was often the case with David Livingstone and John Williams.

Pioneering was a very high-risk activity and it is questionable whether the scale of the risk was appreciated in London, either by the directors or by those setting out with high hopes. It was not physical danger alone that was critical, although tropical illness was largely uncontrollable, but the isolation of a Christian witness amid a culture hardly understood which battered the early groups of missionaries. They fought the fears and disappointments and misunderstandings with a lively sense of spiritual purpose and it is a permanent cause for joy that so many were sustained for a life of service. Those who failed to keep their commitment are largely ignored in missionary histories. In the first century of the Society marriage to a local woman overseas was regularly taken to be a signal of both faith and decency lost. Theological questioning and radicalism meant the severe downgrading of some bright spirits. We therefore note the pioneering groups sent out by the LMS as very mixed in ability, training, intention and suitability with only a few among them reaching the highest levels of public acknowledgment.

This emphasis of the LMS continued throughout its life, though with very restricted scope in the last half century. It was then only in Papua New Guinea that primary, adventurous discovery was called for. It remains, however, a signal achievement of this Society to have been the advance guard of Christian expansion in so many parts of the world. To attempt this overwhelming commission was the calling of the founders of the Society who knew that success was by no means sure. In one of the sermons preached at the formation David Bogue declared: "To attempt is noble. To fail here is more honourable than to succeed in most other pursuits. Should we fail of success, while we may be grieved that the heathen still remain in darkness, we shall have no reason to repent of our undertaking."[1] For the pioneering we can say with confidence that there was more success than failure.

An evangelical society

The revival movements of George Whitfield, John and Charles Wesley stirred the conscience of the English churches during the eighteenth century, blowing away much of the chaff of humbug and laziness that was mixed with the wheat. There was a new seriousness about faith. People's lives were changed. Social concern was not "Lady Bountiful" but radical education. Although there was as much resistance to the movement from ecclesiastical authorities as has been normal throughout history, the effects were very far-reaching. So the missionary societies born at the end of the century were expressions of evangelical conviction. They were not overly concerned with imperial power or with church power. What had taken hold of this group of pastors and church members was the transforming power of the gospel. It was this that gave weight, permanence and mystery to all their planning. We cannot presume that romanticism was absent from their minds, for the voyages of the great explorers, Captain Cook in particular, were much in the public conversation of the day. But they saw through the romantic image of peoples far away to recognize human beings who, like themselves, could be touched by the grace of a loving God.

The Society was thus founded on the conviction of a universal gospel. A similar assurance lay behind the Jesuit outreach of earlier centuries, but the Reformation churches of the seventeenth and eighteenth centuries had been intensely occupied with national freedoms and national provision so that concern for the distant world was itself distant and academic. The evangelical revival brought the issue to the surface again. What does the "all" of the gospel really mean? "I, when I am lifted up, will draw all people to myself" (John 12:32). "Go therefore to all nations" (Matt. 28:19). "Go out therefore to the main streets and invite everyone you can find to the wedding" (Matt. 22:9). "As the result of one misdeed was condemnation for all people, so the result of one righteous act is acquittal and life for all" (Rom. 5:18) "... that the universe, everything in heaven and on earth, might be brought into a unity in Christ" (Eph. 1:10). The "all" contains a great debate. The Calvinist strain in British theology was vigorous. The great stress within it was on the total sovereignty of God whose will is supreme and who wills salvation. But for whom? For all? The other aspect of biblical teaching came to the fore in Calvinism with an emphasis on the few, the narrow way of life and the broad path to destruction.

At the point where the Society was born it was the universal dimension which was most evident. Christ died for all, not for a proportion of the European population. Since that is so then all should know the fact. Preaching to all is an essential obedience. The response is not in human hands. There were those who would categorize a negative response as the judgmental action of God; others who would attribute it to the devil; and yet others who could see it as an entirely human response. The widespread theological agreement was that the same message of repentance and trust in Christ was valid for all classes, all races, all languages and all generations. The early missionaries were indebted to the Wesleyan revival for the strength of this conviction.

Has it remained so throughout the history? The answer is a confident "yes", for there has been no other basis on which resources of people and money and insight and learning have been transmitted. During every period the Society reaffirmed its purpose as gospel-centred. There are two qualifications, however, which have to be made. The first qualification is that gospel for some did not mean a simple preaching of a message which had to be received and accepted for the eternal salvation of the soul. They saw the good news as touching human life in all its captivities. So the great battles with ignorance, fear, illness and poverty occupied centre stage for many who were sent out by the Society from its early days right through to the most recent. The record of the Society in the provision of medical and educational facilities in very needy places shows that this dimension of witness was fully accepted as true to Christ. It was considered to be evangelical, a declaration of the will of God for all human life. More recent divergence between those called evangelical and those called social witnesses would have been anathema to the leaders of the LMS in the nineteenth century. Just as Jesus in his ministry had fused together the healing of the sick, the comfort of the sad, the challenge to the complacent, the preaching of repentance and the way of the cross, so the diverse band of missionaries was justified in regarding all light in human darkness to be God's good gift.

The second qualification is that in the more recent period there was frequent discussion about the calling of God to people of other faiths. In the Congregational churches between the two world wars there was a growth of liberal theology and a greater willingness to accept that God had given a measure of wisdom and goodness through other channels, so that other faiths could not be categorized as no more than devices of evil. This did not mean a lessening of the call to declare what God had done in Christ, but did affect assumptions regarding the presence of God and the judgment of God. Such consideration about the breadth of God's self-revelation has not taken a central place in missionary planning but marked, in the LMS, a departure from old certainties about the clear division between those saved and those damned.

Although the evangelical motive stands as primary in all LMS publications, other, less noble, motives have been suggested. These have to do with status and profit. The majority of those people recruited for service with the LMS, in its early period, came from the emerging British middle class, often with very humble backgrounds and limited educational opportunities. Yet by the middle of the nineteenth century many found themselves in places of considerable influence, living in large houses with several servants, after the style of the local colonial officers. It would be surprising if this did not sometimes lead to an inflated view of the missionary status. "They came to do good," so the jibe runs, "and they did right well."

But such a context certainly did not cover all. Many missionaries lived in considerable hardship, travelling by the most physically demanding means and eating the simplest possible diet. Few developed commercial interests and those who did were reprimanded by colleagues and they usually ended up by leaving the Society. Missionaries were paid very meagre living allowances from London, the figure being based entirely on family need and the local cost of living, not at all on seniority or qualifications or post occupied, and that principle held good right up to 1977. No one grew rich by serving the LMS.

A further accusation is that the Society itself drew finances from the churches which it founded. The basis of this charge is the fact that the local churches were often asked to contribute towards the cost of the service they received. The sums were usually very small and the offering was often in kind rather than cash. The principle was regarded as important, that no church should be utterly dependent on the gifts of people far away but should move towards self-support by its own voluntary giving. Receipts of this kind never covered the full cost of missionary service and certainly did not enrich either the churches or the directors in Britain.

One point where criticism is possible is that in some places the Society obtained sites for churches, schools, manses, etc. either free of charge or on payment of very small fees to local landowners before any formal legal system was developed. In this the missionaries were creatures of their time, seeking the future benefit of Christian work and worship, not sensing any injustice. It is only now as we look back that we sense that advantage was sometimes taken of local goodwill. In each place the Society endeavoured to transfer the titles to land and property to the appropriate local body, and this process was well advanced by 1977.

Concern for the word of grace which is good news, that it may be heard and lived out, remains primary. In 1948 the report of the directors described the harsh conditions which followed the second world war, but concluded:

> As this report clearly shows there have been abundant evidences of God's grace in the increase of evangelistic activity, in the growth of the Christian community overseas, in the increasing confidence of the home churches and in the deepening sense of oneness in the world church. Expectancy is in the air, and it may well be that spiritual renewal is once again at our doors. [2]

Such hope rests in an experience of the power of God.

An ecumenical society

The distinctiveness of the LMS among all the early societies and agencies lay in its professed intent not to be denominational in character. This set it apart from the Baptist missionary arm and the Church of England societies which had been created in response to colonial settlement. The fundamental principle, adopted in 1795, remained crucial until the end:

> As the union of Christians of various denominations in carrying on this great work is a most desirable object, so, to prevent, if possible, any cause of future dissension it is declared to be a fundamental principle of the Missionary Society that its design is not to send Presbyterianism, Independency, Episcopacy, or any other form of church order and government (about which there may be a difference of opinion among serious persons), but the glorious gospel of the blessed God to the heathen; and that it shall be left (as it ought to be left) to the minds of the persons whom God may call into the fellowship of his Son from among them to assume for themselves such a form of church government as to them shall appear most agreeable to the word of God. [3]

Those were remarkable words for 1795 and to date remain so. They were faithfully followed through, for at no point in the history do we find that directors or staff in London were prescribing the Congregational style of church order to which most of them belonged. There was an openness on these matters which could accommodate great variety, both in the recruitment of missionaries and in the ways they developed their work.

This measure of laissez-faire was the ground from which the ecumenical involvement of LMS churches grew, for they knew themselves to be free to reform themselves in relation to other churches. They could seek new unions with a good conscience. This was a slow process and it has to be confessed that through the nineteenth century those churches founded by the LMS could be as partisan and denominational as any. But in the present century the assertion that the unity of Christians is intended to be visible as well as spiritual was very widely accepted. Christians in this particular family found themselves to be key participants in many union schemes, first with non-episcopal sister churches in China, India, Zambia, Madagascar, Papua New Guinea, Jamaica, and then also with episcopal colleagues in South and North India. To have promoted this movement towards unity, and to have contributed much in talent, imagination, hope, tenacity and willingness to learn is one of the clear causes for gratitude in the LMS history. In places which the LMS regarded as "home bases" it was also people from the same tradition who were able to initiate and sustain movement towards unity in England and Wales, Australia and New Zealand. A significant omission from this list is South Africa. Although there has been considerable work done, with the Rev. Joe Wing taking a very significant part, the complexities of racial and tribal difference as well as theological tradition have so far proved stronger than the calling to unite.

A second great benefit which followed the fundamental principle was the freedom to adapt the forms of the church to local conditions and local culture. No one was bound to a prayer book. An Indian ashram could become a model for a church. In Polynesia the leadership positions in the church could imitate those in the old tribes. The surprising fact is that this freedom was relatively little used. In the majority of places the church buildings erected, the forms of worship followed and the church constitutions adopted revealed a great deal of imitation of the English and the Welsh non-conformity of that period.

This points towards the weaknesses that also lie within that basic principle. Where it speaks about those "whom God may call into the fellowship of his Son" there is some unreality. It was bound to be those "whom we have sent out" who were responsible for the early ordering of the life of the churches, and only slowly and hesitantly were local people involved. But that first generation, when the missionary was almost bound to be dominant, set the major elements of church life for very many years after. A pattern could be set with the missionary as the effectual bishop and local Christians obedient to his word. It is now surprising to recall that in 1952 when I was appointed to service in the Cook Islands, the local church constitution ended with the words: "Notwithstanding anything written in this constitution it is accepted by all the churches that the word of the missionary appointed by the LMS to serve in the Cook Islands is supreme." Papacy could go no further! This was the risk which the fundamental principle entailed. The local church could be separated, through personal influence, from the wider body of believers.

There is, however, a deeper problem. The inescapable suggestion of the principle is that faith can be transmitted separately from any ordering of the church. It is a siren call of evangelicals through the ages. Here, they might say, is the meaning of faith, it is to do with you, your heart and mind in the presence of almighty God. It is the basis of your eternal destiny. What kind of group you then join and what pattern of worship it follows and what church government it recognizes is up to you; I, the evangelist, cannot point you in one direction or another. But this divorce is not tenable for most theologians. To be joined to Christ in faith means to be joined to the body of Christ in practice. The nature of the church reflects the character of Christ, the head of the church. It would not be true to say in this connection that the medium is the message, for the church never, at any point in history, has encompassed the fullness of Christ. But the medium and the message are very closely related; they confirm each other. Therefore missionaries who are witnesses of the gospel inevitably declare an understanding of the church by their personal stance, their visible practice, their association, their respect for tradition and their definition of church membership.

A measure of this distance from the theology of the fundamental principle is the increasingly denominational character of the LMS. The vision of an inclusive, ecumenical society gathered "at the funeral of bigotry"[4] and providing a channel of service for people of all persuasions was never fully realized. The Anglican, the Methodist and the Baptist communities in England were committed to a confessional or denominational mission undertaking, not because they were prompted by ill-will towards the LMS but because of the binding together of faith, order and enthusiasms in one bundle. It was a matter of their self-understanding. This meant that the communities supporting the LMS were increasingly Congregational or Independent in their church life. This fact was fully accepted and carried into the constitutional process of 1966.

So we have learnt that the ecumenical engagement does not make progress by ignoring the differences of church order, nor by suggesting that they are only matters of personal preference, but by facing them openly and asking the deepest questions about the relation of faith and order. The LMS was always pointing the way towards a theology and practice of the church which were generous and inclusive; that was its particular gift. It could not deliver, in the missionary enterprise, a solution to the divisions within Protestantism. Hence its ecumenism remained prophetic, a sign in the present of the hope that Christ will lead his people everywhere into the one city where there are no labelled churches any more.

A society of individuals

It was largely through the influence of independent churches that the Society was born with a healthy respect for individualism. It was the paucity of communication which reinforced the pattern. For very long periods the early missionaries were on their own, grappling with unimagined problems, facing the sheer hard labour of language-learning, meeting a tough climate and a strange diet. So they had to be strong individuals. The Society could not dragoon them, nor supervise the way they interpreted their commission. It is not surprising that some became autocratic and enjoyed power, while others maintained feuds with colleagues with the intensity of the Medicis. Most of the missionaries developed their talents with tenacity and a deep sense of purpose. Nowhere was this more evident than in language-learning and Bible translation. Many individuals who had slender academic backgrounds mastered new languages, put them into writing for the first time and produced mature translations. So Henry Nott, a bricklayer by trade, was able to publish the first Tahitian New Testament and, in doing so, set a standard for the written language. In places with ancient written languages, notably India and China, there were strange alphabets and scripts to master and this took years of concentrated effort. Ordinary people were able to do extraordinary things.

This engagement of individualism enabled the Society to maintain a supporting role for a great variety of missionaries. So Van der Kemp came from Holland to South Africa to pioneer among the people then known as the Hottentots, Robert Moffat came from a Scottish Presbyterian background and the Welsh Independents gave themselves sacrificially to Madagascar. There was a freedom about the recruitment process which opened doors for the dedicated individual and this remained a characteristic of the Society throughout. Indeed it was its glory. During one period it offered as a slogan "The Society that sent Livingstone to Africa", but in that case the man stretched even the most elastic of reins and severed his connection with the Society in order to follow his own very personal calling to bring "Christianity, civilization and commerce" to central Africa. In the recent period the Society was able to contain in India missionaries wholly dedicated to the union of the churches and those who opposed it to the end. It enabled the service of many whose theology was sketchy but whose love for others shone like a beacon.

Such individualism was one of the strengths of the pioneering period. It set people free to dare, to risk, to attempt quite new enterprises, to meet new peoples and enter new towns. But this leads to one of the most serious questions which must be asked. "Was the Society which was designed for the pioneering period properly engaged and effectively engaged in the leadership and nurture of churches for the following century?" It is hard to believe that this is what the founding fathers intended. And it was a role for which their theology gave limited sanction. They did not expect that missionaries would carry any strong sense of the church as the whole fellowship through all the centuries, but that they would concentrate entirely on the locality and what happened there. They were thus at the other end of the spectrum from the Roman Catholic missionary movement which, at every point, was emphasizing the bonds which held together the one universal church. So from the start of the Society until about 1930 missionaries were in key positions of local church development, usually without any balancing indigenous leadership. From that date local church people gradually assumed more influence. But that was a long time for the individualists of the LMS to exercise heavy influence on worship patterns, ministry and its training, finance, buildings and theology.

Why did they continue to serve in these positions for so long? All that Roland Allen had described in his two books *Missionary Methods, St Paul's or Ours?* and *The Spontaneous Expansion of the Church* was ignored, for he lamented the overstaying missionary and prescribed a very quick transfer of leadership to local people. The fundamental principle had put all the emphasis on the ministry of evangelism but increasingly missionaries were not serving on the frontiers so much as in the base institutions of the churches.

I see two reasons for this development. First, those who were largely responsible for the direction of affairs during the nineteenth century do not seem to have appreciated the power that missionaries held, a power which easily dominated church life in the shape of benevolent paternalism. It was a power of knowledge — of the Bible, of the world, of western modes of life. It was a power of money — to pay teachers and evangelists, to employ and dismiss, to build a school here and a hospital there. And it was a power of total dedication, that energy, tenacity and whole-hearted self-offering which sweeps others along like dust behind the desert bus. All this power was brought together in regular meetings of all the missionaries in an area and decisions of that meeting must have appeared to local Christians as enigmatic as those from the Vatican. Protestant churches have been notoriously absent-minded about power. Because they live by goodwill and proclaim Christ-likeness it is too easily assumed that no one holds, enjoys or misuses great power over others. But in all the areas of missionary work there was an inevitable accretion of power in missionary hands even as the spokesmen of the Society were rejoicing in partnership. It was only in the last fifty years of the LMS that this issue was fully dealt with. The length of the parental stage of influence added to a sense of dependency which diminished local initiative.

The other root of the prolonged nurture of churches was the reality of deep affection which it is not foolish to call love. Many missionaries were bound to local Christians by such bonds, created by years of steadfast service and by intimate knowledge of language and culture. They could not pack their bags while local people were asking for more teaching, for more health care, for more translations and for more administration. To have gone would have seemed like desertion. In many places it would have left behind considerable institutions without the professional abilities to maintain them. This was a major reason cited in India. In others it was the theological training of the local ministry which was the continuing call. Although the LMS enforced a clear retiring age for missionaries, there were many who could only with difficulty be wrenched from the fellowship where long service had made them at home. And some of those continued to serve in retirement by completing translations or organizing prayer support for their adopted church. Those strong attachments were reflected in reports of missionaries and visiting secretaries and so powerfully influenced the LMS Board. The conviction was established; so long as they need us we will be there. It was only in the context of China that radical change was enforced and there it is hard to see that the indigenous church suffered greatly from the absence of missionary staff.

Thus the Society sustained its highly individualistic missionaries to exercise, for very many years, large influence on local church development. During its last fifty years this was increasingly questioned but transition to fully local leadership was slow. There was, in British church circles, an expectation that the "younger churches" would display a pattern of life similar to that of the parent. There should be a written constitution, a written statement of faith, a regular pattern of ministerial training, full-time ministers ordained for life and audited annual accounts. So although "it should be left to those whom God should call into the fellowship of his Son from among them to assume for themselves such form of church government as to them shall appear most agreeable to the word of God", we do not see much radical innovation; generally conciliar or presbyteral patterns were followed. Gradually the missionaries took less influential positions in these councils and became, in the period of this volume, servants of the local church. But the duration of this process remains as a question mark in the story of so enterprising a Society.

A society able to reform

The British churches sponsored many missionary bodies in the nineteenth century. This was the religious parallel to the emphasis on imperial vocations in the Victorian age, when patriotism, duty, adventure, altruism, greed and class pressure all, in varying measure, sent British people to posts around the globe. Many of the Christian organizations remain after the empire disappeared, and some of them with much the same basis of commitment. They still regard the British churches as, in some respect, the proper base from which to exercise a worldwide ministry. But the LMS was unusual in being able to move through two considerable reforms, in 1966 and 1977, and in that process, to lose its identity as an independent society. Why was it possible for this institution — which shared all the usual defence mechanisms — to embrace radical change?

It is evident that a strong pressure towards change came through the development of the British churches which supported the Society from aggregations of local congregations into self-conscious, organized denominations. This was their story during the century from 1850 to 1950. It particularly affected the English Con-gregationalists who moved from total independency to a connexional system, with the establishment of mutual support and central services which were strengthened to meet the stresses of two world wars. The signal of this change was the adoption of the name the Congregational Church in place of the Congregational Union, for this clearly marked an ecclesial character for the national body which had not been anticipated by the Independents of the nineteenth century. One factor here was the need to deal on an equal basis with the other churches in England, especially in all unity discussions. Another was the dependence of many smaller local churches on national subsidy for the cost of ministry. A third was the call for many specialized services which could only be provided at national level. This movement of thought encompassed the responsibility of the church for mission. What was appropriate for independent local churches was no longer right for a national church. The former could depend on individual enthusiasts; the latter needed a corporate commitment, and this could not be given effect by a Society with individual members. This view was strongly presented by Howard Stanley when he addressed the future of the Congregational Union.

Alongside that emphasis, which we might call organizational, was a theological argument which was clearly expressed in the 1950s by Norman Goodall in the International Missionary Council and as clearly opposed by Max Warren of the Church Missionary Society. If the whole missionary endeavour, both at home and around the world, is a primary function for which the church exists, then the direction and support of that whole enterprise should rest with the representative council of the church. It is not an extra to be tacked on at the side. It is not a haven for a few enthusiasts. It is not an option which a church may pick up on occasion. On the contrary, it is the very stuff of churchliness and so needs to have its constitutional place in the church's life. The opposing view stressed the need for freedom and initiative. The great advances of the church in the nineteenth century had been won by daring, courage, total dedication. Those are not the characteristics of a church assembly. They are stifled by rigid structures. Just as the church needs specialist agencies to deal, for example, with work among children or with drug abuse, so it needs specialists in overseas mission; and they can only be effectively sustained by a body of committed supporters, a voluntary society. This debate continues. For the Congregational churches, however, the former view prevailed, and relationships with the Presbyterians confirmed it.

A third enabling factor was the realism of those leading the Society in the 1950s and 1960s. They were alert to the great changes in the world and the church and were not clogged with nostalgia. One was Stuart Craig, who had been through the period of the communist revolution in China and who could have no illusions about the future role of British people around the world. His keen mind was a moving force in the 1966 reform.

A fourth was the changing situation of churches in Australia and New Zealand which had been traditional partners in the LMS enterprise and also in the Commonwealth Missionary Society. The fact that in both countries the Congregational churches were approaching union led to a radical review of their missionary engagements. The bonds of history and sentiment were loosening so that a London base of operations was no longer appropriate. This was a spur to those in England who sought to move out of the LMS framework into a conciliar body.

Such pressures enabled the LMS to meet reform in a mood of expectancy rather than fear. It is significant that it was alone among British societies in the radical nature of reform but followed quite closely the changes in the Paris Missionary Society which developed into the Communauté Evangélique d'Action Apostolique (CEVAA). Both societies had served a Reformed style of church enterprise in dying European empires; both saw the international round-table as the most appropriate new format; and both had some difficulty in defining the character or emphasis of mission in the new period.

A new form in a new age

The particular gifts of the LMS which make it outstanding among British mission agencies were its pioneering courage, its evangelistic commitment, its ecumenical character, its individualistic style and its ability to face a reform which would end its life as a society. We now have to ask whether the purpose for which it was created (in what now seems a distant age) is fulfilled or carried forward in the new Council for World Mission (CWM). Does the discontinuity of structure enable a continuity in the response made to the call of God? While the pioneering purpose could be set out with clarity from the apostolic commission, can an international council offer as powerful a call? What does international mission require of us today?

The calling of Christ to the apostles was to witness and proclaim the greatness of God in every human community. In missionary history, both Catholic and Protestant, the Matthew version of that call (Matt. 28:20) has been most quoted as the basic authorization. There are other versions: that from Luke in Acts 1:8 stresses witness but not teaching and baptizing; that from Paul in 2 Corinthians 5:18-20 places on the Christian community the reconciliation ministry which carries onward the work of Christ. We have been reminded by Raymond Fung of the World Council of Churches (WCC) that there is a Johannine version also in John 13:34-35 where it is the character of the Christian fellowship by which "everyone will know that you are my disciples". Whichever was the most powerful word in the minds of the apostles the result was the immediate, courageous and sacrificial outflow of witness from the Jerusalem base to the breadth of the Roman empire. That was the model taken by the Catholic missionary enterprise of the fifteenth and sixteenth centuries and then by Protestants in the eighteenth and nineteenth centuries: from a known base, from a secure faith, from a point of departure to the opening world, in order that the wonder of God's gift in Christ may be presented everywhere. A great responsibility was seen to rest on those who had entered the way of faith. On them the light had dawned. To share that light with people who lived and died in darkness far beyond the traditional homeland of faith was a duty and a delight.

A major transition occurred when the Holy Spirit so worked through the witnesses that a community of Christians was born in every nation. There is then no geographical centre for world mission and no periphery, but each congregation is a focus of prayer and action. It has been hard for the traditional sending churches to accept this reality, for the geographical spread is far easier to understand and stress than mission next door in the home country. It is significant that those churches which most consciously call themselves "evangelical" have been least able to accept change in the nature of the world mission. For them there is still a primary evangelistic task to be carried out among "unreached peoples" and the old mission agencies are the means of witness. It would be entirely inappropriate to adopt an exclusive position here. The Spirit calls people in unexpected ways. For those who take the local church with ultimate seriousness as the bearer of the gospel there can only be thanksgiving that everywhere the local church, however small and imperfect, has become the crucial centre of the circle of mission. The spread of Christian faith to new places, new tribes, new language groups, old cities newly pagan and great populations newly secularized will remain an imperative of the gospel, for there is no good news which is a private possession of the churches.

The 1977 reform enabled the Council for World Mission to be internationalized and so to respond to the reality of the church context. All those local churches which had been served through the LMS were enabled to become members of the Council, to sit at the table where decisions are made, and so to share their talents in the common calling. The development of the LMS into the CWM provides a structure to the significant changes in the world Christian map. It removes the UK churches from the position of decision-maker and gives all the churches equal responsibility for the witness in their own areas and equal rights to the concern and resources of all. The calling to go, to witness, is accepted by all, but primarily within their own location. That is not a limitation; it is a starting position. "Beginning at Jerusalem" means that mission is launched exactly where we are gathered at the table of the Lord.

That is never the end of the commitment. "The world is my parish," said John Wesley, not because he harboured imperialist longings but because the outpouring of God's love in Christ is for the healing of the whole human family. So in the new context we anticipate that all churches have associations, involvement, challenges and duties beyond their own borders as a natural part of membership in the one body of Christ. We are still at an early stage of discovering what this means, and the CWM is only one format for our learning process. Certain notes are becoming clear. International mission is not exactly the same thing as church-to-church support. Certainly we all respond to the call of the sister church; we cannot engage in that place on another basis. But the first request that comes may be solely for the support of the organization or infrastructure of the church itself, with very limited outward effect. In faithfulness we not only share resources for building a church office but we ask how that office might serve those who are not yet committed to Christ. We may ask, "please send us an experienced maths teacher", but if that person is to serve only in a privileged private school for the rich, then we may ask whether this is fulfilling the most urgent human need. There is always, in the missionary calling, this note of "going beyond". If it is not a geographical "going" then it is about the "beyond" which is outside the social services, outside the circle of faith, outside the hope of affluence, outside the region of tolerance. Even when we are most devoted to the service of the Christian fellowship itself there is this wider dimension always in our thoughts and plans. This brings to the mission round table the note of challenge. As we read the LMS history it is plain that often the expatriate missionary was able to stir new initiative in a static situation. Now that is what the Holy Spirit enables us to do for one another. It is particularly the churches in the former Christian heartland which now need the loving challenges of colleagues around the world and one test of the missionary organizations is how able they are to give room and resources for this emphasis. We have seen a growth in south-to-south sharing in the CWM with people moving, for example, from North East India to the Pacific islands and from Samoa to Jamaica, thus revealing an international dimension to the life of every church. There has also been a movement from Zambia, India and Jamaica to Britain so that the church with historic mission in its memory may be helped to enter mission today with greater imagination.

At the same time it is evident that church-to-church relations are now predominant in a way that has given a bias to the theological base of the CWM. This is largely due to the separation of "development" and emergency aid in a new channel of service, the ecumenical network which includes the World Council of Churches and regional councils of churches and Christian Aid. A large part of Christian action for the relief of suffering is now moving that way, so the traditional missionary agencies have necessarily to concentrate more on the church side of mission — the training of church workers, the provision of texts, the religious dimension of education, the care of Christian communities.

The risk is plain. The organization can become organizationally handcuffed, a table for church officers to sit at while displaying their financial requests. It is the constant prayer and intention of the partners that this may not be so, in order that the "beyond" of mission can be made evident in every budget and every policy. This is the true inheritance of the LMS. It is a reminder that God loves the world — the actual world as it is with all its corruption and dislocation. This outward, universal dimension reflects the biblical references to the commission given by Christ. It is described in a WCC Faith and Order report as follows:

> The church has been evangelized by God, and thus participating in the revealed mystery of God in Christ enters into the divine mission of evangelizing the world by proclaiming the good news of the kingdom. The church has been reconciled to God and thus becoming a prophetic sign receives from God the ministry of reconciliation within humanity. The church has been gathered by God and thus living as a Spirit-filled communion with Christ is commissioned to share in the gathering of all God's scattered children. [5]

A council dedicated to mission will be challenging the churches to give themselves to these three "beyonds" which are permanent and ecumenical. As we look forward towards the new century we can already see some of the forms that mission will take, and which will appear on future agendas.

1. Mission as people bearing witness in their lives

The outreach of the church from beginning to end is about people who have been touched by the wonder and suffering of Christ reaching out to touch others. There is no impersonal mission concerned only with concepts or planetary systems or cellular division or a computer data base. But the forms of personal sharing are constantly changing and there is no single model of what the word "missionary" means. We live in an age of human mobility which has enabled large numbers to cross national boundaries, by choice to seek work or leisure, by events in the natural world and by compulsion through destitution or war. It would be strange if such mobility is not a route for the Christian mission. The old pattern of being a missionary, which has nowhere been better displayed than in the LMS, lingers like the smell of incense in an ancient temple. Are there new patterns which will enable the face-to-face witness to the gospel?

The first response is to note the new mixed human communities in which very many people live. Every major city in the world has drawn people from other regions or other countries into its life. They live in the barracks of South African townships, the streets of Calcutta, the inner suburbs of London, the ghettos of New York and the hillside shacks of Rio. Often they find it almost impossible to become fully a part of a new human society which has been prejudiced or defensive. So for urban Christians the world over there is a "beyond" in the same street. To make contact and to infuse it with care is a vital area of mission. Often it involves dealing with racism in one of its many forms. It may mean meeting people of other faiths and thus standing at a critical frontier. It is encounter, sharing and friendship. It is being a good neighbour in the very neighbourhood where we are. The theological hesitations regarding dialogue with other faiths tend to disappear when we start out on the road of friendship, for then we meet people and not theologies. This reaching out towards the mixed community is a pressing reality for many Christians in all continents for it is the conversion of a generalized good will into the way we live today, without fear of those who are different from ourselves but confident that we shall meet Christ through them.

There will be more formal and structured service. Certainly there is room in every part of the world church to receive the specialized gifts of others. As an international community it is the most natural thing for churches to share the skills that the witness of the church requires. It is an age of specialization and the attempt by one missionary to do everything cannot serve us today. We are accustomed now to make these personal responses in accordance with government immigration controls as well as church requests. This means that they are usually short-term engagements with precise job descriptions. I expect that the variety of such service will grow, for in recent years the CWM, like most mission agencies, has been rather traditional in the types of service given. The earlier LMS was more enterprising, but of course did not face immigration controls. Are we exchanging musicians and artists, architects and mechanics, AIDS experts and paediatricians, print shop managers and booksellers as readily as the universities of the world share lecturers and the great hospitals share nurses? Yet this remains very much a job-centred vision. There needs to be also a people-centred vision, i.e. we need to see the importance of the person as the witness to Christ and not only the work which is to be done in his name. Although the employment rules in most countries make it difficult to avoid the concentration on function and qualifications, the churches will always value the gift of a colleague from another culture who is able to say: "I offer my life as a disciple of Christ to you, to be part of your fellowship, to serve wherever you see a need and to become a sign of the wider family in the midst." Such an offering will be rare but precious for it has about it the flavour of the giving of Christ to the life of the human family. The international mission agency will provide a channel for this varied service.

One discovery in the new relationship is that made by the traditional "sending" churches which now begin to receive people. They discover that receiving is not easy. For a century the assumption was that those sent by the European churches could be received, accepted, used, respected and loved by colleagues in another culture. It was as though the burden on the senders was considerable but the problems for the receivers negligible. Now the churches of Europe know that this is not so. It is no simple matter to provide the right location, the right introduction, the support, the ease of communication, and the continued links with home which new colleagues need when arriving from overseas. Giving is much more blessed than receiving and it is often a great deal simpler. To discover this leads to greater respect for all those communities around the world where missionaries have been welcomed, despite all the cultural barriers.

There is another kind of international witness which has been made possible by modern communication and holds great possibility for the future. It is the gathering of young people developed by the Taizé community and so far not much noted by the churches which like to concentrate on denominational programmes. But Taizé has been able, with great imagination, to fashion low-cost but large-scale events which bring together young people from many countries and many church traditions. The style of worship developed by the community has been a great bridge-builder across generations and languages, reminding us of the themes which are central to all Christian worship but treating them with fresh simplicity. For young people to discover a fresh spirituality so faithful to apostolic tradition is a great gift. It would be a sign of the ecumenical commitment of the CWM to support youth gatherings of this sort rather than plan its own. Youth exchange will have a continuing place as each church helps to enable the growth of vision in each new generation.

There is also an international calling to serve as a staff member of the new Council. This is a radical change from the LMS tradition. Gone are the all-white faces of a secretariat which was British to the core. From 1977 the Council recruited staff and honorary officers from all the member churches. This was clearly made visible from the inauguration when Mrs Daisy Gopal Ratnam from the Church of South India took over the chair from the Rev. Robert Latham. Staff members present in themselves the ethos of the new Council and their travels inform and challenge the member churches. Since 1977 they have been recruited from Samoa, Jamaica, Hong Kong, India, Sri Lanka and Holland, as well as Britain.

Personal service will always be critical for the development of the one mission of God in the world. As God sent his Son, so the Spirit sends people. They are sent in order that others may be blessed and released and made whole. The mechanics of mission may become very absorbing, for every institution runs the risk of introspection, and the church is no exception. The CWM may appear an ideal construction to be admired by all the structural engineers but could fail to emphasize the sacrificial, imaginative individual service that evokes a response to the gospel. People, therefore, must come ahead of systems, ahead of standing orders, ahead of the theory of mission. The CWM will serve all the member churches well as it enables people to give their best service beyond the immediate circle of faith, in all those human contexts where the way of Christ is not acknowledged.

2. Mission confronting the values of the age

Although the sense of a geographical frontier still draws Christians as being the essential call of God, there is now a growing awareness that another kind of frontier engagement is more critical. The Canberra WCC assembly described it like this:

> There is an urgent need today for a new type of mission, not into foreign lands but into "foreign" structures. By this we mean economic, social and political structures which do not at all conform to Christian moral standards. Naturally, we are aware of the corrupting

tendencies of power which transform anyone who participates in power structures into part of the problem rather than of the solution. It is for this reason that the churches have to make a great and continuous effort in morally equipping their people for their missionary work in the foreign structures of our time.[6]

I would take that theme further by suggesting that structures depend on attitudes, traditions, pressures and values which also may be foreign territory even when they seem part of the very air we breathe. This is where we take note of the power of a dominant culture. For the writers of the New Testament this was the pervasive Roman influence in all aspects of life. For us it is the western technological consumer society which has become dominant, drawing the hopes of people who have only glimpsed it from afar. It is a way of life and thought with great strength which has encouraged invention, efficiency and economic growth. It is supported by and works through the structures which may well be regarded in that quotation as not conforming to Christian moral standards. But it would be hypocritical not to confess our personal satisfaction if we are part of the society where an enormous range of goods and services may be bought and to acknowledge the right of the poor majority to strive for similar goals. It is the poor who are blessed, not poverty; the rich are challenged, not the table set for a feast. Who does not desire to have two pairs of shoes rather than none? No sin is involved. Why should we not give thanks to God for the range of scientific knowledge available since it is a revealing of the wonder of his creation? Who would close down the questioning mind and demand a blind acceptance of dogma? To acknowledge that the modern western civilization has brought us very considerable benefit is a necessary prelude to criticism.

For criticism there has to be. This form of human society has elevated individualism to such an extent that the virtues of community have been demoted. What is the individual desire or dream or inclination or philosophy becomes all-important regardless of the effect on the group. All corporate discipline can be rejected in the name of personal freedom. The results of this for the moral integrity of society have been alarming, especially in the area of marriage and divorce. We would then question the target of individual success which has dominated so much of the western way of life. Every culture has its model of success — in medieval ages in Europe it was in terms of the size of land owned, in parts of Africa the number of cattle owned, and in the Ottoman empire the number of slaves owned. But for modern civilization it is in terms of money and the property that money buys; *that* has become the mark of success. There is a concomitant downgrading of the qualities of honesty, steadfastness, humility, forgiveness, gentleness and grace which earlier Christians saw to be vital signs of the indwelling Spirit. Success is at war with the image of Christ; it would take a macho Christ to be an achiever in the free market. The third major critique must be around the question, at whose cost has affluence been achieved. The world of consumer choice is a very costly enterprise. It has, in our experience, left a poor minority in every western democracy, people who enjoy very few choices for their lives and little hope of change. It has placed burdens on primary producers in the developing world which they cannot carry because the consumers set the terms of trade. Lazarus is at the gate. All this has been part of the downgrading of the spiritual dimension of human life, which is now commonly regarded as a hobby for the few rather than the root of our humanity.

It is this radical displacement of the spiritual quality of life which encourages those operating the major structures of society to set goals such as national security, efficiency and everlasting growth which have the effect of diminishing respect for people as individuals. Economic structures which are very powerful are slipping away from accountability, educational systems from the sense of the ultimate value of each person, security and military forces become stronger than the politicians who profess to control them and the cash value of every social policy becomes the major basis by which it is judged. To evangelize modern societies requires not only the conversion of individuals but the redemption of the values by which we live and the structures that represent them. This is the toughest frontier for mission today. It implies a style of church life which is distinctive, a sceptical attitude to the mass media, a readiness to enter the processes of politics, a determined resistance to "growth at all costs" and a commitment to the disadvantaged sectors of human society. It means also the church's ability to restate the case for the reality of God not in terms of the old logic but through the experience of human love, human need, human hope. The missionary agenda will be about this alternative view of what makes us human and also makes us one community of life on the planet.

3. Mission proclaiming the now and not-yet of the kingdom of God

The justice and peace of the reign of God have been, from the preaching of Jesus in Galilee, primary objectives of all Christian witness. The gospel is about change and it includes the changing of those injustices which stifle and corrupt humanity, so that the world may know a peace based on mutual respect. The church may never forget this and preach a gospel which has no effect on the desperate conditions of those millions who live on the edge of survival. So we are committed, as Christian churches, to a great many causes touching the justice and peace issues of our world. We do this as part of our obedience to the Holy Spirit; but we do it also as citizens in partnership with many others who profess no Christian belief. It is an essential outworking of our discipleship but is never our private calling. Nor is it a romantic tilt at windmills with the expectation of utopia around the corner. The full realization of the reign of God is not in the hands of human authorities, however benevolent they may be. So there is a "not yet", a "beyond" in all our work and witness. So long as human society lasts we shall be struggling with all the negative tendencies within us. We have the ability to corrupt even the most perfect systems and to ignore those with whom we disagree. The achievement of universal suffrage brings only a limited advance in human responsibility. We do not share in this aspect of mission in order to move steadily from a state of wickedness to the realm of bliss, for we know the human story is not like that. Rather we recognize the now of the kingdom, the reign of God here and now in every life of self-sacrifice and devotion, in every expression of truth, in every act of forgiveness, in all those points where new life rises from the tomb of sorrow. But we confess the not yet. The glory is God's and it is his gift which is our end.

This was expressed by the Commission on World Mission and Evangelism of the WCC in an important ecumenical affirmation:

> There is no evangelism without solidarity; there is no Christian solidarity that does not involve sharing the knowledge of the kingdom which is God's promise to the poor of the earth. There is here a double credibility test: proclamation that does not hold forth the promises of the justice of the kingdom to the poor of the earth is a caricature of the gospel; but Christian participation in the struggles for justice which does not point towards the promises of the kingdom also makes a caricature of a Christian understanding of justice. [7]

To preserve this balance is important in every missionary enterprise. The joy of entering into the realm of God's peace is open in every age and every human context. Salvation does not appear gradually with an improving diet or housing. It was there for the disciples in the upper room and for people of every generation since. That kingdom of peace is "at hand", it is "within you". But the realization of God's reign for our immediate society is partial, therefore we wait with patience, and we struggle with all those forces which hinder its fulfilment.

A mission agency will be alert to this double sided coin of grace. It helps us with all the immediacies, the urgent cries of pain and hunger, the bitterness of racial conflict. It is saying to all Christian people: "As we value life so we share the work of God." But it also reminds us of the long-term view, and it is here that the intensely activist mission agencies still have much to learn. We are in the context of God's purpose for the whole creation. It is God who will complete the story in his way in his time and we believe that this means everything brought into obedience to the way of Christ. We have a place in the story but it is a modest place. We are not the perfecters of the human condition. So the mission agency will give a major emphasis to the life of prayer, our waiting on God, and study of what he is doing in the unfolding pattern of life, our confession of ignorance and inadequacy in many things. Mission, if it is truly the mission of God, has a long calendar as well as great urgency.

Indeed the longer-term view compels us to press the question about the objective of the missionary enterprise. After two hundred years we have seen the fulfilment of one great hope, the establishing of a Christian community within every major human community. Often it is only a very small minority but, like the seed and the yeast, has life in it. Is it now our hope and prayer that every minority church will become a majority? Do we expect the other great faiths of humanity to recede while Christianity occupies centre stage? Those who watch the unrolling map could not anticipate this from recent history, for the very enthusiasm of Christian mission has helped to stimulate the resurgence of other faiths in their self-defence. The calling of Christ to his disciples is to share his risen life, to proclaim that hope beyond the grave and to conduct all our human relationships as children of the Father. The little minority church that witnesses in this way is fulfilling the vocation of the apostles. The prayer is always that such witness will be received with faith by many others but the value and integrity of the witness is not determined by numbers.

Nor, I believe, can the witness be limited to the declaration of the faith. To be speakers of a faith requires that we also listen to those whose faith is different but just as sincere. We cannot rule out of theology the possibility that God has spoken "in many and varied ways" through the prophets of other faiths, and to them we must be attentive. Such readiness to listen in no way lessens the commission to declare "the wonderful works of God" in Jesus Christ but it does determine the attitude of heart in which we dare to proclaim Christ as Lord. Missionaries are not proprietors of the gospel but servants of the great mystery which is God in human life, offering his sacrificial love to all. It is surely beyond human vision to know how God will fulfil his "secret purpose... that the universe, everything in heaven and on earth, might be brought into a unity in Christ" (Eph. 1:9-10). We cannot presume that the expanding empire model, a larger Christendom, is the necessary pattern in the mind of God.

For there is another dimension becoming more and more important, the reality of the local church as the critical point for the great universals of the gospel. How we define "local" depends on our church tradition. For some it means the national or ethnic church, for some the diocese, for others the congregation which meets to worship. But if mission is to be the cause for which the church exists, then it is in the local church that this will be evident. If unity is the character of the body of Christ, it is in the locality that we shall see it taking shape. If prayer is the basic language of faith, it is in the local fellowship that we learn to speak. If we are a universal family of God's people then it is the openness of the local community which declares it. So to serve the local church, to honour local gifts, to stimulate local sharing and to secure all the links which bind local churches together will be a true missionary vocation.

These are some of the directions we may anticipate as the story of the LMS flows on through the CWM. The final note must be of thankfulness and expectation. There can only be great thankfulness that the Holy Spirit has been at work through the dedication of many people, people subject to all the limitations of their culture and generation, people who often struggled with faith, people who knew hardship and disappointment, who sometimes assumed too great an understanding of another culture, and yet who were fundamentally faithful to a great vision. What was born as a great commitment, to witness to the grace of God in Christ throughout the world, was blessed with a remarkable result, for Christian communities now, at the end of the century, are testimony to the work of missionaries in the past. In the same way the churches of Europe are a testimony to the mission of the Roman church, and that itself to the apostolic witness. To be part of that remarkable chain of testimony is cause for wonder and gratitude.

And so to expectation. The chain is not completed. The calling continues. The forms in which mission is most appropriately encouraged and sustained will surely change, just as the emphasis will change as the human condition cries for healing, and we cannot anticipate that the structures now in place will last us for a century. They will give way — to the developing unities of church and world. They will project what the family of God is called to be as a sign and foretaste of the kingdom of God. So new styles of personal service and new associations of churches are to be expected. The Christian presence in a torn and very unequal world, where affluence leads to complacency and poverty to bitterness, where for very many people life is still brutal and short, but where the longing for human dignity and peace is never stilled, that presence will take its pattern from a cross and an empty tomb. Mission will always be about suffering which is transformed into healing and joy and renewal. At that point our thankfulness and expectation are one.

NOTES

[1] Richard Lovett, *History of the LMS*, vol. I, London, Oxford University Press, 1899, p.36.

[2] LMS annual report, *Survey 1948*, p.41.

[3] Lovett, *op. cit.*, p.49.

[4] David Bogue at the inaugural service, September 1795, *ibid.*, p.35.

[5] *Church and World*, Faith and Order paper no. 151, Geneva, WCC, 1990, para. 56.

[6] *Signs of the Spirit*, official report of the WCC's seventh assembly, Canberra 1991, ed. Michael Kinnamon, Geneva, WCC, 1991, section I report, para. 46.

[7] WCC, *Mission and Evangelism: An Ecumenical Affirmation*, Geneva, WCC, 1983, para. 34.

Appendix A

APPENDIX A: MISSIONARIES OF LMS/CCWM/CWM 1945-1977

Surname	First names	Degrees etc.	origin	service	YOB	Apptment beg	end	YOD	work	pre/post
ABEL	Robert Owen	MBE	UK	Africa	1904	1929	1934		e	
	1932 m Edith Mary Hope ROBERTSON		UK	Africa	1909	1937	1959			
				Africa		*1932*	*1934*			
				Africa		*1937*	*1959*			
AINSWORTH	Gordon Harry		UK	Guyana	1929	1969	1972	1980	o d	
	1956 m Patricia OGDEN		UK	*Guyana*	1935	*1969*	*1972*			
ALDERTON	Roland Maitland	MB BS FRCS LRCP	UK	Hong Kong	1902	1932	1959		m	
	1935 m Kathleen BLACKMAN		UK	*China*	1903	*1931*	*1935*	1947		
				Hong Kong		*1935*	*1947*			
	1948 m Bessie PARTRIDGE		UK	*Hong Kong*	1900	*1948*	*1959*	1977		
ALDRIDGE	Frances	LRCP LRCS LRFP+S	UK	China	1916	1939	1940		m	
	1940 m Robert Kenneth MCALL (m)			*China*		*1940*	*1946*			
ALLAN	Robert	MB ChB	UK	India	1920	1945	1947		m	
	1945 m Betsy Kellock M.S. KEITH		UK	*India*	1920	*1946*	*1947*			
ALLEN	Clabon James	BSc MA	UK	Malaysia	1938	1966	1979		o d	
				Hong Kong		1979	1981			
	1963 m Margaret Oliver BELL		UK	*Malaysia*	1936	*1966*	*1979*			
				Hong Kong		*1979*	*1981*			
ALLEN	Leslie William		NZ	Papua NG	1915	1946	1955	1961	o d	
	1946 m Cynthia Elfred SOLON		NZ	*Papua NG*	1922	*1946*	*1955*			
ANDERSEN	Neville Arthur	MB BS	Australia	Papua NG	1922	1948	1953		m	
	1947 m Maria Patricia VINES	BA	Australia	*Papua NG*	1923	*1948*	*1953*			
ANDERSON	David Fyfe	MA BEd	UK	China	1903	1929	1952	1986	e	
	1929 m Helen FORRESTER		UK	*China*	1897	*1929*	*1952*	1971		
	1972 m Marion GINGER (m)									
ANDERSON	Susanne Carol		UK	Papua NG	1943	1975	1978		e	

Name	Qual.	Origin	Field					Work
ANDERSON William Wardlaw		S.Africa	S.Rhodesia	1888	1914	1953	1978	o d
1915 m Sheila **BLYTH**		S.Africa	S.Rhodesia	1890	*1915*	*1953*	1976	
ANTHONY Thomas Clifford Lloyd		UK	S.India	1901	1933	1954	1979	o d
1939 m Enid Vivia **HOOPER**		Australia	S.India	1907	*1935*	*1954*		
ARCHER Constance Ruth	SRN SCM	UK	Papua NG	1937	1965	1976		m
ARNOLD Raymond William	BD STM	UK	Madagascar	1923	1950	1968		o te
1956 m Beth **HACKETT**	BA	USA	Madagascar	1932	*1956*	*1968*		
ARTHERN Rosemary Anne		UK	Papua NG	1943	1970	1974		e
ASHBY Winifred		UK	Africa	1920	1952	1955	1971	e
1955 m Revd Dr Alfred **MERRIWEATHER**								
ASHCROFT Anthony Ralph		UK	Madagascar	1930	1958	1974		o d
1957 m Isabel Fraser **MACKIE**		UK	Madagascar	1933	*1958*	*1974*		
ASHTON Frank Richard	OBE MB ChB	UK	Hong Kong	1901	1926	1964	1992	m
1941 m Elizabeth **PATON** (m)								
ASHWELL Katherine		UK	Madagascar	1903	1932	1960	1992	d
AULD Francis	BA BD	UK	Pacific	1913	1947	1954	1980	o d
1949 m Joy **FOWLES** (m)								
AUSTIN Mary	BSc AKC	UK	S.Rhodesia	1931	1961	1966		e

a   = administration
agr   = agriculture
art   = artisan
bld   = building work
staff = office staff of LMS/CWM after or before missionary service
CMS   = missionary of Commonwealth Missionary Society before joining LMS/CWM
PCE   = missionary of Presbyterian Church of England before joining CWM
UCA   = missionary of the Uniting Church in Australia from 1977

c   = communication
d   = district work
e   = education
lit = literature work

m   = medical work
o   = ordained
ship = captain of "John Williams" ship
sw   = social work

(m) means that the person married is a missionary who is listed separately in this appendix.
Years in italics refer to periods that the wives of missionaries have served.

Surname	First names	Degrees etc.	origin	service	YOB	Apptment beg	end	YOD	work	pre/post
BACHE	William George	LTh MCD	Australia	Papua NG	1925	1952	1972	1983	o d a	
1950 m Viola Hilda **BYERLEY**			Australia	Papua NG	1926	1952	1972			
BAGULEY	Frederick Everard	BSc	UK	China	1909	1935	1954	1967	e	
1936 m Beng Tek **LIM**			China	China		1936	1954			
BAILEY	Brian Hudson	OBE	UK	Botswana	1931	1963	1975	1980	o d	staff
1957 m Eleanor **THOMAS**			UK	Botswana	1931	1963	1975			
BAILEY	Harold		UK	S.Rhodesia	1910	1971	1975	1974	e a	
1931 m Mary **LEWIS**			UK	S.Rhodesia	1910	1971	1974			
BAIRD	Edward Simpson		UK	N.Rhodesia	1917	1947	1950		o d	
BAKER	Edna Jane	SRN	UK	South India	1895	1923	1924	1993	m	
1924 m William Thomas **CLEWES** (m)				South India		1924	1949			
BAKER	Edwin Charles		UK	Madagascar	1876	1909	1944	1959	o d	
				Madagascar		1946	1950			
1909 m Elizabeth Maud **HOLDEN**			UK	Madagascar	1879	1909	1944	1966		
				Madagascar		1946	1950			
BAKER	Elsie	MBE SRN CMB	UK	N.Rhodesia	1897	1930	1964	1966	m	
BALCHIN	Frank Kenneth	BA BD ThD	UK	China	1913	1937	1951	1983	o te	
				Singapore		1951	1979			
1937 m Ivy Emily **ANGOOD**			UK	China	1914	1937	1951			
				Singapore		1951	1979			
BALD	Jean Norval Douglas	DipSocSc DipOccTher	UK	South India	1923	1968	1983		m	PCE
BALLARD	Pansy Norah		UK	South India	1913	1940	1951	1990	d	
1952 m Thomas **JACQUES**										
BANHAM	Robert John **RICHARDSON**	BA BD	UK	Zambia	1929	1970	1978		o te	
1954 m Hilda Elizabeth			UK	Zambia	1927	1970	1978			
BARCLAY	Jessie Margaret	BA	UK	Taiwan	1927	1957	1973		e	PCE
BARKHAM	Hazel Patricia	BA	UK	S.Rhodesia	1940	1966	1971		e	

Name	Quals	Origin	Location					Code
BARNES Harold John	OBE	UK	N.Rhodesia	1896	1930	1961	1969	o d
1930 m Evelyn Ida May **GARDINER**		UK	N.Rhodesia	1902	*1930*	*1961*	1991	e
BARR John Snodgrass	MA BSc	UK	China	1900	1924	1952	1970	
			Hong Kong		1953	1966		
1926 m Mary **RAFFO**		USA	China		*1926*	*1930*	1930	
1932 m Ruth **HILL**		USA	China/HK	1903	*1932*	*1966*	1990	e
BARR Margaret Elizabeth	BA LRAM	UK	Hong Kong	1933	1958	1967	1987	d
BARRETT Madge Lilian		UK	S.India	1898	1925	1951		
BATCHELOR David		UK	Madagascar	1939	1965	1969	1977	o d
1966 m Margareta **LJUNGBERG**		Sweden	Madagascar	1937	*1966*	*1969*		
BATTERSBY Joseph Norman		Australia	Papua NG	1914	1969	1977		o d
1942 m Kathleen Mary **ROYLANCE**		UK	Papua NG	1918	*1969*	*1977*		
BAXTER Alexander		UK	China	1882	1907	1927	1960	o te
			China		1933	1950		
1909 m Jeannie Gibson **SMALL**			China	1887	*1907*	*1927*		
			China		*1933*	*1950*		
BAXTER Alexander Morrison	BA	UK	China	1910	1933	1946	1951	d
1935 m Gwyneth **REES**		UK	China	1912	*1933*	*1946*	1980	e
BEARE Stella Mary		UK	N.India	1920	1945	1971	1991	
BEEVERS Robert	M Ed	UK	Papua NG	1930	1955	1972	1989	o d
1954 m Margaret Cowe **NICOLL**		UK	Papua NG	1927	*1955*	*1972*		
BEHARELL Caleb Harley		UK	Papua NG	1881	1906	1929	1951	
			Niue		1945	1949		
1910 m Margaret James **PATTERSON**		Australia	Papua NG	1876	*1910*	*1929*		
			Niue		*1945*	*1949*		m a
BEIGHTON Jennie		Australia	Papua NG	1913	1959	1968	1973	
BELL Ruby Jean		UK	India	1917	1948	1948		o d e
BELLAMY Peter David	MA	UK	Madagascar	1932	1957	1968	1968	
1957 m Elizabeth Ann **WATTS**		UK	Madagascar	1934	*1957*	*1968*		
BENCE Graham Dudley		UK	Papua NG	1930	1953	1958		o d
1952 m Doreen Mary **BULLOCK**		UK	Papua NG	1927	*1953*	*1958*		

Surname	First names	Degrees etc.	origin	service	YOB	Apptment beg	end	YOD	work	pre/post
BENDING 1967 m K. **JACOB**	Eileen		UK	S.India	1925	1952	1967		d	
BENDING 1951 m Mary **GRIMMER**	Geoffrey	BA	UK UK	S.Rhodesia S.Rhodesia	1928 1928	1958 *1958*	1969 *1969*		o d	
BENNETT 1916 m Frederick Lionel **MARLER** (m)	Mary Russell		UK	S.India S.India S.India	1883	1911 *1916* *1941*	1916 *1940* *1950*	1960	d	
BEYNON 1916 m Annie Maud **HARRIS**	Owen Gwynne R.	MPhS	UK UK	China China	1894 1894	1921 *1921*	1948 *1948*	1977 1975	m	
BISHOP	Winifred Mary	LLA	UK	N.Rhodesia	1887	1920	1948	1959	e	
BLACK 1921 m Marion **RIDDELL**	Adam	CA	UK UK	China China	1891 1894	1924 1924	1951 1951	1977 1981	a	staff
BLACKLOCK 1940 m Hazel May **ENDERSBY**	Eric Herbert George	MC OBE AIMTA	UK	Pacific Pacific	1918	1956 *1956*	1966 *1966*	1979	a	staff
BLACKMAN 1935 m Roland Maitland **ALDERTON** (m)	Kathleen		UK	China Hong Kong	1903	1931 *1935*	1935 *1947*	1947	d	
BLACKWELL	Lois Ruth	RGN RMN	Australia	Papua NG	1949	1972	1975		m	
BLEAKLEY	Maggie	MA	UK	China	1887	1915	1951	1958	e	
BLEISCH 1971 m Varena **RAMBOLD**	Christoph		Switz'lnd Switz'lnd	Papua NG Papua NG	1946 1944	1971 *1971*	1980 *1980*		art	
BLOOMFIELD	Gwendoline Emma	SRN SCM	UK	Africa	1908	1947	1971	1986	m	
BOARDMAN	Heather Virginia	Tchg Cert	UK	Papua NG	1947	1972	1976		e	
BOLTON 1937 m Florence Adelaide **NETSCHER**	Leslie William	DipBMngt	UK UK	Africa Africa	1910 1910	1966 *1966*	1971 *1971*	1985	a	
BOLTON	Patricia		UK	Zambia	1937	1971	1977		a	staff

Name	Quals	From	Field					staff
BOWEN David Glyn	BA BD ThM	UK	W.Samoa	1933	1963	1968		te
1963 m Gerda **HOFMAIER**		Germany	W.Samoa	1939	*1963*	*1968*		
BOWERING Beryl	MB BS	Australia	North India	1909	1935	1950		m
BOWERS Mrs Frances May	BA	UK	Africa	1896	1962	1965	1982	e
BOX Ernest Shilston	MA	UK	China	1903	1926	1952	1980	o d
1931 m Margaret **McKINNON**	SRN	UK	China	1902	*1931*	*1952*		
BOX Margaret Hyatt	BSc	UK	China	1906	1933	1951	1993	e
BOXALL Kathleen Minnie		UK	Pacific	1921	1953	1956		e
BOXER Stanley Victor	BSc	UK	China	1887	1914	1927	1949	e
1923 m Jessie Alice **STEVENS**		UK	Hong Kong	1896	*1923*	*1927*	1953	
			China		*1927*	*1948*		
BRADBURY Ethel Frances		UK	Hong Kong	1898	1923	1925	1990	d
1925 m Frederick Maltus **SMITH** (m)			S.India		*1923*	*1925*		
			S.India		*1925*	*1959*		
BRADSHAW John	MSc BA DPh	UK	W.Samoa	1924	1954	1965		te
1954 m Muriel K. **QUICK**	MA BM BCh	UK	W.Samoa	1928	*1954*	*1965*		
BRAGG Lizzie Helmer	MA	UK	South India	1879	1901	1908		
1908 m Herbert Arthur **POPLEY** (m)			South India		*1908*	*1947*	1973	
BRAME Leslie Alfred	MA	UK	China	1914	1939	1949		o d
1941 m Gladys **WORTHINGTON**	SRN	UK	W.Samoa	1910	*1941*	*1960*		e
			China		1949	1949		
			W.Samoa		*1949*	*1960*		
BRAMELD Kathrine		UK	China/HK	1906	1932	1964	1984	d e
BREEZE Gordon Paul	BA BD	UK	North India	1913	1949	1952		o e
1943 m Agnes Craig **MURCHLAND**		UK	North India	1917	*1949*	*1952*		
BROOKS Violet Abigail		UK	N.Rhodesia	1909	1934	1937		
1937 m Norman Howard **PORRITT** (m)			N.Rhodesia		*1937*	*1963*		
BROUWER Willem Hendrik Frits		Neth'Ind	Madagascar	1946	1971	1976		agr
1970 m Gerritje Rika **VAN EEK**		Neth'Ind	Madagascar	1948	*1971*	*1976*		
BROWN Constance Mabel	BA	UK	China	1886	1910	1912	1973	m
1912 m James Lee Hamilton **PATERSON** (m)			China		*1912*	*1949*		

Surname	First names	Degrees etc.	origin	service	YOB	Apptment beg	Apptment end	YOD	work	pre/post
BROWN	Elizabeth Jean	MA	UK	Taiwan	1934	1961	1989		a e	PCE
BROWN	Francis Henry	MA	UK	South India	1907	1932	1958		o d	
1934 m Daphne Graham **ROOK**			UK	South India	1912	1932	1958			
BROWN	Frank Albert		UK	China	1893	1938	1952		m a	staff
				India		1952	1958	1983		
1930 m Robina Antoinette M **SCOTT**			UK	China	1896	1938	1946	1946		
1947 m Hilda **STEPHENS**	MB ChM	UK	China	1906	1947	1952	1981		
				India		1952	1958			
BROWN	Harry Ernest		UK	Africa	1922	1956	1963		bldr	
1959 m Edith **DAVIES** (m)										
BROWN	Herbert Alfred	OBE MA BA PhD	UK	Papua NG	1905	1938	1971	1988	o d	
1944 m Anne **COLE** (m)										
BROWN	Louise Anne	MA SRN SCM	UK	S.Rhodesia	1940	1970	1972		m	
BRYSON	Arnold George		UK	China	1877	1903	1917		o d	
1906 m Norah **LENWOOD** (m)				China		1919	1946	1958		
1950 m Joan **THOMPSON** (m)										
BRYSON	Arthur Frank	MA MB ChB FRCS	UK	China	1910	1938	1952		m	
BRYSON	Janet	MA	UK	Africa	1897	1923	1960	1979	e	
BUCHAN	Annie Gray	SRN	UK	China	1895	1925	1951	1988	m	
BUCK	Thomas Edward		UK	Madagascar	1887	1919	1960	1982	o d	
1914 m Elsie **FRYER**			UK	Madagascar	1888	1919	1960	1976		
BUCKLE	David Malcolm	BA	UK	Papua NG	1940	1972	1976		o d	
1963 m Joan **BRAND**			UK	Papua NG	1943	1972	1976			

Name	Quals	Country	Field					Notes	
BUNTON Hedley Percival	LTh	Australia	China	1906	1932	1950		o d a	
1932 m Clara Margaret **PATON**	BA	Australia	Hong Kong	1908	1958	1974			staff
			China		*1932*	*1950*			
			Hong Kong		*1958*	*1974*			
BURGESS Roger Wilfred	BSc PGCE	UK	Botswana	1950	1975	1979		e	
1974 m Christina Marion **WEST**	BSc PGCE	UK	Botswana	1950	*1975*	*1979*			
BURTON George Eric	MA	UK	Madagascar	1905	1927	1954	1972	o e te	
1929 m Dorcas L. **CHARENSOL**		UK	Madagascar	1898	*1929*	*1954*	1975		
BUSBY Charles Edward	BA BD	UK	China	1888	1921	1953	1980	o d	
1923 m Norah Mellor **THOMPSON**		UK	China	1881	*1921*	*1953*	1958		
BUTLER Frank Howard		Australia	Papua NG	1923	1956	1972		o d	
1956 m Gladys May **CLATWORTHY** (m)									
BUTTER Hilda Mary	MA	UK	Madagascar	1906	1937	1966	1987	e	
BUXTON Frank Charles	BA BD	UK	Malaysia	1926	1959	1964	1964	o d	
1960 m Florence Mary **HOPKINS**	BSc	UK	Malaysia	1929	*1959*	*1964*			
CALVERT Peter	MB ChB DTM&H	NZ	Papua NG	1922	1954	1982	1982	m	
1951 m Linne Bryant **TOMBLESON**	MBE MB ChB DTM&H	NZ	Papua NG	1925	*1954*	*1982*			
CAMPBELL Jean	BSc Dip Soc St	UK	S.Rhodesia	1931	1976	1982	1987	a	
CAMPBELL John Laurie	BA	UK	Madagascar	1919	1949	1956		o d e	
1944 m Dorothy Eileen **BAKER**	SRN SCM	UK	Madagascar	1919	1976	1979	1985		
			Madagascar		*1949*	*1956*			
			Madagascar		*1976*	*1979*			
CAREY Eliza Carswell	MA	UK	S.Rhodesia	1912	1942	1946		e	
CARPENTER Francis Colin		UK	Madagascar	1916	1948	1962		o d	staff
1948 m Phyllis Mary **PUDNEY**		UK	Madagascar	1919	*1948*	*1962*			
CARR Martyn		UK	Papua NG	1942	1966	1972		o d	
1966 m Rachel **JONES**		UK	Papua NG	1945	*1966*	*1972*			
CARRINGTON Rosemary	Tchr Trng	UK	Botswana	1946	1971	1976		e	

Surname	First names	Degrees etc.	origin	service	YOB	Apptment beg	end	YOD	work	pre/post
CARTER Ann 1981 m I. **HOGAN**			NZ	Papua NG	1955	1976	1980			
CATER	Donald Brian	BA MB MRCS LRCP	UK	China	1908	1932	1949	1984	m	
1933 m Constance Amy **GROVE**		MA MB MRCS LRCP	UK	China	1905	*1932*	*1949*	1993		
CATER	Henry William		UK	Cook Islands Africa	1905	1931 1943	1943 1950		o d	
1931 m Elizabeth Annie **WATSON**			UK	Cook Islands Africa	1907	*1931* *1943*	*1943* *1950*			
CAUSER	Marjory	BSc	UK	China	1910	1937	1951/3		e	
CAVE	Harold Livingstone		UK	Zambia	1919	1948	1969	1993	o d	staff
1949 m Sigrid **RODE**			Germany	Zambia	1923	*1948*	*1969*			
CHALLIS	Robert Lye	BA	UK	Cook Islands	1903	1933	1947	1980	o d e	
1933 m Mona **CHESTERTON**		SRN	UK	Cook Islands	1903	*1933*	*1939*	1939		
1941 m Roselyn **CALLANDER**		BA	UK	Cook Islands	1908	*1941*	*1947*			
CHAPMAN	Gilbert Wesley	MB BS DTM&H	Australia	Hong Kong	1929	1959	1969		m	
1955 m Jeannette **CHENNELL**		SRN SCM	Australia	Hong Kong	1930	*1959*	*1969*			
CHAPMAN	William Ronald	BA	UK	Hong Kong	1916	1948	1957		o d e	
1942 m May **COLLIER**			UK	Hong Kong	1913	*1948*	*1957*			
CHAPPLE	Jean Beverley	BA	Australia	Papua NG	1936	1962	1977		e	UCA
CHATTERTON	Percy	OBE KBE LCP LID	UK	Papua NG	1898	1924	1964	1984	e o d	
1924 m Christian Ritchie **FINLAYSON**		MA LTh	UK	Papua NG	1895	*1924*	*1964*	1975	o d	
CHECK	Maru George		NZ	Niue	1913	1948	1956			
1940 m Lois Ida **LAYBOURN**			NZ	Niue	1916	*1948*	*1956*			
CHILDS	Joyce Mary		UK	S.Rhodesia	1926	1949	1965		e	
CHILDS	Susanne Beverley		Australia	N.Rhodesia	1930	1957	1958		e	

Surname	Name	Quals	Origin	Field					Codes
CHUE	Rose Tang	BA	UK	Papua NG	1948	1973	1985		e
CLARK	Doreen	SRN SCM	UK	Papua NG	1928	1958	1962		m
CLARK	Joseph Arthur McChesney	LTh	Australia	China	1912	1940	1945		o d
	1945 m Elizabeth C. WILLIAMS	MA	Australia	Papua NG	1918	1946	*1968*	1969	
CLARKE	John Frederick	BD	UK	Cook Islands	1926	1963	1967		o d te
	1956 m Anne Christine STENING (m)								
CLARKE	Norman		UK	S.Rhodesia	1926	1952	1974		o d a staff
	1952 m Jeanie Elizabeth KING-MEGGAT		UK	S.Rhodesia	1927	1952	*1952*	1992	
CLATWORTHY	Gladys May	SRN SCM	Australia	Papua NG	1922	1949	1956		m
	1956 m Frank Howard BUTLER (m)			Papua NG		*1956*	*1972*		
CLEWES	William Thomas Morris	MA	UK	South India	1891	1923	1949	1984	o d
	1924 m Edna Jane BAKER (m)								
COHEN	John Cranley	SRN SCM	UK	W.Samoa	1931	1956	1970		
	1957 m Claire I. Gretel DAY	SRN SCM	UK	W.Samoa	1929	*1956*	*1970*		
COLE	Anne	SRN SCM	Australia	Papua NG	1902	1941	1944		m
	1944 m Herbert Alfred BROWN (m)	SRN SCM	Australia	Papua NG		*1944*	*1971*	1992	
COLE	Doris Mary	SRN SCM	Australia	Papua NG	1905	1931	1936		m
	1939 m Raymond PERRY (m)			Papua NG		*1939*	*1972*		
COLE	Merlin Edith Annie	SRN SCM	UK	Zambia	1913	1943	1973		m d
COLLINS	Bernard Alan	BA MA DipTh	UK	Papua NG	1948	1974	1991	1989	o d
	1971 m Gwennyth MAHY								
COLLINS	Donald Pickering	BA	UK	Papua NG	1948	*1974*	*1991*		o d
	1941 m May Elizabeth WILSON (m)		UK	South India	1912	1937	1974		
COLTMAN	Kathleen Margaret Lovesey		UK	N.Rhodesia	1922	1947	1960		d
CONNAN	Elizabeth	MRCS LRCP DIP RCOG	UK	Bangladesh	1925	1953	1974	1974	m PCE
CONOLLY	James Harold		UK	Madagascar	1891	1926	1957	1970	lit
	1938 m Janet Ruth WARREN (m)								
COOMBS	Sylvia		UK	Solomon Isles	1946	1971	1990		e staff

Surname	First names	Degrees etc.	origin	service	YOB	Apptment beg	end	YOD	work	pre/post
COOPER	George	BD	UK	N.Rhodesia	1916	1945	1949		o d	
1943 m Mary Olive **MUNN**			UK	N.Rhodesia	1921	1945	1949		o d	
COPP	John Dixon	MA BD BD	Canada	W.Samoa	1908	1939	1947		o te	
1935 m Jean **EVANS**		BA	Canada	W.Samoa		1939	1947			
COURT	Maxwell Arthur	BA LTh	Australia	North India	1930	1961	1967		o d	
1957 m Dulcie Edna **MAYNARD**			Australia	North India	1933	1961	1967			
CRAFT	Reginald Thomas		UK	Botswana	1902	1964	1967		a	
1933 m Lois Mary **LOGAN**			UK	Botswana	1907	1964	1967			
CRAGG	Margaret		UK	South India	1908	1938	1969		d	
CRAIG	Charles Stuart	BA	UK	China	1906	1937	1950	1973	o d	staff
1933 m Audrey Winifred **STUART**			UK	China	1907	1937	1950			
CRIBB	John Bridson		Australia	Papua NG	1927	1955	1969		o d	
1962 m Hazel **FRENCH**			UK	Papua NG	1941	1962	1969			
CROCKER	John Peter	BSc	UK	Bangladesh	1952	1975	1981		o d	
				Zambia		1981	1988			
1974 m Elizabeth M. **NEEDHAM**		BA	UK	Bangladesh	1952	1975	1981			
				Zambia		1981	1988			
CRUCHLEY	Ernest Edward Butler		UK	Zambia	1930	1961	1971		o d	
1955 m Kathleen Mary **AMBROSE**			UK	Zambia	1931	1961	1971			
CULLEN	August Pountney	MA	UK	China	1889	1916	1951	1960	o d	
1919 m Jean Naomi **BATCHAN**			UK	China	1896	1916	1951	1980	o d	
CULLINGFORD	James Donald		UK	Papua NG	1925	1960	1976	1979	o d	
1952 m Molly Eileen **COLEMAN**			UK	Papua NG	1921	1960	1976			
CUMBER	Mary	BA	UK	North India	1910	1938	1961		e	staff
CUMMINS	Douglas Harvery	BA	UK	Papua NG	1922	1954	1955		e	
1954 m Gerda Everdina **DE GEEST**			UK	Papua NG	1921	1954	1955			
CURTIS	William Kenneth	HNC	UK	Gilbert Islands	1911	1973	1976		e	
1964 m Irene Edith **ELMY**			UK	Gilbert Islands	1925	1973	1976			

Name	Qualifications	Country	Field					Notes
CUTTING Cecil George	ARCS MB ChB	UK	South India	1897	1932	1961	1984	m
1931 m Eleanor M. **ALEXANDER**	MA	UK	South India	1906	*1932*	*1961*	1991	
CUTTING Christopher James	MB ChB FRCS	UK	South India	1936	1967	1969		m
1962 m Jean Mackenzie **KERR**	SRN SCM	UK	South India	1938	*1967*	*1969*		
CUTTING William Alexander Murray	MB ChB D Obs RCOG MRCP DCH	UK	South India	1933	1960	1973		m
1958 m Margaret M. **ANDERSON**	MB ChB	UK	South India	1929	*1960*	*1973*		
DANAHAY Grace Helen	SRN SCM	UK	Papua NG	1934	1962	1964		m
DASAPPA Paranjothi	SRN SCM	India	Papua NG / Solomon Isles	1932	1975	1992		m
DAVEY Audrey Vera	MCSP	UK	Papua NG	1927	1963	1969		m
DAVIDSON James Romanes	MB ChB MD	UK	South India	1909	1937	1946	1991	m
1935 m Jean Isabella Moffat **PRINGLE**		UK	South India	1905	*1937*	*1946*		
DAVIES Dilys	SRN	UK	South India	1914	1943	1951	1987	d
DAVIES Edith	SRN	UK	N.Rhodesia	1919	1948	1959		d
1959 m Harry Ernest **BROWN** (m)			Africa		*1959*	*1963*	1990	o d
DAVIES John Edwin	MA	UK	China	1915	1940	1951/6		
1945 m Nelma Holmes **STRANKS**	SRN SCM	Australia	China	1917	1945	*1951/6*		
DEGENHARDT Jean		UK	Bangladesh	1945	1970	1980/2		m PCE
DEVERELL Bruce John	D Min	NZ	Pacific	1930	1957	1987		o e d
1057 m Gweneth **CRYER**	MA MA	NZ	Pacific	1931	*1957*	*1987*		
DEWDNEY Stanley Harcourt		UK	Papua NG	1905	1934	1971	1974	o d
1937 m Madeleine **HOLMES**		UK	Papua NG	1902	*1937*	*1971*		
DEY Emily Maud	SRN	UK	China	1903	1930	1946		m
			Papua NG		1946	1949		
			South India		1949	1950	1952	
DOBSON Frank John		UK	N.Rhodesia	1915	1948	1967		bld a
1941 m Elizabeth Perry **MITCHEL**		UK	N.Rhodesia	1919	*1948*	*1952*		
1953 m Barbara **PEAKE**		UK	N.Rhodesia	1919	*1953*	*1967*		

Surname	First names	Degrees etc.	origin	service	YOB	Apptment beg	Apptment end	YOD	work	pre/post
DOWNS	Evelyn Alice	Tchr Trng	UK	W.Samoa	1897	1922	1948	1985	e	
DOWNWARD	Celia	Tch Dip	UK	China	1911	1938	1951		d e	PCE
				Malaya/Singr	1952	1973				
DUNCAN	Alice Theodora	MA	UK	China	1885	1915	1951	1969	e d	
DUNN	Mary Eardley	SRN SCM RFN	UK	Botswana	1907	1936	1944	1991	m	
				South India		1944	1964			
DUNSTONE	Alan Sydney	MA BD	UK	Papua NG	1930	1964	1976		o te	
	1962 m Alice Wendy **WATTON**		UK	Papua NG	1938	*1964*	*1976*			
DURELL	Dora	SRN SCM	UK	Papua NG	1927	1954	1959		m	
EASTAFF	Ralph Hubert **ANNAN**	MA BD	UK	South India	1884	1920	1950	1967	o d	
	1919 m Jessie Helen **ANNAN**									
	1924 m Gladys May **HARRIES** (m)		UK	South India	1882	*1920*	*1923*	1923		
EASTMAN	George Herbert	OBE	UK	Gilbert Islands	1881	1913	1949	1974	o d	
	1914 m Winifred Hilda **GRIMWADE**		UK	Gilbert Islands	1886	*1913*	*1949*	1977		
EDMANSON	Annie Roxborough		NZ	China	1898	1924	1946	1987	m	
	1946 m William **MILL**									
EDWARDS	Catherine Eleri	BA DipEd	UK	Madagascar	1942	1972	1978		e c	
				Madagascar		1982				
EDWARDS	Ernest James		UK	W.Samoa	1908	1939	1952	1986	o d	staff
	1935 m Phyllis Mary **HUTCHINSON**		UK	W.Samoa	1904	*1939*	*1952*	1986		
EDWARDS	John	BSc	UK	Zambia	1940	1973	1976		o d	
	1966 m Margaret Myra **STEWART**		UK	Zambia	1943	*1973*	*1976*			
ELLIOTT	Linda	SRN SCM	UK	Taiwan	1946	1971	1976/9		m	PCE
ELLIOTT	Peter John Duncan	BA	UK	W.Samoa	1939	1963	1967	1967	e	
	1961 m Celia Ann **SWANN**		UK	W.Samoa	1939	*1963*	*1967*			
ELLIS	Suzannah Jane	BA BD	UK	Papua NG	1897	1926	1931	1989	d	
	1931 m Robert **RANKIN** (m)			Papua NG		*1931*	*1960*			
				Papua NG		1960	1964		te o	

Name	Qualifications	Country	Field	Born	From	To	End	Code	Note
EMMERICH Kurt	LLB BD	Germany	Germany	1903	1946	1950		o d	
1936 m Gertrude **HERRMAN**	PhD	Germany	Germany	1905	1946	1950			
EMMETT Lois Elizabeth	SRN SCM	Australia	Papua NG	1950	1973	1977		m	UCA
ENTRICAN Dorothy Isabel	MB ChB	UK	China	1900	1929	1940		m	
	BAO		Africa		1944	1947			
			China		1947	1951			
			North India		1951	1961			
			Papua NG		1965	1968	1985		
EVANS Elizabeth Marion Wynhall		UK	North India	1917	1949	1961		d	
EVANS Gwyneth Jane	BA	UK	Madagascar	1916	1948	1976		e	
EVANS John Marshall	BA DipTh	UK	South India	1933	1961	1966		o d	
1960 m Anne Elizabeth **GARLAND**		UK	South India	1936	1961	1966			
EVANS Kathleen Beatrice		UK	China	1887	1915	1948	1955	d	
EVANS Noah	DipTh	UK	Guyana	1897	1954	1968	1983	o d	CMS
EVERETT Daphne June	SRN SCM	UK	Zambia	1937	1963	1972		m	
FAIRHALL Constance Grace	SRN LCMB	UK	Papua NG	1906	1932	1967	1993	m d	
FARMER John Graham		UK	Madagascar	1921	1955	1966		lit	
1945 m Violet **DENHAM**		UK	Madagascar	1923	1955	1966			
FENN Edward Richard		Australia	Papua NG	1906	1937	1952	1972	o d	
1937 m Ida Elizabeth Muriel **PROSSER**		Australia	Papua NG	1907	1937	1952			
FENNELL Frederick George	BSc DipEd DipTh	UK	Botswana	1913	1972	1974		e	
1943 m Lisbeth Margaret **JOHNS**		UK	Botswana	1922	1972	1974		d	
FFRENCH Sarah Eleanor		UK	South India	1914	1940	1953	1990	d	
1972 m Alfred **MOVERLEY**									
FINDLATER Ernest		UK	Gilbert Isles	1918	1949	1952	1955	o d	
1949 m Gladys Vera **FORD**		UK	Gilbert Isles	1927	1949	1952			
FIRTH Cyril Bruce	MA	UK	South India	1905	1930	1965		o d te	
1933 m Helen Mary **LEWIS**		UK	South India	1911	1930	1965			
FISHER Cecil Roberts		Australia	Papua NG	1901	1946	1953	1970	art	
1932 m Jessie Anna **ANDERSON**		Australia	Papua NG	1910	1946	1953			

Surname	First names	Degrees etc.	origin	service	YOB	Apptment beg	end	YOD	work	pre/post
FLAWN	Janet		UK	Pacific	1947	1977	1983	1983	e	
FLETCHER	Audrey Mary	SRN SCM	UK	South India	1927	1959	1987	1991	m	
FLETCHER	Hilda Margaret		UK	South India	1914	1944	1972		d	
FOREMAN	Roy	BA	Australia	Nauru	1920	1953	1964	1969	o d	
1944 m Beryl Vivienne **IVES**			Australia	Nauru	1924	1953	*1964*			
FOSTER	Alice Mary	SRN	UK	China	1903	1932	1951		m	
FOWLES	Barbara Joy		UK	W.Samoa	1918	1945	1949		e	
1949 m Francis **AULD** (m)				W.Samoa		1949	*1954*			
FRANCIS	Kenneth David **SADLER** (m)	MA	UK	N.Rhodesia	1910	1934	1963	1979	o d te	
1937 m Mildred Kate										
FRASER	Bessie Gwendoline	MA	UK	South India	1900	1939	1948	1983	e	
FREELAND	Alexena Walker	MA LRAM	UK	S.Rhodesia	1928	1957	1964	1964	e	
FROST	Norman Baldwin		UK	N.Rhodesia	1909	1942	1949		o d	
1935 m Lilian Ivy **TAYLOR**			UK	N.Rhodesia	1909	*1942*	*1949*			
FRY	Beatrice Dorothy	BA	UK	South India	1887	1911	1947	1975	d	
FULLER	Richard Norman	DipTh	UK	Zambia	1936	1962	1970		o d	
1961 m Lauretta Jane **LEE**			UK	Zambia	1939	*1962*	*1970*			
GALE	Godfrey Livingstone	MB ChB FRCS	UK	China	1913	1937	1952	1986	m	
1940 m Elizabeth Durie **THOMSON**			Canada	China	1911	*1940*	*1952*			
GARNICK	Muriel Kathleen	MB ChB	UK	China	1906	1933	1945		m	
1945 m Dennis **BOX**										
GASTON	Arthur Raymond Charles	MA BD	UK	Madagascar	1936	1962	1968		te	
1962 m Evelyn Wilson **MATHER**			UK	Madagascar	1939	*1962*	*1968*			
GIBBON	Muriel Doris		UK	China	1896	1923	1932	1973	d	
1934 m A H Jowett **MURRAY** (m)				China		*1934*	*1946*			
GIFFORD	Florence	SRN SCM	UK	North India	1881	1908	1947	1959	m	

Name	Qualifications	From	Field					
GILBEY, John Edward Mortimer	MA	UK	Madagascar	1924	1948	1970		e a
1949 m Mary Elizabeth Julia **TRINDER**	BA	UK	Madagascar	1924	*1949*	*1970*		
GILLISON, Jean Brotch	SRN	UK	China	1901	1929	1952		m
GILLISON, Keith Harris	MB ChB FRCS	UK	China	1900	1926	1950	1977	m
1927 m Kathleen Francis **SANDERS** (m)								
GILMOUR, Marion	BSc DipEd	UK	Africa	1949	1977	1982		e
GINGER, Marion Emily		UK	China	1906	1933	1951		e d
			Africa		1951	1968		
1972 m David **ANDERSON** (m)								
GOBBETT, Donald Lyon	BA	Australia	S.Rhodesia	1938	1963	1968		e
1961 m Estelle Margaret **KERNICK**	BA	Australia	S.Rhodesia	1939	*1963*	*1968*		
GORNALL, Peter		UK	Guyana		1966	1967		o d
GRAHAM, Keith Irving	MB BS FRACS	Australia	China	1909	1937	1951		m
			South India		1951	1975		
1949 m Barbara **PEDDIE**	BSc	Australia	China	1925	*1949*	*1951*		
			South India		*1951*	*1975*		
GRAY, Edmund Laurence		Australia	Papua NG	1928	1956	1974		o d e
1957 m Laurel **JERREMS**		Australia	Papua NG	1933	*1956*	*1974*		
GREAVES, Ivy Lucy		UK	China	1893	1922	1951/5	1975	o d
GREEN, Alfred		UK	Madagascar	1910	1938	1947	1987	o d
GREEN, Elizabeth Ann (Sally)	SRN SCM	UK	Papua NG	1934	1965	1985		m
GREEN, Samuel Withers	BA BD	UK	China	1894	1922	1927		o e
			China		1934	1939		
			Hong Kong		1948	1960	1976	
1921 m Ruth **VICTORIA**		UK	China	1897	*1922*	*1927*		
			China		*1934*	*1939*		
			Hong Kong		*1948*	*1960*	1971	
GREENHILL, Margaret Anne		Australia	Papua NG	1935	1963	1977		e UCA

Surname	First names	Degrees etc.	origin	service	YOB	Apptment beg	end	YOD	work	pre/post
GREEVES	Perla	MD BSc ChB BAO DRCOG MRCOG	UK	South India	1913	1950	1964	1975	m	staff
GRIFFITHS	Arthur Frank		UK	China	1902	1931	1951	1972	o d	
1932 m Lila Esther Mary RIDER		SRN	UK	China	1906	*1932*	*1951*		o d	
GRIFFITHS	Gerald Robert	BA BD	UK	Africa	1908	1938	1972	1972	o d	
1939 m Eleanor Margaret TENNANT			UK	Africa	1913	*1938*	*1972*		o d	
GRIFFITHS	Winifred Mair	BA	UK	Madagascar	1916	1947	1967		e	
GROSVENOR	John Arthur		UK	Madagascar	1924	1949	1955	1965	o d	
				Madagascar		1958	1965			
1950 m Olga Dorothy LEE			UK	Madagascar	1919	*1949*	*1955*		o d	
				Madagascar		*1958*	*1965*			
GROULT	Eugene Isidore		France	Madagascar	1871	1924	1946	1966	o d	
1892 m Marie Elisabeth VARDON			France	Madagascar	1872	*1924*	*1946*	1954		
GURNEY	Ernest Fred		UK	South India	1894	1924	1946	1969	o d	
1924 m Frances Anna DAVIES			UK	South India		*1924*	*1946*	1972	o d	
HACKER	Edith Annie	SRN	UK	South India	1895	1923	1927	1947	m	
1927 m Wilfred SCOPES (m)				South India		*1927*	*1947*			
HAGYARD	John	BA	UK	Botswana	1926	1965	1972		lit	
1955 m Eileen Mary Canning FARMER			UK	Botswana	1925	*1965*	*1972*			
HAILE	Alfred John	MA	UK	South Africa	1888	1914	1955	1982	o e	
1915 m Dorothy PALMER			UK	South Africa	1889	*1914*	*1918*	1918		
1922 m Ethel PALMER			UK	South Africa	1885	1922	1955	1969		
HAILE	Evelyn Annie	MBE SRN SCM	UK	China	1900	1925	1927	1964	m	
1967 m J.H.L. BURNS				Africa			1957			
HAMBLIN	Mary Kathleen		UK	N.Rhodesia	1915	1942	1952		e	
1952 m James HARRIS										
HAMBLY	Richard Henry	DipTh	UK	W.Samoa	1935	1972	1979		o d	
1963 m Olive Ann HEARN			UK	W.Samoa	1941	*1972*	*1979*			

Name	Qual.	From	Field	b.				
HAMILTON Robert	BD MA	UK	South India	1944	1975	1977	1980	o te
1963 m Susan Edith	BSc	UK	South India	1944	*1975*	*1977*		
HANCOCK Ethel Mary	BSc	UK	China	1879	1920	1947	1968	e
HARDYMAN Arnold Victor	MA BD	UK	Madagascar	1887	1916	1938	1952	o d te
	BA		Madagascar		1944	1950		
1916 m Laura **STUBBS**		UK	Madagascar	1893	*1916*	*1938*		
			Madagascar		*1944*	*1950*		
HARDYMAN James Trenchard	MA BD	UK	Madagascar	1918	1944	1974	1971	o d te
1945 m Marjorie **TUCKER**		UK	Madagascar	1920	*1944*	*1974*		
HARLOW Edgar Augustus	MSR FCS	UK	Hong Kong	1894	1925	1927	1991	m a
			South India		1927	1953		
1923 m Caroline Victoria **BEAL**		UK	Hong Kong	1893	*1925*	*1927*		
			South India		*1927*	*1953*		
HARMAN Douglas John	MB ChB	UK	China	1915	1939	1952		m
			N.Rhodesia		1952	1955		
1939 m Mary Gladys **GUNSTONE**	SRN	UK	China	1914	*1939*	*1952*		
			N.Rhodesia		*1952*	*1955*		
HARMON Frank Henry Brigg		Canada	China	1886	1929	1950	1964	m a
1928 m Marjorie **PORTEOUS**		UK	China	1886	*1929*	*1950*	1966	
HARRIES Anthony Vaughan	BSc PGCE	UK	Bangladesh	1949	1976	1980		e
1973 m Helen Jane **LAING**	MB ChB DipObs	UK	Bangladesh	1950	*1976*	*1980*		
HARRIES Gladys May	BA	Australia	Gilbert Islands	1885	1909	1924		e d
1924 m Ralph Hubert **EASTAFF** (m)						*1950*		
HARRIS Evelyn Winifred Shirley	MB ChB	UK	South India	1935	1963	1966		m
HARRIS John Williams	Tch Cert	Australia	South India	1930	1965	1967		e
HARRISON Muriel Irene		UK	South India	1938	1965	1985		d
1985 m Robin **SLEIGH** (m)					*1965*	*1992*		
HATHAWAY Isabel Emila		UK	Papua NG	1934	1962	1985		e
HAWARD David Edwin	BA	UK	S.Rhodesia	1919	1955	1966		o d
1951 m Sheila A. **THOMPSON**		UK	S.Rhodesia	1926	*1955*	*1966*		

Surname	First names	Degrees etc.	origin	service	YOB	Apptment beg	end	YOD	work	pre/post
HAWARD	Edith Julia	SRN	UK	China	1884	1913	1923		m	
				China		1937	1946			
HAWKINGS	Peggy Barbara		UK	China	1919	1947	1950	1973	d	
				South India		1950	1979			
HAWKRIDGE	Helen Louie	BSc	UK	South India	1890	1915	1922		e d	
				South India		1937	1954	1976		
HAWLEY	Marion Diana	SRN SCM TC	Australia	S.Rhodesia	1929	1958	1963		m	
HAWORTH	Alan	MA MB BCh LRCP DObst RCOG	UK	N.Rhodesia	1928	1956	1958		m	
HAWTHORN	Thomas	MA	UK	China	1918	1947	1951		o e d	
				South India		1952	1958			
				Niue		1961	1966			
				Gilbert Islands		1970	1979			
	1944 m Kathleen **HARPER**	MA	UK	China	1918	*1947*	*1951*			
				South India		*1952*	*1958*			
				Niue		*1961*	*1966*			
				Gilbert Islands		*1970*	*1979*			
HAY	Arthur	MA	UK	N.Rhodesia	1907	1942	1948	1970	o d	
	1936 m Ethel Hope **JOB**		UK	N.Rhodesia	1909	*1942*	*1948*			
HAY	Douglas	Tch Cert	UK	Botswana	1961	1976	1982		e	
HEADLAND	Charles	BSc ARCSc	UK	North India	1878	1909	1946	1958	e	
	1909 m Rose Bertha **NEWBERY**		UK	North India	1879	*1909*	*1946*	1963		
HENDERSON	John	MA	UK	Malaya/Singpr	1922	1922	1950	1977	o d	
	1962 m Daphne Kate **McCANN**	Tch Cert	UK	Malaya/Singpr	1929	*1929*	*1950*	*1977*		
HENSON	Edwin Roland Witham		UK	S.Rhodesia	1916	1951	1965	1991	agr	
	1939 m Irene May **WHITMEE**		UK	S.Rhodesia	1910	*1951*	*1965*	1973		
HENSON	Horace Frederick Paul	BA	UK	Botswana	1926	1954	1960		o d	
HEWES	June Patricia Dorothy		UK	N.Rhodesia	1936	1961	1966	1966	e	

Name	Quals	Country	Field					Notes	Affil
HIGGISON Irene	BSc	Australia	Africa	1920	1948	1964		e	
HOADLEY Jack Herbert DALE	BA BD	UK	W.Samoa	1916	1945	1957	1985	o e d	PCE
1941 m Alice Rose DALE		UK	W.Samoa	1909	1945	1957			
HODGSON Frank Percival	BSc	UK	N.Rhodesia	1918	1947	1960		e	
1945 m Barbara Lucy CLEAVER		UK	N.Rhodesia	1920	1947	1960			
HOLDEN Lilian	SRN SCM	UK	Papua NG	1926	1957	1971		m	
HOLLAMBY Patricia Anne	MBE SRN SCM	UK	Botswana	1931	1963	1976		m	
1976 m Mike DANCE									
HOLMES Christina Sibyl	SRN	UK	Singapore	1913	1949	1950		m	PCE
			Taiwan		1950	1976			
HOLYDAY Bertram Andrew Lockerbie		UK	N.Rhodesia	1907	1950	1964	1993	agr	
1936 m Mary WHARMUND		UK	N.Rhodesia	1913	1950	1964			
HOOD George Archibald	MA PhD	UK	China	1917	1943	1950		o d	PCE
			Malaya/Singpr		1951	1972			staff
1943 m Elizabeth Margaret JAMES		UK	China	1918	1943	1950			PCE
			Malaya/Singpr		1951	1972			
HORSFIELD Donald	BA MA	UK	Papua NG	1937	1965	1983		o e d	
			New Zealand		1983	1987			
1971 m Harokuku AVOHA		PNG	Papua NG	1946	1971	1983			
			New Zealand		1983	1987			
HUGHES Daphne Margaret	BSc	UK	Hong Kong	1937	1964	1967		e	
1967 m Paul BEALE									
HUGHES Trevor Evans		UK	Jamaica	1899	1929	1969	1983	o d	CMS
1928 m Annie Milissa SCHLEIFER		UK	Jamaica	1894	1929	1969			CMS
HUGHES William Henry	BA BSc	UK	Gilbert Islands	1908	1951	1955		e	
1945 m Dorothy GIBBS		UK	Gilbert Islands		1951	1955			
HUNT John William	Craft Certs	UK	Papua NG	1943	1972	1975		e	
m Anne	Cert RSM	UK	Papua NG	1947	1972	1975			
HUNTLEY Charlotte Daisy		UK	Africa	1895	1931	1942	1985	e	
			Africa		1945	1957			

Surname	First names	Degrees etc.	origin	service	YOB	Apptment beg	end	YOD	work	pre/post
HUTCHINS	Sidney John		UK	Cook Islands		1895	1922	1925	o d	CMS
				Madagascar		1928	1949			
				Guyana		1949	1957			
1922 m Florence Caroline **PARKER**			UK	Cook Islands	1898	1922	1925	1957	te	CMS
				Madagascar		1928	1949			
				Guyana		1949	1957			
HUTCHINSON	Dorothy	BA	UK	Hong Kong	1896	1922	1946	1968	e	
INGLIS	David Jackson	MA BD Dip Ed Dip Litt	NZ	Pacific	1924	1967	1975		te	
1953 m Joan Lynley **FORDER**			NZ	Pacific	1933	1967	1975			
IRVING	Robert	BA	UK	Bangladesh	1932	1963	1967		o d	
				Malaysia		1967	1974			
1955 m Patricia **BURRIDGE**				Bangladesh	1933	1963	1967			
				Malaysia		1967	1974			
JAKINS 1954 E.N. **WALKINSHAW**	Marvine	SRN SCM	NZ	South India	1918	1949	1954		m	
JAMES 1967 m Mr **BREWER**	Elizabeth Redcliffe	BA	Australia	China	1913	1938	1953		e	
JAMES	Isaac Roland		UK	Madagascar	1889	1925	1950	1955	o d	
1918 m Gertrude Rendall **LOVELL**			UK	Madagascar	1895	1925	1950	1958		
JAMES	Nicholas Ernest	MB BS MRCS LRCP SRN	UK	South India	1912	1940	1948	1966	m	
1941 m Catherine S. **HYMERS**		SRN	UK	South India		1940	1948			
JAMES	Paul Worsley	MB BS DTM&H DObst RCOG SRN	UK	Zambia	1934	1960	1970		m	
1960 m Margaret G. **SELLICKS**					1936	1960	1970			
JAMESON	Ian Thirkell	MA	UK	Zambia	1902	1960	1963	1991	a	
1928 m Isabel Gladys **JUDD**			UK	Zambia	1900	1960	1963			

Name	Qualifications	From	Field					Code	Note
JENKINS Derek Griffin	MB BS FRCS LRCP	UK	South India	1926	1949	1967		m	
1948 m Mary Georgina **HARDY**	MA		South India	*1924*	*1949*	*1967*			
JENKINS Evelyn Griffin	MA	UK	Hong Kong	1930	1956	1967		e	
JOHNSON Helen Jean	BA	UK	South India	1903	1928	1934		d	
1934 m Montague John **ROLLES** (m)			South India		*1934*	*1956*			
JONES Daniel Owen	MA	UK	Madagascar	1880	1910	1949	1951	o d te	
1912 m Hilda Victoria **SMITH**		UK	Madagascar	*1887*	*1912*	*1949*			
JONES Emlyn		UK	Gilbert Isles	1917	1944	1963	1987	o d e	
1946 m Margaret Alice **ROBERTS**		UK	Gilbert Isles	*1924*	*1944*	*1963*			
JONES Graham John Phipps	MA	UK	Botswana	1914	1961	1969		e	
1939 m Marjorie Frances **WILLIAMS**			Botswana	*1918*	*1961*	*1969*			
JONES John Derek	OBE MA	UK	Botswana	1927	1953			o d	lit
1954 m Joan Ann **TALBERT**		UK	Botswana	*1923*	*1953*				
JONES John Thomas		UK	Madagascar	1889	1922	1952	1952	o d	
1921 m Emily **BOWEN**		UK	Madagascar	*1890*	*1922*	*1926*	*1926*		
1927 m Pauline Madeleine **HIPEAU**		France	Madagascar	*1893*	*1927*	*1952*	*1976*		
JONES Norma Isabella		Australia	Pacific	1923	1948	1954		e	
1954 m Mr **JACKMAN**									
JONES Pearce	MA BD	UK	Jamaica	1920	1963	1986		o d	CMS
1944 m Catherine **CHESTERS**		UK	Jamaica	*1923*	*1963*	*1986*			
JORDAN Thomas Ivor		UK	N.Rhodesia	1911	1943	1949		o e	
1943 m Doris May **SCOURFIELD**		UK	N.Rhodesia	*1914*	*1943*	*1949*			
JUDGE Robin Frank		NZ	Gilbert Islands	1933	1961	1965		e	
1956 m Ruth **MONTGOMERY**		NZ	Gilbert Islands	*1934*	*1961*	*1965*			
JURD Ruby		Australia	Papua NG	1924	1954	1959		e sw	
KEEN Kate Hilda Louise	LTh	UK	China	1887	1913	1929		e d o	
1929 m Walter **HUTLEY** (died 1931)			China		*1932*	*1950*	*1976*		
KENNEDY Mary Forbes	RGN SRN SCM	UK	Papua NG	1934	1960	1975		m	

Surname	First names	Degrees etc.	origin	service	YOB	Apptment beg	end	YOD	work	pre/post
KIBBLE	Walter Frederick	MA PhD	UK	South India	1903	1931	1962	1981	e	
	1930 m Janet Cowan W. **BANNERMAN**		UK	South India		*1931*	*1962*	1976	e	
KIDD	John Brown	BD	UK	Madagascar	1918	1958	1963		o d	
	1942 m Evelyn **PAGE**		UK	Madagascar	1919	*1958*	*1963*		o d	
KIGHTLEY	Percy		UK	Pacific	1897	1936	1963	1972	o d	
	1925 Mabel Emma **DOWLAND**		UK	Pacific	1897	*1936*	*1963*	1975	o d	
KING	David Stansfield	ICIS ICIB	UK	Botswana	1946	1974	1981		e a	
	1970 m Joy Margaret **LAWRENCE**	SRN SCM	UK	Botswana	1949	*1974*	*1981*		e a	
KING	Marjorie	BSc	UK	W.Samoa	1917	1954	1968		e	
KING	Paul Stansfield	BA	UK	S.Rhodesia	1916	1943	1968		o d	
	1943 m Lilian Ethel **PURSEY**		UK	S.Rhodesia	1919	*1943*	*1968*		o d	
KINGSLEY	Sally Rosemary K.	BEd TC	UK	Pacific	1948	1976	1980		e	
KINGSTON	Derek John	MA	UK	Malaysia	1940	1964	1975		o d	
				Singapore		1975				
	1980 m Lai Lan **NG**		Singapore	Singapore	1955	*1980*				
KIRBY	Irene	SRN	UK	South India	1905	1933	1969	1973	m	
KNIGHT	Barbara Blanche	BSc	UK	Hong Kong	1921	1948	1952		e	
	1952 m Edward H. **PATERSON** (m)					*1952*	*1989*			
KNIGHT	Richard Leslie	BSc	UK	N.Rhodesia	1927	1950	1954		d	
	1950 m Joy Edith Stratton **KING**		NZ	N.Rhodesia	1924	*1950*	*1954*		d	
KNIPE	Norman Williams		NZ	Papua NG	1933	1967	1976		o e	
	1960 m Lois Anne **WILLMOTT**		NZ	Papua NG	1937	*1967*	*1976*		o e	
KNOTT	Alan Gordon	BSc	UK	South Africa	1889	1949	1954	1976	o e	
	1919 Edith Grace **OATES**		UK	South Africa	1892	*1949*	*1954*	1989	o e	
LANDSBOROUGH	David	MD FRCP	UK	China	1914	1940	1952		m	PCE
				Taiwan		*1952*	1980			
		MB DS	UK	China	1920	*1947*	*1952*	1993		PCE
	1947 m Jean **CONNAN**			Taiwan		*1952*	*1980*			

Name	Given names	Qualifications	Country	Field	Born				Status
LAPWOOD	Ernest Ralph	MA PhD	UK	China	1909	1932	1952/3	1984	e
1950 m Nancy STUCKEY			UK	China	1907	*1940*	*1952/3*	1993	
LAWRENCE	Gwyneth Ida	SRN	UK	South India	1901	1934	1948	1981	m
LAWSON	Annie Tosh Dunbar	SRN	UK	South India	1897	1928	1947	1964	m d
LEA	Barbara	SRN SCM	UK	Zambia	1918	1945	1976		m d
LEACH	Dorothy Eileen	SRN SCM	UK	Zambia	1924	1955	1965		m
LEE-WOLF	James Philip	MA BD	UK	China	1916	1942	1951/7		o e
1942 m Jean D. McKENDRICK		MB BS LRCP MRCS	UK	China	1916	*1942*	*1951/7*		
LEENHARDT	Roland Pierre André		France	Madagascar	1913	1954	1964	1966	e
1939 m Hilda Renée PEYROT			France	Madagascar	1914	*1954*	*1964*		
LEFEVER	Henry Charles	BA BD PhD	UK	South India	1906	1934	1954		o d
LEGG	Arnold Henry	MA	UK	South India	1899	1924	1967	1980	o d
1928 m Mary Gertrude HEWETT			UK	South India	1904	*1928*	*1967*		
LEGG	Frank Stanley	BA	UK	N.Rhodesia	1919	1950	1959		e
1942 m Lilian Trevanion BROCKETT			UK	N.Rhodesia	1914	*1950*	*1959*		
LEGGE	Douglas Edrick	BSc	UK	China	1920	1947	1950		o d
				Malaysia		1951	1952		
				China		*1947*	*1950*		
1946 m Rene ADAMSON			UK	Malaysia	1922	*1951*	*1952*		
LEHMANN	Dorothea	PhD	Germany	N.Rhodesia	1910	1949	1959	1982	e
LEIGHTON	Rachel Horn	SRN SCM	Australia	Papua NG	1919	1946	1961/6		m
LENWOOD	Norah	MB ChB	UK	China	1876	1905	1906		m
1906 m Arnold George BRYSON (m)			UK	China	1906	*1947*	*1947*		
LEWIS	Aubrey David	BSc	UK	South Africa	1917	1945	1957/60		o e
1943 m Nora Kathleen BELGROVE			UK	South Africa	1912	*1945*	*1957/60*		
LEWIS	Emmeline		UK	North India	1910	1938	1958		d
LEYSHON	Doris Evelyn		UK	North India	1914	1944	1958		d
LINDSAY	Agnes Ellis	MA	UK	China	1901	1929	1949	1968	e d
				Malaysia		1952	1960		

Surname	First names	Degrees etc.	origin	service	YOB	Apptment beg	end	YOD	work	pre/post
LING	May Winifred		UK	North India	1885	1915	1948	1982	d	
LOCHHEAD	Mary	SRN	UK	Madagascar	1889	1920	1952	1967	m	
LOCK	Albert Alfred Frank 1941 m Florence Adelaide **SHEARMAN**	CBE	UK	Botswana	1917	1955	1980	1985	o d a	
	Florence Adelaide		UK	Botswana	1920	*1955*	*1980*			
LONGMAN	Charles Herbert Bell 1913 m Amy **GUTHRIE**	ARCSc	UK	China	1882	1912	1948	1961	e	
	Amy		UK	China	1883	*1913*	*1948*	1963		
LOUGHTON	Jane		UK	Madagascar	1894	1923	1960	1976	d	
LOVELL	Joyce Gertrude	MBE SCM	UK	China Malaysia	1918	1946 1952	1952 1977	1983	m	
LOWRY	Samuel Warnock Patterson 1953 m Elizabeth **JOHNSON**		UK	Gilbert Islands	1924	1955	1964		o d	
	Elizabeth	SRN SCM	UK	Gilbert Islands	1926	*1955*	*1964*			
LUKER	Elizabeth Anne Morris 1962 m Hamilton **CURRIE**	BA	Australia	N.Rhodesia	1926	1953	1962	1988	e	
LUXON	Ellen 1948 m John **SOMERS**		UK	N.Rhodesia	1916	1944	1948		d	
LUXON	Gerald 1913 m Ethel Lilias **MARTIN**		UK	South Africa China Gilbert Islands	1885	1913 1918 1948	1918 1948 1951	1969	e	
	Ethel Lilias		UK	South Africa China Gilbert Islands	1885	*1913* *1918* *1948*	*1918* *1948* *1951*	1971		
MACAULAY	Christine Mary	SRN SCM	UK	Papua NG	1922	1950	1951	1951	m	
MACHIN	Trevor Rawlins 1949 m Dorothy **MELLOR**		UK	S.Rhodesia	1922	1955	1960		e	
	Dorothy		UK	S.Rhodesia	1922	*1955*	*1960*			
MACKIE	Eric Malcolm	BA	UK	Madagascar	1917	1944	1945	1945	o d	

Name	Qual.	Country	Field	Born				Status	Notes
MACKEITH — Anne Vera	BSc	UK	China	1903	1931	1951		e	
MACKEITH — John Stuart **GODFREY**	BA	UK	Hong Kong	1934	1962	1970		m a	
1961 m Ann Veronica **GODFREY**	BSc	UK	Hong Kong	1935	*1962*	*1970*			
MAIN — John Kenneth	MBE MA	UK	Africa	1911	1935	1975		o d a	
1936 m Mary Ruth **BARTLETT**	SRN	UK	Africa	1910	*1935*	*1975*			
MAITLAND — Evelyn		UK	South India	1903	1932	1934		o d	
1934 m Henry Charles **LEFEVER** (m)			South India		*1934*	*1954*			
MARKS — George Maurice	MA	UK	Jamaica	1914	1957	1967	1967	o d	CMS
1951 m Mary Whiteford **HUTSON**		UK	Jamaica	1927	*1957*	*1967*			
MARSDEN — David	MA MA	UK	Singapore	1929	1966	1974		o d	PCE
1954 m Mary Selkirk **GARVEN**	BSc DipBSt	UK	Singapore	1929	*1966*	*1974*			*PCE*
MARSDEN — John Geoffrey	BA MA	UK	South India	1930	1956			o d	
1963 m Ann Elizabeth **TODD**		UK	South India	1940	*1963*				
MARSDEN — George Henry	MA	UK	South India	1894	1923	1957	1957	e	
1919 m Ida **LIGHTFLOWER**		UK	South India	1892	*1923*	*1957*	1971		
MARTIN — Avis Doreen	SRN SCM	UK	Papua NG	1918	1947	1976		m	
MARTIN — Harold Victor	MA BD PhD	UK	South India	1898	1930	1948	1968	o d	
1925 m Hilda Mary **DAVIS**		UK	South India	1900	*1930*	*1948*	1960		
1962 m Patricia Mary **WALKER**									
MARTIN — Henry Roy	BA BD	UK	South India	1930	1961	1980		o d	
1956 m Rose Joy **CARRINGTON**		UK	South India	1932	*1961*	*1980*			
MARTIN — Mabel	SRN	UK	China	1883	1913	1946	1949	m	
MARTIN — Patricia Mary (née **WALKER**)	SRN SCM	UK	Botswana	1932	1972	1982		m	
MATANLE — Richard Percival		UK	Pacific	1919	1955	1959		o a	
1940 m Mary **HAYWARD**		UK	Pacific	1920	*1955*	*1959*			
MATHEWS — Edward John Peter		Australia	N.Rhodesia	1918	1956	1959		o e	
1947 m Rita Clarice **CARR**		Australia	N. Rhodesia	1922	*1956*	*1959*			
MATTHEWS — Rex Williams	BA	Australia	Nauru	1927	1965	1968		o d	
1955 m Gwenneth Joy **TAYLOR**		Australia	Nauru	1931	*1965*	*1968*			

Surname	First names	Degrees etc.	origin	service	YOB	Apptment beg	end	YOD	work	pre/post
MAXFIELD	Edith Eleanor	MBE	UK	Pacific	1913	1945	1977	1987	e	
MCALL	Robert Kenneth	MB ChB	UK	China	1910	1937	1946	1946	m	
1940 m Frances A. M. **ALDRIDGE** (m)										
McILROY	Kathleen Janet	BSc	UK	South India	1907	1935	1968	1988	e d	
McKELVEY	Robert John	BA MTh DPhil	UK	South Africa	1929	1958	1978		o te	
1957 m Martha Esther **SKELLY**			UK	South Africa	1928	1958	1978			
McKENZIE (Mrs)	Vivien	BSc	UK	Papua NG	1925	1974	1975		a	
				Bangladesh		1975	1977			
McPHAIL	Leslie Robert	ACA	NZ	Gilbert Islands	1940	1974	1978		a	
1963 m Patricia Jesse **SHAW**			NZ	Gilbert Islands	1942	1974	1978			
MEREDITH	Richard Glynn	BA Dip Ed	Australia	Papua NG	1921	1956	1958		e	
1945 m Bronwen Myfanwy **WILLIAMS**			Australia	Papua NG	1919	1956	1958			
METCALF	Betty	SRN SCM	UK	Africa	1928	1961	1970		m	
MICKLEBURGH	Hazel Rose		UK	South India	1922	1948	1965	1965	d	
MIDGLEY	Edna May Scott	SRN SCM	UK	S.Rhodesia	1911	1969	1971		m	
MILLEDGE	Geoffrey Wilberforce	LRCP LRCS LRFPS DTM&H BMus	UK	China	1904	1929	1950		m	
				South India		1950	1970			
1029 m Miriam **THOMAS**			UK	China	1902	1929	1950	1991		
				South India		1950	1970			
MILLEDGE	James Sibree	MB ChB FRCP DObst RCOG	UK	South India	1930	1961	1972		m	
1956 m Betty Avril **ASTLE**		MB ChB	UK	South India	1930	1961	1972	1991		
MILLS	Edith Florence	SRN	UK	South India	1900	1926	1946	1991	m	
MILLS	Pamela	BA	UK	Madagascar	1946	1973	1975		e	
MILNE	Dorothy	Tch Cert	UK	South India	1920	1946	1947		e	
1947 m Rodney **TODMAN** (m)			UK	South India		1947	1959			

Name	Qualifications	Origin	Field of service	Born	From	To	Died	Code	Notes
MILNE Emily Sarah 1920 m Evan **REES** (m) died 1922		UK	North India	1878	1918	1920		e	
			North India		1920	1922			
			North India		1922	1948	1960		
MILNE Gwendoline May 1931 m David Eric **URE** (m)		Australia	Papua NG	1901	1929	*1931*		e	
			Papua NG		*1931*	*1965*	1984		
MOODY Helen Irene		UK	China	1896	1925	1950	1956	e	
MOODY Kathleen	M Cert SSc & Admin	UK	Taiwan	1920	1948	1975		e	PCE
MORCH Elizabeth Kirstine	SRN	Denmark	South India	1896	1929	1960	1983	m	
MORRIS Gwendoline Ada		UK	China	1911	1939	1950		d	staff
			South India		1950	1972	1983		
MORTON Olive	BA	UK	South India	1890	1924	1950	1983	e	
MOSS Gwenfron		UK	China	1898	1928	1938		d	
			China		1940	1952	1991		
MOSSOM Margaret Francis 1983 m Arthur **CAYZER**	LTh	Australia	South India	1926	1951	1980		d	
MUIR John Williams 1962 m Dorothy **CLEVERTON**	BA MA	UK	Zambia	1938	1969	1975		o d	
(CLEVERTON Dorothy)		UK	Zambia	1934	*1969*	*1975*		d	
MUMMERY Ethel Ada		UK	South India	1887	1915	1946	1983	o d	
MURPHY William George 1913 m Mabel Annie **BRETT** 1923 m Dorothy **SIBREE**		UK	India	1891	1917	1932		d	
			Cook Islands		1946	1957	1966		
(BRETT)		UK	India	1882	*1917*	*1921*	1921		
(SIBREE)		UK	India	1879	*1923*	*1927*	1927		
MURRAY Arthur Hugh Jowett 1913 m Mary **ROBERTSON** 1932 m Muriel Doris **GIBBON** (m)	MA	UK	China	1888	1912	1946	1981	e o d	
(ROBERTSON)			China		*1913*	*1930*	1930		
MURRAY Elizabeth Helen Sutherland	SRN	UK	China	1894	1922	1955	1965	a	
MYERS Wendy	SRN	UK	Solomon Isles	1941	1973	1975		m	
NAISMITH Rhonda Joan	SRN SCM	Australia	Papua NG	1932	1962	1973		m	

Surname	First names	Degrees etc.	origin	service	YOB	Apptment beg	end	YOD	work	pre/post
NEAVE	James McEwan McKenzie		UK	China	1913	1940	1951	1993	o d	
				Malaysia		1951	1957			staff
1946 m Jenny Stewart **BROWN**		MA ALD	UK	China	1913	*1946*	*1951*	1990		staff
				Malaysia		*1951*	*1957*			
NEEMS	Lewis Hugh Butt		UK	Samoa	1928	1954	1968		o d	
1954 m Eileen Audrey **COVINGTON**			UK	Samoa	1930	*1954*	*1968*			
NEWELL	Honor Olive	OBE MB ChB DTM&H	UK	North India	1899	1927	1971	1983	m	
NICHOLL	Samuel Johnston		UK	Papua NG	1938	1962	1969		e	
1960 m Christine **MANSFIELD**			UK	Papua NG	1939	*1962*	*1969*			
NIXON	Maurice		UK	Papua NG	1906	1931	1967	1979	o d e	
1931 m Jennie Newbold **BOARDMAN**			UK	Papua NG	1904	*1931*	*1967*			
NOBLE	Florence Mary	TC	Australia	South India	1892	1917	1950	1973	e d	
1950 m Jeffrey **BROWN**										
NOBLE	Herbert	OBE BSc	UK	Hong Kong	1905	1937	1964	1964	e	
1937 m Ruth **CHADWICK**			UK	Hong Kong	1906	*1937*	*1964*	1989		
NORWOOD	Clarence Edward	MA	UK	W.Samoa	1904	1959	1967	1985	o d	
1938 m Margaret McFie **GILLIES**			UK	W.Samoa	1907	*1959*	*1967*			
PACKER	Harold Arthur Bevill	BA	UK	N.Rhodesia	1915	1941	1962	1979	e	
1940 m Margaret **GARNER**			UK	N.Rhodesia	1918	*1941*	*1962*			
PAGE	Stanley Stanton		UK	Pacific	1903	1938	1951	1988	ship	
1930 m Mary Hope **HOLDEN**			UK	Pacific	1907	*1938*	*1951*			
PARKER	George Henry	MA BD	UK	South India	1869	1900	1927	1960	o a d te	
				South India		1930	1940			
				South Africa		1940	1947			
1900 m Beatrice **POCHIN**			UK	South Africa	1872	*1900*	*1927*	1965		
				South India		*1930*	*1940*			
				South Africa		*1940*	*1947*			

Name	Quals	Origin	Field				
PARKER Gladys / Dorothy Spencer	SRN	UK	China	1901	1932	1946	m
PARRY David Wyn	MA	UK	Papua NG	1946	1971	1978	e
1968 m Caryl Gillian **BURLEY**		UK	Papua NG	1946	*1971*	*1978*	
PARRY John Edward	MB ChB DTM&H	UK	Zambia	1923	1948	1969	o m
1948 Freda Margaret **CARTER**	SRN SCM	UK	Zambia	1922	*1948*	*1969*	
PARRY John Maldwyn	BA BD	UK	Bangladesh	1946	1973	1978	o d
1970 Yvonne Margaret **DAY**	BSc	UK	Bangladesh	1947	*1973*	*1978*	
PARTRIDGE Wilfred Gordon McDonald	MA	Australia	S.Rhodesia	1912	1946	1967	e
1945 m Nancy Walkden **BROWN**	BA	Australia	S.Rhodesia	1915	*1946*	*1967*	
PATEMAN Emily May	Tchr Trg	UK	Pacific	1893	1922	1953	e
PATERSON Allan MacGregor		UK	Madagascar	1893	1952	1957	o te a stf
1920 m Winifred Hilda **GIDNEY**		UK	Madagascar	1896	*1954*	1962	
PATERSON Donald Edward	MB ChB DMRD MRad MD	UK	China / South India	1918 / 1922	1948 / *1948*	1951 / *1951*	m
1952 m Rachel Elizabeth Lucas **MOORE**		UK	China / South India	1922	1951 / 1951	1964 / 1964	
PATERSON Edward Hamilton	MB BS FRCS	UK	China / Hong Kong	1920	1949 / 1951	1951 / 1989	m
1952 m Barbara **KNIGHT** (m)							
PATERSON James Lee Hamilton	MB ChB	UK	China	1884	1907	1952	m
1912 m Constance Mabel **BROWN** (m)							
PATON Elizabeth Heyer		Australia	Hong Kong	1911	1936	1941	e
1941 m Frank Richard **ASHTON** (m)			Hong Kong	*1941*	*1964*	1971	
PAYNE Peggy Marion		UK	S.Rhodesia	1923	1954	1985	e
PEAKE Ernest Cromwell	MD ChB	UK	China / Hong Kong	1874 / 1946	1899 / 1924	1947 / 1950	m
PEDLEY Richard John	BA	UK	Botswana	1951	1974	1979	e
1974 m Rebecca **ROGERS**	Dip Occ Th	UK	Botswana	1951	*1974*	*1979*	

Surname	First names	Degrees etc.	origin	service	YOB	Apptment beg	Apptment end	YOD	work	pre/post
PELLING	James Norman	BA	UK	S.Rhodesia	1927	1953	1992		o d te	
1954 m Pamela **EASTER**		BA	UK	S.Rhodesia	1930	1954	1992			
PERRETT	Clive Williams	BSc MSc	UK	Papua NG	1947	1972	1974		e	
1971 m Adeline Edith **SINNAMON**			UK	Papua NG	1949	1972	1974			
PERRY	Raymond	LTh	Australia	Papua NG	1906	1939	1972	1990	o d e	
1939 m Doris Mary **COLE** (m)										
PETERSON	Margaret		Australia	Papua NG	1933	1964	1977		e	UCA
PEYROT	Alfred	BTh	France	Madagascar	1910	1947	1962		e	
m 1935 Antoinette **MITCHELL**			France	Madagascar	1907	1947	1962	1980		
PHILLIPS	Joan Avril	SRN SCM	UK	Papua NG	1923	1950	1971		m	
PHILLIPS	John David Forster	BSc	UK	Papua NG	1943	1972	1976		e	
1967 m Penelope Mary **HOBSON**			UK	Papua NG	1948	1972	1976			
PHILLIPS	Leopold Gordon	BD	UK	China	1884	1911	1950	1979	o d e	
1912 m Alice **BRYNING**			UK	China	1885	1912	1950	1987		
PHILLIPS	Ronald John Forster	SRN	UK	N.Rhodesia	1909	1940	1962	1989	o d	
1940 m Phyllis **TUPPER**			UK	N.Rhodesia	1914	1940	1962			
PHILLIPS	Stanley George Forster		UK	W.Samoa	1904	1930	1939	1969	o d	
				W.Samoa		1953	1957			
1931 m Dora Louise **GILBERT**			UK	W.Samoa	1905	1931	1939			
				W.Samoa		1953	1957			
PIDCOCK	Eileen Alice	SRN	Australia	South India	1901	1927	1953	1978	m d	
PLOWRIGHT	Jessie Elaine	SRN SCM	UK	South India	1913	1944	1968	1977	m	
POLLARD	Hilda Margaret	MB ChB	UK	South India	1883	1917	1946	1969	m	
POOLE	Betty	SRN SCM DipNEd	Australia	South India	1929	1959	1970		m	
POPLEY	Herbert Arthur	BA	UK	South India	1878	1901	1947	1960	o d	
1908 m Lizzie Helder **BRAGG** (m)										

Surname	Given names / marriages	Quals	Origin	Location					Notes
PORRITT	Norman Howard	BSc	UK	N.Rhodesia	1901	1927	1963	1985	agr e
	1930 m Mary Bunnell **MAY**								
	1937 m Violet Abigail **BROOKS** (m)		UK	N.Rhodesia	1901	1927	1934	1934	
POTTINGER	James Irvine	MA	UK	Madagascar	1930	1957	1971		o te
	1956 m Katharine Elizabeth **GREEN**	DipTh PhD MA	UK	Madagascar	1933	1957	1971		
POTTS	Colin David		UK	Gilbert Islands	1947	1970	1974		e
				W.Samoa		1978	1981		
	1968 m Jill Mary **OSBORNE**		UK	Gilbert Islands	1947	1970	1974		
				W.Samoa		1978	1981		
PRATT	Joseph James	BA BA	UK	South India	1932	1961	1990		o d
PRESCOTT	Ernest John	FRGS	UK	S.Rhodesia	1918	1950	1954		e
	1940 m Kathleen Winifred **DU PENEAU**		UK	S.Rhodesia	1918	1950	1954		
PRICE	Hugo Gordon Emmanuel		UK	Papua NG	1920	1951	1967		o d e
				Pacific		1970	1974		
	1949 m Mavis Ivy Joshephine **RUNDLETT**		UK	Papua NG	1923	1951	1967		
				Pacific		1970	1974		
RANFORD	Brian Edward	BD	UK	Pacific	1930	1957	1970		o d te
	1954 m Margaret A. **BRADSHAW**	SRN	UK	Pacific	1930	1957	1970		
RANFORD	Ruth Violet	SRN	UK	N.Rhodesia	1913	1937	1947	1981	m
	1948 m J. **BUTLER**								
RANKIN	Robert		UK	Papua NG	1898	1927	1960	1960	o d
	1931 m Suzannah Jane **ELLIS** (m)								
RAWLINGS	Edith Margaret		UK	HK/China	1910	1938	1952/4	1959	d
READ	Phyllis	SRN SCM	UK	China	1913	1938	1950		m
				South India		1950	1951		
				N.Rhodesia		1951	1953		
				South India		1955	1959		
REALI	Sheila Mary	SRN SCM	UK	Papua NG	1934	1966	1977		m
REEKIE	Donald Harold		UK	Pacific	1935	1964	1973		o d
	1956 m Gwendoline Florence **EWINS**		UK	Pacific	1935	1964	1973		

Surname	First names	Degrees etc.	origin	service	YOB	Apptment beg	end	YOD	work	pre/post
REES	Gaynor Mary	DipEd	UK	Botswana	1948	1974	1979		e	
REES	Myfanwy Dyfed	MB ChB	UK	South India	1883	1909	1912		m	
1913 m Thomas C. **WITNEY** (m)				China		1912	1913			
				China		1913	1951	1951		
REES	Vaughan		UK	North India	1891	1922	1961	1974	o d	
1923 m Gladys Annie **WALSH** (m)										
RIBEREAU	Pierre Prosper	Cert Eng Bldg	France	Madagascar	1934	1967	1973		bldr	
1958 m Claude Marguerite **FLAIG**		DipNsg	France	Madagascar	1934	1967	1973			
RICHARDS	Gwyneth	LRCP LRCS LRFPS DRCOG	UK	South India	1926	1951	1958		m	
RIDDOCH	Alvinza	Tch Trg	UK	China	1914	1943	1948		e	PCE
				Singapore		1949	1952			
				Taiwan		1952	1975			
RIDGWELL	Harold Arthur		UK	Madagascar	1882	1912	1947	1975	o d	
1912 m Winifred Ethel **BOULTON**			UK	Madagascar	1886	1912	1947	1968		
1973 m Mrs Dorothy **SANDERS**								1989		
RILEY	Gordon Robert	BA	Australia	N.Rhodesia	1912	1939	1961		o d	
1944 m Margaret **GIBSON**		BA	Australia	N.Rhodesia	1918	1944	1961			
RILEY	Wilfred Theodore	BA	Australia	Papua NG	1916	1943	1951		o d	
1947 m Patricia **DIXON**			Australia	Papua NG	1922	1943	1951			
RIVETT	Eleanor Harriett	MA	Australia	India	1883	1907	1948	1972	e	
ROBERTS	John David	LTh	Australia	Papua NG	1918	1948	1951		o d	
1946 m Jane Yvonne **ZIMMER**			Australia	Papua NG	1928	1948	1951			
ROBERTS	Patience D'Arcy	BA	Australia	South India	1912	1937	1972		d	
ROBERTSON	Christine Blake	MA	UK	S.Rhodesia	1909	1966	1971		e	
ROBERTSON	Ralph	BD	UK	South India	1878	1906	1947	1969	o d e	
1914 m Bertha Doris **EAGAN**			UK	South India	1893	1914	1947	1970		
ROBINS	José Mary	BA	UK	North India	1927	1956	1980		e d	staff

Name	Degrees	Home	Field					Code
ROBINSON John Shawcross		Australia	Nauru	1908	1946	1953	1979	o d
1935 m Helen Sarah **LAY**		Australia	Nauru	1912	*1946*	*1953*		
ROBINSON Patricia Elizabeth		UK	North India	1931	1961	1974		d
ROBINSON Robert Leslie	BSc MA ChB FRCS	UK	South India	1934	1961			m
1979 m Elizabeth Simpson **WILLIAMSON** (m)								
ROBJOHNS Henry Collin	MBE MB BS	Australia	China	1908	1935	1948	1990	m
1934 m Dorothy Elizabeth **HASLAM**	BA	Australia	China	1908	*1935*	*1944*	1944	
1948 m Mabel Humphris **CASHMORE**		Australia		1904			1975	
ROFF Muriel Esther		UK	S. Rhodesia	1930	1958	1973		e
ROGERS Dennis Leslie **WHITTLE**	BA	UK	Hong Kong	1925	1958	1965	1977	o d
1948 m Joan Helen		UK	Hong Kong	1922	*1958*	*1965*		
ROGERS Douglas Malcolm **SPECK**	MA BD	UK	South India	1916	1956	1957		
1948 m Edith Doreen		UK	South India	1928	*1956*	*1957*		
ROGERS Norman Stanley **KENNEDY**	DFC BA	UK	N.Rhodesia	1921	1950	1961		o d
1950 m Sheila Frazer		UK	N.Rhodesia	1929	*1950*	*1961*		
ROLLES Montague John		UK	South India	1908	1932	1956		o d m
1934 m Helen Jean **JOHNSON** (m)								
ROOKE John William		UK	Papua NG	1943	1974	1976		a
ROSS Isabella MacBean	SRN	Australia	S.Rhodesia	1900	1933	1939	1983	m
			South India		1946	1952		
ROWLANDS Edward	BA BD	UK	China	1882	1907	1946	1962	o d
1909 m Florence Mildred **SHERWOOD**		UK	China	1882	*1909*	*1946*	1976	
ROWLANDS Gwendoline Janet		UK	Madagascar	1940	1964	1967		e
1967 m M.Julien **DUCROCQ**								
ROWLANDS William Francis	BA BD	UK	China	1886	1913	1951	1971	o d
1916 m Margaret **CORMACK**		UK	China	1894	*1916*	*1951*	1976	
RUCK Margaret Hephzibah		UK	South India	1939	1965	1965		
RUDOFSKY Sheila Joan	Tchg Cert	UK	Papua NG	1936	1964	1982		e

Surname	First names	Degrees etc.	origin	service	YOB	Apptment beg	end	YOD	work	pre/post
RUMPUS	Friedrich Adolf Arthur **PIPER**	BA	UK	South India	1879	1913	1946	1965	o d	
1914 m Gladys Marion **PIPER**										
SABIN	Margaret Katherine		UK	South India	1882	1914	1946	1969	e	
SADLER	Mildred Kate	SRN	UK	N.Rhodesia	1887	1926	1948	1978	m	
1937 m Kenneth **FRANCIS** (m)			UK	N.Rhodesia	1907	1934	1937			
						1937	1963			
SANDERS	Kathleen Francis		UK	China	1900	1926	1927		d	
1927 m Keith **GILLISON** (m)				China		1927	1950			
SANDILANDS	Alexander	MBE	UK	Botswana	1896	1926	1961	1979	o d lit	
1926 m Doris **WEATHERHEAD**			UK	Botswana	1902	1926	1961	1990		
SANSON	Margaret Craig Gall	RGN RFN SCM DTN	UK	Zambia	1933	1958	1967	1988	m	
1967 m Lloyd **STONE**										
SAUNDERS	Joyce	SRN	UK	Bangladesh	1925	1958	1966		m	PCE
				Bangladesh		1972	1974			
SCARBOROUGH	Charles	Th Cert	UK	Gilbert Islands	1927	1964	1969		o d	
1958 m Dorothea **OLIVER**			UK	Gilbert Islands	1936	1964	1969			
SCHOFIELD	Donald	BA MA	UK	Madagascar	1928	1952	1972		o d	
1952 m Jean **ROWLAND**			UK	Madagascar	1929	1952	1972			
SCOPES	Barrie Downing	MA BD	UK	North India	1932	1956	1971		e	staff
1954 m Elizabeth A. **ROBERTSON**		MA	UK	North India	1930	1956	1971			
SCOPES	Wilfred	MA DD	UK	India	1901	1925	1960	1986	o d te	
1927 m Edith Annie **HACKER** (m)										
1949 m Ruth Mary **MEYER**			USA	India	1904	1949	1960			
SCOTT	Ruth Barbara Eliot	MBE SRN SCM	UK	North India	1915	1944	1976	1981	m	
SEAGER	Alan Edward	MBE BD	UK	Botswana	1912	1941	1977	1987	o d lit	
1941 m Ruth Belle **BROWN**			UK	Botswana	1912	1941	1977			

Surname	Names	Qualifications	Country	Field						
SHARMAN	Margaret 1972 m Robert **SIMPSON**	SRN SCM	UK	Papua NG	1938	1964	1972		m	
SHARPE	Philadelphia Rhoda Acis	SRN	UK	China Botswana	1888	1917 1943	1940 1948	1977	m	
SHAW	Alison Mary	SRN SCM	NZ	Pacific	1933	1960	1964		m	
SHAW	Dorothy Kathleen Havergal	MA	UK	China Hong Kong	1920	1947 1950	1950 1952/3		o d	
SHAW	Frederick John 1929 m Jean Young **GOURLEY**	BA RGN	UK UK	Africa Africa	1901 1895	1937 1937	1958 1958	1968 1982	o d e	
SHEPHERD	Ivor Neal 1955 m Joan Elizabeth **WHITE**	BA	UK UK	Taiwan Taiwan	1930 1933	1958 1958			e	PCE PCE
SHILSTON	Dorothy Mary	BSc	UK	Hong Kong	1900	1929	1960	1976	e	
SHIRT	Charles Ronald 1942 m Sybil Mary **AKHURST**		UK UK	Gilbert Islands Gilbert Islands	1920 1919	1949 1949	1952 1952	1989	e	
SHORT	Frank 1926 m Irene Alice **McCALLA**		UK UK	Hong Kong Hong Kong	1895 1899	1926 1926	1953 1953	1975 1967	o a	
SHORT	Harold James Edwards 1926 m Lilian **STEPHENS**		Australia Australia	Papua NG Papua NG	1887 1885	1921 1926	1953 1953	1962 1964	o d	staff
SHRIMPTON	Mary Yvonne 1955 m L.J. **JULIAN**	SRN SCM HV	UK	South India	1924	1952	1955		m	
SIBREE	Elsie Isabel		UK	Madagascar Madagascar	1881	1904 1930	1921 1954	1969	e	
SIDERMAN	Brian Malcolm 1961 m Brigit Hilligsø **PEDERSEN**		UK Denmark	Zambia Zambia	1934 1933	1962 1962	1975 1975		a	
SILCOCKS	Vera Dorothy A.	JP MBE BSc	UK	Hong Kong	1902	1927	1968	1977	e	
SIRKETT	Monica Mary	Nat Frob Dip	UK	Singapore	1917	1947	1973		e	PCE
SLATER	Noel Brodribb 1915 m Martha Ann **SHIRLEY**	BA LRAM ATCL	UK UK	China China	1885 1887	1913 1915	1951 1951	1961 1971	e d	

Surname	First names	Degrees etc.	origin	service	YOB	Apptment beg	Apptment end	YOD	work	pre/post
SLEIGH	Robin John	BA BSc	UK	South India	1927	1952	1961		o d e	
	1951 m Christine Jean **BODEY**			South India		1978	1992			
	1985 m Muriel Irene **HARRISON** (m)			South India	1928	1952	1961	1981		
SMALL	Albert Edward		UK	China/HK	1901	1928	1961	1970	o d lit	
				Botswana		1961	1967			
	1929 m Barbara **PICKARD**		UK	China/HK	1907	1929	1961	1981		
				Botswana		1961	1967			
SMALL	Hilda		NZ	W.Samoa	1891	1917	1927	1971	e	
				W.Samoa		1951	1955			
SMITH	Alan James		UK	N.Rhodesia	1930	1954	1967	1990	o d	
	1954 m Margaret **GLOVER**		UK	N.Rhodesia	1930	1954	1967			
SMITH	Anne Gertrude Strudwick	SRN SCM	UK	China	1895	1937	1948	1981	m	
SMITH	Anne Poole Sydney	BA	UK	Madagascar	1924	1952	1953		e	
	1953 m Alexander **WALKER** (m)			Madagascar		1953	1961			
SMITH	Dora Helen		UK	South India	1938	1966	1983		e	
SMITH	Dorothy Mack	BSc	UK	South Africa	1888	1915	1924	1953	e	
				S.Rhodesia		1946	1949			
SMITH	Frank Graeme		Australia	Madagascar	1917	1950	1965		o d	
	1943 m Ella May **FICKEL**		Australia	Madagascar	1918	1950	1965			
SMITH	Frederick Maltus **BRADBURY**	MA	UK	South India	1895	1923	1959	1968	e	
	1925 m Ethel Frances **BRADBURY** (m)									
SMITH	Irene Lilian		UK	Hong Kong	1909	1940	1951		d	
				Malaysia		1951	1961			
	1976 m Mr **INGS**									
SMITH	Kenneth Maltus	MBE MA	UK	Africa	1926	1953	1986		e o	
	1953 m Mavis Threfall **ROBERTS**		UK	Africa	1929	1953	1986			

Surname	Forenames	Qualifications	From	Field					
SMITH	Mary Angelina Edith	SRN	UK	Hong Kong	1892	1921	1948	1979	m
SMITH	Mollie	SRN SCM	UK	South India	1916	1951	1981		m
SMITH	Stephen Rider	MA	UK	North India	1934	1966	1972		e
	1960 m Helen E. **SHEPHERD**	DipEd	UK	North India	1937	1966	1972		
SOMERVELL	David Howard	LRCP MRCS	UK	South India	1929	1959	1970		m
	1956 m Margaret **MARCHANT**		UK	South India	1933	1959	1970		
SOMERVELL	James Lionel	BA MB BCh LRCP FRCS	UK	South India	1927	1955	1968		m
	1952 m Katharine Mary **STAPLETON**			South India	1930	1955	1968		
SOMERVELL	Theodore Howard	OBE MA MB BCh FRCS LRCP	UK	South India	1890	1925	1954	1975	m
	1925 m Margaret Hope **SIMPSON**			South India		1925	1954		
SOUTHGATE	Dora Hilda	BA	UK	South India	1899	1925	1954	1993	d
SPARKES	Carmen Ida	SRN	UK	South India	1899	1926	1947	1987	m
SPENCER	Aileen	Tchr Trng	UK	China	1892	1925	1952	1987	e
SPENCER	Ethelwyn Mabel		UK	S.Rhodesia	1912	1961	1963		e
SPENCER	Gordon Meredith **MORRIS**		UK	N.Rhodesia	1926	1959	1964		e
	1952 m Shirley **MORRIS**		UK	N.Rhodesia	1932	1959	1964		
SPICER	Eva Dykes	MBE MA	UK	China	1898	1923	1951		e
				Nigeria		1951	1959		
SPIVEY	David Arthur	BD	UK	Gilbert Islands	1937	1969	1971		o d
	1964 m Ann **SUNLEY**		UK	Gilbert Islands	1947	1969	1971		
SPIVEY	John Henry		UK	Gilbert Islands	1904	1928	1956	1985	o d
	1928 m Constance Mary **BRIGGS**		UK	Gilbert Islands	1904	1928	1956	1987	
SPONG	Bernard		UK	South Africa	1930	1962	1980		o d c
	1956 Margot **BELL**		UK	South Africa	1934	1962	1980		
SPRINGHAM	Olive Carol	SRN SCM RSCN	UK	South India	1934	1965	1971		m
STANYON	Lottie	BA	UK	South India	1892	1919	1953	1978	e d
STARK	Elsie Lilian	BA	UK	Madagascar	1917	1943	1972		e staff

Surname	First names	Degrees etc.	origin	service	YOB	Apptment beg	end	YOD	work	pre/post
STENING	Anne Christine		UK	China	1923	1948	1951		e	
				Singapore		1951	1954			
1956 m John Frederick **CLARKE** (m)				Cook Islands		1963	1967			
STEVENSON	Mrs Leila Mary	LAMDA Dip Tchg	UK	W.Samoa	1917	1975	1976			
STEWART	Cecil Ernest	DipTh SSt	UK	S.Rhodesia	1920	1969	1973		o d	
1947 m Doris Elizabeth **SHARP**		DipTh SSt	UK	S.Rhodesia	1919	1969	1973			
STICKLAND	Gladys May	SRN SCM	UK	China	1905	1932	1950	1986	m	
				Zambia		1951	1966			
STILLWELL	Olive Henrietta	MA	Australia	North India	1890	1920	1953	1982	e	
STOLTON	Jean Elizabeth	BA	UK	North India	1936	1963	1991		e	
STOREY	Peter	Agr Trng	UK	Taiwan	1937	1963	1980		agr	PCE
				Nepal		1980	1990			
1956 m Agnes **WATSON**			UK	Taiwan	1936	1963	1980			PCE
				Nepal		1980	1990			
STREETER	Marjorie		UK	South India	1896	1921	1926	1968	e	
1926 m Bernard **THOMAS** (m)				South India		1926	1961			
STURNEY	John Brian		UK	Cook Islands	1931	1957	1965		o d te	
1955 m Rita Mary **RODGERS**			UK	Cook Islands	1930	1957	1965			
STYNES	Brenda	SRN SCM	UK	Pacific	1944	1973	1975		m	
SYDENHAM	Annie	MRCS LRCP	UK	Hong Kong	1894	1924	1955	1968	m	
SYKES	George Leonard	MA EdB	UK	Gilbert Islands	1937	1966	1974		e	
1966 m Lesley Hyslop **DAVIDSON**			UK	Gilbert Islands	1946	1966	1974			
SYMES	Philip	BSc ARCS	UK	S.Rhodesia	1934	1960	1972		e	
1959 m Joyce Elizabeth **BURTON**			UK	S.Rhodesia	1939	1960	1972			
TAYLOR	Dorothy England		UK	North India	1897	1925	1944	1959	e	
				North India		1949	1959			

Name	Quals		Field					staff
TAYLOR Eileen D. Blanchard	SRN SCM	UK	N.Rhodesia	1918	1947	1969		m
1971 m G.F. **SEYMOUR**								
1985 m Jack **ASHWORTH**								
TAYLOR Elsie Jean	SRN SCM	UK	Africa	1930	1959	1967		m
TAYLOR Ethel Gertrude	MBE PKT SRN	UK	China	1897	1928	1952	1993	m
TAYLOR Harold		UK	Niue	1906	1929	1946		o d
			Africa		1946	1955	1968	
1929 m Beatrice **WOOTTON**		UK	Niue	1898	*1929*	*1946*		
			Africa		*1946*	*1955*		
TAYLOR Mary Ann Violet	MBE	UK	Africa	1894	1926	1956	1988	m d
THOMAS Alun Lloyd	MB ChB	UK	Hong Kong	1908	1939	1951		m
1941 m Elizabeth Jean **MACDONALD**		USA	Hong Kong	1919	*1941*	*1951*		
THOMAS Bernard	MA BA	UK	South India	1898	1924	1961	1982	e
1926 m Marjorie **STREETER** (m)								
THOMAS Gwyneth	SRN BTA SCM	UK	Zambia	1939	1966	1975		m
THOMAS Iorwerth Lewis	MA	UK	India	1916	1940	1970		o e
1945 m Jean Mary **MURRAY**		UK	South India	1918	*1945*	*1970*		
THOMAS Lewis John		UK	South India	1883	1911	1949	1970	o d
1913 m Hannah E. **MATTHEWS**		UK	South India	1882	*1913*	*1949*	1964	
THOMPSON Arthur Herbert		UK	Guyana	1916	1966	1969	1981	o d
1947 m Sheila Marjorie **HYNDS**		UK	Guyana	1925	*1966*	*1969*		
THOMPSON Dorothy Joan	MA MB ChB MRCS LRCP MRCOG	UK	South India	1909	1936	1950	1973	m
1950 m A.G. **BRYSON**								
THOMPSON Humphrey Curtis	BSc	UK	South Africa	1904	1932	1972	1991	o d
1932 m Florence A. M. **BUDGE-HARMER**		UK	South Africa	1906	*1932*	*1972*	1974	
THOMPSON Robert Stanley H.G.	BSc	UK	China	1907	1931	1952		e
1931 m Minnie **ADAMS**	BSc	UK	China	1906	*1931*	*1952*	1978	o d

Surname	First names	Degrees etc.	origin	service	YOB	Apptment beg	end	YOD	work	pre/post
THORNTON 1990 m Mr **MITCHELL**	Audrey Joy	Dip Ed	UK	South India	1935	1962	1970		d	
THOROGOOD 1952 m Jannett Lindsay P. **CAMERON**	Bernard George	MA	UK Australia	Pacific Pacific	1927 1923	1952 *1952*	1970 *1970*	1988	o d te	staff
THURSTON 1945 m Doreen Elizabeth **YOUNGS**	Arthur George		Australia Australia	Papua NG Papua NG	1919 1923	1965 *1965*	1971 *1971*	1991	a	
TIDBALL	Eleanor Elizabeth		UK	South India	1889	1920	1946	1947	d	
TIERNEY	Celia		Australia	Papua NG	1921	1946	1949		m	
TILNEY	Pamela Doreen	Tchg Cert Hld Dip	UK	Zambia	1934	1962	1967		e	
TODMAN 1941 m Margaret Winifred **DRAKE**	Arnold John	MA	UK UK	South India South India	1917 1920	1942 *1942*	1966 *1966*		o d	staff
TODMAN 1947 m Dorothy **MILNE** (m)	Rodney Claud F.	MB ChB	UK	South India	1919	1945	1959		m	
TROWELL 1943 m Vera **KILHAM**	Gordon Watson	MSc BA	UK UK	South India South India	1903 1909	1925 *1934*	1963 *1963*	1984 1969	e o a	
TUDOR 1961 m Nerys Llwyd **WILLIAMS**	John Hywel	MA TTC MA MB BS	UK UK	Taiwan Taiwan	1932 1937	1974 *1974*	1979 *1979*		o d	
TURBERVILLE 1927 m Jane Campbell **LAWSON**	Geoffrey	MA	UK UK	W.Samoa W.Samoa	1899 1899	1959 *1959*	1963 *1963*	1993 1976	e	
TURNBULL	Evelyn Joyce	BA	UK	South India	1914	1940	1965	1988	d	
TURNER	Jane Somerville		UK	China	1905	1932	1952	1982	d	
TURNER-SMITH 1961 m Gillian **RAINBOW**	Ronald Francis	BSc PhD	UK UK	Hong Kong Hong Kong	1937 1940	1967 *1967*	1987 *1987*		e	
UNDY 1954 m Sheila **CHEETHAM**	Harry	LLB	UK UK	S.Rhodesia S.Rhodesia	1932 1932	1959 *1959*	1974 *1974*		e o d	
URE 1931 m Gwendoline May **MILNE** (m)	David Eric	MLC LTh	Australia	Pacific	1900	1929	1965	1988	o d	

Name	Qualifications	Area	Origin					Code
USHER Gladys Francis Marion		North India	UK	1890	1920	1949	1949	e
VARLEY Alice Mary	BA	South India	UK	1889	1913	1930		e
1930 m Edward **BARNES** (m) died 1941		South India			*1936*	*1941*		
		South India			1941	1950		
WALDEN Alfred Edward	BSc AIC	South India	UK	1893	1926	1937	1968	o e
1919 m Ella Howison **HENDERSON**		Africa	UK	1896	1937	1959	1987	
		South India			*1926*	*1937*		
		Africa			1937	*1959*		
WALES Derek Malcolm	MA BD	Zambia	UK	1936	1973	1978		o d
1965 m Elizabeth Anne **MORGAN**		Zambia	UK	1939	*1973*	*1978*		
WALKER Alexander	MA	Madagascar	UK	1912	1944	1961	1992	o d
1953 m Anne Poole Sydney **SMITH** (m)								
WALKER Eric	MB ChB MRCP SRN	South India	UK	1943	1974	1976		m
m Susan					*1974*	*1976*		
WALLACE Ruth Marjorie	BA	South India	UK	1947	1947	1957		e
WALSH Gladys Annie		North India	UK	1921	1920	1923		d
1923 m Vaughan **REES** (m)		North India		1892	*1923*	1961	1968	
WARD Ernest Victor		Pacific	UK	1919	1946	1952		ship
1941 m Jane **HATTRICK**		Pacific	UK	1921	*1946*	*1952*		
WARD Geoffrey Michael	BD	Papua NG	UK	1939	1961	1973	1973	o d
1961 m Shirley May **WALFORD**	BA	Papua NG	UK	1938	*1961*	*1973*		
WARD Maud	MBE SRN	Hong Kong	UK	1890	1920	1951		m
WARDLE Robert Stuart		Gilbert Islands	UK	1899	1965	1967	1974	a
1927 m Sara Ann **MARR**		Gilbert Islands	UK	1903	*1965*	*1967*		
WAREHAM Jean Monica	MA	Zambia	UK	1909	1937	1970		e
WARREN Janet Ruth	MA	Madagascar	UK	1905	1935	1938		e
1938 m James **CONOLLY** (m)		Madagascar			*1938*	*1953*		

Surname	First names	Degrees etc.	origin	service	YOB	Apptment beg	Apptment end	YOD	work	pre/post
WATKINS	Amy Kathleen	BA	UK	China	1912	1938	1946		e	
WATSON	Jean Mary	SRN SCM	UK	South India	1930	1957	1962		m	
WATTS	Ruth	BA	Australia	W.Samoa	1922	1949	1951		e	
WELFORD	Elizabeth Joyce	MB ChB	UK	South India	1906	1932	1952		m	
WENYON	Winifred Phyllis	SRN SCM	UK	Africa	1910	1947	1968		m d	
WHEELER	Nora		UK	China	1888	1916	1952	1963	d	
WHITE	John Francis	MA BD	UK	China	1915	1943	1950	1960	o d	
				Africa		1950	1960			
1943 m Lucy Doreen **FFRENCH**			UK	China	1911	*1943*	*1950*	1993		
				Africa		*1950*	*1960*			
WHITFIELD	John Noel Berridge	MA	UK	Madagascar	1889	1923	1952	1962	o d	
1916 m Constance Muriel **SENNITT**			UK	Madagascar	1894	*1923*	*1952*	1991		
WHYTE	Francis William **MACDONALD**	BA	Australia	North India	1912	1939	1959	1967	o d a	
1939 m Nina Alice **MACDONALD**		BSc	Australia	North India	1914	*1939*	*1959*			
WHYTE	Henry William	MA	Australia	India	1882	1908	1929		o d a	
				W.Samoa		1939	1951			
1909 m Ruby Addison **FLOWER**			Australia	India	1882	*1908*	*1929*	1979		
				W.Samoa		*1939*	*1951*			
WICKINGS	Harold Frederick	MA	UK	China	1901	1930	1956	1992	o d e	
1930 m Mary Dorothy Louisa **THORP**			UK	China	1900	*1930*	*1956*	1983		
WIGHTMAN	Harry Sheavyn	MA	UK	South India	1907	1934	1956	1992	o d	
1935 m Elizabeth Carolyn **EDDY**			UK	South India	1911	*1934*	*1956*	1973		
WILKINSON	Stephen Dennis		UK	Madagascar	1945	1972				e
1972 m Hardy Rahoby **RAHARIJAONA**			Mdgcr	Madagascar	1939	*1972*				

Name	Qual	Origin	Field					Code
WILLCOCKS Alan Luther **MEREDITH**		UK	Botswana	1939	1971	1977		o d
1963 m Catherine **MEREDITH**		UK	Botswana	1942	1971	1977		
WILLIAMS Helen		Australia	Papua NG	1915	1945	1947		m
WILLIAMS Muriel		UK	N.Rhodesia	1922	1959	1964		e
1966 m Murray **SANDERSON**								
WILLIAMS Terence		UK	Guyana	1938	1965	1968		o d
1962 m Stella Jessamine **WILKINSON**		UK	Guyana	1942	1965	1968		
WILLIAMSON Edwin		UK	Botswana	1930	1969	1974		a
1954 m Iris Lilian **TUNKS**		UK	Botswana	1932	1969	1974		
WILLIAMSON Elizabeth Simpson		UK	South India	1937	1966	1979		d
1979 m Leslie **ROBINSON** (m)			South India		1979			
WILLIAMSON Jessie Tulloch	MA	UK	North India	1882	1911	1917		e
			North India		1923	1946	1983	
WILLS Edith Sanders		UK	China	1887	1926	1946	1952	d
WILSON Elizabeth Hester	Tchg Cert	UK	Papua NG	1947	1972	1977		e
WILSON Freda May	BA	NZ	South India	1912	1941	1961	1961	e
WILSON May Elizabeth		UK	South India	1911	1935	1941		d
1941 m Donald **COLLINS** (m)			South India		1941	1974		
WING Audrey	SRN SCM	UK	Botswana	1926	1954	1963		m
WING Joseph		UK	Africa	1923	1950	1957		o d a
			Africa		1962	1970		
1951 m Marjorie **PEGG**		UK	Africa	1926	1950	1957	1992	
			Africa		1962	1970		
WITNEY Thomas Charles	BA	UK	South India	1886	1910	1951	1952	o d te
1913 m Myfanwy Dyfed **REES** (m)								
WOFFENDEN Donald Trevor	SRN	UK	Zambia	1929	1956	1967		o d
1953 m Margaret Louise **DAVIS**		UK	Zambia	1929	1956	1967		

Surname	First names	Degrees etc.	origin	service	YOB	Apptment beg	Apptment end	YOD	work	pre/post
WOOD	Hilda Maud		UK	South India	1907	1933	1959		d	
WOOD	Mary Myfanwy		UK	China	1882	1908	1948	1967	e	
WOODLAND	Margaret	SRN SCM HV	UK	Papua NG	1915	1950	1956		m	
WOOLLARD	Joyce Mansfield		UK	South India	1923	1948	1989		d	
WRAY	Helen Katherine		UK	Botswana	1937	1963	1965		e	
WRIGHT	Christine	SRN SCM Dip TrMed Dip Cb	UK	Papua NG/Solomon Isles	1944	1971	1976		m	
WRIGHT	Christopher Preston Wheeler	BA	UK	Africa	1943	1968	1980		e a	
	1968 m Susan Mary **GREEN**			Africa	1948	*1968*	*1980*			
YATES	Stephen	BSc	UK	Papua NG	1911	1947	1968		e	
	1941 m Freda Millicent **COOK**	FIL	UK	Papua NG	1913	*1947*	*1968*	1984		
YOUNG	Jennifer Helen	Tchg Cert	Australia	Papua NG	1940	1973	1977		e	UCA
ZIMMERMAN	Hansjürg		Switz'lnd	South India	1920	1948	1955	1983	e	
	1950 m Miriam **COREY**		USA	South India	1915	*1948*	*1955*		o d	

Appendix B

APPENDIX B: ASSOCIATES OF LMS/CCWM/CWM 1954 - 1978

SURNAME (Married)	First names / Surname	Degrees/Certs (First name)	Year of birth	Origin	Countries of Service	Years of Service	Work
ABEL / Edith (Dr) / 1963 m	Margaret / **GRANT**	DRCOG / Ian	1933	UK	N.Rhodesia/Zambia	1960 1970	Medical Officer
AGGER / 1973 m	Patricia Winifred / **HARMS**	BA PGCE / Myron	1945	UK	Botswana	1971 1974	Teacher
ALLARD	Margaret	SRN SCM	1945	UK	Malawi	1968 1970	Physiotherapist
ALLARD	Rosemary	SRN RSCN	1942	UK	Zambia	1969 1970	Nursing Sister
ANTROBUS	Felicity		1947	UK	Zambia	1971 1972	Nurse
ARMSTRONG (Mrs)	Heather Belle	Teacher Training	1948	Aust	Papua New Guinea	1971 1973	Teacher
ASTLEY	John	Teacher Training	1941	UK	Zambia	1969 1972	Teacher
ATKINSON	Robert Bryant	BA	1935	UK	Kenya	1961 1968	Teacher
AUSTEN	Jennifer Pauline	BSc Tchg Cert	1945	UK	Kenya	1971 1977	Teacher
AUSTIN	Kitty		1912	UK	Papua New Guinea	1972 1973	Secretary/Bookkeeper
AUSTIN*	Mary	BSc AKC	1931	UK	S. Rhodesia	1967 1972	Teacher/SCM Secretary
BAILEY*	Harold		1910	UK	South Africa	1975 1978	Administration
BALLARD	John Oman	MA	1924	UK	Tanganyika / Cyprus / Borneo	1954 1958 / 1960 / 1961 1963	Civil Servant
BANWELL	Gerald	FRCS MRCOG	1927	UK	Hong Kong	1961 1964	Doctor

Surname	Name	Qualification	Born	Country	Location	From	To	Occupation
BARNES 1960 m	Kathleen / Martin	Tchg Cert	1933	UK	N. Rhodesia	1957	1966	Teacher/Housewife
BARR*	Margaret Elizabeth (Betty)	BA LRAM	1933	UK	Hong Kong	1967	1972	Teacher
BEADON	Richard George (Captain)	Nautical Trng, Tech Tchg Cert	1937	UK	Fiji	1970	1976	Navigation Instructor, Ship Captain
BEADON (Mrs)	Denise Ann		1942	UK	Fiji	1970	1976	Housewife
BEALE (Mrs)	Daphne (née HUGHES)	BSc		UK	Hong Kong	1968	1970	Teacher
BECK (Mrs)	Mary	Social Sc Dip	1917	UK	Zambia / Zambia	1971 / 1975	1973 / 1978	Social worker
BENT	Dora Mabel Lucy		1900	UK	Hong Kong	1961	1968	Hospital Administration
BENTALL	Peter Hamilton	BSc	1940	USA	Kenya	1971	1977	Engineer
BLAKE	Enid Grace	SRN SCM	1919	UK	Gilbert Islands	1967	1969	Sister Tutor
BLYTH	John Francis	BSc PhD	1946	UK	Malawi	1974	1978	Land Husbandry Officer
BOLTON*	Patricia		1937	UK	Zambia	1971	1975	Secretary
BROWN	Francis Jesse	DLC	1933	UK	Zambia	1965	1968	Teacher
BROWN (Mrs)	Kathlyn Margaret	Teacher Training	1939	UK	Zambia	1965	1968	Housewife/Teacher
BORTHWICK 1968 m	Frances Marianne HADFIELD / Edwin		1944	UK	Botswana	1966	1968	Secretary in Diplomatic Service
BURDON	Anne Catherine	Teacher Training	1941	UK	Hong Kong	1968	1972	Teacher
BURGESS *	John Hopkins	BSc	1952	UK	South Africa	1975	1977	Field Geologist

* Missionary before or after being an associate.

SURNAME (Married)	First names / Surname	Degrees/ Certs / First name)	Year of birth	Origin	Countries of Service	Years of Service	Work
BURGESS * (Mrs)	Mary Elizabeth	Dip in Nutrition	1951	UK	South Africa	1975 1977	Housewife
BURTON	Andrew Clifford		1950	UK	Papua New Guinea	1971 1973	Volunteer Electrician
BUTLER	Victor			UK	Zambia	1971 1977	Lecturer in Public Admin
BUTLER (Mrs)	Susan Joan		1946	UK	Zambia	1971 1977	Housewife
BUTTFIELD	Grace Margaret	Nursing Training	1901	UK	N. Rhodesia	1956 1960	Nurse
CADWALLADER	Robin John	BA	1943	UK	Panama Zambia	1968 1970 / 1970 1975	Civil Engineer
CAMPBELL*	Jean	BSc	1931	UK	Uganda	1958 1963	Research Biochemist
CARR*	Martyn		1942	UK	Papua New Guinea	1973 1975	School Chaplain
CARR (Mrs)	Rachel (née JONES)		1945	UK	Papua New Guinea	1973 1975	Housewife
CARTER	Michael John		1932	UK	Uganda	1956 1963	Trade Development Officer
CATLING	Joy Susan (Dr)	MB BS DObst RCOG DA	1940	UK	Hong Kong	1968 1975	Anaesthetist
CHAPMAN	Gilbert Wesley	Medical Qualifications	1929	UK	Hong Kong	1969 1970	Doctor
CHAPMAN (Mrs)	Jeanette Constance	SRN SCM Inft Welf Cert	1930	UK	Hong Kong	1969 1970	Housewife
CHAPMAN	Rosemary		1939	UK	Kenya	1969 1973	Teacher

Surname	Forename	Qualification	Birth	Country	Field	From	To	Role
CHILDS	Joyce	Teacher Training	1926	UK	Rhodesia	1972	1977	Teacher
CLINTON (Mrs)	Iris Annie (née CORBIN)	Teaching	1901	UK	Rhodesia	1962	1971	School Secretary
COATES (Mrs)	Lilian (née JONES)		1928	UK	N. Rhodesia	1954	1963	Nurse/Housewife
CONDON	Michael John	Teacher Training	1930	UK	Zambia	1968	1972	Teacher Trainer
CONDON (Mrs)	Rosemary June	Teacher Training	1930	UK	Zambia	1968	1972	Teacher
COOPER	Jean	Occupational therapy	1926	UK	Kenya	1968	1976	Teacher Trainer
COOMBS*	Sylvia	Teacher Training	1946	UK	Sierre Leone	1967	1969	Teacher
COUCH	Gwendoline Alice	Teacher Training	1922	UK	Nigeria	1960	1964	Teacher Trainer
CRAWFORD	Margaret Elizabeth	BA PGCE	1944	UK	Kenya / Papua New Guinea	1968 / 1973	1971 / 1978	Teacher
CULLINGFORD	David Wilray John		1922	UK	South India	1962	1963	Anaesthetist
CULVER	Frederick Lloyd	BA DipEd BD	1912	UK	Gilbert Islands / Papua New Guinea	1967 / 1970	1970 / 1972	Teacher
DALEY	Philip Alexander		1928		Nigeria / Hong Kong	1954 / 1959	1959 / 1978	Forestry Officer
DALEY (Mrs)	Elizabeth (née WALDEN)	SRN	1931	UK	Nigeria / Hong Kong	1954 / 1959	1959 / 1978	Housewife
DANCE* (Mrs)	Pat (née HOLLAMBY)	MBE SRN SCM	1931	UK	Botswana	1977	1978	Nurse/Housewife
DAVIES	Herbert John	B Law	1941	UK	Papua New Guinea	1972	1976	Bible translator
DAVISON	Jeffrey Cooper	BSc Cert Ed	1944	UK	Ghana	1967	1968	Teacher

SURNAME (Married)	First names / Surname	Degrees/Certs / First name)	Year of birth	Origin	Countries of Service	Years of Service		Work
DAVEY	Audrey	Physiotherapy Trng	1927	UK	Uganda	1960	1963	Physiotherapist
DEACON (Mrs)	Sheila E. (née ROBSON)	BA PGCE	1930	UK	Nigeria	1965	1966	Teacher/Housewife
DEY	Jennifer Jane	BA Dip Soc Sc	1941	Aust	Indonesia	1964	1970	Lecturer
DOHERTY (Mrs)	Harriet Rita (née ALSOP)	BSc Tchr Training	1908	UK	Nigeria	1963	1968	Principal Secondary School
EARP	Denis	MA	1929	UK	Iraq	1954	1960	Engineer
EARP (Mrs)	Audrey (née WINSOR)		1931	UK	Iraq	1954	1960	Housewife
EDONI (Mrs)	Gail Alison (née STOW)		1944	Aust	Papua New Guinea	1971	1975	Secretary
FAIRHALL *	Constance Grace	MBE SRN SCM	1906	UK	Papua New Guinea	1967	1971	Welfare Officer
FAIRSERVICE	Robin Andrew	BSc MICE AMIPE	1935	UK	Ceylon/Sri Lanka	1969	1971	Engineer
FEATHERSTONE	Michael John	BSc MICE	1939	UK	Tanzania	1965	1968	Water Engineer
FEATHERSTONE (Mrs)	Tessa	BA PGCE	1941	UK	Tanzania	1965	1968	Housewife/Teacher
FERGUSON	John	MA BD	1921	UK	Nigeria USA	1956 1966	1966 1969	Professor
FERGUSON (Mrs)	Elnora	BA Social Sc Cert	1929	UK	Nigeria USA	1956 1966	1966 1969	Housewife
FEWSTER	Peter	BSc ARIC	1928	UK	Botswana	1965	1973	Teacher

Name	Given names / Spouse	Qualifications	Birth	Nat.	Country	From	To	Occupation
FEWSTER (Mrs)	Patricia Diane		1935	UK	Botswana	1965	1973	Housewife
FIRTH	David Norman Lewis	MA PGCE	1934	UK	Nigeria	1959	1963	Education Officer
FIRTH (Mrs)	Shirley Jean (née **ROLLES**)	BA Soc Sc Cert	1936	UK	Nigeria	1959	1963	Housewife
FOORD	Kathleen Mary	SRN SCM	1904	UK	Kenya	1955	1958	Matron, midwifery training
FOURIE (Mrs)	Kathleen (née **BARNES**)	Teaching Certificate	1933	UK	N.Rhodesia South Africa	1957 1966	1966 1976	Teacher/ Housewife
FOX	Anthony Henry	BSc	1936	UK	Malaysia Singapore Libya	1963 1967 1972	1967 1970 1973	Engineer
FOX (Mrs)	Ann Christine		1938	UK	Malaysia Singapore Libya	1963 1967 1972	1967 1970 1973	Housewife
FRANKS (Mrs)	Margaret Ann	Teacher Training	1937	UK	Zambia Botswana	1967 1973	1971 1975	Teacher
GARRETT	John Allen	MA BD	1920	Aust	Fiji	1968	1978	Theological Lecturer
GARRETT (Mrs)	Alice Roberta	MA	1926	USA	Fiji	1968	1978	Journalist
GOBBETT *	Donald	BA	1938	Aust	S. Rhodesia	1969	1973	Teacher Trainer
GOBBETT * (Mrs)	Estelle		1939	Aust	S. Rhodesia	1969	1973	Housewife
GRANT (Mrs)	Margaret (née **ABEL**)	DRCOG	1933	UK	N.Rhod./Zambia	1960	1970	Medical Officer
GRAY 1961 m	Jean **MARSHALL**	David	1926	UK	Malaysia	1955	1960	Almoner
GREENE 1972 m	Eileen Nancy **HORNSBY**	BA Tchr Training Stanley	1930	UK	N.Rhodesia Singapore	1955 1969	1969 1972	Teacher

SURNAME (Married)	First names / Surname	Degrees/ Certs First name)	Year of birth	Origin	Countries of Service	Years of Service		Work
GREEVES *	Perla (Dr)	BSc MB BCh MRCOG	1912	UK	South Africa	1970	1977	Doctor
HALIBURTON	Gordon	BEd MA	1928	Can.	Sierre Leone	1957	1977	University Lecturer
HARRIS	Vera May	Teacher Training	1917	UK	Zambia	1965	1968	Teacher trainer
HARRISON	Trevor John	BA Cert Ed	1937	UK	Uganda	1966	1972	University Lecturer
HART	Norman	BA	1930	UK	Uganda Zambia/USA Kenya/W.Germany	1958 1966 1970	1965 1969 1978	Journalist
HAYWARD (Mrs)	Anita (née PAUL)	BSc	1937	UK	Ghana Papua New Guinea	1963 1968	1968 1971	Teacher/ Housewife
HICKS (Mrs)	Alice (née SOMERVILLE)	SRN SCM	1921	UK	Kenya	1960	1973	Nurse/ Housewife
HODGES	Peter Frederick Alan (Capt)		1929	UK	Singapore	1966	1968	Officer in Royal Marines
HULETT	Keith		1942	UK	Singapore	1967	1971	Cook in Royal Marines
HULETT (Mrs)	Lesley Constance		1943	UK	Singapore	1967	1971	Housewife
HUMPHREYS	Mary	BSc Teaching Cert	1914	UK	Nigeria	1966	1971	Headmistress
IVES	David Robert	Chartered Surveying	1933	UK	S.Rhodesia	1959	1964	Valuation Officer
JACOB * (Mrs)	Eileen (née BENDING)		1925	UK	South India	1977	1978	Housewife

Surname	Name	Qualification	Born		Country	From	To	Occupation
JOHNS (Mrs)	Myfanwy (née HARRIES)		1937	UK	Liberia	1968	1970	Housewife
JONES *	Leslie George William Phipps	BA	1912	UK	Malawi	1969	1978	Teacher
JONES (Mrs)* 1957 m	Evelyn		1917	UK	Malawi	1969	1978	Teacher
JONES	Lilian COATES	John	1928	UK	N.Rhodesia	1954	1957	Nurse
JONES	Martin	BA	1945	UK	Uganda Zambia	1967 1970	1972 1972	Agricultaralist
KEMP	Anthony	ARIBA	1929	UK	South Africa	1958	1961	Architect public works
KEMP (Mrs)	Gwynneth Blodwin		1929	UK	South Africa	1958	1961	Housewife
KEMP	Graham Grove		1947	UK	Papua New Guinea	1974	1975	Foreman instructor
KEMP (Mrs)	Maureen Joan	SRN	1950	UK	Papua New Guinea	1974	1975	Nurse
KIMBER	Audrey	Rad Dip	1918	UK	Congo (Zaire)	1968	1972	Radiographer
KING	Robert Shirley	BA	1920	UK	Tanganyika/	1959	1962	District Officer
KING (Mrs)	Mary (née ROWELL)	Physio-therapy training	1927	UK	Tanzania	1959	1962	Housewife/ Physiotherapist
KINNERSLEY	Stewart Conrad	B Com AIB	1923	UK	East Pakistan Burma India/W.Pakistan	1954 1956 1963	1956 1957 1968	Banker
KINNERSLEY (Mrs)	Helen		1926	UK	India West Pakistan	1963 1963	1963 1968	Housewife; former BMS missionary
KIRBY	Hugh Arthur John	BSc	1943	UK	Tanzania	1966	1968	Agricultural Chemist
KENDALL	William John	MA PhD	1934	UK	Zambia	1974	1976	University lecturer
KENDALL (Mrs)	Maureen Elizabeth	BA	1937	UK	Zambia	1974	1976	Housewife

SURNAME (Married)	First names Surname	Degrees/Certs First name	Year of birth	Origin	Countries of Service	Years of Service	Work
KENNEDY *	Mary Forbes (Myra)	RGN SCM	1934	UK	Papua New Guinea	1975 1978	Nurse
KNOWLES	Ian Charles	BA	1950	UK	Papua New Guinea	1974 1977	Teacher
LADE (Mrs)	Helen Mann	BA DipEd	1909	Aust	Papua New Guinea	1971 1972	Teacher
LANGLEY	Gordon	Tchng Cert	1928	UK	S.Rhodesia	1956 1964	Teacher
LANGLEY (Mrs)	Mary		1932	UK	S.Rhodesia	1956 1964	Housewife
LEACH	Dorothy Eileen	SRN SCM	1924	UK	Zambia	1968 1978	Nurse
LEGG *	Frank Stanley	BA	1919	UK	N.Rhodesia/Zambia	1959 1978	Teacher
LEGG (Mrs) *	Lilian Trevanion		1914	UK	N.Rhodesia/Zambia	1959 1978	Housewife
LEHMANN *	Dorothea	PhD	1910	Germ	N.Rhodesia/Zambia	1959 1978	Women's Welfare Officer
LEVERETT 1962 m LEAVER	Maureen	Physiotherapy training	1936	UK	Singapore	1959 1963	Physiotherapist
LEWIS	Nancy Ruth	Tchg Cert	1933	UK	Zambia	1967 1970	Teacher
LEWIS *	Aubrey David (Revd)	BSc	1917	UK	Ghana	1960 1962	Teacher
LEWIS * (Mrs)	Nora Kathleen (née BELGROVE)		1912	UK	Ghana	1960 1962	Housewife
LOCKWOOD 1975 m RIDGWAY	Sheila Jean	BSc Cert Ed Robert	1942	UK	Grand Cayman Botswana	1969 1974 1976 1978	Teacher
LUKEY	Frank William	BSc	1940	UK	Ghana	1966 1971	University lecturer

Surname	Name	Qualifications	Born	Origin	Country	From	To	Role
LUKEY (Mrs)	Barbara Mary	BA Teaching Dip	1940	UK	Ghana	1966	1971	Housewife
LOMAX	Robert William	BA	1947	UK	Zambia Papua New Guinea	1971 1976	1974 1978	Teacher
MALIPHANT	Gordon Keith	BSc PhD ARIC	1926	UK	Trinidad Indonesia	1954	1978	Research soil chemist
MALIPHANT (Mrs)	Margaret Joyce		1930	UK	Trinidad Indonesia	1954	1978	Housewife
MARSHALL (Mrs)	Jean (née GRAY)		1926	UK	Singapore	1955	1976	Hospital almoner/ Housewife
MARTIN	Elizabeth Gertrude (Betty)		1901	UK	Kenya	1954	1963	Christian Council rural work
MAYNARD * (Mrs)	Margaret (née ROWLEY)		1904	UK	South India	1969	1971	Superintendent church industry
McILROY *	Kathleen	BSc	1907	UK	South India	1969	1978	Superintendent church industry
MICHAELSON (Mrs)	Gwendoline Agnes		1920	UK	Singapore	1965	1968	Housewife
MITCHELL	David Charles	BA LLB	1934	Aust	Bechuanaland	1960	1962	Assistant District Commissioner
MITCHELL (Mrs)	Diana Ethel Ruth	MA	1936	Aust	Bechuanaland	1960	1962	Housewife
MOODY	Christine (Dr)		1914	UK	Ghana Jamaica Philippines	1958 1969 1971	1968 1971 1972	Medical Officer
MORGAN	David John	FIST	1921	UK	Uganda Brazil Nigeria	1961 1970 1974	1967 1973 1977	Teacher in Technical Institute

SURNAME (Married)	First names Surname	Degrees/Certs First name)	Year of birth	Origin	Countries of Service	Years of Service	Work
MORGAN (Mrs)	Doris Mary		1923	UK	Uganda Brazil Nigeria	1963 1970 1974	Housewife
						1967 1973 1977	
MORRIS 1970 m	Wendy **SMALL**	Murray	1947	Aust	Papua New Guinea	1968	1970	Secretary
MORRIS 1972 m	Yvonne **POTTS**	SRN RSCN Obst Cert Gordon		UK	Zambia	1971	1972	Nurse
MUIR *	John Williams	MA	1938	UK	Zambia	1975	1977	Lecturer in Technical Institute
MUIR (Mrs)*	Dorothy		1934	UK	Zambia	1975	1977	Housewife
MUNSTER	Peter Maxwell	BA DipEd	1934	Aust	Papua New Guinea	1969	1977	Teacher trainer
MUNSTER (Mrs)	Judith Rosalynd	Dip Phys Educ A Mus A	1941	Aust	Papua New Guinea	1969	1977	Teacher
NG'AMBI (Mrs)	Jean Ann (née **PEARCE**)	Teacher Training	1941	UK	Zambia	1969	1978	Teacher/ Housewife
NICHOLLS	Brian William		1931	UK	N.Rhodesia/Zambia	1957	1971	Civil servant
NICHOLLS (Mrs)	Ruth Barbara	Teacher Training	1937	UK	Zambia	1964	1970	Housewife
ODDY	Barbara May	BA DipEd	1908	UK	S.Rhodesia	1956	1970	Teacher
ODELL	Jack Lawrence	Dip Poultry Husbandry	1937	UK	Nyasaland/Malawi	1962	1969	Poultry Officer
PACKER *	Harold Arthur Bevill	BA	1915	UK	S.Rhodesia	1975	1978	Teacher Trainer
PALMER 1976 m	Mary Ann **SINUYANDI**	SRN	1950	UK	Zambia	1972	1978	Nurse

Surname	Name	Quals	Born	Country	Field	From	To	Occupation
PARRY *	David	MA	1946	UK	Papua New Guinea	1971	1973	Teacher
PARRY (Mrs)*	Gillian (Jill)		1946	UK	Papua New Guinea	1971	1973	Housewife
PARRY *	John (Revd Dr)	MB ChB DTM&H	1923	UK	Zambia	1970	1972	Doctor
PARRY (Mrs)*	Freda	SRN SCM	1922	UK	Zambia	1970	1972	Nurse & housewife
PARTRIDGE*	William G. MacDonald	MA	1912	Aust	S.Rhodesia	1968	1978	Principal, Teacher Training College
PAUL 1964 m	Anita Claire HAYWARD Peter	BSc PGCE	1937	UK	Ghana	1963	1968	Teacher/
					Papua New Guinea	1968	1971	Housewife
PEARCE	Donald James	BSc	1944	UK	Uganda	1966	1969	Teacher Trainer
PEARCE 1975 m	Jean Ann NG'AMBI Kelvin		1941	UK	Zambia	1969	1978	Teacher Trainer/ Housewife
PEART	Josephine May	SRN SCM	1945	UK	Zambia	1971	1975	Nurse
PERKS	John		1897	Aust	Papua New Guinea	1971	1974	Businessman
PHILLIPS *	John David Forster	BSc	1943	UK	Papua New Guinea	1972	1973	Teacher
PHILLIPS * (Mrs)	Penelope Mary (née HOBSON)		1948	UK	Papua New Guinea	1972	1973	Housewife
PINNELL	Alan		1943	UK	Japan	1965	1976	Civil servant
PINNELL (Mrs)	Christine (née BURGHART)	RK Cert	1942	UK	Japan	1965	1976	Housewife
POLKINGHORNE	Brian Trevor (Revd)	LTh RDA MATA	1937	Aust	Tanzania	1970	1977	Agricultural Instructor
POLKINGHORNE (Mrs)	Jillian Kaye		1941	Aust	Tanzania	1970	1977	Housewife
POTTER	Jean (née PALMER)	BA Cert Ed	1933	UK	Nyasaland/Malawi	1956	1967	Housewife
POTTS *	Colin	Tchg Cert	1947	UK	Gilbert Islands	1970	1974	Teacher
POTTS (Mrs) *	Jill		1947	UK	Gilbert Islands	1970	1974	Housewife

SURNAME (Married)	First names Surname	Degrees/ Certs First name)	Year of birth	Origin	Countries of Service	Years of Service	Work
PRATT (Mrs) *	Rosemary (née **ARTHERN**)		1943	UK	Papua New Guinea	1974 1977	Teacher
PUTNAM	Stanley George	BSc Cert Ed	1925	UK	Gilbert Islands	1967 1970	Headmaster Secondary School
RAPLEY	William George		1931	UK	Gilbert Islands	1973 1975	Broadcasting Engineer
RAPLEY (Mrs)	Doreen Beryl		1935	UK	Gilbert Islands	1973 1975	Housewife
READ	Kenneth	BA	1926	UK	Tanganyika/ Tanzania	1955 1969	District Officer/ Teacher
READ (Mrs)	Patricia		1931	UK	Tanganyika/ Tanzania	1963 1969	Housewife
REDMAN	Margaret Marion	Cert Inst Mngt	1940	UK	Hong Kong	1965 1968	Dietician
REID	Donald Sutherland	MA	1932	UK	Sierra Leone Nigeria	1963 1965 1965 1968	Engineer
RIDGE	Jessie Christine (Dr)	MB ChB	1903	UK	Papua New Guinea	1968 1970	Doctor
RIDGWAY	Robert Broughton	BSc PhD	1946	UK	Botswana	1976 1978	Land use planner
RIDGWAY (Mrs)	Sheila (née **LOCKWOOD**)		1942	UK	Botswana	1976 1978	Housewife
RILEY	Richard Woodburne	BA	1930	UK	Iraq Hong Kong	1957 1961 1959 1965	Construction Engineer
RILEY (Mrs)	Ruth Longworth		1927	UK	Iraq Hong Kong	1957 1961 1959 1965	Housewife

ROBINSON	Sylvia Joan	Tchg Cert	1937	UK	S.Rhodesia	1967	1978	Teacher Trainer
ROGERS	Ralph Thomas	Tchr Trng	1916	UK	Kenya	1956	1963	Teacher Trainer
ROGERS (Mrs)	Kathleen Theresa		1927	UK	Kenya	1956	1963	Housewife
ROSS-BROWN	Dermot Macaragh	BSc MSc	1940	UK	Ghana	1967	1969	Mining Engineer
ROWELL	John Gerrard	BA AIS	1929	UK	Malawi	1969	1972	Agricultural Statistician
ROWELL (Mrs)	Elizabeth Jane	Teacher Training	1932	UK	Malawi	1969	1972	Housewife
RUSSELL	Johnston	BSc Tchr Trng	1943	UK	Botswana	1968	1973	Asst Manager, Bookshop
RUSSELL (Mrs)	Margaret (née WORKMAN)		1945	UK	Botswana	1968	1973	Housewife
RYALL	Paul Clifford	MA MSc AMICE MIHE DTE	1934	UK	Papua New Guinea Ghana Fiji	1967 1970 1972	1969 1972 1975	Civil engineer/ Professor
SALVI-MARCROFT (Mrs)	June		1933	UK	Cameroon	1963	1963	Housewife
SANKEY	Ronald Ernest		1923	UK	New Hebrides	1964	1967	Police Superintendent
SANKEY (Mrs)	Dorothy Eva		1922	UK	New Hebrides	1964	1967	Housewife
SANSON * 1967 m	Margaret Craig Gail STONE	RGN SCM Trop Dis Cert Lloyd	1933	UK	Zambia	1967	1970	Leprosy Settlement Administration
SAVAGE	Brian Anthony	BSc	1943	UK	Gilbert Islands Gilbert Islands	1965 1970	1967 1972	Teacher
SCOPES	Peter Gray	MA PGCE	1928	UK	Tanganyika/ Tanzania	1954	1969	Education Officer

SURNAME (Married)	First names Surname	Degrees/ Certs First name)	Year of birth	Origin	Countries of Service	Years of Service		Work
SCULLY	David Ross	Radio-graphy Trng	1938	UK	South India	1969	1970	Radiographer
SEAL (Mrs)	Ruth M. (née **PORRITT**)	Teacher Training	1939	UK	N.Rhodesia/Zambia	1961	1965	Teacher
SEXTON	Margaret Ethel	SRN SCM	1925	UK	S.Rhodesia Tripoli	1958 1961	1961 1963	Army Nurse
SIMS	Grace		1915	Aust	South India	1969	1978	Superintendent Church Industry
SINUYANDI (Mrs)	Mary (née **PALMER**)	SRN	1950	UK	Zambia	1976	1978	Nurse/ Housewife
SMALL (Mrs)	Wendy (née **MORRIS**)		1947	Aust	Papua New Guinea	1968	1970	Clerical Asst/ Housewife
SOMERVILLE 1966 m	Alice May **HICK**	SRN SCM	1921	UK	Kenya	1960	1968	Sister tutor/ Housewife
STANFIELD	Paget	MD MRCP DCh	1926	UK	Uganda	1962	1973	Lecturer in Paediatrics
STAPLETON	Richard Philip	RICS	1947	UK	Ghana	1971	1973	Surveyor
STAPLETON (Mrs)	Margaret Lesley	DipEd	1948	UK	Ghana	1971	1973	Teacher Trainer
STEVENSON	William Handforth	MA BLitt	1928	UK	Ghana Nigeria	1957 1960	1960 1969	University staff
STEVENSON (Mrs)	Kathleen Joyce	MA	1929	UK	Ghana Nigeria	1957 1960	1960 1969	Housewife
STONE (Mrs)	Margaret (née **SANSON**)	SRN SCM	1933	UK	Zambia	1967	1970	Leprosy Settle-ment Nurse

Surname	Given names	Qualifications	Birth	Country	Service area	From	To	Occupation
STOW 1973 m	Gail Alison		1944	Aust	Papua New Guinea	1971	1975	Secretary
TADESSE (Mrs)	EDONI Valerie (née TONG)	J.W.	1936	UK	Zambia / West Germany	1971 / 1973	1973 / 1976	Housewife
TAYLOR	Richard Stuart	BSc PGCE	1936	UK	Nigeria	1965	1967	University Teacher
TILNEY *	Pamela Doreen	Teaching Certificate	1934	UK	Zambia	1967	1970	Teacher
TONG 1971 m	Valerie Jane TADESSE	Zawdu	1936	UK	Zambia	1969	1971	Admin, Christian Broadcasting
TUCKER	Bessie Lorna	F S Radiographers	1922	UK	South India	1965	1969	Radiographer
WARREN	Joan Barbara	BA PGCE	1940	UK	Tanzania	1966	1971	Teacher
WATSON	Edward John	Teacher Training	1937	UK	Gilbert Islands	1965	1972	Teacher
WATSON	Jennifer	BA	1943	UK	Botswana	1971	1973	Teacher
WATSON	Lloyd Stewart	B Eng	1940	Aust	Malaysia	1967	1971	Administrator
WATSON (Mrs)	Elizabeth Agatha	BA	1945	Aust	Botswana	1967	1971	Teacher
WATT	Daphne Eleanor		1934	Aust	Papua New Guinea	1968	1973	Hostel matron
WATTS	Shirley Olive	BA	1940	UK	Jamaica	1967	1969	Teacher
WEIR	Harold Gibson (Revd)	AUA (Soc St) LTh AASA	1921	Aust	Japan	1964	1965	Researcher in Crime Prevention
WEIR (Mrs)	Gwendoline Mary		1920	Aust	Japan	1964	1965	Housewife
WEIR	Robyn Evelyn		1945	Aust	Japan	1964	1965	Nurse
WESTON	Keith	AIB	1938	UK	Ceylon/Sri Lanka / Malaysia / Hong Kong	1965 / 1967 / 1972	1967 / 1976	Banker

SURNAME (Married)	First names Surname	Degrees/ Certs First name)	Year of birth	Origin	Countries of Service	Years of Service		Work
WESTON	Sylvia May	BSc Dip Ed	1912	UK	Ghana	1963	1967	Teacher
WILKINS	David Gordon	BA LRCP MRCS	1937	UK	Hong Kong	1964	1969	Medical Officer
WILKINS (Mrs)	Angela Mary	Teacher Training	1938	UK	Hong Kong	1964	1969	Housewife
WILLMER	Doris Kathleen	Teacher Training	1912	UK	South India	1973	1974	Teacher
WRIGHT	Janet	Teaching Certificate	1932	UK	S.Rhodesia	1955	1959	Teacher
WRIGHT *	Christine	SRN RMN	1944	UK	Papua New Guinea	1971	1973	Nurse
WRIGHT	Wallace Wheldon	ASIA	1906	UK	Tanganyika	1957	1960	Accountant

Appendix C

APPENDIX C: STAFF OF LMS/CCWM/CWM 1945 - 1977

(A list of staff, most with ten years or more service)

Name	Designation	Years
ALLARDYCE Mrs G.H.	In charge of voluntary workers	1925 - 1963
BELL Mr Arthur C.	Exhibition & Visual Aids Dept	1949 - 1992
BOWERS Mrs Frances	Women's Secretary	1946 - 1962
	Secretary for Madagascar	1950 - 1960
	Candidates & Personnel Secretary	1960 - 1962
BIGGS Miss Dorothy	Assistant Education Officer	1945 - 1966
BROCKIS Mr George	Finance Department / Cashier	1902 - 1960
BROWN Revd T. Cocker	Secretary for Africa & China	1934 - 1946
	Special LMS Envoy to China	1946 - 1947
BUCKSTONE Miss Ida	Loans & Exhibitions, Visual Aids	1916 - 1964
CALDER Revd James M.	District Secretary for Scotland & Ireland	1936 - 1951
CAMERON Mr Robert	Financial Agent in Australia and New Zealand	1940 - 1959
CHIRGWIN Revd Arthur M.	Assistant Home Secretary, Field/Foreign Secretary	1920 - 1932
	General Secretary	1932 - 1950
CHIRNSIDE Mr Tom C.	Treasurer	1966 - 1977
COCKS Revd Norman F.	Secretary in Australia and New Zealand	1945 - 1970
CRAIG Revd Charles S.	Secretary for India & Islands	1950 - 1966
	General Secretary	1966 - 1971
CROSS Miss Edna	Secretary to General Secretary	1938 - 1967
CUMBER Miss Mary	Personnel Secretary	1962 - 1974
DEANE Miss Nellie	Welsh Office Secretary	1922 - 1958
DIAMOND Mr Howard	Assistant Treasurer	1928 - 1952
EDWARDS Revd Ernest J.	District Secretary, Organisation & Field Officer	1953 - 1956
	General Secretary, Commonwealth Miss Soc	1956 - 1966
	Overseas Secretary for Pacific, Caribbean & Africa	1968 - 1975

EDWARDS Revd R.E.	District Secretary for Wales & Monmouth	1950 - 1966
FAIRHALL Miss Muriel	LMS Girls Auxiliary	1936 - 1943
	Secretary to Candidates Department	1945 - 1968
FLETCHER Irene	Librarian & Archivist	1942 - 1972
GORDON Revd I.B.	Financial Agent in New Zealand	
GRIFFITHS Revd A. Frank	Foreign Secretary	1955 - 1968
HOLLOWAY Miss Edith	Secretary to Overseas Secretaries & General Secretary	1945 - 1969
HUBNER Miss P.E.	Secretary to Overseas Secretaries	1919 - 1962
HURST Revd H.Leonard	District Secretary in N W England	1929 - 1934
	Secretary in Australia and New Zealand	1934 - 1945
	Secretary for India, Madagascar & the Islands	1945 - 1950
	Home Secretary	1950 - 1956
	Editor	1953 - 1958
JANES Revd Maxwell O.	General Secretary	1950 - 1966
	Consultant Secretary	1966 - 1967
JONES Miss Elsie	Pilots Secretary	1948 - 1966
	Home Department	1940 - 1966
LATHAM Revd Robert O.	Education Officer	1946 - 1956
	Home Secretary	1956 - 1966
McLENNAN W.B.	Assistant Secretary, Australia and New Zealand	1960 - 1968
MORRIS Revd W.T.	District Secretary for Wales & Monmouth	1938 - 1949
NEW Miss Mary h.	Home Department	1913 - 1950
	Watchers Prayer Union Secretary	1936 - 1950
NORTHCOTT Revd Cecil	Home Secretary & Literary Superintendent	1936 - 1950
ORCHARD Revd Ronald	District Secretary in NE England	1937 - 1944
	Assistant Secretary	1944 - 1946
	Secretary for Africa & China	1946 - 1955
PATERSON Revd Allan M.	District Secretary for London & Home Counties	1939 - 1952
PILKINGTON Mr R. Austin	Treasurer	1933 - 1944
	Joint Treasurer	1944 - 1947

Name	Designation	Years
PILPEL Dr Olga	Assistant Editor & Joint Editor	1954 - 1967
RUTHERFORD Revd E.Joyce	Women's Secretary	1930 - 1945
SEARLE Miss Marjorie	Office Secretary, Sydney office	1924 - 1969
SIMMONS Revd Donald S.	Assistant Home Secretary	1956 - 1966
SMITH Mr J.Rider	Joint Treasurer	1944 - 1947
	Treasurer	1947 - 1965
SPEARING Mr Austen	Financial Secretary	1953 - 1966
THOMAS Revd Harold	District Secretary in NW England	1935 - 1947
	District Secretary in NE England	1947 - 1954
	Reception & Organization Officer	1954 - 1958
TIMMIS Miss Faith I.	Finance Department	1915 - 1960
TOMS Miss Janet	Assistant to Women's Secretary	1949 - 1959
	Secretary, Watchers Prayer Union	1950 - 1959
	Secretary for Deputation	1952 - 1959
TODMAN Revd Arnold J.	Overseas Secretary for India & East Asia	1966 - 1977
	Overseas Secretary for Madagascar	1968 - 1977
WILTON Revd Stanley	Assistant Secretary for Education	1956 - 1966

Contributors

The Rev. Dr *Bernard G. Thorogood*, formerly general secretary of the United Reformed Church in the UK, was an LMS missionary in the Pacific from 1952 to 1970, and CCWM/CWM general secretary from 1970 to 1980. He is a well known ecumenical leader who has served on the executive committee of the British Council of Churches, and on the central committee of the World Council of Churches. He is the author of several books on the Christian faith and on mission.

The late Rev. *Joseph Wing* was an LMS missionary in South Africa during the years 1950-57 and 1962-70. From 1967 to 1987 he was the general secretary of the United Congregational Church of Southern Africa and also served for many years as secretary of the South African Church Unity Commission. From 1987 to 1989 he was the president of the Federal Theological Seminary in Pietermaritzburg.

The Rev. Dr *John Parry* was an LMS medical missionary in Zambia from 1948 to 1969.

The Rev. *Donald Schofield* was an LMS missionary in Madagascar from 1952 to 1972.

The Rev. *Iorwerth Thomas* was an LMS missionary in South India from 1940 to 1970.

Miss *José Robins* was an LMS/CWM missionary in North India from 1956 to 1980.

The Rev. Dr *George Hood*, a Presbyterian Church of England missionary in China from 1943 to 1950 and in Malaysia-Singapore from 1951 to 1972, served as a CWM overseas secretary from 1972 to 1977 and then became a tutor at St Andrew's Missionary Training College, Selly Oak, Birmingham. He is the author of a book on China, *Neither Bang nor Whimper*.

The Rev. *Frank Butler* was an LMS missionary in Papua New Guinea from 1956 to 1972.

The Rev. Dr *John Garrett*, a research associate of the Pacific Theological College, Fiji, is the author of several books on the Pacific including *To Live among the Stars* and *Footsteps in the Sea*.

The Rev. *Pearce Jones* was a CMS/CWM missionary in Jamaica from 1963 to 1986.

The Rev. Dr *Robert Latham* served on the home staff of the LMS as education secretary from 1946 to 1956 and as home secretary from 1956 to 1966 before becoming CCEW/URC church life secretary from 1966 to 1980.

Index

Words in italics are either local language words or names of publications. Acronyms are explained.